MR NICE &
MRS MARKS

MR NICE &
MRS MARKS

JUDY MARKS

EBURY
PRESS

First published by Ebury Press in Great Britain 2006

1 3 5 7 9 10 8 6 4 2

Text © Judy Marks 2006

Ebury Press, an imprint of Ebury Publishing.
Random House, 20 Vauxhall Bridge Road, London SW1V 2SA

Random House Australia (Pty) Limited
20 Alfred Street, Milsons Point, Sydney, New South Wales 2061, Australia

Random House New Zealand Limited
18 Poland Road, Glenfield, Auckland 10, New Zealand

Random House (Pty) Limited
Isle of Houghton, Corner of Boundary Road & Carse O'Gowrie,
Houghton 2198, South Africa

The Random House Group Limited Reg. No. 954009

www.randomhouse.co.uk

A CIP catalogue record for this book is available from the British Library

All photography © Howard & Judy Marks unless otherwise stated

Cover design by Two Associates
Typeset by seagulls.net

ISBN 9780091909189 (From January 2007)
ISBN 009190918X

Papers used by Ebury Press are natural, recyclable products
made from wood grown in sustainable forests.

Printed and bound in Great Britain by Clays Ltd, St Ives PLC

Copies are available at special rates for bulk order.
Contact the sales development team on 020 7840 8487
or visit www.booksforpromotions.co.uk for more information.

To my wonderful daughters Amber and Francesca

And with special thanks to my son Patrick.

Acknowledgments.

I would like to thank the following for their help and support. Ann Blain, Lynne Franks, David Godwin, Andrew Goodfellow, George Lane, Amber Marks, Francesca Marks, Howard Marks, Patrick Marks, Anna Nielsen, Frances Richardson, Mick and Bee Tyson, Jodie Webb and Eric, Rebecca and Isabella Woolger, and the staff at Ebury Press and all others who have supported and encouraged me.

Special thanks to Bridie Woodward for choosing the cover photographs and David Leigh for kindly allowing me to use dialogue from his book *High Time*.

Contents

Prologue

I lay on the dirty, stained mattress on the top bunk while small brown cockroaches ran in and out of the bed's metal frame, centimetres from my face. On the wall opposite the room's big metal door was a barred window with dirty frosted glass, slightly open at the top. I stared up at the smoke-stained 12-foot-high ceiling, which was damp in patches, causing the plaster to hang down. Mice shuffled among the debris of weeks-old breadcrumbs and spilt coffee grounds. Eleven women shared this room. Some were sleeping; others, like me, lay immobilized, lost in thought. A young, thin Spanish woman with syringe-bruised arms, pock-marked skin and greasy black curly hair falling about her shoulders shambled up and down the room, stopping only to retch at the toilet in the corner.

I thought, not for the first time, of the bathroom in my house in Mallorca. The terracotta tiles, the mural on the wall, the massage shower, the huge bathtub, the massive mirror above the washbasin and the smell of pine disinfectant. The bathroom I shared with these strangers was a partitioned-off corner of the main room. The partition walls were seven feet high and made of flimsy, slightly transparent wire-reinforced plastic. In the corner of the 'bathroom' stood a cracked white sink, filthy and smeared with toothpaste, matted hair blocking the plughole. Next to the sink was the toilet. Vomit and excrement covered the toilet bowl, floors and walls. The bowl leaked; water or urine trickled across the floor. There was no bath, no shower and no mirror.

From the lower bunk opposite me, a pregnant black woman stifled a sob. When I first entered this room, desperate for someone to talk to I had asked her if she spoke English. She stared back at me with large lifeless brown eyes and mumbled a barely audible 'yes'. I assumed she had no time for conversation or for me. I now realized it was not unfriendliness, but fear. Most of the women in the room were afraid. Only the Spanish junkie and a woman who seemed to be her friend were unfazed by the surroundings. Now and then, the junkie or her friend would yell out of the window in Spanish I didn't understand and a voice (from I don't know where) would shout back. I had tried to see where the main part of the prison was through the opening at the top of the window, but all I could see was what looked like an uninhabited derelict building.

A month after my arrest, as I sat in the yard of Palma prison reading letters from my children, a guard told me to pack my belongings. I was leaving for Madrid.

Sick with dread at moving further from my children, I climbed into the back of a prison van. It hurtled to the docks, sirens blaring. Out of the barred window I glimpsed the magnificent cathedral of Palma. Built into the old city walls were bars and discos Howard and I had been to. I looked up and saw the terrace of the Abraxus bar under the old windmill, where shoeless Geoff the Chef had sold munchies to the stoned clientele. Closed and shuttered by day, at night these bars would be heaving with people, the sounds of music drifting over the bay. I wondered if Howard or I would ever be among those crowds again.

High on the hill overlooking the port was Bellver Castle and the woods where we went walking with the children, where Amber and Francesca invented such happy games. I shuddered at the thought of the nightmare they were now living.

Two armed guards ushered me on to the ferry bound for Valencia. Their guns pointed the way far down into the depths of the ship. I entered a tiny windowless cell close to the engine room; the guards bolted and locked the door. I was alone.

An hour later I felt the ferry begin to move; the engines were noisy. I thought of all the passengers high above me. People excited about going on holiday, waving goodbye to friends and relatives standing on the dockside. I lay down on the cold bunk. Hours later, I felt a change in the ship's movement and engine noise. My guards unlocked the heavy door, signalled me out with their guns and led me up on to the crowded deck. Children pointed and adults stared as my armed guards marched me in handcuffs along the deck. I straightened my back, breathed in deeply, stuck my nose in the air and pretended not to notice.

As the ship came in to dock, I saw a police van parked below. It was waiting for me. With automatic rifles pointed at my back, I descended the gangplank, each footstep causing it to creak and shake. Once on land I was directed to the waiting van. My guards took out sheets of forms, religiously signing each page, then handed them to my new escorts to sign. We drove through the streets to Valencia's women's prison. On arrival, the sheaves of paper appeared again. Signatures were added then they were handed over to the prison warden for yet more signatures before I was sent to an empty cell once more. The prison warden closed and bolted the door behind me.

During the evening I heard the door unlock and another woman enter. Her complexion was unhealthily pale. We nodded to each other and she lay down on the other bed in the cell. I fell into a fitful sleep, but woke during the night to the noise of my companion doubled over in pain, clutching her stomach. She was sweating; her eyes and nose were running. I called for a warden and eventually one came. She looked at the young woman and told me in English that she was 'suffering from the heroin'. She left, banging and bolting the cell door. I lay awake, listening to my young companion in our grey tomb.

The following day I entered the main part of the prison. It surrounded a large courtyard filled with purple and orange bougainvillea. Women sat around reading, knitting, talking or sunbathing. A few children played among them.

A smiling-faced middle-aged woman, with long, curly, light brown hair approached me.

'You must be the Englishwoman who was in *Ingresos* last night.'

I was relieved. I hadn't spoken to anyone for days.

'Hi, you speak English,' I said.

'Ah yes.' She laughed. 'In Holland we speak English, as well as Dutch and German. I am Johanna.'

'I'm Judy,' I replied and put out my hand, which she took and held warmly.

'So, Judy, what brings you to Hotel Valencia?'

'I'm going to Madrid, but I don't know when.'

'Ha, Madrid.' She patted my hand. 'They will not tell you when, but you will probably be here for four days or so.'

'Do you know what Madrid is like?' I noticed that anyone I mentioned Madrid to looked the other way, but not Johanna.

'I have been there,' she said. 'I might as well tell you, it's rough. There are many fights and stabbings. More drugs in there, I think, than on the streets. My best advice is do not see anything and mind your own business. The Nigerians run the jail; nothing happens without their say-so.'

'Is it that bad?' I whispered, trying to hide the alarm in my voice.

'Look, I have a friend there. Her name is Lillian, she's Belgian. I will write to her and ask her to help you. When you get there, a functionary will talk to you. Tell the functionary you have a friend in department two and they will put you in her dormitory.'

'Thanks, Johanna.' But the fear remained.

Over the next few days I spent all the time I could with Johanna. She had a degree in modern literature, and worked in the prison library. She supplied me with a few English books, but I was too distraught to read. She had been in jail awaiting trial for over two years. In Spain, prisoners on remand on serious charges can spend up to four years without trial. Joanna's crime was supplying false documents, many of them. In spite of the circumstances, I found her jolly and good company.

Early in the morning and eight days after my arrival in Valencia, my cell was unlocked and a warden told me I was leaving. She gave me a *bocadillo* to eat, along with some yoghurt and a bottle of water, and wished me '*buena suerte*' as she patted me on the back. Since my arrest, the Spanish prison authorities had treated me with nothing but kindness; I guessed they had read the papers and seen the televised news reports. The previous evening I had phoned home and spoken to the children. They tried to sound brave, but I knew by the awkward silences from normally talkative children that it was pretence.

Madrid is 250 miles from Valencia. We travelled in a big, slow prison bus. I was the only passenger, and although I felt like a caged animal, I welcomed the drive. My guards were friendly and did not handcuff me. They allowed me to sit in the front cage so I could see out. For the last few weeks I'd had only brick walls to stare at. As we left the city behind we passed orchards of Valencian oranges, and palm groves that hinted at the region's Moorish past. I widened my eyes and savoured the view, the passing villages and towns and the architecture of the buildings; details I had never taken notice of before. The August sunshine had dried the fields golden-brown. Mountains in the distance, with villages scattered on their sides and the occasional castle perched on an edge, beckoned to a hidden Spain. We drove for most of the morning, stopping briefly to eat our *bocadillos*, when the guards shared their red wine with me.

As we approached Madrid, the traffic grew heavier and traffic lights appeared with more frequency. On the outskirts I turned my head from side to side, swallowing up all the sights, the busy cafés and restaurants. Another world; a place where people lingered over lunch and drinks and strolled arm in arm. I envied the women shopping, the mothers with their children. Suddenly the hairs on the back of my neck bristled and a cold chill swept over my body despite the heat of a Spanish summer day. The van turned a few more corners and arrived at tall, black, heavily guarded gates and armed towers. Perhaps, having been in prison, I had become sensitized to the smell of human despair.

How long would I be here? Would I walk out a free woman? The gates opened slowly, the van rolled through into the compound and the gates closed behind, a hard clink of metal against metal. One of my guards unlocked my cage. I clambered out, stiff after the long drive. The guard gave me my suitcase; his look was sympathetic. He handed me over to the female warden at the inner gate with the inevitable papers that received yet more signatures and dates. I shook hands with the guards and wished them a safe journey back to Valencia. They in turn wished me luck and hoped that I would soon be back in Palma with my children. I felt no bitterness towards them, only envy. They were staying overnight in Madrid, they had told me, having never been to the city before. I hadn't been to Madrid before either. They were spending the night in a hotel before returning to Valencia and their families. I was spending the night and who knew how many more in Yeserias, then the most notorious women's prison in Europe.

CHAPTER ONE
On the Move

I lay in my cot in the dark, frightened, trying to sleep. The wind was bellowing outside, clamouring around the house, jolting the windowpanes. Flashes of lightning filled the sky followed by thunder.

'They're coming to get you. They're going to take you away. They're going to get you tonight. I can hear them. Ssh! Can you hear them? They're coming.'

As the whispering voice continued, I crawled beneath my covers, taking comfort from the smell of freshly laundered sheets. There I remained, too terrified to move. I imagined black figures clambering through the window, taking me away into the murkiness. The whispering voice explained that I was a kidnapped Russian princess, that this was evident in my blonde hair and blue eyes, and that my real parents had sent men to claim me back.

The murmuring voice belonged to my brother George – two years my senior – who regularly took the kind of pleasure in scaring me that only older brothers know how to enjoy so fully.

Back then I was the youngest of four children. The eldest was Patrick: nine years my senior. Tall for his age, with dark brown hair and brown eyes. I remember him playing with his chemistry set in the garden shed. Then Natasha: three years younger than him, slim with the same brown eyes and short dark brown hair, playing her recorder or helping my mother cook. Four years later George arrived. Natasha would have nothing to do with George at first as my mother had joked that she was giving birth to an elephant. Natasha was upset when she didn't.

I was born into a well-to-do family which, like most families in the 1950s, revolved round the man of the house in his role as provider. In practical terms this meant bedding down in a new town wherever our father's business took him and, once you'd had time to make a few friends, moving on to somewhere else. My father's name was Kenneth Lane. The bright son of a naval submarine captain, he had grown up in Gosport, Hampshire, and then studied nuclear physics at Cambridge under the tutelage of C.P. Snow, master of Christ's College and novelist. Father was of average height and build with brown eyes and thinning hair. He was gently spoken and had a deep love of classical music and books. He and my mother Peggy had met during the war in Pencoed, south Wales. My mother, with her elder sister Kay, had come over from Belfast and got work showing film reels to the troops stationed near Bridgend. My father, a nuclear physicist, was in the area on a research project.

By the late 1950s, when I was born, my father was a busy executive working at English Electric, at the time the largest hi-tech company in the UK. C.P. Snow was a director of the company. Father's office was in a large building on the Strand. We lived in Stevenage and my father would disappear for the train each morning at the appointed time, under a bowler hat with an umbrella trailing from his arm. When I asked my mother what he did, she said, 'He sits, my darling, in an office and drinks coffee all day.' Later, when asked my father's occupation by a teacher, I repeated my mother's answer.

Once, when I was about six, I visited my father in his office. He was sitting behind a large desk reading some papers and drinking coffee.

My mother's hobby was going to auctions. One room in our house became so crammed with oddities she had bought it was almost impossible to open the door. She would also pick up odd assortments of people, old ladies and tramps, whom she'd bring home and feed with tea and scones in the kitchen.

My mother came from a large Belfast Catholic family. Her

father, Patrick Murphy – a police officer in the RUC – had been shot dead on Easter Sunday 1942, leaving my grandmother Bridget with nine children. Six men were convicted of the murder and sentenced to death. The famous republican Joe Cahill was one of them. Only one of the gang of six, Tom Williams, was hanged for the crime. The British government – after a plea from Pope Pius X11 – chose to show clemency. Joe Cahill served seven and a half years. My grandmother had travelled to Buckingham Palace to receive the George Cross in my grandfather's honour. My grandmother and various sisters and brothers of my mother's regularly visited from Ireland, always bringing laughter and gaiety into the house.

Mother was the free spirit. Always full of life and mischief, her green eyes constantly sparkled with vitality, a smile was never far from her lips and her wackiness was priceless. Apart from a girl who came to help clean two hours a week, my mother took care of everything herself. I loved going shopping with her, bathing in her confidence and charm as she chatted and laughed with everyone we met. I even helped her canvas in the local elections. (My parents were both politically and socially active in the Conservative Party.) My mother made the difficult task of knocking on people's doors into fun, gamely engaging whoever she encountered.

I was a happy tomboyish girl. At the age of four I terrified my mother by diving off the balcony outside her bedroom, after a bet with George. George was, in contrast to me, a rather serious child. He wore glasses and usually had his dark head in an I-Spy book. Despite that, and all the tormenting he liked to do, George and I were friends and spent most of our time together. My mother, a great believer in fresh air, shooed us out early in the morning, no matter the weather. We explored the local woods and fields and spent hours inventing games, climbing trees or playing hide-and-seek.

In 1960, when I was six, Father moved us to Arkley in north London. He'd bought a plot of land on which he was building a modish home he called Lane House. When it came time to move in, the house was still full of builders and so, much to the disdain of our new neighbours, my father rented two caravans and installed them in the front garden. It was while we were living in the caravans that my grandmother Bridget died during a routine varicose vein operation – the first time I had seen my mother cry.

George and I attended the local primary school, and Patrick and Natasha went to local grammars. My mother became pregnant again and, on Easter Sunday 1961, gave birth to a beautiful little girl named Diana. She became known, even before her birth, as Masha. My mother told me she was my Easter present. I adored her. During the last week of the pregnancy, George and I were shipped off to stay with 'the Holy People', arranged through the local Roman Catholic church. We had a wonderful time. The Holy People had an enormous house with massive gardens and endless secret passages, where stuffed bears appeared out of hidden cupboards like scenes straight out of Enid Blyton's Famous Five books.

One nasty incident marred these carefree days. George and I were playing in the woods behind our house one day when we were captured by a gang of boys of about twelve years old. They tied George up and told me to take my knickers down, jeering and poking me with sticks. I cried and whimpered as they stood round me. George fearlessly negotiated with them, took down his shorts and pants, and allowed them to whip him to save my honour, virginity and whatever else might have been at stake. Accordingly on release we ran all the way home. We never went back to those woods again.

I liked my new school and I had a new best friend. Penny and I first bonded because we were the only children in the playground whose parents didn't have a television set. Our parents, who became friends with one another, finally gave in to our constant nagging and acquired sets in the autumn of 1963. Penny's viewing was subject to parental censorship. There was some of this in our house too, but soon we were living on a depraved diet of *Dr Who* and *Ready, Steady, Go*.

Family holidays were fun; we'd go camping as we explored Europe. A couple of days before returning to England my father would laboriously make lists of every purchase we had made on holiday for UK customs: two buckets and spades, four bottles of suntan lotion, two tubes of insect repellent. My mother, meanwhile, would be secretly stashing bottles of wine in the boot.

We were all growing up, some faster than others. Patrick chose to have little to do with George or me, save to treat us as a nuisance. He'd be irritated if I wandered by mistake into a room where he had a young woman sitting on his knee. Patrick had his eighteenth birthday at home, with a jazz band playing hit songs like Acker Bilk's 'Stranger On The Shore'. All the young women had short skirts, beehive hairstyles and stiletto heels. The shoes ruined my parents' fashionable vinyl floors.

In 1964 my father was promoted to managing director of English Electric's Transformer Division in Stafford and we were on the move again. Natasha was the most upset. She had just discovered the Biba boutique and the Marquee club, where she screamed and swooned at Manfred Mann. Patrick didn't care. He had finished his A levels and secured himself a deferred place reading English Literature at the new and trendy University of Sussex. With his Beatle-length dark brown hair, he and a friend set off to hitch-hike around the United States just as Beatlemania was taking America by storm. When he returned he had a crew-cut and patched Levis. The patches he explained to me were from young women who had ripped their dresses up to repair his jeans. He smiled at me when he returned and for once did not seem displeased to see me.

Around the same time I noticed my mother was putting on weight. I accompanied my father to the family doctor and from the waiting room I could hear him talking worriedly. The doctor tried to soothe my father, telling him it was not unheard of for women of my mother's age to have a baby. My mother was forty-one. On 28 January 1965 my little brother Marcus Sextus Lane joined the family. And I fell in love again.

Meanwhile, having found no house to suit his tastes, my father had bought another plot of land in a village called Acton Trussell on the outskirts of Stafford, where another, much larger Lane House with a swimming pool began to take shape. We moved in the summer of 1965, shortly after Edward Heath had become the new Tory leader.

The village was small and isolated. There was Top Lane, Bottom Lane and Middle Lane – that was it. An occasional bus service, no pub and the nearest we had to a village shop was at the top of a steep climb up the narrowest thread of a path that wound its way through a rambling bracken-filled garden to a house where two old spinsters lived. They worked out of their front room and sold basic stuff such as teabags, sugar and Ovaltine.

The driveway up to our house was at least a quarter of a mile long and began with a cattle grid. The house followed an ultra-modern design. We had underfloor central heating, a vast hallway with Italian marble floors, a temperature-controlled wine cellar and a heated swimming pool. At the back of the house by the pool my father had built a large room called the playroom. It was mainly for us as teenagers to entertain our friends in and to decorate as we wished. He had thoughtfully built an outside toilet so our visitors would not need to enter the main house. From our house we could see vast expanses of countryside. North, four miles in the distance, the county town of Stafford touched the skyline.

Stafford was a typical market town with a high street and not much more. At the northern end of town was a large Victorian prison, still in use, next to a square aptly named Gaol Square. The prison fascinated me. As we drove by I would stare in wonder at the rows of unhappy-looking women and children who queued in all kinds of weather, waiting to be let in the massive iron gates to see their husbands and fathers. An air of oppression radiated from the prison's high barbed-wire-covered walls. When you walked by you could sometimes hear a prisoner shouting out of his window on the top floor. A shiver ran through me whenever I was near the place.

Natasha did her A levels at the local girls' high school, George attended the boys' grammar and I went to St Joseph's Convent to do my eleven-plus. I became best friends with Alison Williams, who lived on a nearby farm. Her brothers, who were excitingly a bit older, were both becoming farmers like their dad Jim. She taught me to ride on her white horse Silver. I loved it, and her scruffy homely home with dogs and cats curled up on comfortable sofas. It was in contrast to the stark lines of our modern house.

This was a time when the age gap between me and George felt at its greatest. George had become fascinated by Dalí and the Marquis de Sade. His I-Spy books were replaced by Oscar Wilde and Edgar Allan Poe. He was thirteen years old. Ian Brady and Myra Hindley had been arrested for the Moors murders and George pored over any newspaper cuttings he could get his hands on. My mother began to notice and I would see her in George's room flicking through his books and things with a worried frown on her face. My only obsession was with *The Sound of Music*, which my friends and I would re-enact during break times.

In September 1966 I joined Natasha at the high school. Natasha had herself a boyfriend named Martin, an art student at the local college. He and his best friend Snowy were frequent visitors to the playroom. I soon developed a crush on Snowy with his long blonde hair and Citroën 2CV. Martin painted the playroom for us in psychedelic and groovy designs and Natasha began her own impromptu party period. Hordes of people would come and our parents hardly batted an eyelid. Our house gained a reputation for miles around as the place to hang out.

My parents had their own kind of social life, though, which was just as active. They cultivated a wide circle of friends among their peers in the neighbouring community: doctors, lawyers, solicitors, architects, judges and magistrates. They were always either dressed up to go out to a dinner party or hosting one themselves. We children were excluded from such events, except for doing the dishes. One night after a large dinner party and much washing-up, I had gone to bed exhausted, only to be awoken by loud laughter. I crept from my room and looked out onto the terrace to see all the male dinner guests stripped to their white Marks and Spencer underpants and string vests frolicking in the pool. The women were standing around giggling, clutching onto their sides or their pearls, when a few of the drunker ones ripped off their dresses and joined the men in the pool. I was aghast. I was glad my mother didn't swim and decided I didn't wish to know if my father was in the pool or not.

I found it difficult to fit in at school. The girls made fun of me for my 'posh' London accent. Many of their parents worked for my father and they resented me for being the boss's daughter. It didn't help that I was frequently taken to school in my father's gleaming white Daimler Sovereign, or dropped off by my father's chauffeur in one of the company cars. The other girls stood about in groups, whispering and laughing at me.

Seeing my distress, my mother sent me off to a Young Conservatives party in the hope it might cheer me up and I might meet some 'nice' children. But I found it thoroughly boring, apart from having my first cigarette.

One girl from school did befriend me. Her name was Suzanne and the fact that her father was a foreman at my father's factory didn't seem to bother her. Suzanne had long curly brown hair and exotic dark skin; her mother was Lebanese. She lived in the centre of town in a small terraced house in which the walls and floors were covered with oriental carpets. I was besotted by Suzanne's older brother, Frank, who had a band called Salem's Red Scarf. He played at youth clubs and at school dances and I begged my mother to let me go. She firmly refused. I was, however, allowed to visit Suzanne on Saturday afternoons. Every time I knocked on the door I prayed that tall dark handsome Frank with his deep mysterious Middle Eastern eyes would open the door and fall madly in love with me. It never happened. Suzanne and I spent the afternoons walking up and down the high street puffing on cigarettes, pretending not to watch the boys while they pretended not to watch us.

Patrick returned home from Sussex during holidays, often bringing one or more of his friends. For his twenty-first birthday he brought eight of his friends with him. My mother thought they were a wonderful bunch and took great satisfaction in their lack of interest in alcohol. She watched delightedly out of the kitchen window, over the top of the rose garden she so lovingly tended, as they whizzed up and down the drive on the children's bikes, playing with the children's toys and laughing at Masha and Marcus's antics. Frisbees flew through the air and the sounds of Procol Harum, Cream and the Beatles echoed out of the playroom and around the grounds of our house, but it did not occur to my parents, or to me for that matter, that they were all out of their heads on LSD, amphetamines, marijuana and heroin. Things would never be the same again.

CHAPTER TWO
A Pope and a Son

It was one of those nasty English days when rain came down in thick grey gusts. I sat in the kitchen looking out of the window at the lights of Stafford glimmering in the distance.

'I wish it would stop raining,' said George, joining me at the window.

We were in charge of Masha, aged seven, and three-year-old Marcus, while our parents had driven down to London, two and a half hours away. We were waiting for my father's car to come up the drive. They were late and a fluttering sense of foreboding had started to fill me. I switched on the television to watch *Top of the Pops* but couldn't concentrate.

When we finally heard the car purring up the driveway, it was 7.45. Relieved, I put on the kettle to make a pot of tea. It took them a long time to come in from the garage, but eventually I heard their slow footsteps in the hall. The kitchen clock read 8.00. I turned to face the door as I heard it creak open. The sight of my mother's face numbed me: it was pale and blotchy-red from crying. As her misty green eyes met mine she broke into tears. My heart dropped. I went to hug her and she fell into my arms. My father stood there, a sopping umbrella in his hand. He looked ashen, and tears welled in his brown eyes. Masha sat on the floor silently watching, her Sindy doll naked in her hands. Marcus continued playing next to her with his Lego. George, not knowing what else to do, carried on making

16

the tea. 'Mummy, what's wrong?' I asked with dread. My mother sobbed bitterly against my body. Finally she took a deep breath and whispered through her tears, 'I've got cancer. They're going to cut my breast off next week.'

It was the autumn of 1967. She was only forty-three years old. My father took her from me and led her to the sitting room. I looked out of the window. The rain had stopped and I was staring out into darkness.

As autumn turned to winter, an air of stifling depression settled over the house. After the operation, my mother returned home and began radiotherapy treatment. Each morning a large white ambulance arrived to take her to hospital and each afternoon it brought her back home. Bit by bit she began to show signs of recovery. Her green eyes twinkled with laughter in her still young face. Her black, shoulder-length hair came back to health and the kitchen radio blasted out the latest pop hits. The children starting laughing, giggling and squabbling again.

One evening I heard the purr of my father's car as he slowly drove up to the house. I saw my mother rush to her drawer in the kitchen and pull out a brush for her hair before she put on her red lipstick in front of the kitchen mirror. Daddy always drove up the driveway at a crawl. I guess he took satisfaction at admiring the house he had helped design and the garden he had worked so hard on.

He entered the kitchen with a boyish spring. He looked less strained than he had in a long while. He smiled at us all and bounced Masha and then Marcus into the air, his few remaining strands of grey hair falling across his face as my mother prepared their gin and tonics.

'Okay, everyone into the dining room. I have an announcement to make,' he said, and smiled at my mother as she handed him his drink.

We sat down at the polished teak table. The smell of freshly mowed lawn drifted in through the open window.

'We're all going to Italy next week. We shall put the car on the ferry to France and then drive down,' he announced, looking at us each in turn. 'We shall go to Rome, where I have arranged an audience with the Pope.'

George and I looked at each other, not sure what to think.

My father continued. 'George, I want you to help me with the itinerary, and Judy to help your mother with the packing. Patrick will join us to help with the driving.'

My mother smiled happily at my father. She rose from her seat and kissed him on his bald patch. I was excited. I had never been to Italy and an audience with the Pope sounded very grand.

The journey seemed endless. We had two overnight stops. For much of the car journey I slept as we travelled mile after mile on the autostradas – the yellow headlights streaming past us. I was awoken on the third afternoon by the sound of car horns honking. We had reached Rome and my father was doing battle with the crazy, chaotic streets while my brother tried to make sense of the map and give directions. I rubbed my eyes clear and looked out of the window. We were crossing a bridge with statues along its parapet, and then past piazzas with fountains, churches, icons and monuments on every corner. We passed the main train station and drove down smaller streets where women hung out over balconies draped with laundry, shouting at neighbours across narrow rubbish-filled streets. A short while later I heard Patrick call out to my father, 'Look, there are the Spanish Steps. We must be near the hotel.'

I looked at majestic-looking steps thronged with people and decorated with pink azaleas. Teenage boys stood gawking at teenage girls, and tourists sat on the steps reading guidebooks and consulting maps. Shortly after passing the steps, we pulled up outside a spacious historical villa just off the Via Conditti. A porter came rushing down the steps to help with the baggage and ushered us into the hotel.

Most of the week we spent sightseeing and shopping. The Coliseum was the place in Rome that most captured my thirteen-year-old imagination. I imagined I could hear the cries of the condemned echoing out of the walls, the roar of lions as they chased their prey. It amazed me to see, instead of lions, hundreds of scrawny cats prancing about in the warm sunlight. I wondered if they contained the souls of their long-gone relatives and that was why they congregated there.

Time came for our audience with the Pope. We made our way to St Peter's in the Vatican City. St Peter's was enormous inside but not a cavernous space, rather a clutter of marble and gold with something to look at on every square centimetre of wall. I thought we'd be sitting with the Pope in some smart room with overstuffed sofas drinking cups of tea, talking in hushed tones and being terribly polite. In fact, the audience was to take place in the Palazzo Apostolico and, to my surprise, hundreds of other people were also making their way there. We showed our blue tickets at the entrance, then went to seats by the main altar.

It took a while to fill up. Masha and Marcus became bored and fidgeted. Sitting close by were a group of nuns clutching their rosary beads and praying silently with eyes closed. Next to them were a couple of stern-faced priests gazing at the frescoes on the ceiling. Behind them sat a frail elderly couple who constantly looked over their shoulders as if they were afraid of missing something. Eventually, we heard a great echoing of voices drifting in from outside, followed by thunderous applause. I too looked over my shoulder towards the entrance. The atmosphere had grown tense. The nuns had stopped praying and opened their eyes, which they now directed towards the cathedral's opening, as did the priests and all the other people I could see.

I, like my father, had never been a great believer in the Catholic Church and found my weekly trips to Mass a chore. It was all done for the love of my mother. Yet I felt my heart begin to beat faster as I caught sight of the Pope being carried in on a large decorated gold throne followed by all his cardinals. The procession made its way up the aisle; the Pope waved to the packed congregation. When he reached the altar and his throne was gently set down, he rose from his dais. With his arms outstretched as if to enfold everyone, his eyes sent out messages of warmth and love. He was small and frail, and he looked a little as if he wanted to fly down the steps and embrace all the people. The cardinals were big ravens who clustered round him and held him back. Throughout the Latin Mass that followed, there was among the congregation a strong sense of reverence and seriousness and a deep murmur of prayer.

At the end of the Mass, after blessing the congregation, the Pope started to make his way slowly and falteringly down the steps, two cardinals guiding him in case he fell. He made his way to where we were now standing. I was mesmerized. I couldn't take my eyes off him. He shook hands with my father and whispered a few words in Italian. Then he took hold of my mother's hands and kissed her gently on the forehead and blessed her. He smiled delightedly at Masha and Marcus, tousled their hair and gave them each a large silver medallion before kissing them on their heads. He took my hands and kissed me on the forehead and whispered a blessing in Italian as he gazed into my enraptured eyes. I never wanted to wash my face again. He shook hands with George and blessed him, and then the Pope held his hand out to Patrick. Patrick looked at him coldly, his hands firmly in his trouser pockets. The Pope, with his hand still held out, locked eyes with Patrick's. I heard my mother gasp. The Pope turned to look at her and smiled as if to say it doesn't matter. I saw my father's face tighten. My father was an atheist, but he had organized this entire holiday knowing how deeply my mother felt about her religion and how momentous this was for her. Patrick's eyes were bloodshot, his face stern and full of contempt. The Pope withdrew his hand, smiled gently at Patrick and moved on.

Later that night I heard my mother crying as my father tried to comfort her.

'It's the drugs, darling; it's all the drugs he's had. He doesn't think straight.'

It was the first time I realized Patrick had a drug problem. The whispered conversations I had heard between my parents over the last few months began to make sense. I knew Patrick smoked dope. I had seen that when we visited him in Brighton. I had no idea that he was also using heroin, or that one of the friends who'd come to his twenty-first, Maggie, had since died of a heroin overdose.

When I came down for breakfast the following morning, I saw my father and Patrick deep in conversation in a small seating area next to the hotel reception. I hid by the doorway and listened.

'I just hate the hypocrisy of the Church. All its wealth and how it keeps its followers in poverty. Telling women it's sinful to practise contraception, so they become trapped in a cycle of poverty and pregnancy all their lives. All those works of art – the money could help so many people. I hate it,' Patrick said, with his young voice rising in emotion.

'It's all very well to have your views, Patrick,' said my father. 'But why couldn't you have had the decency to behave in front of your mother? What harm would it have done to shake his hand?'

'Yeah, I'm sorry, Dad, but when he stood so smugly in front of me I just felt such anger. I will go and apologize to Mum.'

'I think that's the least you can do,' my father replied in a weary voice.

A couple of days later we packed for the long drive back to England.

On the outskirts of Milan the car broke down. The mechanics told us it would be at least two weeks for the spare parts needed to fix it to arrive. We abandoned the car and flew home from Milan. My first plane ride.

Natasha finished her A levels in June and accepted a place reading English Literature at Essex. Patrick had finished his degree and to keep away from the drug scene at Sussex he returned home. He took a job teaching at the local polytechnic while he considered his next career move. One night he got drunk with one of his colleagues. He left his friend's flat in the early hours to buy some cigarettes. The only machine he found was in a locked-up petrol station. He leapt through the double-glazed window, put his money in the machine, took his cigarettes and calmly went back to his mate's flat. The next morning the local newspaper's front page headline read: 'Police Follow Trail of Blood.'

My parents were mortified. My mother hastily arranged a string of dinner parties inviting suitable guests. Patrick received a caution.

Shortly after this, much to my parents' surprise, Patrick decided to straighten out his life and become an accountant. He moved down to London and started training with Price Waterhouse.

George had taken over the entertaining in the playroom and

began to throw his own parties. It was at one of these that I smoked my first joint. I was sitting outside by the pool, my legs dangling in the water. It was a clear evening under a nearly full moon. A boy sat down beside me and swung his legs into the pool. It was a face I had often spotted in town and had fancied. To my impressionable mind he looked like a Rolling Stone.

'Hi, you're George's sister, would you like a drag on this?' he said as he handed me the cone-shaped joint. It was as simple as that.

I took it from him and inhaled. And soon everything became dream-like. The people wandering round the garden, chatting and laughing, were in slow motion. My feeling for the music drifting out of the playroom, Arthur Brown's 'Fire' – something I will never forget – became heightened. We sat there by the water in silence, sharing the joint, not feeling any need to talk.

George saw me and grinned. 'Good stuff, Judy.'

'It's brilliant,' I replied, grinning back. I felt cool and grown-up and very much part of the crowd.

The boy's name I discovered was Ollie and he was an apprentice printer four years older than me. He was tall with long brown shoulder-length hair, warm brown eyes and a square jaw at the bottom of a long narrow face.

The following spring, when I was fourteen, he asked me to come to a festival with him in Droitwich, at the Chateau Impney hotel. A crowd of us headed off by train. As we waited on the platform, Ollie handed me a pill. 'Enjoy,' he said.

'What is it?'

'LSD. Don't worry, I'll look after you.'

There was a lot in the newspapers around this time about LSD. The Beatles' song 'Lucy In The Sky With Diamonds' had caused an uproar when people claimed it was about the drug, which the Beatles denied. The drug sounded interesting. I trusted Ollie and so I swallowed it. By the time we reached Birmingham New Street, where we needed to change for Droitwich Spa, every hair on Ollie's arm and chest was a moving coloured snake. I felt like I was walking on air and kept saying, 'Wow, look at that,' as a rubbish bin would walk or a phone would talk and people appeared as a myriad of colours. We giggled madly.

We made it to the chateau. Music drifted around the grounds and Ollie and I made love for the first time in a sheltered spot among buttercups. I remember it as a place of clear light and the sweet aroma of hashish mingling with the smell of summery green. As our bodies merged and the colourful snakes on his arms caressed me I felt an amazing closeness to him.

Hours later, returning home, the hallucinations had subsided but I still felt otherworldly. I worried about seeing my mother. I was certain she'd be able to tell I was out of it.

From then on, we took acid just about every weekend. George and I competed to see who could take the most at once. Ollie and I would go off to Cannock Chase, an area of beautiful woods and heathlands, losing ourselves in our fantasies and making love. The world seemed a place of endless bliss.

It was July 1969, the first moon landing, and my mother learnt from her consultant at Guy's, Dr Black, that the cancer had spread to her lymph nodes and she would have to have them removed. I was a sad girl when I attended the Stones' free concert in Hyde Park. I cried for Brian Jones, my mother and me as Mick Jagger let loose hundreds of butterflies. I couldn't understand how they could put Neil Armstrong on the moon and not cure a mere something like cancer.

My mother occasionally found hashish in George's room and confiscated it. After the experience with Patrick she was worried that George would become an addict too. For some reason I failed to understand, my parents never suspected me. My mother even confided her worries about George to me. Meanwhile my drug-taking continued unchecked. There began to be casualties among our friends. One friend took some acid he never really came back from. Others we knew were facing prison after being caught in possession of hashish. And my mother was in and out of hospital.

My periods had stopped and what I most notably did not do was think. At school I had received no sex education except for playground talk. My mother became embarrassed when I asked her for sanitary towels, so there was no sex education from that quarter. The thought of being pregnant did not enter my mind. If it had entered

Ollie's I don't know, but I find it hard to imagine it did not. He was older and much more experienced than me.

Eventually I confided in a girlfriend. She came with me to buy a pregnancy-testing kit, which I used at her house.

As soon as I was sure, I met Ollie after school for a coffee in Jenks on the high street.

'Ollie, I'm pregnant,' I said quietly and calmly though I was sick and frightened.

'Oh my God. What are you going to do?'

'Don't you mean what are *we* going to do?'

'My parents are going to kill me,' he said.

'And what do you think mine are going to do to me?'

'We'll have to get rid of it.'

I went home alone and upset. I had thought Ollie would have a solution. I also knew that, much as I liked him, I had no wish to marry him. That evening before going to bed I followed the only advice he'd given me and drank a couple of large glasses of gin and had a steaming hot bath. I repeated this for at least a week and it did nothing else but make me feel wretched every morning. I have never touched a drop of gin since.

I started to tell my closest friends at school and they started knitting clothes for the baby. For weeks I tried to find the courage to tell my parents. Should I tell my mother or my father? What should I say? Would they kick me out? Would I be sent away to a Catholic institution for unwed mothers? I could no longer put it off. I was nearly five months pregnant when I finally chose to tell my father. It was at the end of October, just before my sixteenth birthday. My mother was in Guy's hospital and my father, George, me and the little ones were staying in a hotel in London. I kept wandering from our room to my father's room, taking a deep breath as I raised my hand to knock at his door, before bottling out and returning to my room. George, who now knew, was losing patience with me.

'Judy, for goodness' sake, you have to tell him now.'

Finally my hand made contact with his door. He came and opened it.

'Judy, is everything all right?'

He looked tired and weary. I hated the thought of piling yet more worry on him.

'Daddy, I have to talk to you.'

'Yes, of course. Come in and sit down.' After I'd managed to get the words out, he asked quietly, 'Are you sure?'

'Yes, I did a test,' I said, staring at a spot on the carpet.

'How many weeks?'

'Nearly five months.'

'Oh, Judy, why didn't you tell me before?'

I was so relieved at the gentleness in his voice that I went to hug him. I knelt on the floor with my head in his lap. He stroked my hair gently. I didn't envy his task of breaking the news to my mother.

They were as understanding as they could be, but in private far from happy. They asked if I wanted to marry Ollie and seemed relieved when I said no. Ollie still came to the house but my mother was cool towards him. We stopped taking drugs but we still made love. I was expelled from the convent school I now attended. The headmistress, Sister Mary Marks, who I was very fond of, gave me ten Hail Marys and ten Our Fathers to say before I collected my belongings and left.

My parents' solution was that I have the baby adopted. They made contact with the Catholic Church to arrange it. I was enrolled at the local college of further education to finish my O levels.

Sitting in the college common room one day looking at my swollen belly, the truth of what was happening hit me. I felt and then saw a kick, closely followed by another one. It wasn't just an annoying object, an inconvenience arresting my life – it was a precious little baby, my baby, just like my beloved younger brother and sister. The idea of giving it away suddenly appalled me. I began wildly to think of how I could keep it. I considered moving into a rented house some friends of mine had in Stafford near the jail. I could go on the dole, I thought. I could marry Ollie. It then occurred to me that if I had the baby at home, there was no way my parents would give it away. They would fall in love with it just as I had done. I decided not to tell anyone when I went into labour.

One morning in late March I went for my antenatal appointment at the local hospital. I had a terrible lower back pain.

'Ooh, I think the wee bairn is coming,' said the nurse as soon as she examined me.

'When?' I asked, alarmed.

'Impossible to say, lovey, but as soon as your contractions start, call for the ambulance.'

I went home. The backache worsened throughout the day.

'Are you all right, Judy?' my mother asked as she saw me wince.

'I'm fine, Mummy,' I lied.

My father was away in London and it was only my mother, George and the little ones at home. I found it impossible to relax. As the day wore on I was unable to sit down. I felt overwhelmed by the enormity of what was happening. By eight in the evening the contractions were coming about every twelve minutes. I still said nothing. I said good night to my mother at nine and retired to my room. The contractions became stronger and stronger as I paced my room. By midnight they were about three minutes apart, intense, painful. I was groaning. My mother opened my door.

'Judy, the ambulance is on its way.'

Within an hour of arriving at the hospital I had given birth to a baby boy. He was immediately whisked away from me.

The following morning I awoke. Nurses were coming into the ward carrying babies which they gently placed into eagerly waiting mothers' arms. I lay waiting for them to bring my son. He didn't come.

'Nurse, will you please bring me my baby?'

She avoided my eyes. 'I'll have a word with matron.'

Three days I remained in the hospital; for three days I pleaded to see my son. I was kept subdued with tranquillizers before my father came and took me home. At home my father asked me to sign some forms. The adoption papers. I ran to my room and wept. The doctor came and gave me an injection. Every day my parents asked me again to sign the papers. Every day I spent crying in my bed.

George begged me to pull myself together. Ollie kept phoning but I refused to accept his calls; girlfriends came around and tried to talk to me but nothing helped. Then one morning on the way to the bathroom I heard sobbing. It was my mother; she looked so frail and sad. I realized what a selfish bitch I had been.

'I'm sorry, Mummy. I'll sign the papers. But can I please just see him one time to say goodbye?'

Five days later my mother drove me to a large house in Worcester. As I sat in a garden filled with purple rhododendrons, a nurse brought me my son. I looked in awe at this beautiful little creature, with his blue eyes and bald head. I cherished the half-hour I had with him and wondered if I would ever see him again.

The adoption agency had told me that he was going to a professional family and that they already had an adopted daughter and son. I prayed that they would be loving and take good care of my son.

My father was now spending much time in the south of England. He was working for a company in Crawley, Sussex. Over the summer my father took my mother, Masha, Marcus and me to the US. In Los Angeles my mother visited a cancer specialist who told her that her body had become riddled with the disease.

CHAPTER THREE
Nuclear Physics

Because of my mother's declining health, Masha and Marcus were to start at Catholic boarding schools in September. My parents decided to sell the house and rent one for a while and buy a flat in Brighton. They thought I should leave Stafford and start afresh in Brighton. I was all for this.

Tony Iommi, the guitarist from Black Sabbath, bought our house. He came to view it on a couple of occasions, each time in a different coloured Lamborghini. On each occasion I blagged a lift off him into town, hoping my friends would see me, but they never did.

My father bought a large flat in a Regency mansion block overlooking the sea in Kemp Town, Brighton, an area popular with writers, artists and students. I moved down. Within a few hours of my being there, the phone rang.

'Hi, Judy, it's Jude, we're having a dinner party tonight. Would you like to come?'

'Thanks, Jude, I'd love to.'

'See you about eight o'clock then.'

Jude was Patrick's girlfriend; she shared a flat with a computer analyst called Arthur. Their flat was also in a mansion block in Kemp Town, just off St James Street. I felt nervous as I pressed the doorbell. Patrick opened the door, gave me a big smile and a hug and ushered me in. He looked smart, a respectable businessman. He'd recently begun dressing in expensive suits and getting good haircuts.

I was in awe of Patrick's friends, who to me were sophisticated and intelligent. I was too scared to say anything in case they thought me silly, stupid or too young. That evening there were seven people there; all the guests were Sussex graduates. Arthur gave me a glass of red wine and we took our places at the oak dining table. I noticed that two chairs remained unoccupied and vaguely wondered whose they were. The doorbell rang. Arthur jumped up eagerly.

'That will be Howard and Rosie I expect.' He went out into the hallway.

There settled around the room an air of excited anticipation. Shortly afterwards, a strong-featured man entered the room. He was about six foot in height, in his late twenties with dark longish hair and brilliant blue dancing eyes. He wore a pink shirt over slightly round shoulders and, although slim, his dark trousers rested under a pot belly. Over his arm he carried a dark jacket.

'Evening,' he said, with a Welsh valley lilt that could have belonged to Richard Burton; intelligent, smiling eyes encompassed everyone in the room. A tiny, dainty-looking woman accompanied him. She had brown shoulder-length hair, brown saucer-like eyes and delicate features.

Patrick stood up and kissed the woman and shook the man's hand.

'I'd like to introduce you to my little sister Judy; she's just moved here to take her A levels. Judy, these are my good friends Howard and Rosie.'

Howard smiled at me, his blue eyes crinkling at the corners. 'Welcome to Brighton, Judy.'

Rosie smiled too, her eyes warm. 'I'm sure you'll like it here,' she said.

'What A levels are you studying? I taught A levels at a crammer college in London. I might be of some help,' Howard said.

'History, English lit and sociology,' I replied.

'I'm afraid I'm a bit of a science man.'

'Bloody genius he is,' I heard someone shout out.

'Just Welsh devilry,' Howard bantered back. He grinned at me mischievously. 'I studied nuclear physics,' he said.

'That's what my father studied.'

'Really? Patrick never told me. Oxford?'

'No, Cambridge.'

'I studied history, Judy,' Rosie said. 'Get Patrick to give you my number and give me a call if you need any help.'

Howard and Rosie took their places at the dinner table. Immediately, Howard took from his jacket pocket some skins, a large lump of hashish and some tobacco, and proceeded to roll a joint. I noticed a certain sensuality as he licked each skin, his lips full and generous, his hands soft, narrow with long elegant fingers, the nails blackened from crumbling hash. The task accomplished, he lit the joint, closed his eyes and inhaled the smoke deep into his lungs, a look of contentment spreading over his face. After a few more drags, he handed the joint to the woman next to him and started to roll another one. I noticed the other women present had difficulty keeping their eyes off him and the men also competed for his attention. The joint came to me, the first I had had since my pregnancy. I took a couple of drags before passing it on. I felt my body melting, pieces of talk, laughter, giggles and music floated around, above and below me. Suddenly everyone at the table seemed shadowy. I started to feel faint and had difficulty keeping my eyes open. I noticed another joint about to reach me. I excused myself from the room on the pretence of needing the bathroom. I was walking towards the bathroom, my legs feeling unsteady, when Jude's bed caught my attention. I stumbled towards it, collapsed and passed out.

I settled happily into life in Brighton. The contrast with Stafford couldn't have been greater. The city was fun, cosmopolitan and slightly bizarre. The Lanes with their narrow paved streets full of pavement cafés, antiques and jewellery shops were always a delight to walk round. The North Laine area below the station was full of slightly seedy streets where Graham Greene had set many of the scenes in *Brighton Rock*. The Royal Pavilion, the seaside palace of George IV, with its Chinese-style interior and Indian mogul exterior, was eccentricity itself.

I quickly made many friends; they were almost all students or ex-students of Sussex University. Two Kemp Town pubs became my locals: the Barley Mow and the Harvey. The Barley Mow was run by a family; it played good music, made excellent Welsh rarebit and had a dartboard. The Harvey was run by a Hungarian woman, Friedl, and her husband Charles. It had a jukebox, dartboard and pinball machine and was popular for its cheap lunchtime goulash. Both pubs were well liked by students.

One evening I entered the Harvey. My eyes met Howard's. I had not forgotten him and I blushed as I recalled how I'd passed out.

'Hey, Judy, let me get you a drink,' he called over to me.

I was flattered that he remembered my name. Rosie, who was standing next to him, turned round and a beautiful smile lit up her face.

'Judy, good to see you again. Let me introduce you to my ex-husband Richard.'

The man sitting next to her on a bar stool turned round to look at me. As he did so he spilt his pint of Guinness and knocked Rosie's half-pint of bitter all over her expensive-looking tan-coloured suede miniskirt. The moment froze. Then, blustering, Richard picked up some napkins and tried to wipe Rosie's skirt. As he did this the contents of his shoulder bag spilled out: Gitanes, keys, lighters, a Lloyd's chequebook and scribbled-on scraps of paper joined the puddle of Guinness and bitter on the stained pub floor.

'Richard, look what you've done! You've ruined my skirt. I'm soaking wet. Howard, please take me home.' Rosie stormed out of the pub.

'Sorry, Judy, I owe you a drink. Next time I promise.' Howard left.

I spent the evening in the pub with Richard Powis. It was the start of a long, deep platonic friendship. He was fourteen years older than me, ex-Oxford, now a maths lecturer at Sussex University. He came from a wealthy family and a large trust fund supplemented his income. He was the archetypal eccentric academic. His flat, in beautiful Regency Sussex Square, had unopened mail tossed carelessly to one side, which often lead to the disconnection of the electricity and telephone. His passion was to spend hours puzzling over mathematical equations. He had a young daughter with Rosie, called Emily, otherwise known as Muffin. He walked with a sway, coloured clogs on his feet stamping on the pavement. From his shoulder dangled a brown leather bag, which he constantly mislaid, along with his brown thick-lensed glasses. His light brown hair, usually uncombed, stuck up in tufts. He drove a bright orange BMW.

I was not to see Howard or Rosie for a while after that incident, apart from one occasion when I spotted them kissing in their white Saab. I learnt from Richard that Rosie had became pregnant and that they had moved to London and then to Oxford.

One evening in the Barley Mow I befriended a guy called Rick Conroy.

'Can I buy you a drink?' he'd asked.

'Thank you. A half of lager, please.'

He was tall and slim with long yellowy-brown hair falling over his shoulders rather like a lion's mane, pale blue innocent eyes, a beard and moustache. He was dressed in a denim shirt and jeans, brown leather bomber jacket and brown motorbike boots. He was, I decided, easily lovable.

'Are you at Sussex?'

'No,' I said, feeling a blush spread across my face. 'My brother was, though. Patrick Lane.'

'You're kidding! Patrick and I used to be good friends. We were in the same year. Does he have any other beautiful sisters hidden away?'

I laughed. 'I have a sister at Essex and a younger sister at boarding school. I also have two more brothers. One of them is doing the hippie trail to Afghanistan and the other is at boarding school.'

'And what about you?'

'I'm at Lewes tech, doing my A levels.'

'No way – my ex-girlfriend works there. Jackie, teaches English, long blonde hair.'

'You're joking, that's my teacher.'

It turned out he did his first degree in nuclear physics – I wondered vaguely why I was meeting all these handsome nuclear physicists – and was now doing a PhD on the Chinese Cultural Revolution. He'd spent a year studying Chinese. During the evening I liked him more and more.

'What's Patrick doing? I heard he'd become an accountant.'

'Yeah, that's right. But now he's working for some chap called Graham Plinston, who's got an oriental carpet shop called Hamdullah in Warwick Place, Little Venice. And a property company called Zeitgeist.'

We went back to his flat. He walked with a limp, an injury from a serious motorbike crash. He shared the flat with tall and skinny Al – another nuclear physicist. Rick and I became lovers; he put me on the pill.

It was round at Rick's one evening with several other students that I heard a girl, Lucy, who had been away in Australia for a year, ask Al what had happened to Richard and Rosie's marriage.

'Oh, it was all a horrible mess. Rosie had not long had Richard's baby when this couple from Oxford moved down, Howard and Ilze. They all used to hang out together and drink in the Harvey,' said Al.

'Yeah, it was a horrible atmosphere in there at that time. I stopped going,' said Rick.

'Why?' I asked.

'Well, it became pretty obvious that something was going on between Howard and Rosie. You never knew who was going home with whom. Ilze and Richard were both pretty devastated. Then Howard and Rosie moved in together and Ilze left town,' said Al.

'Richard seems fine about it all now,' I said.

'Well, he did start drinking a lot. And I would often see him on campus looking pretty down. He adores his daughter,' said Rick.

My mother joined me in Brighton and my father came at weekends. My mother was now on a large number of drugs and spent a lot of time sleeping. I turned seventeen, passed my driving test and had the use of my mother's little Fiat Panda, which was just as well, as driving was now difficult for her.

Patrick visited from time to time. He had bought himself a second-hand white BMW, as well as a mews house in Kentish Town and an old mill in the Dordogne, both of which he intended to renovate. He began to make frequent trips to Ireland, returning dressed in Irish tweed and always with some present for my mother from her beloved country. This, with the newfound wealth, began to arouse my mother's suspicions.

'Ken, do you think he's gun-running?' she asked my father one night.

'No, I don't think so.' He chuckled. 'I met his partner Graham for dinner last week and he seems a straightforward business chap. Went to Oxford. Seems to think it's a sensible time to invest in property in southern Ireland.'

My mother continued to look worried. When she joked to Patrick one Sunday lunch about him smuggling guns to Ireland he laughed but looked vaguely uncomfortable. The situation in Ireland had progressively worsened throughout 1971. New emergency powers such as internment had been brought in and there was among the young intellectuals and others then much sympathy for the Irish cause.

In the summer I went with my girlfriend Julia on my first trip to Amsterdam. We stayed in an old canal-side house belonging to her American boyfriend Paul. He had just returned from a Sufi retreat in Switzerland and excitedly described an experience he'd had on the top of a mountain.

'Wow, man, it was the most profound crap I've ever had. Just like squatting on top of the world. I really felt at one with myself. What an experience, man.'

I remained silent, unsure what a suitable comment would be.

Paul became our guide to Amsterdam. He took us round the red-light district where I gazed in amazement at the young women sitting in shop windows waiting to be hired. He took us to the well-known Paradiso club and to many bars and restaurants. All this we did in a stupefied stoned haze. He had loads of money and insisted on paying for everything.

We were sitting round at Paul's house one afternoon in an incense-filled room with Ravi Shankar playing on the stereo, drinking cups of herbal tea and eating hash cakes, when an American couple arrived, carrying three rucksacks.

'Judy, this is Chris and Angie,' said Paul.

After some small talk they said they'd better start working. I watched intrigued as Paul, Angie and Chris began carefully unpicking the stitches of the rucksack straps, removing the padding inside and then replacing it with hashish wrapped in plastic. It was black Afghani, pressed into thin soles just under a quarter of an inch thick. When they had finished it was impossible to tell the straps had been tampered with. I was impressed. The three of them, with the rucksacks, flew to Chicago the following day. Julia remained tense and worried until Paul phoned and said everything was cool. I learnt that this was a regular occurrence and was how Paul made his money. Until this point I had never given much thought how the hash I smoked got to England or anywhere else.

I joined my parents and the little ones in Paris. We were on our way to visit Patrick at his mill in the Dordogne. My mother felt it was important for Patrick that she saw it before she died. I hated it when she talked like that. I could not imagine life without her, and refused to think of it.

We did a tour of the wine regions of Burgundy and Beaune; my father bought extensively to build up his wine collection and had it shipped back to England. We then drove across to the Dordogne. The mill stood on the side of a little country lane just outside the small village of Mollière. A foie gras farm backed onto his land and the snorts from the truffle-hunting pigs intermittently sliced through the peaceful whirring of the flies. The mill was far from habitable so Patrick and Jude were camping in the grounds. We stayed in a small hotel in the tiny town of Beaumont. The hotel had an excellent restaurant. It was here that Patrick introduced us to the delights of the dessert wine Monbazillac, and where I first sampled foie gras and truffles courtesy of his neighbours. One night over dinner Jude leant over to me.

'Do you remember our friends Howard and Rosie, Judy? They were at my flat for dinner that night you came around.'

'Yes,' I said, as an image of those sensuous lips and long elegant hands swept through my mind.

'We've just heard they've had a baby girl.'

Back in England my father bought a small yacht, a Westerly. It had been a dream of his for a long time and my mother now encouraged it. She was fretting about how he would cope when she was gone and thought the yacht would keep him occupied.

I applied and was offered a place following a gap year to read English Literature at Sussex. I turned eighteen. I broke up with Rick. Christmas came and went. My mother became visibly weaker. The doctors had advised her to walk at least two miles every day to build up her leg bones and muscles. George, now back from Afghanistan, made her cups of tea with added marijuana.

'Do you think it's a good idea?' I asked.

'I know it will help her,' he said. 'Have you not noticed she doesn't take so many pills when she's had this tea?'

It was true; she seemed to need fewer of the painkillers that made her so drowsy.

'In Afghanistan and India, they set great store by the medicinal value of marijuana,' George said.

Each evening I accompanied my mother on a walk along the seafront. If we'd had one of George's cups of tea, the walk was punctuated with giggles and silly jokes.

'Let's walk along the pier, Judy. Ooh look, that house says it's a friendship house. Let's go and make some friends.' It reminded me of the days when I was small and accompanied her as she canvassed for the Conservative Party. I'm not sure if my mother knew what was in the tea.

I began missing college because I couldn't bear to leave her alone. I would tell her that my lectures had been cancelled or it was revision time. I think she knew it wasn't true. I felt that every minute I spent with her was precious. At weekends, when my father was home, she put on a tremendous show of strength. Many weekends we'd spend sailing and she'd manage to hide from him the exhaustion that was so evident during the week. The little ones came home for the Easter holidays. It was hard watching my mother decline and caring for a confused younger brother and sister.

My father got himself a new job in King's Lynn, Norfolk. My mother was to go with him for the weekend to meet his new colleagues. We went shopping in Brighton for some new outfits for her. A couple of the outfits had to be altered and she told the saleswoman she would collect them after the weekend. It was me who collected them.

I kissed my mother and father goodbye.

That night she slipped on the floor of their hotel bathroom and broke her legs. She was immediately taken to Guy's Hospital, London, where her consultant worked. I was not unduly worried. Broken legs mend, I assured Masha and Marcus. I didn't realize the cancer had eaten its way into her bones. After a few days my father came down to Brighton from the hospital to check the children were okay. In the early morning of 8 April 1973, the hospital called. My mother's long fight with cancer was over.

My father was distraught. He asked me to drive him up to the hospital and berated himself for not being there.

'She couldn't stand the thought of being fifty,' he said, as if to comfort himself. She would have been fifty the following January.

I drove him up to London, leaving the little ones with George. My father had to deal with the details involved with death. I asked the hospital staff if I could see my mother. I was desperately hoping that it was some dreadful mistake. My father advised against it but I insisted. After a half-hour wait I was shown into the morgue. My mother was wheeled out to me. I gasped. She looked like Mummy but when I went to kiss her she was cold like marble and an empty shell.

I managed to hold it together and drive my father back home. Once the door to the flat was open I lost it, and despite the desperate, confused, unhappy eyes of Masha and Marcus I ran to my room. I didn't think I would or could ever stop crying.

The funeral was held a few days later at a crematorium, near Gatwick. My mother's family flew over from Belfast. Masha stood so small with her lips quivering; Marcus was silent, not really understanding. George, Natasha and Patrick all stood with heads bowed, tears in their eyes. My father looked crushed.

I watched in an almost detached way as the loathsome working whirr of machinery, barely hidden by the piped music, carried my mother's coffin like a piece of luggage on a airport conveyor belt through the black curtain and into the furnace.

CHAPTER FOUR
Oriental Carpets

'Hello.'

'Richard, it's Judy, are you okay? I've been trying to get you for days,' I said, relieved to hear his voice. I had been feeling slightly lonely since breaking up with Rick and losing my mother.

'Judy, great, let's go out for dinner. I've been in Amsterdam. I'll pick you up in half an hour.'

'Okay, great.' I put the phone down.

We drove to Little Preston Street, a street brimming with restaurants. We chose a small Italian one with red and white table-cloths. I noticed Richard had dark circles under his eyes as if from lack of sleep.

'So, Richard, what were you doing in Amsterdam?'

'Long story and I beg you not to tell anyone what I'm going to tell you.'

'You know you can trust me, Richard,' I said.

'Will you swear?'

'I promise. I swear not to repeat a word you say.'

'Basically, Howard asked me to deliver $50,000 to this mad Irishman Jim McCann. A real lunatic,' Richard said, as he attempted to wipe tiredness from his eyes.

'$50,000? Bloody hell. What exactly does Howard do? I thought he owned a dress shop in Oxford.'

'Anna Belinda – that's just a front for him. The two girls who run it have no idea what he really gets up to. He smuggles loads of hash with Graham. Lately they've been doing loads through southern Ireland with this lunatic Jim. Claims he's with the IRA. Wouldn't surprise me. Scary nutcase he is and not fond of your brother.'

'Is Patrick involved in this too?' I asked.

'For sure. He's Graham's accountant and troubleshooter.'

I thought of my mother and her suspicions about Patrick. A mother's intuition. She wasn't far out; just had the commodity and direction wrong. I thought of Paul and his friends in Amsterdam – I'd been impressed. Howard became even more exciting and attractive to me, although I wasn't too sure about the IRA connection. Sympathy and support for the Irish cause had dwindled since the October 1971 Post Office Tower bombing.

'Rosie is getting so fed up with it all. He's hardly ever at home,' Richard said. 'And she's positive he's having affairs.'

'Really? How old is the baby now?'

'About six months. I'm going to Oxford at the weekend. Want to come?'

'I'd love to, but I'm way behind with all my essays and I've got Masha and Marcus home for their half-term.'

'Yeah, of course. Poor kids.'

At the end of half-term I took the children up to Euston Station to join their respective school parties. Patrick had suggested that instead of going straight back to Brighton, I call by the carpet shop. Ever since Richard's revelations I'd been intrigued to see the Warwick Place set-up.

It was early evening when I reached a small, genteel street just off Warwick Road near the Regent's Park canal. On the corner was a pub, the Warwick Castle; next to it was the carpet shop. Patrick lived above the shop. I rang the bell.

'Judy, come straight up,' called Patrick's voice through the intercom. I walked up to the first floor where Patrick was waiting for me.

'Come in, let me introduce you to Graham,' Patrick said as he ushered me into a large light office. A small man stood up and held out his hand to me.

'Hi, nice to meet you,' he said. Apart from longish light-brown hair, he looked every bit the straight executive, dressed as he was in a grey suit with flared trousers and blue striped shirt.

'I'll leave you two to it. I'm going to the pub. See you there,' Graham said.

'So, what do you think of my office, Judy?'

My eyes scanned the office. It had two antique wooden desks with large expensive-looking black leather office chairs, a leather Chesterfield sofa and several filing cabinets. On the cream walls hung a couple of Hockney prints.

'Very smart, Patrick,' I said. He looked pleased. There was, I noted, no sign of anything untoward.

'Come and I'll show you my quarters.' He showed me the next floor where he had a large light-filled double bedroom, bathroom and small kitchen.

'Where does Graham live?'

'He's got a large house nearby in Maryland Road. He lives with his woman Mandy and their two kids,' Patrick replied. 'Now, time for the pub.'

We walked down the stairs and out the front door.

'Let me quickly show you the shop,' he said.

He unlocked the door to the shop. Every bit of wall was covered in exotic-looking carpet; the shop window was also full. Heaps of carpets in all sorts of colours and designs lay piled up on the floor.

'This is a Yakyal carpet from Turkey,' he said, pointing at a carpet in dark red and blue. 'They use natural dyes made from vine leaves, wild mint, walnut shell and buckthorn. The women and girls who weave these carpets shift all their feelings and thoughts onto them. And this one over here is a Kayseri kilim. We have nearly all types of carpets and kilims here from Afghanistan, Uzbekistan, Iran and Turkey. Anyhow, that's enough. To the pub.'

Patrick's knowledge of the carpets surprised me. I could see he was genuinely fascinated by them and their origins, as well as proud of his shop and office.

We walked into the pub. Graham sat huddled in a corner with a craggy-faced blond-haired man.

'What do you want to drink, Judy?' Patrick asked.

'Just half a lager, please.'

Patrick ordered a pint of bitter for himself and suggested we took the drinks outside. I was wearing high-platform yellow clogs and as I stepped out onto the pavement I failed to notice the uneven paving stones. I stumbled and a man whose green silk suit became washed by my lager caught me.

'Oh, I'm so sorry,' I said, mortified, as I raised my eyes to meet brilliant blue laughing ones.

'Well now, if it isn't Judy christening my brand-new Yves St Laurent suit,' purred the soft Welsh voice.

I felt a deep blush creep up and over my face. 'I'm so sorry, Howard. Please can I buy you a drink?'

'Yeah, okay. A pint of bitter – in a straight glass, mind. I can't stand those beer mugs,' he said before smiling at me.

I left Howard and Patrick talking while I went to get the drinks, mindful this time of the pavement on my return. It was a sunny mild evening at the end of May. I noticed that Patrick and Howard were of a similar height, but that Patrick stood ramrod-straight while Howard hunched his shoulders. I handed Howard his beer, feeling terrible about the large wet patch on his suit jacket and trousers.

Howard offered me a cigarette. Both Patrick and Howard smoked filterless full-strength Capstan, which were the most poison-ous of all the attractively packaged poisons available. I had picked up Richard's habit of smoking Gitanes and declined the offer.

'These are the strongest cigarettes in the world. Top of the list,' Patrick said.

'Yeah, I read they've got more nicotine in them than any other brand, and there's no filter to stop it going straight into your lungs,' Howard said and inhaled deeply.

Patrick laughed.

'Jude's coming up for dinner tonight, why don't you stay, Judy?' asked Patrick.

'Good idea. Rosie will be here soon and I'm sure will want to see you,' Howard said, his eyes crinkling at the corners.

Dinner was in an expensive French restaurant, Didier's, next door to the carpet shop. The staff knew Patrick, Graham and Howard well. I got the impression they ate there nearly every day. There were about twelve of us: Graham, Howard, Patrick, Jude, Rosie, Mandy (Graham's wife), Stu (the craggy-faced man), his wife Fran, and a few more whose names I no longer recall. Mandy was tall with an open, friendly face, good features and a gracious figure. Stu, I learnt, was a carpet dealer; his wife Fran was a small, dizzy-looking woman with bleached blonde hair. Graham ordered bottles of champagne, which was not, as far as I could tell, to celebrate anything in particular. Conversation over dinner was mainly about President Nixon and the Watergate affair. Televised hearings into the alleged cover-up had just started showing in the States. There was talk, too, of the miners' strikes and power cuts.

'I've just bought tons of candles from Holland. If they strike again this winter I'll be laughing,' Howard said.

Rosie, I noticed, was quiet the entire evening. She looked far from happy. I accidentally dropped my lighter on the floor and as I bent to pick it up I saw to my shock Howard's legs playing with Fran's legs under the table. Did Rosie know? Was this why she looked so unhappy? I thought about what Richard had said.

Graham picked up the bill for dinner, which I could see was well over a hundred pounds, if not two. He paid in cash. The average wage in England at this time was £16 a week.

Two weeks later on my way home from college I drove past the Barley Mow and decided to drop in for a quick drink. I was putting off going back to the flat. It had felt so empty since my mother's death, especially now the children had returned to school. I had my history A level the following morning and intended having an early night.

I went into the pub, and there were Arthur and Howard playing snap with their credit cards. They both looked delighted to see me and jumped up at the same time to ask me what I wanted to drink. Arthur made it first to the bar to get me a lager. Howard and I sat down at the table.

'So how are you, Judy?'

'I'm fine. I've got my history A level tomorrow, so I mustn't be out late.'

'Mmm, we'll just have to make sure we get you to bed early, won't we?'

His voice purred and his eyes were full of sexuality and mischief. I looked down at the floor. Luckily attention was taken from me by a tall, good-looking man in a soft leather jacket who walked into the pub and put his arm around Howard's shoulders.

'Hey, Howard, how you doing?' he said. He had a rugby-player's build and light-brown hair.

'Hey, Johnny, good to see you. Do you know Judy?' asked Howard.

'No, I haven't had the pleasure,' Johnny said as he smiled at me.

'Judy, this is Johnny Martin.'

The pub began to fill up. Rick came in with his new girlfriend, Anne; Richard Powis and others turned up. Howard challenged me to a game of darts and won. A bunch of us went for dinner at a restaurant called the Salamander, where the tables were covered in orange and brown floral-pattern cloths. Howard picked up the bill and we all trooped back to the pub.

At the doors, Howard pulled me to one side.

'Judy, I really need a joint. Is your place nearby?'

Butterflies filled my stomach. 'Sure, I'm just round the corner. Here's my car,' I said, pointing at my Fiat.

'I'm not getting in that.' He looked horrified.

I was hurt. I was fond of my little car. Something Richard had said a few days earlier echoed in my ear. 'First he takes my wife and kid and now he's gone and bought the same car as me, even the same colour.' I'd been surprised at the bitterness in Richard's voice. I hadn't heard him speak like that before.

'I'm sorry it's not a BMW, Howard, but my flat is only one minute away.'

'Okay, let's go,' he said. He opened the door and crammed himself in.

As soon as we got to my flat, Howard rolled a joint. I put Lou Reed's 'Walk On The Wild Side' on the stereo. We sat on the floor, our backs against the sofa. He handed me the joint and it made me feel light and delicious. His arm worked its way around me. He kissed me, and I breathed in his smell, mingled with that of the Afghani hash. I tasted his mouth on mine, and felt the warmth of his arms on my back, pulling me into the heat of his body.

I was still wrapped in Howard's arms when I woke the following morning. I didn't want to move. The night had been long and delightful, and all my good intentions had gone up in smoke.

I looked at my watch: 9.00. Shit. I had to get to college. I had an exam. I was going to be late. Howard stirred, his arm stretching out to the ashtray to retrieve a half-smoked joint.

'Howard, I have to go to college. I'll just be a couple of hours. Will you still be here when I get back?' I asked.

'No. I've got to get to London and back to Oxford tonight. And before I leave Brighton I've got to see Johnny. I'm sending him to Italy next week to rent me a house and to await some material I have arriving there.'

That was that. I wondered what kind of material was arriving but I said nothing. I reluctantly climbed out of bed, showered and dressed. He was still lying in my bed rolling yet another joint when I went to kiss him goodbye.

'Good luck with the exam, Jude. I'm sure I'll see you again soon.'

'Bye, Howard.'

I arrived at college forty minutes late. They wouldn't let me into the exam room. I was cross with myself. Then I jumped into the car and drove home hoping Howard would still be there. He'd left.

My father, who had taken no time off work since my mother's death, had a few business meetings in Switzerland, Germany and France. With my exams done (apart from the history one, which I never retook), he asked if I would chauffeur him so he could make it into a break. I happily agreed. While we were away we discussed how to entertain Masha and Marcus over the long summer holidays. He decided I should take the children on the yacht to Cherbourg, then sail to Alderney and to Guernsey where he would meet us. I didn't have much idea about sailing but he said he would find someone to help with the sailing.

My father also talked to me about a large house in Primrose Hill he had just bought. It needed total renovation and he had employed Julian Samson, who was Graham Plinston's property developer, to do this for him. The idea was that this would be a good investment and the family home.

'You're not going to sell the Brighton flat, are you?' I asked.

'No, don't worry. Not unless I have to.'

On returning to Brighton I met Richard for dinner at the Salamander. I thought wistfully of my night with Howard. In fact, I thought of him often. The only thing I felt bad about was Rosie.

'I'm driving Rosie and the kids to Ibiza next week,' Richard said, as the waiter poured our wine.

'Is she going on holiday there?' I asked.

'Between you and me I think she's leaving Howard. Mandy is down there at the moment and is looking for a villa for Rosie to rent. I'm driving her down in Howard's BMW, so if you want to borrow mine while I'm gone you're very welcome.'

'Hey, Richard, that's very generous of you.' I rather liked the idea of gadding about town in a BMW. 'But what makes you think Rosie is leaving him?' I asked.

'Because he's never at home, and when he is, it's like a circus with people constantly coming and going. The madman McCann phones up ranting and raving at all times of the day and night. The deals are getting more and more hectic and his womanizing is really getting her down.'

Guilt tore into me.

Richard left the following week. I took full advantage of having his car. I drove up to London to visit George who was living in Patrick's Kentish Town house, though it was only just habitable. He was working as a brickie for Julian Samson. All George wanted was to save up enough money to return to Afghanistan. He had some of our old friends from Stafford down visiting. We dropped some acid and went to Dingwalls in Camden. Driving home with the car full of tripped-out passengers, I was stopped by the police on three occasions. Once driving the wrong way up a one-way street, once for stopping at a traffic light I couldn't work out the colour of, and once for driving round a roundabout too many times. On each occasion I leapt out of the car and smiled a Cheshire-cat grin at the officers. I was dressed in a checked red and yellow micro minidress with matching thigh-high striped socks. The officers were all really nice and seemed to be amused. But on each occasion they advised me to get home as soon as possible.

Richard returned and was relieved to find his car gleaming clean and in one piece.

'How was the trip?' I asked.

'Cool, really cool. Ibiza's a great place. It's full of the international jetset, the young hip and wealthy, rich hippies, poor hippies, dope dealers and smugglers. It's a Pandora's box. I'm going down again towards the end of the summer if you want to come.'

'Yeah, that sounds great. My father's promised me a holiday at the end of the summer. So we could go then.'

'Brilliant, it's a date.'

Rick had suggested to my father that his twin brother Chris, a sailor, should accompany me and the children on our sailing trip. We set off one grey afternoon from Shoreham Marina. My father looked a sad solitary figure as we pulled away from the shore. Our first leg was down the coast to Littlehampton, a distance of 16-odd miles by road. At Littlehampton, much to my surprise, I met a friend, who took me for a drink. He expressed some concerns about the trip. When I returned to the boat, I was astounded to see the galley table had been turned into a double bed.

'What's going on?' I asked.

Masha and Marcus sat silently watching me.

Chris gave me a sleazy smile. 'I thought it would be a good idea. We're going to be with each other a while. I thought we should get to know each other better. I mean, you know my brother well.'

'Well, think again,' I said, shaking with fury. 'I'm taking the kids for a walk, and when I return I want to see the table back in place.'

It was not a good start. He sulked. The following morning we sailed to the Isle of Wight. The journey was uneventful and Chris and I spoke only when necessary. The following morning at five we set off for Cherbourg; it was grey and overcast as we watched the Isle of Wight receding into the distance. The first three or four hours were fine. The children took turns at the wheel under Chris's watchful gaze. But then it began to rain and the children complained of being cold and feeling sick. We were ill equipped – we had no wet gear. A heavy fog began to descend. Chris looked worried. We had no radar and we were crossing the busiest shipping lane in the world in thick fog. The old rule of 'steam gives way to sail' was irrelevant if a large container ship could not see us. If they hit us they probably wouldn't even know. The wind had dropped and we had to sail under engine.

Sailing in fog is an eerie, frightening experience. The cold damp air pressed against my skin. Marcus's party trick was to make a noise like a foghorn. It used to drive me mad – I never thought I would beg him to make it. So there we sat huddled in the cockpit with Marcus acting as the foghorn. Chris and I took it in turns to steer or sit up in the bow trying to see through the fog.

After fifteen hours at sea, we saw a buoy. Written on it was 'Cherbourg No 1'. I was so relieved I smiled at Chris. Masha and Marcus whooped with relief. Soon we made out the massive outer breakwater of Cherbourg harbour. It was a great feeling of comfort when we motored into the marina and tied up to a pontoon.

A week later, after a two-day stop in Alderney, where the children and I stayed with Mandy's parents, we arrived in St Peter Port, Guernsey. My father and sister Natasha joined us, and much to my relief Chris flew back to England. The sailing horror wasn't quite over, however. My father decided we'd sail to Sark. Countless boats have been wrecked and thousands of lives lost on the coasts of Guernsey, Sark and the group of rocks known as Les Casquettes. Rocks are not the only dangers. There are also strong tides and unpredictable weather. We left St Peter Port mid-morning, carefully picking our way through the jagged pinnacles and small islands along the nine-mile route to Sark.

Finding the entrance to La Creux harbour was like trying to find the way into a secret cove. We were approaching the harbour at low tide; my father hadn't taken into account that it needed approaching at high tide. More jagged rocks emerged as the water level dropped. The waves hissed and sizzled against them. My father paled; Masha was crying. Marcus began his foghorn noise. With frayed nerves we all told him to be quiet. Natasha and I lay on our stomachs at the bow, heads hanging over the side on rock watch. Ragged-looking rocks were all around and just below us. In front of us, teasingly, was the harbour against a backdrop of sheer rock. Luckily for us the sea was almost mirror calm. An extremely anxious few hours followed until the tide turned and we were able to motor into what is probably the tiniest harbour in the world.

'As soon as I get back to London I'm going to do a sailing course and get my master's certificate,' said Natasha.

'Good idea. I think I'll do the same,' agreed my father.

'I really think you should have radar fitted before you take the boat back across the Channel,' I said. I didn't fancy doing that trip again, or any other sailing trip. But Natasha had been fired with a love of sailing. Back in London, she immediately enrolled on a sailing course. This was to shape her life for years to come.

CHAPTER FIVE
Escape

Richard and I drove down through France. The weather was wonderful and we smoked endless amounts of dope. The Grateful Dead played on the car stereo throughout the journey. With the car windows open and warm air blowing in my hair, I felt free. I had not realized what a strain I had been under, what with the worry about my father and his depression and loneliness, and the responsibility of looking after Masha and Marcus. When we had returned from our sailing adventures, my father and Natasha, now in London, had both had to go back to work. The children stayed with me in Brighton until they returned to school.

Much as I loved them all, it was a relief to be away.

We arrived in Barcelona on a late afternoon in September. The ferry to Ibiza was not to leave for several hours so we filled in the time by people-watching in a bar on the Ramblas.

'Richard, why do so many people come to Ibiza?' I asked.

'Oh, it's beautiful and it's been popular for years. In the fifties beatniks came in search of parties and jazz. Then in the sixties it became popular with American draft dodgers, escaping the Vietnam War. That kind of put it on the hippie map.'

'Doesn't Frank Zappa have a house on the island?' I asked.

'Yes, and Mike Oldfield, Nina and Frederick and some of the Floyd, and a whole bunch of others.'

The ferry, slightly rusty, was far from luxurious, although our cabin with its two single beds and washbasin was clean and comfortable enough. We climbed a metal staircase to the top deck and in the warm night air watched the lights of Barcelona disappear before we went to the bar. Our fellow passengers were a mixture of lorry drivers and long-haired hippies, and a few families with overtired children. Sleeping bags and rucksacks filled the boat's lounges where the hippies had targeted their chairs for the nine-hour voyage.

Early the following morning I rushed to the top deck to see Ibiza from the sea. The old city of Ibiza stood proudly high on a hill overlooking the bay, crisp early sunlight bathing its protective Renaissance walls. It had been built on a promontory jutting into the sea. As we entered the natural harbour I had a strong feeling there was something magical about the place. I wasn't sure if this was because of my relief at being away from all the strains of family, or something bigger than us I didn't understand. A small flotilla of fishing boats was making its way out to sea; fishing nets lay on the old harbour walls. Men on the dock were ready with ropes to throw to the ferry.

Richard had told me that Victoria, who was helping Rosie look after the children, would meet us. As we drove off the ferry, pungent smells of sewage hit me. It was a smell anyone who spends any time in Ibiza gets accustomed to. We parked the car and walked to the terrace bar of the Hotel Montesol, a colonial-style building on the main plaza in an area between the city walls and port known as Sa Penya.

'There's Vicky,' Richard said.

I saw a tall thin girl with large breasts and, under a straw hat, wavy dark-blonde hair almost reaching her waist. When we reached her, Richard gave her a huge hug.

'Muffin is so excited – she can't wait to see you,' said Victoria.

'Me too. Vic, this is Judy.'

She held out her hand; I took it and was surprised at her firm grip. She was, I reckoned, about four years older than me and slightly taller.

'Good to meet you at last. I've heard a lot about you,' she said in a quiet voice and smiled.

'Good to meet you too,' I said.

'Would you like a quick drink before we go up to the finca?'

I looked to see what Victoria was drinking. It looked like chocolate. 'What's that?'

'La bomba – it's delicious. Chocolate and brandy. You can have it hot or cold. I like it hot in the morning.'

'I'll have one,' said Richard.

'Yes, I'd like to try one,' I said.

We pulled out cane rattan chairs and sat down. A waiter came and Victoria ordered our drinks.

'So Rosie's left the house in Santa Eulalia?' said Richard.

'Yes, she just couldn't stand it after Howard had been down. It was complete madness. People were forever turning up, which is what she had come here to escape from. The last straw was when Jim McCann arrived,' Victoria said.

'God, that lunatic,' said Richard.

'That's putting it mildly. First he arrives with this Irish girl Anne, then a few days later a Dutch girl called Sylvia arrives and he's taking it in turns to sleep with them both. The atmosphere was horrible. Rosie was furious with Howard for bringing all the chaos. He left to go back to London or somewhere.'

'Yeah, I saw him briefly in Brighton. Says he hates it out here with all the hippy shit,' said Richard.

'It's not really his scene,' said Victoria.

I thought of Howard with his pints of bitter and his green silk suit, and couldn't really imagine him here.

'So did McCann leave too?' Richard asked.

'Unfortunately not. Things got worse. Mandy and her kids were staying with us and Jim was furious with her and seemed ready to lose it.'

'Good lord, why?'

'Well, Mandy started spending time with an American guy called Skip, she bumped into here. He was a junkie and Mandy was increasingly under his influence. Graham was very upset and worried. Jim was angry with Mandy. He said Graham couldn't operate properly with her fucking his head, so she had to go,' Victoria said.

'So what happened?'

'Rosie and I, fearful for Mandy, managed to lock him in one of the upstairs rooms and get Mandy out of the house. She went and hid out in a house up in the hills. Then she, Skip and the kids went back to her palace in the old Kasbah in Tangiers.'

'And McCann?'

'He was spitting mad with Rosie and me. He left a few days later with Sylvia, after despatching Anne back to Belfast.'

The more I heard about Jim McCann the less I wanted to meet him. Richard went quiet. I presumed it was from the thought of Jim McCann being in the same house as his daughter.

Our drinks arrived. Victoria was right, the hot chocolate and brandy was delicious. The café terrace was beginning to fill up. A couple of tables were occupied with families we'd seen on the ferry; a few Spanish businessmen were having discussions over *café con leche* with small glasses of brandy. Some tables were occupied by suntanned hippies in colourful clothes and dark sunglasses, drinking freshly squeezed orange juice. On the other side of the street, two policemen watched the café. They were dressed in green military-style uniforms and wore dark glasses and black patent-leather hats, which resembled dog bowls, with flaps at the back that hung down to their shoulders.

'Are they the local police?' I asked Victoria.

'No, they're the Guardia Civil.'

We followed Victoria out to her car, a white Renault 4 that she had driven down from England piled high with Rosie's stuff, kilims, clothes, toys and sound system.

'I'll drive round to you, and then just follow me,' she said.

We drove out of Ibiza town on the San Juan road and very soon we were in the countryside, a patchwork of almond, olive and fig trees and pine-covered hills. About thirty-five minutes later, after having driven up dirt tracks for at least twenty minutes, we arrived in front of an isolated whitewashed finca, high in the hills above the small village of San Carlos. The smell of pine trees filled the air. Howard's orange BMW was parked outside; Richard parked his alongside. Muffin came running barefoot out of the house, her blonde hair, bleached by the sun, flying.

'Daddy, Daddy,' she called, as she hurled her four-year-old body into Richard's arms.

Rosie appeared in the doorway, with her and Howard's daughter Myfanwy, otherwise known as Podge, in her arms.

'Hey, Judy, welcome,' she said.

I walked over and gave her a kiss. 'I'm so pleased to be here, it's such a beautiful island.'

'You're going to love it – it's so chilled and peaceful and there are some wonderful people about.'

The interior of the house was one large room with beamed ceilings, simply furnished but covered with oriental carpets. All the bedrooms led off this room. To the side of the house was a kitchen and bathroom.

Later in the day Victoria and I drove down into San Carlos. In the village square was a church that looked like a beautiful house except for the small bell gable and cross on the roof. There was a small shop selling basics where Victoria picked up some bread. We then went to a little bar, Anita's, run by an Ibizan woman, on the corner of a track that led down to the beaches.

'This is the only place for miles with a telephone and it's where we collect our post.'

The bar had flagstone floors and a vine-covered courtyard. One or two of the customers called out greetings to Victoria. In the corner a girl with long multi-plaited gold hair sat reading tarot cards. At another table a man was hunched over reading *The Dice Man*.

'This place does the best tortilla on the island. Do you want one?'

'Yes, please, I'm starving,' I said.

We ordered two tortillas and two beers and talked about the people she knew, including a Dutch doctor who liked to try to persuade people to get a hole drilled in their head to expand their consciousness. A couple more hippies walked in with bongos in their hands.

'It's great down here in the evening with everyone chilling, smoking joints, playing guitars or drums and singing. We'll do it one night,' Victoria said.

'Do the locals not mind all the hippies, smoking dope and

everything?' I asked.

'The *Ibicencos* are I think one of the most tolerant people in the world. They're really friendly. I think it quite amuses them. They call the hippies *peluto*, the "hairies". Some of the locals have started growing dope that they sell. It was a poor island with only agriculture and salt, now it's got foreign revenue flowing in. The Guardia Civil are the ones you have to look out for. They're Franco's police from the mainland and can be heavy.'

In the early evening of the following day, after a lazy time on the beach, Victoria drove me into Ibiza town. We parked the car and walked up towards the old city walls. The nearer we got, the narrower and more tortuous the streets became. We crossed over a drawbridge and as we passed through the main gate we had to stand to one side as a group of orange-clad Hare Krishna disciples danced by singing their mantra. Hippy stalls stood in the shade beneath the old city walls. The stalls sold candles, joss sticks, tie-die everything, obscure mystical figures and Che Guevara and marijuana leaf posters. Victoria made her way to one selling bronze bracelets. A beautiful Peruvian man was the owner.

'Hey, Lucio.'

'Victoria, *cómo estás*?' He leant over the trestle table and gave her a kiss on each cheek.

'*Muy bien. Esta es mi amiga*, Judy. Judy, this is Lucio.'

Lucio held out his hand and I looked into beautiful warm, liquid brown eyes I could have drowned in. He leant over the table and kissed me too.

As we walked away I said, 'He is gorgeous.'

'Don't tell me about it! But no go, he's Rosie's,' she replied. 'He is a special, peaceful man.'

Good for Rosie, I thought. We carried on walking and passed an ancient cobbled courtyard opening immediately on to the main square. I saw men walking holding hands with other men.

'Vic, am I seeing right?'

She laughed and said, 'You haven't seen anything yet.'

The main square was full of restaurants crowded with clients, trendy boutiques and craft shops. Traditionally black-clad Ibizans made their way among the crowds, apparently untouched by time or change. We walked up another cobbled street full of lively bars with customers spilling out onto the street. People were dressed in the most fantastic costumes.

'Take a look at this lot, Jude,' said Vic.

Five or six gay men were standing outside a bar dressed in outrageous clothes and jewellery. One was swathed in ostrich feathers and wore exquisite make-up, fishnet stockings and pink high heels. Nearby a bunch of local children played with a ball. Not something you would see in England or anywhere else I could think of. I loved it.

Two days later, as Richard looked after the children, Rosie and Victoria took me to a full-moon party. We drove down steep, winding tracks to reach a wide sandy beach that sloped softly down to shallow, crystal-clear water. It was in a wide bay dotted with tiny rocky islands. We arrived just before sunset and the beach was already crowded with an astonishing assortment of people. As the sun fell and the moon and stars rose, the bongo players started up, joined by the sound of tambourines, Jew's harps, maracas and the Indian tabla.

We walked through the crowds to a large rock where a group of people sat cross-legged in a circle smoking joints. By the side was a large, dark-haired man with an enormous belly cooking steaks on a barbecue. I recognized Lucio, who on seeing Rosie leapt to his feet and made his way towards her, enveloping her in a warm embrace. I continued with Victoria into the circle. I was introduced to Martinique, a henna-haired French beauty, and Ricardo, a young Argentinian. Armando, another Argentinian, was the man cooking. Then Victoria introduced me to a man with long blond hair who looked like a Roman god. Our eyes locked. My stomach fluttered.

'Judy, this is Arendt. Arendt, our friend Judy,' said Victoria.

He stood up. He was tall and slim, dressed in a loose-fitting white shirt and white linen trousers, which enhanced his golden tan and his long slim legs. He took my hand and gestured to me to sit down beside him. Victoria winked at me and went to talk to another group of people. Arendt handed me a joint. I took it and inhaled deeply.

'So, how do you know Victoria?' Arendt asked in a strong Dutch accent.

'Through Rosie and Howard.'

'And how do you know Howard and Rosie?'

'Through my brother Patrick.'

'Not Patrick who works for Graham?'

'Yeah, do you know him?'

'Well yes, Howard, Graham and I are in the middle of a lot of business together.'

'Ah, right,' I said. I decided it probably wasn't best to ask what kind of business. Just then Armando handed us beautifully cooked chargrilled steaks with salad and potatoes. We ate in silence as a large moon bathed us in its light. Conversation and music floated above my head. I heard Martinique proclaiming that Ibiza was powerful mystically and psychologically and exerted a force over those who strayed on to it. I believed it. I could feel it.

'Shall we go for a walk?' asked Arendt.

'Good idea,' I said, and got to my feet as Arendt also rose. We smiled at each other. He slipped his arm round my shoulder. As we walked a young girl with eyes the colour and shape of almonds and skin the colour of *café con leche* walked by on her hands. Further on was a juggler and then a clown. Small groups sat clustered round fires with food cooking on them. Some people walked round naked adorned only with beads. Others strummed guitars, while all the time the drums kept up a steady background beat.

Rosie came up to me and whispered, 'Go for it, Jude. I'll drop by and pick you up tomorrow lunchtime.' She and Lucio grinned at me before they disappeared into the crowd.

Arendt bent down and kissed me softly.

'Would you like to come up to my place?' he asked.

'Yes, I'd like that,' I said, as I thought, why not?

We walked, arms around each other, away from the beach and up through the pine trees to Arendt's car. It was a large American jeep. I climbed in and we began the drive to his finca. Like Rosie's it was up miles of dirt track; it was in the hills near the village of San

Juan. Unlike Rosie's, it was well furnished. Oriental rugs covered the rough stone floors and white walls. A huge hi-fi system was in the main room, with hundreds of LPs and tapes strewn about. There was a large terrace, and the moon shone a silvery light on pine forests that reached down to the sea.

Arendt put on *Goat's Head Soup*, then sat down at a circular antique pine table in the room and laid two lines of white powder onto a mirror. He handed me a rolled-up $100 bill.

'What is it?' I asked.

He laughed. 'Cocaine – have you never had any?'

'No,' I said, and for some reason felt embarrassed.

'Well, you're in for a good time. Come sit by me and watch.'

I watched him snort half of one line up one nostril and the other half up the other nostril.

'Here – want to try?'

For the second time that night, I thought, why not?

I took the note from him and leant over the mirror with the dollar bill up my nostril. It was not, I thought as I looked at my reflection, an attractive image. The powder almost immediately hit the back of my throat and numbed it. I was soon feeling a rush of euphoria. I grinned widely at Arendt.

My body filled with erotic energy. He rose and scooped me up and carried me through to a room with an inviting bed with gleaming white sheets. He kicked the door behind him, set me down and pulled me to him. Somehow his clothes seemed simply to drop off him, as did mine, landing in untidy heaps on the flowing patterns of the carpet beneath our bare feet before we collapsed in lust between the crisp cotton sheets.

We woke late the following morning. It had been an adventurous night.

We sat in the shade on the terrace drinking freshly squeezed orange juice and ensaimadas, brought up freshly from the village by Arendt's maid Juanita. Followed by two more lines of coke.

Below us we heard the sounds of a car struggling up the dirt tracks. Now and then glimpses of orange appeared among the trees.

'Here's Rosie, to steal you away from me,' Arendt said.

I laughed. 'I'm here for another week.'

Ten minutes later Rosie joined us on the terrace. She smiled warmly at me, then turned to Arendt. 'I've just spoken to Howard,' she said to him.

'Judy, will you excuse us for a bit while I speak to Rosie?'

As they moved to another room I heard Rosie saying, 'It seems like a lot of heat is spreading out from the Vegas bust.'

Twenty minutes later they re-emerged on the terrace. Arendt seemed distracted. Rosie wrote a number down for him to call Howard on.

'Judy, we must go,' said Rosie.

Arendt and I kissed goodbye.

'I'll call by the house in a couple of days,' he said.

As Rosie and I drove back to her house, she suddenly said, 'You know, I should never have left Richard. Do you know why I fell for him? He was the only guy I knew who liked Bob Dylan as much as me.' She laughed. 'But it was wrong to take Muffin away from him.'

'But you fell in love with Howard and now you have another beautiful daughter.'

'Yes, but I'm nearly always on my own. I didn't leave Richard for that.'

I saw Arendt once more for dinner and a night of fun before Richard and I drove back to Brighton. Richard had to go back to teaching and my father had enrolled me on a secretarial course for my gap year. We were both sad to leave Ibiza, but Richard was particularly sad at leaving Muffin.

We settled back into life in Brighton. Thoughts of Howard still occupied my mind, much as I tried to prevent them. My father spent the odd weekend in Brighton. He seemed less depressed; I suspected he was dating.

One particular weekend in early October he asked if I had spoken to Patrick. I said no and asked why.

'Well, I got a strange call from him early in the week. He said he was fed up with the rat race and was going to live a simple life in France. He and Jude caught the ferry two nights ago. Terribly sudden decision, I thought, especially as Jude is pregnant.'

'I haven't spoken to him since I've been back,' I said. I wondered if this had anything to do with the 'heat' I had heard Rosie referring to.

'And then yesterday I couldn't get hold of Julian, so I tried Graham at his office and the shop and there was no reply. Eventually Julian phoned me, and when I asked about Graham he was a bit evasive.'

'How's the house coming on?' I asked, wanting to change the subject.

'Oh, like they always do. Slowly. But Julian's doing a good job.'

A couple of days later I saw Richard and repeated my conversation with my father.

'Yeah. Rosie said a load of dope they'd sent in some pop-group speakers had been seized in Las Vegas. Maybe they're all going to lie low for a bit.'

'Where's Howard at the moment?' I asked.

'No idea. He's not in Ibiza and he's not in Oxford.'

Early November, Masha and Marcus joined me for half-term. They both seemed more settled, although Marcus said he hated his school. A couple of weeks after they'd gone back, I got a frantic call from Richard.

'Judy, can you drive me to Gatwick, now?'

'Yeah, of course. What's up?' I said, thinking something must be wrong with Muffin.

'Howard and Arendt have been arrested at Arendt's house in Amsterdam. Howard has been sent to jail back here. Rosie wants me to fly out and drive her and the kids home.'

'Oh my God. When do you want to leave?'

'I'll be round in twenty minutes. Can you be waiting downstairs?'

'Of course.'

CHAPTER SIX
Ibiza

Howard spent three weeks on remand in Brixton prison before a magistrate released him, on £50,000 bail, to stay with his parents in Kenfig Hill, Wales. He had put up £10,000 of his own money, the rest guaranteed by his parents and a family friend.

Muffin spent most weekends with Richard in Brighton, and Richard and I drove to Oxford to pick her up from Rosie. Rosie had moved out of the little cottage she and Howard owned in Yarnton, a small village close to Oxford. After it had been raided and ransacked by the police, she couldn't face living in it on her own. She rented the top two floors of her friend Kate Collingham's house in Oxford, and occasionally drove with Myfanwy to Kenfig Hill to visit Howard.

There was much talk about Howard's plight in the pubs of Brighton. There were rumours that Howard had made a statement to the police implicating Johnny Martin, that he had told them of the villa in Italy that Johnny had rented for him. Johnny was questioned on several occasions but never arrested.

The carpet shop, I learnt from George, had closed down.

I continued with my course. The first Christmas without my mother loomed. Patrick announced he would not be home.

George suggested I put some hash in the Christmas cake to cheer up my father.

'Do you think that's a good idea? What about Masha and Marcus?'

'They never eat Christmas cake,' he said.

'That's true. I'll think about it.'

What I did was crumble a tiny piece of hash in one half of the cake, and covered that half with extra cherries.

It was a sad Christmas. Mummy's sense of humour was sorely missed. Natasha, George and I played many board games with the children. Richard had bought us a huge white jigsaw puzzle, which kept us all occupied, if maddened. I bottled out of giving my father any cake, but George didn't. In the evening, my father watched television with tears of laughter running down his cheeks and Natasha giggled at how quickly the wine had gone to her head.

I heard from Richard that Howard had had his bail transferred to Rosie's place at Kate's in Oxford.

Easter was late in 1974. I drove the children and Natasha (who didn't have a licence) in our father's car to the mill in France. Jude was heavily pregnant. She and Patrick were living a simple life. They had restored the mill on a pittance; Patrick had done most of the work himself, including making the furniture. They grew their own vegetables. While we were there, marrows were on the menu. Jude had an astonishing ability to invent a different way to cook marrow nightly. Patrick spent his days painting on an easel at the side of the road, wearing a black beret and attracting passing tourists. He really was the great romantic. He had also built a snail farm out of wooden planks and plastic sheeting covered in salt. The salt was supposed to stop the snails climbing up the sides of the enclosure and escaping, but one morning he woke up to discover they'd all gone. This distressed him greatly.

Patrick and Jude had integrated well into the local community, who could see they were struggling and adopted them. The farm next door kept them supplied with foie gras and eggs. It was in many ways an idyllic existence.

Patrick never mentioned Howard or Graham, and I had a feeling I should not bring them up. For Patrick that part of his life had gone.

My father joined us for a week before we all drove back to England. Once I was back in Brighton, I phoned Richard.

'Oh, Judy, so glad you're back,' he said. 'I'll come and see you, is that okay?'

'Sure, I'll open a bottle of wine.'

Half an hour later Richard stomped into the flat. He flung his leather bag down on the kitchen counter. I handed him a glass of red wine and he guzzled it.

'Want a line?' he said.

I had noticed since we came back from Ibiza that this was becoming a regular habit of Richard's. Luckily, the allowance from my father didn't allow it to become one for me. Cocaine in those days was a rich man's drug. But I indulged when Richard invited me to. He laid out two long fat lines. We snorted.

'Howard's disappeared,' he said.

'What do you mean, he's disappeared?' I laughed. I had a vision of Howard, joint in hand, vanishing in a puff of smoke. 'Puff the Magic Dragon' played in my head.

'It's serious, Judy.'

I looked at Richard and realized how exhausted he was.

'What's happened?'

'A couple of days before Easter, a man turned up at Kate's front door. Told her he was from Customs and Excise and asked for Howard. A few minutes later this man takes Howard away.'

'So have Customs rearrested him?'

'No, that's the whole thing. Customs say it was nothing to do with them. The police are investigating and endlessly questioning Rosie.'

'Good grief. How is Rosie?'

'Well, obviously upset and worried. Won't say much to me.'

'But if the man wasn't Customs, who was he?' I asked.

'Nobody knows. That's the whole thing. Howard's disappeared and his trial is due to begin early next month.'

Howard's trial went on at the Old Bailey in early May without him. The other four defendants in the case, whom I had never met, were found guilty. They had been charged with conspiracy to export hashish to the US hidden in loudspeakers.

The day after the trial, the *Daily Mirror* went to town. The whole of the front page carried the story of Howard's disappearance. It carried a mugshot of Howard's profile, in which to me he looked so handsome. I cut it out and put it under my pillow. The story was fascinating. It had Howard tied up with the IRA, MI6 and the Italian mafia. The suggestion was that one of these groups had abducted him. The *Mail* followed with the story that the police were investigating the possibility that Howard had been executed by the IRA. What with all the stories I had heard about McCann, I worried it might be true.

I phoned Richard. 'Have you seen the papers?'

'Yes, pretty mad stuff,' said Richard.

'Is any of it true?'

'Well, Howard had mentioned MI6 to me, and they do recruit from Oxbridge. And McCann claims he's IRA and Rosie said something to me about Howard being beaten up a few weeks ago.'

'Oh my God. I hope he's all right. How's Rosie coping? It must be awful for her.'

'I'm going to go down and take her and the kids somewhere quiet for the weekend.'

'Good idea. Give her my love,' I said.

I worried about Howard and wondered if he was all right.

It was early June. George had left to go back to Afghanistan. Richard called.

'Hey, Judy, I fancy going to Ibiza again. Want to come?'

'I'd love to, but I have no money,' I said.

'Don't worry. My treat. I have a friend Susie down there. She's rented a villa and we can stay with her. You must know her.'

'Yes, I've met John and Susie a couple of times. I like them. They were Sussex contemporaries of Patrick's.'

'Well, they've split up now,' he said. 'John went and bought this old yacht, thought it was a good investment. Now Susie's got the job of restoring her.'

I phoned my father to ask if I could go. He said it was fine; Masha and Marcus could spend the summer at Patrick's.

Once again Richard and I found ourselves on the rusty ferry approaching the old harbour. I felt excited to be back. I couldn't wait to see Victoria again – she was meeting the ferry and taking us up to Susie's.

Driving off the ferry I noticed the smell of Ibiza town had not improved. We parked and walked to the Montesol, and there was Victoria, grinning widely.

'Hey, you guys, great to see you,' she said, hugging us both.

We ordered la bombas. I looked around; nothing seemed to have changed since last summer. Even the bar's clientele looked the same.

'How's Rosie, Richard?' asked Victoria.

'Oh, up and down. She's sold the house in Yarnton and is going to buy a house with a couple of friends.'

'God, what a terrible time for her,' said Victoria. 'And the kids, how are they?'

'Well, Muffin worried me. I think she picked up on all the tension, started having a few tantrums. She seems calmer now. Podge is still too young, I think, to have noticed anything amiss.'

'All those newspaper headlines got the gossipmongers here busy,' said Victoria.

'So what are you doing here now Rosie's left?' I asked.

'I'm staying at Susie's and helping her with the yacht. It's a beautiful old ketch. I'll take you guys down tomorrow to see her,' said Victoria. 'It should be an exciting day. They're going to haul her out of the water and put her on the hard dock.'

We followed Victoria, who still had Rosie's Renault 4, six kilometres up the San Antonio road. Near a sign to the village of San Rafael we turned off on to a cart track and drove up through gnarled pines and past blinking goats. We finally reached a two-storey finca with crimson bougainvillea climbing up its white walls. Susie was standing on the first-floor balcony waving to us, before she came down and greeted us.

Susie was slightly shorter than me. She had an attractive face and dark-brown shoulder-length hair, which had been bleached to a lighter shade by the sun.

'Hey, welcome. Great to see you both.'

The finca was not as isolated as Rosie's house had been. Through the trees about four hundred yards away I could see another house. In the distance I could hear dogs barking.

Rosie's oriental carpets were dotted around the finca. Outside a covered veranda ran the length of the house. It was furnished with cane chairs, sofas and large cushions. Susie slept in the room upstairs, which had its own balcony. She showed us into a room that led off the end of the veranda. There were two single mattresses on the floor and one bedside table and nothing else. It was definitely going to be living out of a suitcase. A door at the end of the room opened onto the bedroom next door, which could also be accessed from the finca's main room.

As we sat on the terrace Susie brought out lemonade made with freshly squeezed lemons.

'So, Vic, who are your neighbours?' I asked.

'In that house there,' she said, as she indicated the house I could see through the trees, 'are four guys. Two English, one Dutch and one American. They have a boat, and have discovered the old Ibizan smuggling routes. They're okay. I don't have that much to do with them, they're pretty reclusive. Further down the path a really nice Argentinian couple live with their Ibizan hound. They're coming over for a barbecue tonight.'

'Vicky, have you got any dope?' asked Richard.

'Only enough for a couple of joints,' she said. 'But the guys staying in the room next to you will get you some if you want.'

'Who are they?' I asked.

'Two guys from Leeds, Kevin and Larry. Susie is letting them stay here in return for sanding the decks and doing other bits and bobs.'

Early the following morning we all went into Ibiza town. We drove down to the port to where Susie's yacht was moored. She was a beautiful 57-foot wooden ketch called *Minoru*. She had been built on the Clyde in 1909 and named after the horse that won the Epsom Derby that year.

Kevin and Larry were there. A couple of years older than me, they had long dirty hair, tanned bodies and bloodshot eyes. They had spent the night sleeping on the deck.

'These guys obviously did the town last night,' Victoria whispered. They looked a bit dodgy to me.

The yacht had to be lifted out of the water in order for the hull to be cleaned and repaired. A cradle was put under the boat and yoked to a wheel. A mule then walked in seemingly endless circles working the machinery that slowly lifted the yacht out of the water. The process took the entire day.

Richard and I left Victoria and Susie by the yacht and went to La Tierra, a little cave-like bar with tables outside. We ordered horchata, a drink made from chufa, the roots of a plant originally found in North Africa and imported to Valencia by the Moors. It tasted of almonds. The bar was on the right-hand side of a little plaza that sloped down to the port and was full of tourists. Down by the port was a small wooden hut belonging to the Guardia Civil.

As Richard and I sat in the bar, we saw the Guardia dragging two shirtless, handcuffed hippies towards the hut. They threw them unceremoniously inside before shutting the door and clapping each other on the back, pleased smiles on their faces. A couple more Guardia turned up; much joking appeared to go on between them. They glanced up at our bar and then by turns went into the hut. Each one came out after spending about five minutes in the hut, a wide grin on his face as he wiped his hands on his green trousers. I looked at the other customers in the bar. I was amazed to see that none of their faces seemed to register the shock I was feeling, even though they were watching every bit intently as I was.

'Richard, isn't that a bit heavy?'

'Looks it, but I'm wondering if it isn't a bit of a show for the tourists.'

Show or not, I prayed I would never have any contact with the Guardia.

A few days later I was up at the finca, reading on the veranda. I saw Victoria walking towards me from the house next door.

'Jeez, those guys are spitting mad,' she said.

'Why, what's up?'

'They buried ten kilos in the woods and someone has dug it up and disappeared with it. They wanted to know if we knew anything about it.'

'Why do they think we would know anything about it?'

'Beats me. They were wondering if we knew or had seen or heard anything.'

Early the following morning I was woken by shouting and banging. The door opened and Susie's head appeared.

'Hey, Judy, Richard – the Guardia are here and they want everyone on the veranda now.'

She came into our room and banged on Kevin and Larry's door.

'Kevin, Larry – the Guardia are here and they want everyone on the veranda. Be quick, they want to search the house.'

Panicked voices could be heard through the closed door. Susie repeated herself and told them to be quick. She turned round and looked at us as I was wiping sleep from my eyes.

'Best be quick,' she said.

Richard was searching his trouser pockets; he pulled out a small lump of hash and ate it before quickly dressing. I pulled on a pair of shorts and a T-shirt and followed Richard outside.

Victoria was already on the veranda. There were four sunglasses-wearing Guardia standing round Susie, who was smiling and chatting to them. They appeared charmed by her. I sat on a cushion next to Victoria; Richard slumped into a cane armchair next to us. Kevin and Larry appeared at the door of our room. Kevin stumbled over to us, yawning and rubbing his eyes. Larry, on seeing the Guardia, darted back inside before reappearing a minute later. He joined us too.

'Where did you put it?' Kevin whispered to Larry.

Larry hesitated before quietly answering, 'I threw it in a case.'

'What did you throw in a case?' Victoria asked.

'We had a kilo,' Kevin whispered.

'Oh God,' groaned Richard.

'What case did you put it in?' I asked.

Larry looked down at the ground. We all looked at him, waiting for an answer.

'What case, man?' said Kevin.

'A black one, lying on the floor, just behind that door.'

I felt the blood drain from my face.

'That's Jude's case,' Victoria said.

Larry said nothing.

'Are you saying, Larry, that you have just thrown a kilo of hash in my case?'

'Sorry. I'll tell them it's mine,' Larry said, still staring at the ground.

I wasn't sure that would make much difference.

This was Franco's Spain. The Guardia were not known to fool around. A kilo of hash and you were looking at ten years. I felt sick. I had this tight little ball of fear forming in my stomach. Susie, totally unaware of what was in her house, was offering to make *café con leche* for the Guardia. While she went into the kitchen to prepare the coffees, two Guardia went upstairs to search Susie's room. They were up there about eight minutes before coming back down and searching Victoria's room. The other two Guardia leant languidly against a wall, watching us through their dark sunglasses. Guns hung at their sides.

We were all silent on the veranda, lost in our own thoughts. Masha and Marcus's faces flashed in front of me. What would they think of their sister being in jail? I missed them. I could see the disappointed face of my father.

They finished in Victoria's room and went on to the main room, then to Larry and Kevin's, using the entrance off the main room. I waited for them to emerge from my room, triumphantly holding a kilo of dope high in the air, demanding to know who was the owner of the black suitcase.

Susie came out of the kitchen with a tray of steaming cups of coffee. One of the watching Guardia took the tray from her while the other one called his comrades. The two searching Guardia came out and beamed at Susie. They stood around with the mugs in their hands flirting with Susie, who flirted and giggled back. It seemed like for ever that we sat there listening to their voices. Then all off a sudden they were calling out *adios*, as they climbed into their van and drove off.

Victoria leapt to her feet and gave Susie an enormous hug. 'Good one, Susie.'

Susie looked startled, not understanding. Victoria took her to one side and explained the situation to her. She was not amused.

Richard, Kevin, Larry and I sat in stunned silence, hardly believing they were gone.

Susie asked Larry and Kevin to leave.

'Larry, given that you decided to hide the dope in my case, I reckon I should lay claim to it,' I said.

'Absolutely,' said Victoria.

'Hear, hear,' agreed Richard. 'You put us all at risk.'

'Did you have anything to do with the guys' stuff next door?' Victoria asked.

'What stuff?' Larry said in his heavy Leeds accent, looking sheepish.

'The guys next door had some dope disappear. They're far from happy about it.'

'We don't know anything about that. Do we, Larry?' Kevin said.

'Come on, let's get out of here, man,' Larry said to Kevin.

They went into the house, grabbed their rucksacks and left, without arguing about the kilo.

'Why do you think the Guardia came here?' Susie asked.

'Maybe they were suspicious of Kevin and Larry,' I said.

'Perhaps the guys next door tipped them off, thinking we had their dope,' Richard suggested.

'But if we did, surely they wouldn't want the Guardia finding it,' I said.

'They wouldn't expect us to hide it all here. It could have been a test to see if anything was found, like a couple of kilos,' Victoria said.

'Well, please, don't you lot have any amounts like that kept here,' Susie said, unaware that the kilo was still in the house.

The guys next door denied to Vic that they had sent the Guardia. We weren't convinced. We were never to see Larry or Kevin again. After breaking a piece of the dope off for personal use, I hid the rest in the woods. It dawned on me that if I sold some of it I could stay in Ibiza a lot longer.

The next day Susie joined me on the veranda. 'Judy, would you like to stay on and help on the yacht? I can't pay you, but I can give you room and board.'

'I'd love to, Susie. That would be great.'

With room and board and money from the dope, I'd be okay for the whole summer.

The following week, at the beginning of July, Richard returned to England and I started working on the yacht. The idea of returning to Brighton and starting at Sussex began to lose its appeal. The summer went by in a cloud of smoke and hard physical work on the boat. Full-moon parties still happened on the beaches, especially Benirras beach, up in the hills near San Juan and a couple of other locations. Two clubs opened in town, Pasha's and Amnesia. It was the beginning of the commercial club scene in Ibiza. We stayed well clear of them. They didn't have anywhere near the atmosphere of the free parties.

Susie returned to England for a week. Harry, a Dutch friend of Arendt's and fellow smuggler, came down from Amsterdam and stayed in Arendt's finca.

'How's Arendt?' I asked him.

'Oh he's fine. Bit cross about the statement your friend Howard made to the police. He's out on bail but can't leave Holland at the moment.'

Harry asked Victoria and me to sail with him on his small yacht to Mallorca. Neither of us had been to Mallorca before and thought it might be fun. I'd got over my dislike of sailing; in the warmth of the Mediterranean I found it a very different activity. We left early the following morning for the fourteen-hour sail.

It was dark when we arrived and moored in the Real Club Nautico. Harry went immediately to a phone box and then told us he had to meet 'someone'. It became fairly obvious that he was up to something. He left us in the club bar and disappeared with an empty briefcase. The feel of Mallorca was very different to Ibiza. It seemed a lot straighter and smelt of money and luxury.

A couple of hours later Harry returned, with a full briefcase and a couple of carrier bags.

'We better turn in; we'll have to leave early in the morning.'

Victoria and I looked at each other. It didn't seem like we were going to get much of a chance to see Palma. Back on the yacht, Harry stashed the briefcase and carrier bags into a locker. I strongly suspected they were full of money.

When we reached Ibiza the following evening it was dark. Harry sailed as near to a beach as he could get and told us it was better if we took the dinghy and rowed ashore rather than return to port with him. We were learning that on Ibiza one didn't ask questions. We lowered the rubber dinghy into the water before carefully climbing in ourselves.

Harry sailed off and Vic and I began rowing towards the beach. It was a fairly new moon in a clear cloudless night. The sea was calm.

'Jude.' Victoria broke the silence. 'This dinghy is sinking.'

I had noticed this as well, but had hoped it was my imagination. The beach was still another hundred-odd yards away. We started rowing faster. We each had a small rucksack with clothes and passports in and didn't want them getting wet.

Thirty yards from the shore we abandoned the dinghy, and with the sea up to our chests and rucksacks on our heads we waded to the beach with absolutely no idea how we would get back to Ibiza town.

'Bloody Harry,' Victoria fumed. I couldn't help but agree.

Susie returned from England with a six-foot-two, blond, handsomely rugged South African. 'Judy, Vic, this is Jeff,' she said.

'Hi, ladies,' he responded, with blue smiling eyes.

Jeff, after assessing the yacht, advised Susie to take her back to Southampton. 'It will be much cheaper and the work will be done more efficiently,' he'd told her. Then to me he said, 'Jude, ever used an electric drill?'

'Uh, no,' I replied.

'Well, now's your chance. I want you to build bunks for you and Vic, and a galley, and I'll need a chart table.'

I looked at him blankly.

'I'll take care of mine and Susie's bunk. I don't want it collapsing.' He gave me a cheeky grin.

Right, I thought, I'll show him.

'Vic, I want you to help me finish pitching the decks and fixing
up the electrics. Hopefully we can be out of here by the end of
September.'

'What about the plumbing?' asked Susie.

'We'll take plenty of water, and the lavatory will be the sea,'
Jeff replied.

It was going to be a very basic interior.

The yacht was put back into the water. Susie employed two
Danish guys to build a new fibreglass wheelhouse. The following
weeks were a buzz of activity. Victoria, Susie, Jeff and I began work
on the yacht early in the morning before it became too hot. The day
would begin with la bomba and an *ensaimada*.

At the end of August, Richard came back down to visit.

'You're very brown, Richard. Has it been hot in England?'

'I've been in Italy. I drove Rosie and the kids down to see
Howard.'

'Howard,' Victoria and I said in unison.

'Yeah, he's living in this luxury villa in Pineta di Arenzano,
near Genoa.'

'So what happened to him?' I asked agog.

'Oh, he staged the whole abduction thing himself. Reckons that
if everyone thinks he's been kidnapped his parents won't lose the
bail money.'

'Good grief. How did Rosie take it?'

'She knew all along.'

'No wonder she looked so thin and haggard if she had to
pretend she didn't know where he was all the time,' I said.

He pulled some photos out of his bag and showed them to us.
They were photos of Muffin taken in Howard's villa. She was sitting
on a marble floor in a large room with a terrace in the background
overlooking the sea.

'Where's Rosie now?' I asked.

'Back in Oxford.'

'And Howard?'

'He's staying in Italy, seems to like it there.'

'So is it over between them?'

'Yeah, I'd say so. They can't really be together. Rosie was fed up even before this latest charade.'

Richard stayed ten days and then left for England. I found it hard to banish thoughts of Howard from my mind.

I became adept with my drill and took pride in what I was building. I even had praise from Jeff, who was pleased with his chart table. The yacht had been out of the water such a long time the wooden planks of the hull had shrunk and it was possible to recognize people walking on the dock through the spaces between them.

Jeff was busy stripping the engine we'd nicknamed 'evil Arthur'. Then he reckoned we'd be ready to leave.

The night before we were due to leave, Victoria and I hit the town in a big way. We went to La Tierra bar. It was owned by Arlene, an American woman, and was full of our friends of all nationalities. As we walked into the bar, J.J. Cale's 'After Midnight' was playing. Before we knew it, after way too many drinks, dawn was breaking. We stayed the remainder of the night in a friend's house in the old town and failed to wake at all the following morning. When we finally surfaced and staggered with colossal hangovers to the yacht, we were met by a disgruntled Jeff and Susie.

'Right, girls, tonight you're staying with us. I'm not letting you out of my sight,' Jeff informed us.

The following morning we finally left Ibiza. The first two days of the voyage went well: the sun shone, we had a good wind, and now and then a dolphin would surface and dive alongside. The dry planks let in constant streams of water and for the first three days we had to constantly pump out the bilges until the planks swelled up. During the night we took it in turns to do two-hour watches. On the afternoon of the fourth day, grey clouds hung ominously in the sky, while ahead we saw white tips on ever increasing waves. The wind was growing stronger by the hour.

'It doesn't look good, girls. I think we're in for a tough one,' said Jeff.

Victoria and I exchanged anxious looks. By nightfall, the storm had increased in its intensity. When Jeff woke me for my 2 a.m. watch I was aghast to see the waves towering above the boat, a big grey wall that looked like it would swamp us. But the sea carried us up and down into the trough on the other side, just like a cork. Jeff had lowered the mainsail and put up the storm-sail; we had changed our course and were running off with the storm towards the Moroccan coast. He told me to wake him if need be. I was frightened, battling this monstrous sea on my own, but I also felt fascinated by the intensity and the noise as the wind pounded the rigging and the massive waves grew out of the darkness of the moonless night.

Two hours later I nervously secured the wheel to remain on course and went to get Victoria. She awoke with a start. Her hair was dishevelled and her green eyes were startled. She leapt out of bed and joined me in the cockpit just as an enormous wave broke on deck and drenched us.

'What's it all about, anyway,' she cried.

'I don't think now's the time to start being philosophical. Look, I'm not going to be able to get back to sleep. I'll sit with you.'

It was a long night as we huddled together in the cockpit, looking at the coast of Africa getting closer and closer. By dawn the storm had begun to subside and by early afternoon the wind had dropped and the sea had calmed. But we remained stuck in the strong east-going Alboran current off the Moroccan coast for days, surviving on porridge and Ibizan honey and rationed water.

We finally escaped the current and sailed to the little fishing village of Estepona in Andalucia, where we anchored stern-to against the fishing wharf at the cost of 15 pesetas a night. Here we were able to restock with food and water.

Two days later, after a five-hour sail, we saw the rock of Gibraltar rise majestically out of the Mediterranean sea. Isolated, it towered above the surrounding countryside as we sailed into the port and moored in the old naval destroyer pens right by the town.

Gibraltar is a strange place. Its British atmosphere is in striking contrast with its Spanish neighbour. Franco had ordered its border closed in June 1969 because of the ongoing dispute over its sovereignty. Gibraltar is a stopping-off point for a whole variety of vessels that use it to restock or refuel.

We moored next to a trimaran. Its owner stood on the main hull. He was tall, in his mid-twenties, with high cheekbones and a square jaw. He had longish blond hair and long tanned limbs that reminded me of Arendt.

We went in search of the public baths. It was strange walking up Main Street and seeing familiar high-street shops like Boots in a Mediterranean climate. After we'd cleaned ourselves up and changed, we went to a pub, where we saw our neighbour from the trimaran. He came over and joined us.

'Hi, I'm Donald, and this is my partner Joe,' he said in a Californian accent, indicating another tall man with dark hair and soft brown eyes.

'I'm Jeff and this is Susie, Victoria and Judy.' Jeff shook Donald's and then Joe's hands.

'Hi,' we three girls said.

We spent a couple of hours with them chatting about boats and sailing before we returned to *Minoru* and an early night. Jeff intended to spend only four nights in Gibraltar before we started on the trek to England. For the next two, we tidied up *Minoru* and stocked up with food and water from Lipton's on Main Street. The evenings Victoria and I spent with Donald and Joe, who seemed intent on wining and dining us before taking us back to their boat for nightcap joints.

'Why don't you girls join us on our trip back to the States?' said Donald.

'It's a tempting offer, Donald, but we couldn't let Jeff and Susie down.'

We set off early one morning a couple of days later for the trip back to Southampton. Jeff reckoned it would take about ten days depending on the weather. He warned us it might be a bit of a rough trip. We sailed out of the port, then passed through the Pillars of Hercules, past Tarifa point and out into the Atlantic Ocean. The wind was strong and the waves rough. That night there was a splintering sound as the spreaders that stabilize the mast broke. There was no choice but to turn round and run with the currents back to Gibraltar.

A couple of days later I was having dinner with Donald. We got on together well.

'Judy, there's no reason not to join our boat now,' he said.

Susie had decided to leave *Minoru* in Gibraltar to get repaired.

'I'll make it worth your while.'

'How?'

'By $20,000,' he said, looking me right in the eye.

'$20,000? What do I have to do for that?'

'Nothing, just help us sail and cook.'

'What, I just sail with you from here to the States and you'll give me $20,000?'

'Well, we'll be doing a detour down the coast of Morocco, where we'll be picking up a load. It'll be fun. The boat's a million times more comfortable than what you're on.'

'That wouldn't be difficult.' I laughed.

The offer was tempting. The $20,000 was tempting. I liked Donald and we got on well. But since I had heard from Richard about Howard, I couldn't stop thinking about him. I wanted to go and find him.

'I'll sleep on it and let you know tomorrow,' I said.

The following morning over breakfast Susie said she was going to book her plane ticket back to London. Jeff was staying in Gibraltar to supervise the work on the yacht. Victoria thought she would perhaps get a lift back to Ibiza. It was then that I made up my mind.

'Can you book mine as well, Susie. I'm going to go and find Howard.'

Susie and Victoria looked at me.

'That sounds very determined, Judy,' said Susie.

'Yes, I am,' I said, realizing how much I longed for him.

'Well, that's fine, Jude. I just hope he doesn't make you as unhappy as he made Rosie,' Victoria said.

CHAPTER SEVEN
Empty Crates

I arrived back in England towards the end of October. I had by this point decided against going to Sussex. I phoned Richard.

'You're back – great,' he said. 'Let's have dinner and catch up on each other's news.'

I filled Richard in on the adventures of the boat and then asked about Howard.

'He's still in Italy as far as I know.'

'I'd quite like to go and visit him. Do you think he'd mind?'

'You know Howard, he loves having people around. I'm going down to visit Rosie this weekend. Want to come?'

'Yes, I would. How is she?'

'Not bad. You know she bought a Victorian schoolhouse with Howard's old friend Julian Peto and his wife Viv in a village called Northleigh just outside Oxford. They've converted it and divided it in half. I think it's working out well for her. They've got two kids, so it's nice for Muffin and Podge too.'

We arrived about lunchtime on Saturday. We parked the car and walked across the old schoolyard, which was littered with children's bikes and toys, straight through the open front door into the wellington-filled hallway and on into the living room, where we saw, to our astonishment, Howard reclining on the sofa. Julian, a tall, fair-haired man with glasses perched precariously on the tip of his nose, burst into loud laughter at the look on our faces. Howard, who was smoking a large joint that looked like it was part of his anatomy, smiled sheepishly at us.

'Good lord, Howard. What on earth are you doing here?' Richard asked. 'I thought you were still hiding out in Italy.'

'I was until last night. Then my sister phoned and told me the *Daily Mirror* was trying to interview her at her place in Padua, and that they knew I was in Italy and that my parents had been to visit me, so I reasoned the last place they would look for me would be here,' Howard explained.

'Yeah, so he just walks into the Victoria Arms last night, drunk as a skunk,' Julian said, breaking once more into his characteristic donkey laugh as he flipped back a blond lock that had strayed over his glasses. He had been Howard's closest friend since the day they met at Balliol.

'And only yesterday I had Inspector Fairweather here, grilling me again. You know, the one from the Thames Valley Police, in charge of investigating Howard's disappearance.' It was Rosie, who'd come in and was glaring at Howard. She looked tired, I thought, and seemed to have lost a lot of weight. We hugged each other. I asked Howard what he was going to do now.

'Well, for starters, don't call me Howard any more. Call me Albi; it's an anagram for bail.' He grinned. 'And then I was going to ask you if you could drop me off in London on your way back to Brighton. It won't be long before word gets out I was in the pub last night.'

'Of course we will,' said Richard.

The afternoon passed by pleasantly. Howard and Richard entertained their daughters and played the board game Go, and I chatted to Julian and Viv. Later we took Muffin and Julian's kids Josh and Anna for a long walk. Rosie was quiet and busied herself cleaning the house.

On the drive to London I asked Albi if he had anywhere to stay. He said he wasn't sure. I told him he could stay with me in Brighton if he liked, while he sorted out what he was going to do. He grinned a lazy sensuous grin and accepted my invitation with what seemed like relief. I was delighted. I wanted risk. I wanted excitement. I was too naïve to stop and think about the implications of harbouring a fugitive; too young to consider consequences.

Richard dropped us off at my flat. Howard and I spent the evening lying on the floor, getting stoned on magical Nepalese hash. He put *Clear Spot* by Captain Beefheart and the Magic Band on the record player. When 'Her Eyes Are A Blue Million Miles' came on, he said, 'This song is for you, Jude; it always reminds me of you.' There was no denying the sexual attraction between us was as strong as ever.

Later, as we lay naked in my bed, his arm wrapped round my shoulders, our legs entwined, I asked Albi about his disappearance.

'All the newspapers said you'd been kidnapped or something,' I said.

'I'm glad they think that otherwise my parents might lose the £50,000 bail they've posted,' he said, as he laughed and reached for the half-smoked joint in the ashtray.

'I worried when I saw all those newspaper headlines. My favourite photo of you was the one in the *Daily Mirror*. I slept with it under my pillow.' I felt myself begin to blush.

Albi seemed flattered at this revelation of mine. He looked at me, his brilliant blue eyes gleaming with pleasure under bushy eyebrows. 'I always wanted to be famous, but I never thought it would be like this.' He laughed. 'Did you see that newspaper report where some guy confessed to murdering me and burying me beneath a bridge near Bristol?'

'Yes, but luckily by then I'd heard from Richard that you were fine.'

'You know, Jude,' he said, pulling on the joint and inhaling deeply, 'what hurt badly was when I heard my parents were getting over my disappearance or death.'

My eyes widened in surprise. I sat up and looked at him.

'Did they not know you were okay? Surely you let them know?'

'I tried to. I wrote a letter to Bernard Simons, my solicitor, saying that I had gone away voluntarily and I was well. Anyway, they know now. They came out to see my sister and me in Italy. We took a two-week tour in this Winnebago I had. But I couldn't risk them knowing before.'

I was still grieving badly for my mother and I couldn't imagine how he could make his parents go through such agony. 'How could you let them suffer like that, Albi?'

'Yeah, I know, I'm not proud of it. I worried and felt bad. But they're okay now. I'm just worried the Old Bailey judge will decide to forfeit my bail.'

As I lay back in his arm it occurred to me that under the charming façade was a man who was ruthless. I quickly dismissed the thought. I was fascinated by him.

'So were you in Italy all the time?'

'No. At first after I skipped I stayed with an old teaching friend of mine Dai on the Isle of Dogs while I grew a moustache. Then, when all the press started, Dai wasn't happy and thought I should go abroad. I got a phony passport and a pair of prescription glasses. Did you know, Jude, that smoking loads of dope gives you long sight?' He giggled. 'Anyhow, then I went with a friend called Sheila to Denmark, then flew to Genoa, Italy.'

'What happened to Sheila?' I asked.

'I became bored and sent her home.'

I was glad he was no longer with her and prayed I wouldn't bore him so easily.

'And what was all that about the mafia beating you up? Was that true or did Rosie invent it?'

'Oh that happened, Jude, when I was on bail. It was scary. Ernie, my American partner, sent this guy over to pick up money I'd left in a safe-deposit box in Amsterdam. He was so heavy-looking, straight out of an American gangster movie. I met him in London and I gave him a letter to gain access to the box and off he went. Two days later I go to see him in his London hotel room and as I sit down he whacks me hard round the face. He then starts screaming at me that I'm a liar and a cheat, the money wasn't there and that I'd ripped Ernie off. He even threatened to throw me down the lift shaft and he had four other equally heavy guys with him ready to do just that. I was terrified. I asked him to phone Ernie, as the authorities had obviously got to the box first. He said I had four hours to get $10,000 or my family and I would be dead. So I went and phoned my father. Luckily I had a suitcase under my bed in Wales with the cash.'

'Did you tell your father what it was about?'

'Yeah. I met him at the Severn Bridge and he could see I'd taken a knocking. So then I drove like the clappers back to the hoods in the London hotel and when I get to his room he's smiling. Said he'd talked to Ernie and everything was fine.'

I breathed deeply at the thought of his near miss. 'Albi, did you work for MI6?' I was beginning to feel like an interrogator. I was also beginning to feel comfortable calling him Albi.

He turned on the pillow and looked at me.

'Yes, Jude. I was recruited by an old friend of mine from Oxford, Hamilton McMillan. I did a couple of assignments for them. The first job they wanted me to do was go to a party and pick up this chick who worked for the Czech embassy. She never showed up. It was a pity – I'd seen a photo of her and she was unusually attractive.' He paused and inhaled on his joint.

'Then, of course, my Irish dealings interested them. They ignored my dope dealing because they thought I could give them information on the IRA. They also wanted me to open branches of Anna Belinda, my clothes shop, in Amsterdam and Dublin and let them put some people in as representatives of the company.'

I hung on to his every word. I felt privileged to have him next to me in my bed; dazzled, as I always had been, by his looks, his charm and his wonderful voice. I was falling in love hopelessly.

The following day I went out to do some food shopping. Passing the newsagent's, I caught sight of the *Daily Mirror*. The headline read 'He's Alive' and had a large photograph of Howard underneath it. I bought a copy and rushed home. The reporter, Edward Laxton, who'd tried to interview Linda in Padua, had written an article titled 'Why the Mafia Hid Howard'.

Two days later the headlines read: 'Whereabouts of mystery man known by police'. I started to feel paranoid, and I didn't think it was because of all the dope I was smoking. Then I realized they still thought he was in Italy. On 31 October the story in the papers informed us that, despite the police knowing Howard's whereabouts, bail money would not have to be forfeit. Delighted but puzzled, Albi concluded the authorities didn't want any revelations about his spying activities after the recent Littlejohn and Kenneth Lennon scandals.

Kenneth Littlejohn and his brother Keith had been bank robbers. MI6 had recruited them and paid them, and other agents in Ireland, large sums of money to infiltrate and inform on the IRA. More importantly, they also paid them to act as agent provocateurs, organizing and conducting bank robberies and bomb attacks on police stations in the Republic of Ireland, knowing these raids would be blamed on the IRA. When Kenneth Littlejohn was arrested after a large bank robbery in the republic, he named his employers in court, acutely embarrassing the British government. In March 1974, Kenneth Littlejohn escaped from jail in Dublin and found his way to Amsterdam, where he freely gave interviews to the press. Much criticism was directed at MI6 for employing criminals. Yet more embarrassment for the security services came with the case of an Irishman called Kenneth Lennon. He was found dead in a ditch in Chipstead, Surrey, on 13 April 1974, a few days after making a statement to the National Council for Civil Liberties that was then made public. In the statement he alleged that Special Branch officers had pressured him into becoming an informant and infiltrating a branch of Sinn Fein. He'd been shot dead.

It would seem that, luckily for Albi, the MI6 and the government did not need any more bad publicity.

The following day we celebrated my twentieth birthday with much love, champagne and strong Afghani hash. Albi, thankful his parents were not to lose their money, began to relax, and the media circus, much to our relief, died down. Albi started inviting his friends around. One friend who would call down from London was a character I knew only as Cyril. He was a chemistry graduate, of slight build, about five foot seven, who wore brown-rimmed glasses with thick lenses and dressed in nondescript clothes to blend in with the background. He was acutely paranoid; he saw police and customs officers hiding everywhere. Cyril kept Albi well supplied with hash.

One day, when Albi was having a hushed private meeting with Cyril in the sitting room, Richard and I sat in the kitchen. Richard laid out two lines of cocaine and as Richard and I snorted them, Albi walked in. Without a word he walked out again. After Richard had left, Albi said, 'Jude, if I ever see you taking cocaine again I will leave and never have anything else to do with you. It is the devil's drug and it only distorts personalities. I don't trust anyone who takes it. Please don't do it again.'

'I promise I won't, Albi,' I said, and I meant it. I felt like a chastised schoolchild, and guilty for upsetting him so much. I'd had no idea how much he despised cocaine.

My father's phone bill began to take a hammering. Albi contacted Ernie, his Californian partner, whom he referred to as Pete, now also a fugitive over the speaker scam. Phone calls in the middle of the night began to be the norm. A squeaky Californian voice would say, 'Hi, this is Peter, can I talk to Albi please,' and I would hand over the phone. In the evenings I cooked large meals for whoever was passing by because Albi was nervous about going out. He renewed his friendship with Johnny Martin, who now had his own building firm. Albi was drinking through my father's wine collection and beginning to enjoy the taste of good red wine. He'd managed to sell his Winnebago in Italy, and was also making money selling ounces of dope to the local students.

Albi could not stay in my flat for ever. Although the house in London was now ready, Christmas was looming, and my family would be spending it in Brighton. I raised the subject with him.

'I know, love,' he said. 'London would be the best place for me because it's large and anonymous.' Then he added, 'You'll come with me, won't you?'

Relief flooded through me. He wasn't just going to move out and leave me.

'Of course I will, but I'll have to stay here for Christmas to help with the kids.'

'Is your brother Patrick coming home?'

'No, he's still too nervous.'

'Why? He's not been charged with anything,' Albi said.

'Well, I guess because he was Graham's accountant and had close links with you,' I said. Then I laughed. 'And his snails might run away again.'

Shortly before Christmas I rented a flat in Cranmer Court, Chelsea. Albi moved into it before my family arrived in Brighton. I realized I would have to let my father know what I was going to do, but I didn't think it prudent to tell him I had decided to live with an infamous fugitive dope dealer. George returned from Afghanistan just before Christmas. He thought it would be a good idea for me to take a course teaching English as a foreign language. My father agreed, although he was disappointed I hadn't taken my place at Sussex, and offered me the basement flat of the house in London.

I phoned Albi. He was delighted. We'd have access to two places, and we needn't tell anyone about my father's house. As soon as the children went back to school, I moved to London and enrolled at International House to begin my course.

Pete phoned from California. 'I'm sending my girlfriend Patti to see you guys.'

A few days later she bounced through the door. She was likeable, in her early twenties, small, slim and tanned. She wore brown leather pants, an amber-coloured angora sweater and a beige suede jacket with matching bag, a gold Rolex on her wrist and a thick gold chain round her neck.

'Here, Albi, a present from Pete.' She handed over a brown paper package.

It contained $10,000 in used $100 bills.

'Now, here's what Pete wants you to do for him. He has a man, DB, at JFK airport, who can clear anything through customs as long as it arrives on an Alitalia flight and is smellproof. The code we'll use for Alitalia will be Dorothy. Pete already has someone supplying him with Thai grass. Can you supply good-quality hashish?'

'Of course, no problem. Tell Pete I'll be in touch at the earliest opportunity with the costing.'

Later, after Patti had left and we were in bed, Albi said, 'Jude, this is an opportunity of a lifetime, but I've lost all my good contacts. I don't know how I'm going to pull this one off. If I do, I might achieve my ambition of having a million pounds by the time I'm thirty.'

While I worked at my course, Albi spent his time trying to solve the problem of supplying Pete with his hashish. Fred, a Sussex graduate Howard had worked with before, had contacts in Beirut. He arranged that machine parts returned under warranty would be flown from Beirut via Rome to New York. Pete sent over the investment needed to buy the hash and to pay for all the other expenses. Fred left for Beirut and phoned a couple of weeks later to say the load was on its way. Albi phoned Pete to give him the airway bill number. We sat back and waited.

Pete phoned and said, 'Dorothy has arrived.'

We opened a bottle of champagne. A few hours later Pete called again and said that all the crates were empty, except for one, which contained a small wooden boat.

Pete's man at JFK was furious; Albi was embarrassed and angry. Fred denied having ripped us off. We never found out what happened.

Pete was philosophical. 'Don't worry, Albi, we'll try again. But perhaps you should use someone else next time.'

'Wow,' I said to Albi later over dinner in an Indian restaurant. 'Pete sounds remarkable. He's just lost all that money and he wants you to have another go.'

'He is, Jude,' he said, still clearly unhappy about the mystery of the Beirut load. 'He forgave me for the statement I made to the Dutch police. Everyone else said I'd grassed.'

Just after Albi's arrest in Amsterdam, two British Customs and Excise guys had turned up. They questioned him for over ten hours. They told him they'd arrested Ernie's man, James Gater, in London and that he was cooperating, and that they'd already arrested three others in London, who were also cooperating. They had accounts with Howard's name, Ernie's and a guy called Jim Morris.

'They questioned me a lot about Graham Plinston,' said Albi. 'They wouldn't let me see a lawyer. I blamed it all on Graham and

Ernie. They drew up a statement and I signed it. Graham and a lot of others are not happy about it. I guess it was quite detailed.'

'There were rumours in Brighton you'd grassed up Johnny.'

'I didn't tell them anything they didn't already know. I never mentioned the Irish scams or your brother. I'll never grass again. Anyhow, then they persuaded me to go voluntarily back to the UK to Brixton prison. The smell of the nick I'll never forget, Jude. It's dreadful. I never want to go back there.'

'How did they persuade you to come back? Surely you would have been better off under Dutch law? I thought they were liberal about marijuana offences.'

'I didn't know enough about the law and at that point I was so tired. They said if I didn't agree to return to the UK I'd do four years in Holland and then they would extradite me to the UK to be tried again. Then the Americans might want to try me in the US. Anyhow, I sent a copy of my statement to Ernie; he was cool and told me not to worry.'

After the JFK fiasco Cyril became increasingly nervous. Whenever he visited us in Chelsea he would pace back and forth across the room, constantly peeking out of the windows and chewing his lips.

'You've got to get out of this gaff. We'll have to find you some-where else to live, man. Too many people have this number. Lie low for a while.'

'I think he's right, Albi. Too many people know where you are,' I said.

Albi agreed that perhaps he had been a bit foolhardy. Cyril found us a bright modern flat overlooking Regent's Park, which was far more convenient for me because it was close to the house in Primrose Hill. We hired a van and moved all the expensive stereo equipment, records and gadgets Albi had bought into the new flat. Cyril gave me strict instructions to clean the Cranmer Court flat so that no fingerprints or clues to our identity remained. Wearing rubber gloves, I spent hours meticulously cleaning every door handle and surface.

'I've got to get hold of Durrani, Jude,' said Albi to me that night, lying in our new bed.

'Who's he?'

'Oh you'd like him. He's an Afghani. His grandfather's brother was king of Afghanistan. He used to supply Graham and me with a lot of the dope we sold in England. He's the one I need to supply me with the hashish to send to Pete.' His shoulders sagged into the pillows.

'Do you know how to get hold of him?'

'I'll just have to ring all his old numbers and contacts and hope something gives.' He sounded less than confident.

Albi was in luck. Durrani got a message to him that he would meet him in London in a month, providing Albi could stay out of the newspapers.

I was studying in the basement flat in Primrose Hill when the phone rang.

'Jude, I'm on my way round. Pack a case, we've got to get out of London,' said Albi.

'What's happened?' I asked.

'I'll tell you when I get there, just be ready to leave.'

I felt a twist of alarm in my stomach. I wandered round in circles, picked up Levi's and T-shirts, packed a dress and then unpacked it for another. Albi arrived twenty minutes later. I heard his key in the lock and ran into the hall.

'Albi, whatever is it?' I asked. I saw Cyril behind him, standing outside on the pavement. His shoulders were hunched and he was chewing his bottom lip as he checked that no eyes were on him before he entered the flat.

'What's going on, man?' asked Cyril.

'The *Daily Mirror* has just turned up at the Regent's Park flat. At least I think it was them. I was looking out the window and saw four men running to the entrance. One was carrying a large camera; something told me they were coming for me. I ran down the stairs and got to the main door just as they were coming in. I carried on walking and one of them took a photograph of me. One of them said, "That's not him," and I went out and took a cab to the zoo, phoned Jude, then took a cab here.'

'This is bad, man, this is bad.' Cyril shook his head, his hair falling across his eyes. He pushed his hands deep into his pockets and looked at the floor. 'Is there anything in the flat with your name on, Jude?'

'No,' I said, wondering whether I had been careless. I was certain I hadn't been. It was Cyril who told me always to take that precaution.

'Do you have any ID on you, man?' Cyril asked Albi.

'Yeah, I've got my Albert Lane driving licence. I grabbed it as I ran out the door.'

'I've got your new John Phelan one here, Albi,' I said.

'That's good,' said Cyril. 'If they're on to Jude, at least you can use that. Now what I suggest you do is leave London tonight. Go and disappear to some other big city, like Liverpool, Ken Dodd land, man, and lie low.'

'I've only got fifty pounds on me. I had to leave in such a rush I've left over eight thousand pounds in the flat,' Albi said. He lowered himself into an armchair.

'Jeez, this is a mess. It's bad, man. I dread to think what else they are going to find. The police will be all over the joint.' Cyril shook his head again.

'I think Liverpool sounds a good idea, Albi. I don't think I have ever been there,' I said.

'Are you sure that's okay, love? What about your course?' Albi asked.

I thought about my nearly completed course. Maybe in a week or so I could come back and finish it. I thought back to my history A level exam. He was bad news for my academic education.

'What's most important now, Albi, is your security.'

'That's right, man,' Cyril agreed. 'I've got the car outside. I'll drive you up now in case they know about Jude and come snooping round here. I can let you have three hundred. Sorry it's not more.'

'Thanks, Cyril,' I said.

I picked up my belongings and we set off. I lay on the back seat;

conversation was scarce. The worried frown remained on Cyril's face and Albi looked morose. It took about five hours before Cyril was bidding us farewell outside the Holiday Inn, Liverpool.

'Jude, look after him,' he said, then he drove off.

CHAPTER EIGHT
Mr and Mrs Tunnicliffe

Albi and I checked into the hotel as Mr and Mrs Albert Lane and ordered the *Daily Mirror* for the following morning, Saturday, 19 April 1975.

In the morning, the *Daily Mirror* was put under the door. On the front page was a large photo of Albi with his moustache and spectacles. The headline read: 'The Face of a Fugitive'.

Albi rushed to the bathroom and shaved off the moustache. He covered his hair in Brylcreem and brushed it back, like a 1950s teddy boy. I wasn't sure I liked the new look, but I understood its necessity. I disposed of his glasses outside the hotel.

'Jude, we'll have to find some cheap place to live; we don't have the money to stay here.'

'Okay, I'll go down to the lobby and get the local paper.'

We scoured the newspaper and finally found a bedsit in the Sheill Park area for £4 a week. It was a miserable room with a shared kitchen and bathroom. I set about cleaning it and making it as comfortable as possible. There was a phone box on the corner of the street, and Albi made good use of it. He gave the number out to contacts who phoned him at prearranged times. There was a workers' café nearby where we ate sausage butties served by a Liz Taylor look alike. We spent our days reading books about the mafia – Lucky Luciano, Joe Costello, Al Capone – and consumed ample amounts of hashish, which Cyril delivered to us regularly. And we explored

Liverpool. We were on the ferry across the Mersey when we lost part of Albi's disguise – his wig – to a gust of wind.

One day Albi emerged from the phone box saying, 'Jude, I must get hold of Durrani now. Pete's got Japanese airlines sorted out. He calls them Wayne.'

I laughed at the name. 'It's June now, Albi. There's been no mention of you in the newspapers for ages. Try calling him and getting him to meet you in Manchester.'

'Good idea, love.'

Albi came back from the phone box in a happy mood. 'Durrani has agreed to send a load on credit. God, I can't wait to move out of this miserable shit hole.'

I looked at the filthy peeling wallpaper and cracked plaster and agreed with him. We'd borrowed money from friends but there wasn't enough to improve our surroundings greatly. But summer was under way and the weather was glorious. It was becoming one of the hottest summers on record. 'Hot enough to fry an egg on the pavement,' said the tabloid press. I had an idea.

'Albi, why don't we buy a second-hand van and go camping?'

'Brilliant! There are nearly always phone boxes near campsites. Yeah, let's do that. Leave the filthy bedsit.'

We bought an old blue Bedford van, a tent, a cooking stove, a mattress, a sleeping bag, a television (which connected to the van battery) and the AA guide to the camping sites of Great Britain. We set off like a couple of excited kids and had a wonderful time touring England. We stayed in provincial towns, played mini-golf, went for long walks, and spent evenings in pubs playing darts or lying under the stars watching television or just talking. The only drawback during this camping lark was Howard's insistence that we pitch the tent by the telephone box, which was almost always next to the toilet block.

Towards the end of June, Durrani got a message to Albi: the load was on its way. A dhow had carried 700 pounds of the best Pakistani black hashish to Karachi where it was flown to Dubai and then to Rome, where Alitalia carried it to JFK.

Albi came back to the tent late one night, a Cheshire cat grin on his face. 'Dorothy's done it! We're rich, Jude.' To celebrate we rolled several large joints and spent the rest of the night making sweet love.

In mid-August friends of ours lent us their house in Brighton. We were waiting for Pete to send the money from Albi's share of the profits. After paying off the debt for the failed Lebanese load, Albi had grossed about $80,000, most of which Pete was to look after in the States. Pete had also suggested to us that we might be safer living in the States, but we had to work out how to get visas, and a passport for Albi.

On 13 August Albi turned thirty. I bought him a cake and loads of presents. He spent the day in a strange mood, silently chain-smoking joints. I didn't know what was up. It might have been because he hadn't achieved his ambition of becoming a millionaire by thirty. But the following day he was back to his normal self.

'Hey, Jude, look at this.' He waved a copy of the *Daily Mirror* in front of me. 'There's a competition for the best legs in Britain. I'm going to enter you into it.'

He dressed me up in stockings and garter belts and took photos of my legs, but he never got round to sending the pictures in.

During this time in Brighton we met Phil Sparrowhawk. The introduction came through his elder brother, Tony, another ex-Sussex student. Phil was a jack-of-all-trades. He was about five foot ten with reddish-blond hair, a few freckles and wire-rimmed glasses. He had a quiet voice, a slight stutter and a south London accent. His father and his uncle Ernie were bookmakers; Uncle Ernie had opened the first betting shop in Epsom. Before the gaming laws had changed in the early 1960s, they had taken bets in pubs, clubs and offices. Phil's first big money had been when he bet on Nijinsky, ridden by Lester Piggott in the Epsom Derby of 1970. Phil was a good source of false identities, of which Albi was beginning to build up an impressive number. Phil and Albi set up offices together at 38A High Street, Ewell, Surrey. This office supplied us with references for bank accounts and for flat rentals. Albi asked me to open a bank account in Harrods, London, and get a safe-deposit box in the vault. He bought me a large green jewellery box and asked me to store it there in preparation for the arrival of the money from Pete. I also rented a flat on Sutherland Ave, W9. It was a small studio flat with a payphone in the living room.

Pete sent a courier over with the money. I stashed most of it in the jewellery box in Harrods. Because we had enjoyed ourselves so much travelling around England we decided to carry on, but this time not stay in a tent. We equipped ourselves with the AA hotel guide to Great Britain.

We spent a couple of weeks in Norfolk, where we rented a small cottage near Castle Rising castle about five miles north of King's Lynn. We spent our time sampling the excellent local beers and restaurants. We drove to Stafford and I showed Howard my old house. I took him for a walk on Cannock Chase and relayed my adventures on acid. We went to Matlock Bath, in Derbyshire, and stayed in a wonderful hotel where they had a thermal-fed heated indoor plunge pool, where we went for midnight dips. They also had a tennis court. We walked into the village and kitted ourselves out with the most expensive gear and rackets available, then made our way to the court, where a few children were practising their game, supervised by their mothers. On seeing us approaching, the mothers clearly thought we were professionals and shooed their children off the court. After watching us floundering around for twenty minutes, they politely asked if the children could get back to practising for a match the following day. We left feeling rather humiliated.

We travelled to the Lake District and stayed at a hotel called Overwater Hall. Albi had during this time developed a passion for watching *Kojak*, so we had an early dinner and rushed to the television lounge. About halfway through the programme, the owner of the hotel wandered in and said, 'It is beyond me that anyone having the good taste to stay in Overwater Hall could watch this mindless rubbish.' He then left the room. Albi and I giggled in astonishment.

Next we toured Scotland.

'Hey, Jude, let's rent a boat and explore the Caledonian Canal.'

'Great idea.'

We rented a boat for a week, but moved off again within a few hours. It stank of fibreglass. We didn't even bother to ask for our money back.

'I think we should go back to London now, Jude. Pete's ready to do another one. I must set up meetings.'

We returned to London and settled into Sutherland Avenue. Many weekends Julian Peto would come and stay. He'd recently split from his wife and had a new girlfriend, Helen.

Durrani sent another load. Pete phoned in the middle of the night. 'Hey, guys, open the champagne.'

We moved into a bigger flat, in Marloes Road, W8, just off Kensington High Street. I was beginning to notice that whenever we moved, Albi made himself scarce as I began packing and re-appeared only once all the hard work had been done.

It was in this flat that I first met Howard's parents. They came up to London to visit us shortly before Christmas 1975. His mother Edna was at the time a primary schoolteacher and his father Dennis a stevedore at Port Talbot steel works in charge of unloading iron ore. They struck me as pleasant, ordinary people. It was obvious from the first meeting that they doted on their son, especially his mother.

My father had remarried, sold the London house and moved permanently to Brighton. Marcus was now boarding at Brighton College, while Masha remained at her convent in Buckinghamshire. Patrick continued living the simple life in France with Jude and their baby daughter Peggy. George had gone to Iran, where he was working as a teacher for the British Council.

Natasha was living in Hackney. Her local was the Jolly Farmers, a pub run and owned by the ex-Arsenal player Peter Storey. Here Howard and I spent many evenings. Peter Storey kept unconventional pub hours. From lunchtime onwards he rarely closed and we often drank there until the early hours of the morning. Occasionally Alan Ball and Bobby Moore were there and we shared drinks and jokes with them.

My sister had become politicized at Essex and had been on the fringes of the Angry Brigade. Unknown to us then, one of our drinking companions, a German girl we knew as Anna, was in fact Astrid Proll, the Baader-Meinhof fugitive. And unknown to her, Albi was also a fugitive.

We were living in Marloes Road when we first met Tom Sunde. Tom was Pete's right-hand man; Pete had asked him to fly to London to meet us. He arrived with a collection of Waylon Jennings records, a country singer Albi admired. Albi's favourite track was 'Ladies Love Outlaws'.

Tom was about five foot ten, brown-eyed, smart but casually dressed, nearly bald, with a small moustache. I never quite figured him out even in those early days. He told us he had avoided being drafted to Vietnam by pretending to be mad.

'Yeah, I just ran into the army recruitment service saying, "Give me a gun, give me a gun. I want to shoot all those yellow-skinned fuckers." So they sent me off to a psychiatric unit and proclaimed I was mentally unfit. I've got the paper back home to prove it.'

There was a nervous energy about Tom. It was almost impossible for him to be still. If he was sitting down his foot was always tapping, while his thumb and forefinger fiddled with his moustache. It was Tom who introduced us to the dubious delights of McDonald's. Albi daily went for what he called his Big Mac Attack. He also became addicted to watching *General Hospital* in the afternoons.

On one of his forays to McDonald's, Albi met an old Oxford acquaintance, Anthony Woodhead. They got talking and soon another deal was being hatched. Woodhead took us out for dinner in the West End to discuss the deal, and introduced us to the delights of Japanese food.

Since Albi didn't have a passport, he asked me if I would mind flying to Zurich and opening a bank account. I happily agreed. I was now twenty-one but entitled to reasonable plane fares as a young person. I had been to Geneva before with my father but I had never been to Zurich; I was excited. I booked into a small hotel on the

Bahnhofstrasse, feeling very grown-up. But I was shy that first evening eating dinner on my own in the hotel's Italian restaurant and buried my head in a book.

The following morning, after breakfast in a pavement café, I walked goggle-eyed up the Bahnhofstrasse. It was the most expensive shopping street I'd ever been in, its elegant shops interspersed with banks. I'd read in the guidebook that vaults of gold are buried beneath its pavements. I could believe it.

I selected the headquarters of the Credit Suisse bank. I walked nervously through revolving doors into an impressive interior of smart, efficient calm and approached a desk behind which sat a young man in an impeccable grey suit and sombre tie.

'May I help you, madam?' he said.

'Yes, I'd like to open a numbered account.'

'Certainly, madam. If you would like to give me your passport we can open it straight away.'

'I would like you to hold all the mail relating to my account here, please,' I said, following Albi's instructions, as I handed him my passport.

'No problem, madam.'

'And I would like to open a safety-deposit box too.'

'Certainly, madam, my colleague at the desk over there will help you with that.' He indicated another smartly dressed young man at a desk nearby. 'How much would madam like to open the account with?'

'Five hundred Swiss francs. Is there any limit on how much I can hold in my account?'

'Certainly not, madam. You can bring lorryloads in if you wish. We don't mind.' He seemed amused at my question and smiled at me. What a great country, I thought, no longer feeling nervous.

Within half an hour of walking into the bank I had myself a numbered account and a safe-deposit box in the bank vaults. The key to this was kept in an envelope sealed with red wax with my signature scrawled across it, which was placed in a large safe. I was most impressed.

* * *

In London our social circle was growing. Albi was meeting up with old friends and we began to make new friends. We kept our address and phone number tightly guarded, however. Deals seemed to be going on all over the place. Albi was forever doing a circuit of phone boxes.

One night we went out for dinner with Denys Irving and his pregnant wife Merdelle. Albi brought up the difficulties of having to use phone boxes all the time. He complained about the bags of coins he had to carry round and how people abroad often didn't understand the beep-beep sound that British phone boxes made.

'What you need is a machine using two telephone lines with a black box between that reroutes calls. When anyone calls up from anywhere in the world, the box will automatically dial them to whatever number you are at without them knowing your number,' said Denys.

'That sounds exactly like what I need. But does such a thing exist?'

'No, but I can try making you one,' said Denys.

'That would be fantastic. I'll pay you. We've got a spare room in our flat you can use to make it. That's all right, isn't it, Jude?' asked Albi.

'Of course it is,' I said. I liked Denys. In looks and build he reminded me of my brother Patrick.

Denys started working at our flat a couple of days later.

'Jude, can you go to Switzerland for me?' Albi asked one evening.

'Yeah, sure. When?' I asked.

'In a couple of days. I'd like you to meet Tom in Geneva. He'll give you $300,000. Then I want you to go to Zurich and give $250,000 to Woodhead and put the other $50,000 in your account. I don't want Tom and Woodhead meeting each other.'

A few days later I did exactly that.

Within a short time my trips to Switzerland became more frequent.

Denys worked round at the flat on the telephone project. We spent a lot of time together. He was a keen hang-glider. Albi asked

Pete to send him the latest model from the States. It arrived and Denys was delighted. He told me about a hang-gliding race across the English Channel he was due to take part in. He said he was going to practise that weekend.

He went quiet for a moment. 'Jude, last night I had this horrible nightmare. I dreamt I crashed while I was taking part in the race.'

'Well, perhaps you shouldn't do it,' I said, feeling worried now.

'I'm sure it's fine. It's not for a couple of weeks anyhow.' But he continued to look preoccupied for the next couple of days.

That weekend a freak wind hurled Denys and his new hang-glider into a cliff. His wife had given birth the week before to a beautiful baby boy they'd named Arthur. She was distraught; she never really recovered.

Albi felt responsible. I felt I should have persuaded Denys to listen to his nightmare. He was far too good a man to have died such a violent death and at such a young age.

It was the early summer of 1976 and Pete was putting more pressure on us to move to the States, but Albi wasn't confident that any of his false ID would stand up to scrutiny. I had an idea.

'Albi, I have some friends in Stafford who have never been abroad. They're pretty broke with two small kids and I'm sure if we made it worth their while he would happily apply for a passport for you.'

'Are they married?'

'Yes.'

'Well, Jude, it would be even more brilliant if we got both their passports. It would be so much safer if we travelled as a married couple,' he said.

I could see his point.

'How soon can you go and see them?' he asked.

'I'll go tomorrow if you like.'

The next morning I caught the train to Stafford. Gill and Anthony lived in a small terraced house in the street next to where my old friend Suzanne lived. I wasn't sure what they would make of my suggestion. Gill was a year younger than me and Anthony five years older. They had married when Gill was sixteen and now they had two children. As it was they were delighted to see me. They were very obviously hard up. Anthony was a TV engineer and Gill was busy looking after the two children.

I asked them if they had been abroad or were likely to.

'Bloody hell, Judy, I can hardly afford the bus to visit my mum,' Gill said laughing.

'We've never even been to London,' said Anthony.

The passport idea came up in a discussion. They hummed and hawed.

'We'll have to think about it, Judy,' said Anthony. Gill nodded.

'Look,' I said, 'while you're thinking about it please be our guests in London for the weekend. Our treat.'

'That would be fantastic,' said Gill, her eyes gleaming.

'Yeah, you can take the kids to see Buckingham Palace,' I said, pleased to see the joy on their faces.

Friday night the Tunnicliffe family arrived at Euston. We put them up at the Lancaster Gate hotel and Albi proceeded to work his charm on them. And it worked. When they left on Monday morning they had agreed to apply for passports for us.

They filled in their application forms and had their photographs taken and asked their GP to verify them. Albi then went up to Stafford and collected the forms and photos and rented a flat in Birmingham in Anthony Tunnicliffe's name. New application forms were filled in giving the Birmingham address. Phil forged the Tunnicliffes' doctor's signature on the form and on the back of Albi's and my photos.

Ten days later two full passports arrived at the Birmingham address. It was then a question of applying for American visas. Albi set up a company called Insight Video in Birmingham, which employed Anthony Tunnicliffe as general manager and Gill Tunnicliffe as secretary. A Tunnicliffe bank account was opened at a Birmingham branch of the Midland Bank and visa application forms were filled out. These were sent off along with the Tunnicliffe passports to the United States embassy in Grosvenor Square. They were sent back with visas valid for multiple entries not exceeding two months each visit. Albi was ecstatic.

We began our preparations to leave for the States. We memorized our new identity details, date of birth, place of birth, names of parents, and tested each other endlessly. We were both nervous.

At this point our thinking was that the move to the States was for the long term. We had a series of farewell parties with friends and family. Finally the day of departure came.

We flew out of Birmingham airport in early November 1976 on an old-fashioned propeller plane to Brussels. I kept telling myself I was Gillian now. We were relieved when we cleared customs with no problems. We celebrated that evening over large bowls of steaming mussels in the beautiful Grand Place.

Albi was happy to be travelling again. The following day we flew to Zurich. We had arranged to meet Patrick, Jude and Peggy there and spent a rather drunken couple of days with them, Albi and Patrick once again enjoying each other's company.

We took money out of the safe-deposit box and went shopping on the Bahnhofstrasse, a shopper's paradise with some of the best and most expensive merchandise in the world. We bought ourselves a complete new wardrobe of clothes and a set of matching suitcases. It was fun.

Patrick, Jude and Peggy waved us off from the station as we caught a train to Frankfurt. In Frankfurt we were beginning to feel more comfortable with our identities. Our passports were hardly glanced at. We looked like a normal, happy, well-dressed young couple. From here Albi booked our tickets to New York. Except for Phil, and the real Tunnicliffes of course, no one knew our new identity.

Normally on a flight or a train journey Albi and I would drink plenty of wine, but we decided we needed to keep our heads straight in case we were questioned in New York. As it was, there were no problems. The immigration man welcomed us to New York. Only when we were in the taxi hurtling towards the Big Apple did we breathe a sigh of relief.

'We've done it, Jude,' Albi said as he squeezed my hand and kissed me.

CHAPTER NINE
A Bite of the Apple

The cab sped towards central Manhattan. We'd asked the driver to take us to a central Holiday Inn, thinking it would be anonymous and of the same standard as the ones in England. He pulled up in front of an old grey building on the West side near Times Square. An air of decay hung over the building and the rubbish-strewn street.

The young woman behind the reception desk had bleached Farrah Fawcett hair cascading around her shoulders. She smiled a Hollywood smile, showing a mouth full of perfect white teeth, making me wonder why Americans had more teeth than any other nationality.

Our room contained the standard Holiday Inn two double beds. Wallpaper peeled from the walls and the ceiling had damp patches. The plumbing was antiquated but we were too exhausted to care.

We had breakfast the next morning in one of the many covered pavement restaurants, a stack of pancakes with maple syrup.

'Jude, I think we should find an apartment before we phone Pete and let him know we've arrived.'

'But he might know of places and be able to advise.'

'I think it will make us more independent and less of a burden to him. And I don't want to stay in that hotel another night. Let's book into the Plaza,' he said.

The Plaza I was not going to argue with. I had stayed there with my parents and loved it. Once settled into the Plaza we contacted a

101

couple of real estate agencies. We viewed a succession of places and finally settled on a two-bedroom furnished apartment above a trendy singles bar, Maxwell Plums, on the corner of 65th and 2nd. We took out a six-month lease.

We then began a serious Manhattan tourist trip.

New York in 1976 was teetering on the verge of bankruptcy. The city's decline was obvious, from its rubbish-covered badly repaired streets to its graffiti-daubed subway cars. Crime was growing out of control with soaring murder rates and arson attacks that consumed entire ghetto blocks. Times Square and the area around Madison Square Gardens seemed overrun by prostitutes and their pimps.

Central Park, which had become a running joke in Johnny Carson's nightly television monologue, was a no-go area unless you wanted to risk rape, mugging or murder. But despite all this, the restless energy in this huge urban sprawl was infectious.

We took a horse-drawn cab ride from outside the Plaza Hotel around the small section of Central Park that was considered safe. We took a helicopter ride from Pier 6 on the East River and had the unforgettable experience of flying round the Manhattan skyline and between the Twin Towers before circling the Statue of Liberty and flying over Ellis and Governors islands.

We took a taxi downtown, bumping and flying over the appalling New York streets. We explored Little Italy, surprised by the number of funeral parlours. As we walked the streets we remembered all the mafia books we had read in Liverpool. We ventured into China Town, Greenwich Village and the financial district, before taking the lift to the top of the Empire State Building. New York we loved.

Walking up 5th Avenue early one evening after an unexpected storm that blew out of nowhere and lasted at the most half an hour, Christmas was evident. Santas stood in the streets calling out season's greetings. The trees that lined the shopping avenues were sparkling with fairy lights; overhead, dangling perilously between the buildings, were more elaborate Christmas lights. A thin blanket of white powder covered 5th Avenue making everything for a short while look clean and pure.

We phoned Pete and he told us to fly to Denver, Colorado. On Tuesday 25 November we arrived at Denver airport. A chauffeur-driven limousine drove us up into the snow-covered Rockies to a large and luxurious Swiss-chalet-style house in a valley on the outskirts of the resort town of Vail.

Finally I was to meet Pete. The face behind the voice on the phone.

Tom Sunde was pacing up and down the driveway fiddling with his moustache as we drove through the gate. Pete's girlfriend Patti appeared at the front door with a welcoming smile. Tom paid the chauffeur and carried the cases into the house. We followed Patti into a large comfortable living room with a ceiling-high Christmas tree and a blazing log fire. A tall, slightly overweight man with thinning light-brown hair, bushy beard and moustache and clear blue intelligent eyes appeared in a doorway. He looked to me like a big warm cuddly bear.

'Hey, Judy, Albi welcome,' he said in the squeaky voice I knew so well. He gave Albi a huge bear bug before pulling me into a warm embrace.

We had arrived two days before Thanksgiving and Patti cooked us a wonderful dinner and served some excellent wine while Pete regaled us with stories.

'Yeah, so I hit eighteen and finish high school and my dad says I don't want to see you again until you've made a million dollars.'

'What did you do?' I asked.

'I went out and made two million. I flew to Europe, bought a jeep, drove to Pakistan, had a false floor put in it, filled it with 700 pounds of the finest Pakistani hash. Then drove back to Europe and sent the jeep back to the States. I repeated it and got a few friends to do the same. Then I went and saw Dad and asked him if I'd done okay,' said Pete.

'Was he pleased?'

'Yeah, he said I'd done well.'

I noticed during the visit that Tom did whatever Pete told him to. I also noticed that he was good at doing the chores that Patti and Pete hated, like washing the car or taking out the rubbish and filling and emptying the dishwasher. He constantly sought their approval.

'You know what,' Pete remarked to Albi and me one evening. 'Tom reminds me of my favourite dog, a Doberman; they're always faithful and loyal to their masters.'

The rest of our stay in Colorado consisted of horse-riding, which I loved and Albi hated, too much television, endless games of backgammon and eating fine foods and drinking copious bottles of good red wine and Dom Perignon.

Pete and Patti wanted us to spend Christmas with them in Miami, where they had an apartment in Coconut Grove. The five of us flew first-class from Denver. Albi and I checked into the Mutiny hotel, across the road from Pete and Patti's apartment. It over-looked the bay where Pete kept a small 35-foot-yacht. We had a luxurious suite with a mirrored ceiling, sauna and jacuzzi.

'This is the life, Jude,' Albi said as we lay in each other's arms in the huge king-size bed, looking at our reflections in the mirror above.

A couple of days later we took out a year's rental on an unfurnished two-bedroomed apartment in a condominium complex overlooking Biscayne Bay. In the public area there was a huge pool, jacuzzi and tennis courts. There were also two large snooker rooms. Patti took me out in her silver Porsche and we spent an entire day shopping to furnish the apartment. Sofas, king-size beds, dining table and chairs, bric-a-brac, every kitchen gadget you could possibly imagine and a massive desk for Albi with a magnificent leather office chair and two smaller matching chairs.

It astounded me. Not just the cost, which was phenomenal, but that an entire household could be bought in a day and delivered the following morning. Albi loved it. He took care of buying the sound system and a solid metal safe, which was immediately packed with $100 bills.

We settled happily into life in Miami. We had tennis lessons and swam daily. Albi took a driving test and got a Florida driving licence in the name of Tunnicliffe. He bought a green Cadillac Seville from a mafia friend of Pete's.

I found Christmas in Miami strange, with its combination of warm sunshine and Santa Clauses. I missed my family. Christmas Eve dinner we had at Pete and Patti's with Tom and a New Yorker called Alan Schwarz, who was Pete's hashish and marijuana wholesaler, and his wife Jackie and their one-year-old son. Pete and Albi had bought Patti and me several pieces of gold jewellery. Alan had bought his son a model of a freight container airport, complete with forklift trucks, container crates and warehouses, and models of airport workers, custom officers and even a sniffer dog.

To celebrate New Year Albi and I drove in our new Cadillac down to Key West. We rented a small motorboat and cruised around the bay until we spotted what looked like a shark and swiftly returned to shore. We had a wonderful time. It was the only significant trip we made in the Cadillac.

One evening Pete took us in a limousine to one of the flashy Miami hotels to introduce Albi to a couple of mobsters. We were shown up to a large luxurious suite. The men went into a separate room while we molls remained in the living room. One of the mob's girlfriends rolled several joints, all of which I shared. When the guys came back to join us I was incoherent and had no control of my limbs, though my mind remained clear. It was a horrid state to be in. It was time to leave but I couldn't stand up. Albi's face was tight. Patti and Pete, laughing at me, pulled me to my feet. Now I had to work out how to walk. I looked at my feet, wondering how to make them move. By this time everyone was laughing except Albi. Pete took one of my arms and Albi the other, and Patti guided me from the back, pushing one leg and then the other, out into the corridor to the lift. Albi's voice hissed into my ear, 'Get yourself together.' I felt a sharp kick on my shin, and another one when we reached the lobby floor.

I was pulled out of the lift, still desperately trying to regain control of my movements.

'Stop embarrassing me like this,' Albi muttered.

I wanted to say I don't mean to. But I couldn't remember how to talk.

It seemed to take an eternity to make it across the vast, marble, palm-filled lobby and out to the waiting limousine. I felt like the entire place was watching me. When we reached our condominium, thankfully, I had regained some of my mobility. As I climbed out of the limousine I managed to say sorry to Pete and Patti. They told me not to worry and wished us a good night.

Once up in the apartment, Albi started on me.

'How dare you humiliate me like that in front of the mob? I'm meant to be the biggest smuggler in England and my girlfriend can't take a few joints. How will they take me seriously? I've never felt so humiliated in my life.'

I gave up smoking.

I later learnt from Patti that a couple of the joints had been laced with some other drug. I still refrained from smoking.

In the middle of January our two-month permitted stay was running out, so Albi and I decided to fly to Canada and then re-enter the United States after a couple of weeks. We went first to our apartment in New York. It looked drab after the luxury we had quickly become accustomed to, so we booked into the Waldorf Astoria. New York was experiencing the coldest winter since 1950. It was so cold the official advice was not to go out unless you absolutely had to, and if you did, to wear a scarf covering the face as it was harmful to breathe in the cold air.

We flew to Toronto, where it was even colder and the snow was several feet deep.

'Let's go to the west coast, Albi. It's warmer there.'

'Okay, I'll book the flights.'

We flew first class the following day to Vancouver on a Canadian Pacific flight. We were both impressed at the silver service. We checked into the Bayshore Inn, where Howard Hughes had a few years previously maintained the penthouse suite, and watched seaplanes taking off outside the windows. We bought a guidebook and went about being tourists again.

One evening we went to the planetarium. At the end of the show, as the lights began to brighten, Albi clutched my arm.

'Jude, I don't believe it. It can't be.'

'Who, Albi?'

'It's Marty, my oldest friend from Kenfig Hill.'

I looked to where his eyes were fixed. A man with thinning strawberry-blond hair was looking at Albi with mouth agape. We stood up and made our way towards him.

'I don't fucking believe it. I don't fucking believe it. What the fuck are you doing here?' he said in a strong Welsh accent.

'I could ask you the same,' Albi replied, a big smile on his face.

Marty Langford came back to our hotel room with us. Albi hadn't seen him since September 1973 when the heat from the speaker bust had hit. They had a lot to catch up on. Marty had fled to Dublin where he had been looked after by Jim McCann and Sylvia, who was now Jim's wife. They were now all living together in a wood and glass mansion in Brunswick Beach, Vancouver. McCann was living under the name James Kennedy and claiming he was a close relative of the late president. Marty and Albi chatted well into the night. I went to bed.

In the morning, Albi woke me with a room service order of breakfast.

'Jude, Jim is bound to be round soon knocking on the door.'

So I was about to meet the infamous McCann. I wasn't sure how I felt about it. Curious, that's for sure.

'I think it's best I don't tell him you're Patrick's sister.'

'Why?'

'Patrick and Jim had a huge row about your grandfather. Patrick said Joe Cahill had murdered your grandfather. Jim completely exploded and said Cahill was a good man and never shot anyone. And if your grandfather was shot he probably deserved it. They nearly came to blows and Jim said that if Patrick ever set foot in Ireland again he would have him shot.'

'Bloody hell. Yes, I think it's better he doesn't know. I'll go out shopping or for a massage or something when he gets here.'

Shortly afterwards there was a knock on the door. I opened it to a dark-haired man with a pointed nose and protruding teeth. He was slightly taller than me. He wore a white trench coat with its collar up, the belt tied tight around a middle-aged paunch. He scrutinized me from head to foot.

'What, you're cradle-snatching now, H'ard, you Welsh pervert,' he said in a thick Belfast accent.

Albi looked embarrassed. 'Jim, this is Judy,' he said.

'Judy, what's a pretty young slip of a thing doing with a Welsh wanker like him?'

'Helping him wank,' I said.

Jim burst out laughing. 'Yeah, I can believe he can't even do that on his own,' he replied. 'The girl's got spunk, H'ard. The girl's got spunk,' he said to Albi as I was treated to another all-over inspection.

'Okay, I'm going out now. I'll leave you two to it,' I said and left the room.

Later that evening we met up for dinner with Jim and Sylvia in Trader Vic's in the lobby of our hotel. Sylvia was my height, slim with large breasts and long blonde hair. She was attractive and I guessed not that much older than me. She was gentle in manner and I warmed to her. They had a little daughter called Siobhan who was being baby-sat by Marty.

McCann spent the evening showing off about his Venezuelan oil interests and his company, Ashling Multi-Media, which had an office in the Guinness Tower and was financing the film *Equus*. He named-dropped continuously and boasted of a close friendship with James Coburn and his wife Beverly.

'And all you're doing, H'ard, is the same old shit. I've got money, I've got real money. I'm one of the real shakers and movers. I live life in the fast lane. You understand what I'm saying now, H'ard.'

It was certainly the case that the restaurant staff treated 'Mr Kennedy' with a great deal of respect. Jim McCann was larger than life. He was from Belfast and from 1959 onwards had been jailed several times. In London he was a petty criminal with a history of cheque fraud, stealing cars and receiving stolen property. He had also worked as a debt collector for the landlord Nicholas van Hoogstraten.

Although he was frequently disowned by the IRA, he was adept at what he called 'playing the green card'. He had escaped from Crumlin Road jail in the early 1970s where he had been imprisoned for throwing petrol bombs at Queen's University, which he considered 'a citadel of Brit rule'. At the time Howard met him, he was wanted by the Wiltshire police for burglary, the Cambridge and Manchester police for fraud, and the Belfast police for the petrol bomb and escaping from Crumlin Road. But it was Jim who had been responsible for smuggling all Graham and Howard's dope through Shannon airport a few years earlier. Probably by playing the 'green card'.

We left Vancouver. Jim and Albi swapped contact details. We flew to San Francisco, where we met up with Pete, Patti and Tom, and checked into the Mark Hopkins hotel on the top of Nob Hill.

A load of Thai weed had just been cleared through JFK and Pete had decided to sell it in California. We had dinner at a Mexican restaurant and Pete introduced us to tequila – a mistake. Albi and I got outrageously drunk. Albi was so drunk at one stage he was whispering sweet nothings to a stainless-steel bar attached to the counter. The most unfortunate thing, though, was that Albi started insulting Pete, telling him among many other things that he was boring and stupid.

The following morning we awoke with the most atrocious hangovers either of us had ever experienced. We couldn't remember how we had got back to our hotel room. Despite this, we decided to carry on with our planned tourist trip. We made our way to Union Square where we tried and failed to eat breakfast. We then took a cable car down to Fisherman's Wharf.

'It's time for a hair of the dog, Jude.'

'Just don't mention the word tequila,' I said.

We sat in a waterfront bar sipping lagers as memories from the night before seeped back into our fogged brains. We both cringed with shame.

'Do you think Pete will talk to us again?' I asked.

'That's what I'm worried about. We're completely fucked if he doesn't,' Albi said.

To our immense relief, Pete and Patti found the whole thing hysterical and got much fun out of teasing us. I've never touched tequila since.

We stayed in San Francisco for about three weeks as the money from the load rolled in. Every few days we moved to another five-star hotel before we all flew back to Miami.

One afternoon we were round at Pete and Patti's drinking rum and orange. Pete, who was a gambling man, decided he wanted to go to a casino. Within an hour a limousine had been called and the five of us were on our way to Miami airport, where we boarded the four-hour flight to Puerto Rico.

'Where's Puerto Rico?' I whispered.

'I've no idea,' Albi whispered back.

In the early evening we checked into a beachside hotel and casino resort. From the balcony of our suite we looked out over a white sandy beach with swaying palm trees. We had a buffet dinner in the hotel restaurant. After dinner, Pete, Tom and Albi went to the casino. Patti and I went to our rooms; we'd been drinking all day and I was exhausted.

The following day we spent on the beach. The boys had hangovers they were busily curing with Mai Tais. Pete was happy; he'd done well on the tables playing blackjack.

'You know, you guys, you really ought to go and check out Las Vegas,' Pete said.

'Yeah, that's real fun. Take in a couple of shows while you're there,' said Patti.

'I'd like to do that. But I'd like to study blackjack more before I go,' said Albi.

'I've got a couple of books I can give you,' said Pete.

Back in the apartment in Miami we pulled out an atlas to find out where we'd been. The island of Puerto Rico lay 1,000 miles south-east of Miami near the Dominican Republic.

Albi spent the next couple of weeks studying Pete's gambling books. We were excited by the idea of Las Vegas. Yet again the characters we'd read about in the miserable bedsit in Liverpool came to mind, in particular Bugsy Siegel and his Flamingo hotel. And Elvis Presley had appeared in Las Vegas the previous December – Albi was a fan and hoped he might do a show when we were there.

We flew first class, as had become our habit, to Las Vegas. All during the flight Albi studied his gambling books and was irritated if I talked to him. We checked into the MGM Grand on the Las Vegas strip, a garish building put up in 1973 and the largest hotel in the world at the time. Our suite was definitely over the top. It had velvet wallpaper in the living room with matching furniture and the biggest TV I had ever seen. The bedroom had the normal king-size bed with mirrored ceilings, another large TV and was decorated in fuchsia pink. The pink and purple marble bathroom had a double bath with gold taps, a Jacuzzi and 'his' and 'hers' sinks.

Albi checked what shows were on. The most interesting one appeared to be Linda Lovelace, the lead actress from the porno movie *Deep Throat*. She was famous for her ability to swallow a cock so deep that she only stopped when she bumped into the balls. We went to see her. It was a stand-up comedy act that we found distinctly unfunny.

Then we hit the gaming rooms. I had never been into a casino before. It was a huge brightly lit room full of people but with a relaxed atmosphere. Smartly dressed waiters and scantily dressed waitresses wandered round serving glasses of free champagne.

We wandered around for a bit watching the different tables. We had decided to allow ourselves $1,000 each to play on whatever we wished, and agreed to meet in two hours. Albi got immersed in a blackjack table. I wandered round and found myself sitting at a baccarat table. I had never gambled before and never have since. Within an hour I had won over $16,000. I rushed off to find Albi. He was still at the blackjack table, not looking very happy. He only had $200 left. When I told him of my winnings he was astounded.

What magic was in me that night I have no idea. I hit the one-arm bandits and kept winning. We went down into the basement where the Spanish game Jai Alai was being played. We placed bets. I won. Albi lost. Six games I bet on in total and each time I picked the winner. The next day my luck had gone and so I quit. Albi sulked for three weeks.

* * *

We returned to New York and rented a much larger apartment in the Pavilion building on the corner of East 77th Street and York Avenue. Pete had a couple of warehouses full of furniture we used to furnish it. The apartment above Maxwell Plums we lent to a friend from London and his visitors, who included among many the Guinness sisters Sabrina, Miranda and Anita, Jane Bonham Carter and Rebecca Fraser.

Phil Sparrowhawk came out to visit. Albi was sending him to Thailand. He left with a suitcase full of cash. My sister Natasha came to stay for a week. Durrani phoned; he was in New York. Albi invited him for lunch.

I was interested to meet him. He arrived as I was preparing the Sunday roast. He was taller than average, his dark hair well cut and conditioned, with just enough grey to make him look distinguished. He was attractive, with deep-set brown eyes and brown hawk-like face and a good body, immaculately dressed in a Savile Row suit. Albi had told me he only ever drank Johnnie Walker Black Label so I had gone out to buy some. To me that Sunday he was the perfect gentleman and guest.

He agreed to send a consignment of Afghani hash to New York.

Our next visitor was McCann. He claimed he was staying in New York as a guest of Jackie Onassis. She never attended any of the restaurant dinners Jim constantly organized with odd assortments of people. One of his favourite places to host dinner was Elaine's on 88th Street, a restaurant popular with celebrities and literary types. It was a cosy no-frills kind of place with red painted walls, serving Italian American food.

When Jim returned to Vancouver he was arrested by the Royal Canadian Mounted Police. They claimed to have proof that he was not James Kennedy but a British fugitive called James McCann. Jim strenuously denied this and created a media storm. Sylvia appeared on television giving interviews about the injustice of the arrest. His lawyers battered the courts with appeals and pleas for bail. After three months of McCann madness, the Canadians let him out on bail. He fled the country.

I noticed that my period was late. I wondered if I was pregnant.

I got myself a pregnancy kit – it was positive. I wondered how Albi would feel.

I was scared. I was living with a drug smuggler and a fugitive in a foreign land. Wouldn't it be irresponsible to have a baby in such circumstances? What if we were caught? I couldn't bear the thought of having another child taken from me. At the same time I could not think of anyone else in the entire world whose baby I would rather have.

Later that night as I lay in his arms in bed I told him.

'Albi, I'm pregnant.'

'Are you sure?'

'Yes.'

'How do you feel about it?'

I voiced my concerns to him.

'Jude, I can't tell you what to do, nor would it be right given my position to persuade you either way. I might get arrested any day and spend years in jail. But I promise you that if you keep the baby I will look after you and it to the best of my ability.'

He pulled me tightly into his arms and kissed me gently. The night was filled with much love.

The following day I made an appointment to see a gynaecologist recommended to me by Alan Schwarz's wife Jackie. The gynaecologist confirmed my pregnancy and said I was in good health.

I returned to the apartment and told Albi that I was going to keep the baby, but that I wished to be me, Judy, again. A huge grin of relief broke out on his face.

'I'm so happy, Jude. We'll go back and live in Europe. I've had enough of all this have-a-nice-day shit anyway. We'll keep this apartment on for a while in case I have to come over. And once the baby's born we can all stay here.'

'Are you sure – what about our Cadillac and the Miami apartment?'

'We'll sell the car, we've hardly used it anyhow, and just give our notice in on the apartment and store the furniture until we find somewhere we want to live in Europe. Don't worry, Jude. What is important is you and our baby.'

We continued to divide our time between Miami and New York. Alan Schwarz introduced us to all the hip and cool places in Manhattan. We met celebrities such as Margaux Hemingway and Bernie Cornfield. We were having fun. The New York scene was in full swing. Punk rock was emerging; the Ramones, Richard Hell and the Voidoids and Blondie had started appearing at CBGB's in the Bowery.

Money was rolling in. We flew to San Francisco to pick up some more. Once again we stayed at the Mark Hopkins. I had started suffering from morning sickness. While we were staying there, Albi developed a mean little trick. In the morning while I was sleeping he would order undercooked boiled eggs from room service. He'd then wake me and once I'd opened my eyes pour the contents of the egg into a bowl. He'd laugh loudly at the speed at which I leapt out of bed for the bathroom.

We returned to New York via Miami. It was the last time we were to visit the Miami apartment. It felt sad.

We arrived back in New York on 16 May 1977, the day five people were killed when a New York Airways helicopter, idling on top of the Pan Am building, toppled over, sending a huge rotor blade flying. The following week we flew from Washington to Paris on Concorde.

CHAPTER TEN
Campione

We arrived at Charles de Gaulle airport late in the afternoon. An Air France limousine took us to the Meridien hotel. It was a good feeling to be back in Europe with its familiar sights and smells. Cyril flew over from London the following day, bringing with him my real passport. I felt hugely relieved to be me again. It was only then that I realized how stressed I had been living under a false ID.

Albi told me to take some money and go shopping while he and Cyril were discussing business. I took a wad of French francs and made my way to the Rue du Faubourg St-Honore, a street lined with boutiques. After buying some underwear and a crocodile handbag I had no money left. I returned to the hotel.

'That was quick, Jude,' Albi said.

'I ran out of money.'

'But you had the equivalent of $3,000.'

'Good grief, was it that much?' I hadn't got my head round the value of the franc against the dollar. I laughed. 'Well, I got a nice bag.'

A few days later we flew to Nice. We were going to visit Durrani, who had a villa in the Alpes-Maritimes. We checked into the Carlton in Cannes and the following day we rented a Mercedes. We drove up into the mountains, with the heady smell of flowers and clean air drifting in through the car windows. Lavender grew wild by the side of the road. Durrani's house was a couple of kilometres outside the small town of Grasse, perfume capital of the world. It was a large villa with honeysuckle and jasmine climbing its walls. The garden had sweetly scented flowers around a kidney-shaped pool.

Durrani looked relaxed and happy dressed in shorts and a designer T-shirt. He introduced me to his Lebanese guest called Omar, whom Albi knew from days gone by. Two Filipinos waited on us as we had lunch of bouillabaisse with toast and rouille by the pool. Durrani opened a bottle of vintage Chateauneuf-du-Pape. After lunch the men retired to the living room to discuss business and I lay by the pool flicking through Durrani's large assortment of newly published magazines.

On the way back to Cannes, on Durrani's recommendation we stopped off at Grasse. As we walked along the tiny streets and up and down ancient steps around the seventeenth- and eighteenth-century buildings a new scent hit us every few yards. Albi bought me a bottle of Bal à Versailles by Jean Desprez, which remains one of my favourite fragrances.

We spent a few days on the Riviera with Durrani, who was a superb guide to all the best restaurants. From Nice we flew back to Paris. Jim McCann was waiting for us. He'd fled there from Vancouver, broke after having to leave so much behind. Unknown to me, Jim and Albi had come up with a plan to rip off Pete. Tom flew into Paris to discuss funding for Albi and Jim's mythical deal. I flew to England to catch up with my family, leaving them in Paris.

Masha was now sixteen and about to sit her O levels; Marcus was twelve. Natasha had a job on a yacht in the Mediterranean, and George was now in Jordan teaching English to the Jordanian air force.

I stayed with Merdelle and little Arthur in London. Denys's older brother, who was a lawyer, came for dinner one night.

'Where are you going to have the baby, Judy?' he asked.

'I'm not sure yet. We haven't decided.'

'Well you do know, don't you, that if you're not married and you have the baby outside the UK the baby will have no right to British citizenship.'

'Even though I'm English?'

'That's right, unless you put an English father on the birth certificate. And it might not be a good idea putting one of Howard's false IDs down. Could cause all sorts of difficulties at some stage.'

'That's discrimination against women.'

'Well, I don't know about that. But it is the law,' he said.

I phoned Albi in Paris the following day repeating the conversation.

'Don't worry, Jude. We'll go back to London for the birth. Now, Jude, I've got a favour to ask you. I've given Pete your number there as a contact for me. He thinks I'm going to Thailand. I'm not. I'm trying to raise money for a scam Jim and I want to do. I'll have to ask you to tell him some bullshit.'

'You can't do that to Pete,' I said.

'Look, Jude, it's complicated. I'll explain it all when we're face to face. Okay, love?'

'I don't like lying, especially to someone who's been so good to us.'

He started to sound exasperated. 'Look, Jude, it's hard enough being out here with Jim. Just please do what I ask you.'

'Okay,' I replied, feeling unhappy.

'When he rings tell him I've left Paris and everything is going to plan and to phone you again in a couple of days. Got that?'

'Yeah.'

'Good girl. I'll phone tomorrow. Take care.'

I spent the rest of the day playing with Arthur while Merdelle went out for an acting audition. Arthur took his first steps that afternoon. I felt sad that Denys wasn't there to see. And I prayed that Pete wouldn't call. He did, at midnight.

'Hey, Jude, how you doing? We miss you guys. How's the bun in the oven?'

'Hi, Pete, yeah I miss you too. The baby is doing fine,' I said.

'Great, and what's the news on Albi?'

'Uh good,' I said, feeling a blush spreading across my face. 'He's left Paris and says to tell you everything is going to plan and if you call in a couple of days there should be some more news.'

'Okay, sounds good. Talk in a couple of days.'

I put the phone down feeling distinctly uneasy. Albi phoned the following morning. 'Hey, Jude, did Pete call?'

'Yes, I told him what you told me to. He's going to call back in a couple of days.'

'Okay, Jude, when he calls back I want you to tell him I've been taken ill with something called devil's grip.'

'What?'

'Devil's grip. I'll explain more to you later. Got to go now. I'll call this evening. Okay, love? I'm missing you.'

'Miss you too,' I said. I disliked this deceit more and more.

Where he had discovered this disease I have no idea. I tried looking it up and eventually found a reference in the local library. The more general name for it was Bornholm disease; it was also known as the grasp of the phantom. I remembered a story Albi had told me about when he was a young boy. He had, while in perfectly good health, persuaded his parents and local doctor that he had undulant fever by inventing symptoms and by flicking the thermometer reading up. He was so convincing he ended up being placed in the isolation ward of the local hospital.

For a week I continued, under Albi's instruction, to lie to Pete. I hated it.

Finally he asked me to ask Pete to call him in Paris. I felt a huge relief.

I flew to Paris the following day. I was so pleased to see Albi I found it impossible to remain cross with him over Pete.

'Can you please not ask me to lie like that again?'

'Okay. It was just necessary at the time.'

'Supposing he finds out you ripped him off?'

'I don't see how he could.'

As it turns out, he did. Tom had been suspicious. About a year later when Tom was visiting Phil Sparrowhawk in Thailand, Phil told Tom about the rip-off. And Tom told Pete. Amazingly Pete shrugged it off. As far as he was concerned I was just following my man's instructions. And Albi was a naughty boy. Although knowing Pete, I'm sure he was hurt.

'Jude, do you think Patrick is bored with snail farming yet?' said Albi.

'I don't know. Why?'

'Well, Graham was always pleased with the accountancy work he did for him. I was thinking it might be sensible to use Patrick to open some foreign bank accounts and offshore accounts. I don't know much about all that.'

'We could go down and ask him.'

The following day we hired a BMW and left Paris for the drive to the Dordogne. We booked into a small hotel in Sarlat. Patrick, Jude and Peggy joined us for dinner. By pure coincidence, Jude and I were almost the same number of weeks pregnant.

Patrick and Albi discussed banking and Jude and I discussed pregnancies. By the end of the evening it was agreed that Patrick would fly off on an all-expenses-paid fact-finding mission to discover offshore banks and tax havens.

While Patrick was away, Jude and Peggy joined us for a holiday. We stayed in a wonderful hotel in the Pyrénées-Orientales, the Château de Riell. It was with much curiosity from the hotel staff that Mr Tunnicliffe booked into the hotel with a pregnant Mrs Judy Lane and a pregnant Miss Judy Lane. We spent a week playing tennis daily and enjoying the nearby thermal spas; Jude relaxed being away from the mill. On our way back to the Dordogne we couldn't resist calling into the town of Albi, north-east of Toulouse. The centre is dominated by a Gothic cathedral. Wandering round its interior we came across a statue dedicated to St Judith. We both took this as the ultimate sign we were meant to be together.

We dropped Jude and Peggy back at the mill. We then drove to Italy, which is where we wanted to live because of our love of the language, food and wine. We arrived in Milan, where the taxi-drivers were on strike. Chaos was everywhere; horns hooted loudly, groups of men stood around arguing and gesticulating wildly. We checked into the Palace hotel, which Albi informed me was mafia-owned.

'The guy who threatened me in London always said I should stay here.'

'Why?' I asked.

'Don't know really. I guess he has connections here. I'm always curious about running into him again,' he said.

Albi tried all evening to phone New York from our room. A

load from Lebanon was about to arrive in JFK. He was unable to get a connection on the antiquated phone system. In frustration he slammed down the phone with too much force and smashed a beautiful thick-glassed coffee table.

'I'm going to have to fly to New York. This is impossible,' he said. He was in a foul mood.

'Look, Albi,' I said. I'd been reading the guidebooks, as usual. 'The Swiss canton of Ticino just over the border is Italian-speaking. Let's go there. We at least know the phones work in Switzerland.' I realized from Albi's temper tantrum that Italy would be difficult to live in. We checked out of the hotel and paid a hefty price for the damaged table.

We drove from Milan to Lago Maggiore. Small villages and towns overlooked the lake, stacked up perilously on the rocky slopes. The northern part of the lake is in Switzerland; we passed over the border and arrived at the beautiful lakeside town of Locarno, known for its annual film festival.

We booked into a lakeside hotel and Albi tested the phone. It worked. We fell in love with the area. The town was an Italian city in appearance, language, food and culture. The climate was mild, almost Mediterranean, promoting the growth of palms, mimosa and jasmine. We spent a week exploring the area. Albi loved being so close to the Italian border.

'Jude, this is where I want to live.'

'I agree, but I'd like to check out Lugano first.'

'Okay, you do that, while I go to Zurich to meet Patrick. I'll meet you in Lugano in three days.'

Albi left the following morning for the drive to Zurich. I decided to catch the scenic train to Lugano. It involved a couple of changes, which was exhausting for me with my big case and pregnancy, but it was worth it. The train crossed fragile-looking bridges over deep gorges and hugged hairpin bends on vertical drops. Small villages with old stonewalled houses and towering village church spires clung to the mountainsides; lush green vineyards covered sun-facing slopes.

Eventually I arrived in the lakeside town of Lugano. Like Locarno it had an Italian feel, the usual narrow streets, pleasant squares and shopping arcades. The buildings were painted beautiful shades of dusty pink, beige and cream. I booked into the stately looking Splendide. I explored Lugano and studied guidebooks. Albi arrived by train from Zurich a couple of days later in the early evening.

'Jude, that's a fantastic train ride. I had the most superb lunch and beautiful views and it only takes three hours. This is definitely the place to be.'

Later we sat on our hotel balcony sipping champagne. I pointed to a village the other side of the lake and told Albi I'd like to go there for lunch tomorrow. I showed him the guidebook: 'An Italian enclave surrounded by Swiss territory opposite the city of Lugano.' He liked the sound of it.

The following morning we hired a silver two-seated open-topped Mercedes. We drove up the side of lake Lugano. Red-roofed houses in green lawns contrasted with the blue of the lake. We followed the signs to Campione d'Italia. Passing under a stone arch hosting an Italian flag, we were back on Italian soil, with none of the usual border-crossing formalities: no passports and no border guards. We followed the road until we reached a fork, then rather than drive back down to the lake we continued up the hill until we could go no further. We had reached the gates of an imposing bougainvillea-clad villa. Its roof sported a garden of wild antennas and was guarded by Japanese private armed security. We turned round rather rapidly and tried to take another turning up the mountain, but that road ended at a tennis stadium. We were in Italy but unable to get anywhere else in Italy. There is only one road in and out of Campione.

'Jude, this place is crazy.'

We drove down to the lakeside through a wonderful mix of modern and old architecture. On the waterfront sat a large modern casino, built by Benito Mussolini. This explained the aura of wealth. We later learnt that the casino's revenue provided the residents with their municipal services, so they had no local taxes to pay. A secret tunnel, which seemed not to be much of a secret, led from the casino to the local priest's palatial house.

Switzerland as a rule does not grant residency to anyone who is not Swiss. In Campione, however, foreigners have no problems getting residency. At this time, Campione was one of the world's least-known and most unusual tax havens.

'Let's look for somewhere to have lunch,' said Albi.

'Good idea. I'm starving.'

We parked the car in the casino car park and strolled along the waterfront holding hands, overlooked by fanciful wrought-iron balconies. Small cobbled streets rose off to our left. Ducks bobbed about on the water to our right. Ferries went around the lake, stopping at the small villages. Small, colourful fishing boats were tied to a collapsing wooden pier.

We liked the look of a restaurant called the Taverna, and were ushered to our table by a faultlessly dressed waiter who spoke perfect English. We sat on the shaded terrace overlooking the lake, and ate wonderful Italian food and drank Brunello di Montalcino. We marvelled at the anomalies of Campione. The policeman lounging in the bar, with his glass of grappa and a cigarette, wore an Italian uniform but his car had Swiss plates; the telephones were Swiss; the postbox was Italian but accepted Swiss stamps. The official currency was the Swiss franc but Italian lires were accepted as well. It seemed that everything that was good about Italy and everything that was good about Switzerland had joined up inside Campione without any accompanying negatives.

As we drank espresso and sambuca, as if to confuse us further a London black taxi with Swiss plates parked opposite the restaurant. Out of it climbed five people: a good-looking fifty-year-old German man, a blonde woman, a Rastafarian, a well-dressed Michael Caine lookalike and a man who looked like a real-life Michael Corleone.

The place reverberated with life, glamour, money and a sense of intrigue. Albi and I decided we wanted to live here.

A couple of days later Albi had to leave for New York. The Beirut load had arrived. I drove him to Malpensa airport.

'Jude, while I'm gone, try to find somewhere nice for us to live. I'll be back in seven to ten days.'

When he got back, I had rented a furnished flat in 22 Via Totone, Campione. References were unnecessary; money was what spoke in Campione. I bought a small Mini and opened an account for household bills in the Union Banco in Lugano.

We made arrangements with Rosie for me to fly to England to pick up Podge. Two days after Podge and I arrived back in Campione, Albi announced he was off to the US again.

'But, Albi, Podge has come out to spend time with you. You haven't seen her for months.'

'Yeah I know, but it can't be helped.'

He left. Rosie was, unsurprisingly, unimpressed. I enjoyed Podge's company, not knowing anyone in the area and not speaking the language. We took boat rides everywhere, fed the ducks, discovered a mad zoo near the Italian border and were surprised at how quickly the time went. Albi arrived back in time for his parents' and sister's visit. Podge flew back to England with them.

Our baby was due around the middle of October. At the beginning of September we locked up the Campione flat and took a combination of train and ferry to Victoria station. We booked into Blake's in Roland Gardens, SW7.

The following day we had lunch at an Indian restaurant. Nik Douglas and Penny Slinger were there; we'd got to know them before we left for the States. They lived near Blake's in Gledhow Gardens, SW5. Penny was a surrealist artist with a first-class honours degree. Nik had a varied career. In the early 1960s he had produced sounds and managed pop groups before moving to Ibiza. He had also travelled extensively in India, Tibet and Nepal and published books on Eastern culture and religion. When we first met them, they were working together on several art and literary projects.

'Albi, Judy, great to see you,' said Penny.

'We thought you were still in the States,' said Nik.

'Judy, you're pregnant. Congratulations,' Penny said, smiling widely.

'Thank you,' we replied together.

'Where are you having the baby?' asked Penny.

'I don't know. We've only just got back from Europe. I've got to find a doctor and we have to find somewhere to live,' I said.

'I've got the best doctor. His speciality is gynaecology. He believes in natural birth.'

'That's brilliant – that's just what I want.'

She gave me his number and address. Dr Basil Lee, 64 Redcliffe Gardens, SW10.

'If you guys need a reference for a flat, let me know,' said Nik.

I phoned the doctor at once and made an appointment for the following afternoon. Albi and I liked him immediately. He told us he delivered his private patients' babies at St Theresa's hospital in Wimbledon, so we started flat-hunting in that area. Eventually we found a pleasant three-bedroom flat in a quiet street in Richmond.

The baby arrived on 29 October. Albi was there throughout; he even helped Dr Lee cut the umbilical cord. She was a beautiful little baby girl. Far too beautiful for any of the names we had chosen for her. She remained unnamed until my twenty-third birthday when Penny came to visit us. She took one look at my beautiful baby and said, 'She's told me her name is Amber.'

It instinctively felt right.

Albi proudly drove us home from the hospital. The following day we went to register her birth. Albi was stoned. I gave my details, and was expecting Albi to say his name was Albert Lane. He instead came out with the name Albert Waylon Jennings and said he was a singer for the group Laughing Grass. I couldn't start arguing with him in front of the registrar.

Life was peaceful at the Richmond flat. I loved being a mother. I spent hours just staring with wonder at the beautiful little girl Albi and I had created. Only a few people had our phone number, one of them being Pete, another Marty. After Jim had fled Vancouver, Marty had made his way back to England and was living in London. As I was breastfeeding nine-day-old Amber in the middle of the night, the phone rang. I assumed it was Pete. Albi stretched his hand out of the bedcovers to answer it.

'Hello,' he said. He suddenly held the phone away from his ear.

'You fucking Welsh fucking arsehole. You've ripped me off,' was the tirade I could hear drifting from the mouthpiece across the room to my armchair. Jim had decided Howard had not given him a big enough share of the money they had ripped off Pete.

'Jim, I don't know what you're on about. Let's talk in the morning.'

Albi put the phone down. Half an hour later, once Amber was sleeping peacefully, the phone rang again.

'Jim, please, the baby's sleeping,' I heard Albi say.

For the rest of the night the calls continued. Each time waking Amber. The following day we were all exhausted.

'Who gave him our number, Albi?'

'I don't know. I can only think it was Marty.'

'Did you tell him not to give the number to anyone?'

'Of course I did.'

The following night the calls began again. Eventually Albi left the phone off the hook.

'Jude, we'll have to move. Jim says he's going to blow up my parents' house and stuff like that,' he said. He looked tired and worried.

'Do you think he would?' I asked.

'To be honest, Jude, when he's in one of these moods there's no telling what madness he will do.'

'Was it Marty who gave him our number?'

'Yes.'

'Albi, I have a baby to look after now. Will you please not ever give Marty our phone number again.'

'Yeah, I'm sorry, love.'

I phoned around and found a short-let serviced apartment in Chelsea Cloisters that was available that day. I began packing. Albi went out.

Moving with a small baby and all the paraphernalia that went with it was a lot of work. But I loved her so much it didn't bother me. I found it, however, very hard to think kindly towards Marty.

Amber, at two weeks old, was on the run.

CHAPTER ELEVEN
Goodbye to Mr Nice

The flat in Chelsea Cloisters was small, scruffy and absurdly expensive. We stayed there for a couple of weeks before moving into a flat in Queensgate. For Christmas 1977 we booked into the Metropole hotel in Brighton. We had lunch with Richard Powis, his new girlfriend Lisette, and Rosie, Muffin and Podge.

We saw Masha. She had moved out of my father's flat and into a flat with her boyfriend Chris. It was to be the first of a few disastrous relationships. She had put on a lot of weight and seemed depressed. The last time I had seen her she was as slim as me. She told me that Chris wouldn't let her out on her own because he hated other men looking at her. I worried about her.

Marcus was a typical twelve-year-old. I had brought him a skateboard back from the States, which delighted him. Natasha was still sailing in the Mediterranean and George was still in the Middle East.

We wanted to move back to Campione but Albi was feeling insecure about the safety of the Tunnicliffe passport, given McCann's recent behaviour. The search was on for a new passport.

Shortly after McCann's telephone terrorism, we heard he'd been arrested by a combination of French and German police on the French Riviera. The Germans wanted him for bombing a British army base at Mönchengladbach in 1973. Anne McNulty, Jim's ex-girlfriend, had been discovered in Hamburg in 1973 with a carload of Jim's hash and a false passport. Jim, as a self-promoted spokesperson for the IRA, phoned the juvenile detention centre she was held in and threatened bomb attacks if she did not receive a light sentence. He then paid someone to plant three bombs outside the army camp. The bombs had not hurt anyone but had shattered a few windows. She got seven months.

Jim started his new media antics with aplomb, much as he had in Canada, but using the opposite arguments. He said he was James McCann, a fundraiser for the IRA, not James Kennedy. He claimed he was a political prisoner. In France then there was much support for political prisoners. Shortly before McCann's arrest the French government had handed over to the Germans a lawyer for the Baader-Meinhof group. There had been many protests in France about this decision. When the Italians tried to claim a supporter of the Red Brigade who was living in France, and the Spanish wanted back a member of the Basque group ETA, supporters of political asylum came out in force. The courts denied the extraditions. The same lawyers who defended the ETA case took on McCann's case. The French courts eventually refused to extradite McCann to Germany. The reason given was that his blowing up of a British army base was a political act. He received political asylum.

While we were back in England, Albi became involved in various ventures. He financed a recording studio called Archipelago with his friends Sally Minford and Michael O'Connell. He helped Nik and Penny, and thanks was accordingly given to 'Albion Jennings' in their book *Sexual Secrets*. We spent many evenings round at Nik and Penny's and met various interesting people, who included the renowned psychiatrist R.D. Laing and best-selling author Lyall Watson.

We met up for dinner with Anthony Woodhead. He said he had a bent customs officer in San Francisco airport. He wanted Albi to send a ton of Pakistani hash. He and Albi spent dinner discussing the deal and the investment needed. Durrani was to send the hash in boxes marked as containing surgical equipment. Two weeks later

Woodhead called to say the load had arrived. Did Albi want to send someone over to collect the money?

Albi asked Johnny Martin to go. Johnny went and waited in the Mark Hopkins on Nob Hill. Albi told him to expect just over $1,000,000; 25 per cent was due to Albi and the rest to Durrani and his partner. But nothing was heard of Anthony Woodhead again, except vague rumours he had moved to Nicaragua. He had ripped us off. Albi was furious.

Nik introduced Albi to a man in Norfolk called Donald Nice (pronounced 'neece'). He had just finished twelve years in prison for murder and was willing to sell his passport to Albi for £1,000. From March 1978 Albi assumed this identity, using the pronunciation 'nice'.

Another man introduced to us around this time was an electrician Nik had met in Nepal. His name was John Denbigh, but he was also known as Old John. He was tall with long hair and a resemblance to Mick Jagger. He wore beads and had amulets and semi-precious stones about his person, and drove an old London taxi. Brought up on the streets of Fulham, he had the accent to match. He still lived in the flat he had as a child, with his older brother Nigel and his attractive dark-haired girlfriend Liz, who was to become a dear friend.

John's Nepalese connections interested Albi. I found John hard to understand; he had a tendency to talk in riddles. However, before long a deal was fixed and Pete sent Tom Sunde to meet Old John in Kathmandu with the finance.

Durrani was back in London. He invited us for lunch at his Knightsbridge house in Trevor Square, SW3. A couple of days later he suffered a heart attack. Howard visited him in Westminster hospital. He returned home very saddened and told me that Durrani looked appalling and how he had to lean right over to hear what he had to say.

'There was a close friend of Durrani's with him, a Pakistani called Malik. He is staying the night with him. I'll go and visit him again tomorrow. Will you come with me Jude?'

'Of course,' I said. But I never did as the following day Durrani suffered another massive heart attack and died. He was forty-two.

* * *

In March 1978 we returned to Campione. It was good to be back. Patrick, Jude, Peggy and their new baby Bridie came to visit. They loved Campione. Albi decided to invest in Patrick, setting up a tax consultancy business called Overseas United Investors with a weekly newsletter, *The Offshore Banking Report*. Patrick was taking care of moving money round for Albi when needed. They were to have our apartment while we rented another one.

Albi introduced Patrick and Nik. They got on well together, and Nik employed Patrick as his financial adviser. Patrick set about opening a string of companies for Nik. A couple of the companies Mr Nice became consultant to, and he became the managing director of Worldwide Entertainments. These legitimate companies provided a front for his dope smuggling.

In June Albi had to go to Pakistan to meet a friend of Durrani's called Raoul. It was his first visit to a dope-producing country and his excitement was clear. While he was gone I rented a large unfurnished flat down the road from Patrick and Jude, with views over the lake. I arranged for our furniture from the States to be sent over. I also put in an order with a garage in Zurich for a BMW as a birthday present for Albi.

Albi flew back from Karachi to Frankfurt. Amber and I met him there. He had a serious case of dysentery. We drove to Oestrich in the Rhine valley and booked into a lovely old hotel called the Schwan. It was near where Albi had done his first dope deal.

Albi consulted the hotel doctor, who told him the cure for dysentery was red wine.

'The best doctor I've ever seen, Jude,' he said. That night we drank on doctor's orders.

'Let's drive back to Campione through France and tour the vineyards.'

'That's sounds like a nice plan,' I said. I thought back to when I had done a similar trip with my parents.

'Yeah, we can build ourselves a good wine collection.'

We arrived back in Campione a couple of days after our furniture arrived. Patrick and Jude had kindly unpacked most of it. To celebrate their hard work Patrick opened one of our good bottles of Brunello di Montalcino.

Natasha phoned from Greece. She had met a man she thought Albi would find interesting. He was Stuart Prentiss, a Californian hashish smuggler. He owned a yacht-chartering business based in Kerrera, a small island off the coast of Oban in Scotland. Albi arranged to meet him in Palma de Mallorca. At this meeting it was agreed that Albi would arrange for Stuart's boat to be filled up with a ton of Moroccan hash. The loading would take place offshore, close to Al Hoceima. This area of the Mediterranean coast is sparsely populated because of the inhospitable Rif mountains, also famous as the source of Moroccan cannabis. Stuart would then sail it to Scotland.

In August, Albi, Amber and I flew from Zurich to New York. We had given up the New York apartment by this time; we stayed at the Plaza. Albi had a series of meetings. We went to Studio 54 with Alan Schwarz and Margaux Hemingway. Diana Ross, Andy Warhol and Christopher Reeves were also there. Alan took us to Regine's on the corner of Park Avenue and 59th Street. It was the most chic, expensive, classy club in New York at that time. Donald and Ivana Trump were there the same evening we were.

We then flew to San Francisco; Pete and Patti were now living on Nob Hill. Albi and I had asked Pete to be Amber's godfather and he had happily agreed. While we were visiting Pete and Patti, a load of Thai marijuana flown into JFK got busted by the Drug Enforcement Administration (DEA). Sixteen New Yorkers were arrested. Luckily none of them knew Pete or Albi. DB (Pete's man at JFK) was not one of them, for reasons we didn't understand. Between 1975 and August 1978 twenty-four loads had been imported into JFK, totalling 55,000 pounds of marijuana and hashish. There was a lot for Albi and Pete to discuss. Was this the end of the JFK scams?

From San Francisco we flew to Los Angeles, where Julian Peto was working. He was there with Helen and her daughter Rosie. After only one night in LA, Albi flew back to Europe for more meetings. Amber and I stayed on with Julian and Helen for a few more days before joining Albi in Campione.

It was the beginning of October when the phone rang in the Campione flat.

'Jude, that was Natasha's friend Stuart. He wants us to fly to Scotland and check out his island where the Moroccan is going to land. How soon will you be ready to go?'

'Two days,' I said.

We flew from Milan to London, checking into Blake's hotel, and then flew with Natasha to Glasgow, where we hired a car and drove to Oban. Here we caught a passenger and bicycle ferry for the ten-minute ride to the tiny island of Kerrera. There is just one tiny piece of road by the jetty; the rest of the island is accessible only by foot or bike. Stuart was waiting to greet us as we stepped off the ferry. He was a tall, stooped, bearded man, dressed in a checked jacket with leather patches on the elbows, and brown trousers and green wellingtons. We followed him to a rented isolated farmhouse called Mount Pleasant; his wife Dianne was there. Natasha and Dianne took Amber for a walk while Stuart took Albi and I off to show us the proposed landing site.

We boarded a small motor launch. It bumped through the Firth of Lorn, round the northern tip of the island and out into the Bay of Oban. The sea had become choppy. Albi looked distinctly wet, unhappy and frightened. He hated sailing. Between Kerrera and the Isle of Mull, a light blinked through the mist. 'That's Grass Point. It has an old stone quay that's no longer used except by the occasional leisure craft,' said Stuart. I giggled at the name. It must be a good omen. We anchored in a tiny creek and clambered over slimy rocks and up a muddy grass slope to a small stone farmhouse with a barn to its right. 'This is Bar nam boc, where Dianne and I got married, and I still own the lease. There is no way on to this island except like this or by the one-man ferry you came over on. I thought we could store the load here,' said Stuart.

Albi seemed pleased with the set-up, despite hating the boat journey.

We returned to Campione in time for Amber's first birthday. In December we came back to London and rented a flat in Clive Court, a mansion block off the Edgware Road. The Moroccan load was due to land in Scotland. It landed successfully. Every day for a week, Albi had someone drive 300 pounds down to London, where it was sold to various dealers. The whole deal worked smoothly.

'Stuart, let's do another one,' Albi said.

'No, that's greedy. I'll do another one next year. It's best not to push one's luck,' said Stuart.

I agreed with him.

We stayed in the Edgware Road flat for Christmas. Despite Albi's fugitive status we socialized widely. One evening at the Zanzibar we nearly bumped into Bernard Simons, Howard's solicitor. Bernard did a double-take before discreetly looking away. At a Christmas party we met an American man called Tom Baker, and the singer P.J. Proby. Proby was probably the first male of the twentieth century to wear his hair in a ponytail. He had a string of British hits and was known for his exhausting stage performances, tight trousers and frilled shirts. At a show in Croydon in January 1965, he burst out of his skin-tight velvet bell-bottoms. The females in the audience went wild, and he appeared on the front cover of every newspaper in the country. Two days later at another concert it happened again. After that he was banned for a while from theatres and TV stations in England.

Tom Baker, an actor turned film director, wanted to make a film called *Life After Elvis*, which would star Proby. Albi had always harboured dreams of been a pop star and realized this might be the nearest he would get. Wealthy with success in the dope business, he was happy to help with the finance.

We hired the Nashville Rooms off the Old Brompton Road. Proby was billed to appear and Tom Baker was to film it. As it turned out, Proby got drunk and refused to go onstage. I tried coaxing him, to no avail, as did Albi, Phil and Tom. The audience were restive and beginning to get angry. Albi, who had now drunk nearly as much as Proby, decided to go onstage and impersonate Elvis. The audience booed. I cringed. Then a whole host of would-be Elvises climbed on to the stage and tried to get the microphone out of Albi's hands. He stubbornly refused. Occasionally an Elvis would succeed, only to have the microphone snatched back by Albi. A friend came over to me.

'Jude, you have to get him off that stage. Apart from embarrass-ing himself, anyone could recognize him and call the police.'

'Easier said than done,' I said as I watched Albi warbling and writhing drunkenly around.

Finally we got him off. We received a copy of the filmed footage. It made amusing viewing for me, if not for Albi.

We went back to Campione via Paris. Phil came to visit with his girl-friend Shirley. I, like nearly all the other Campione residents, did my weekly shopping in Italy in the border town of Chiasso, which halved the shopping bill. We had lunch in the Taverna, then, after extracting a promise from Albi and Phil that they would be at home to help unload the shopping, Shirley, Amber and I set off.

We arrived back at the flat with a carload of food and wine. There was no sign of Albi and Phil. Unloading shopping in our new block was hard work. There were about ten steep steps to climb up to the lift in the sweltering heat and with a nine-month-old baby it was not easy.

We eventually finished getting all the shopping up and stored it away.

'Where do you think they are?' Shirley asked.

'Drunk in a bar I don't doubt,' I said.

'Should we go and look for them?'

'Let's have a cup of tea first,' I said.

A little later we drove down to the lakeside and parked the car in the casino car park. It didn't take us long to find them. They were in Tonino's bar, next door to the Taverna, and they were, as we had expected, drunk. But that is putting it mildly. Neither of them could sit up straight and neither of them could speak properly. Albi was trying to have a conversation in Italian with an old man sitting next to him. He greeted me with what I think were endearments but his words were so slurred it was hard to be sure. He held his arms out to hug me and fell off his stool.

'How the hell are we going to get them to the car?' Shirley asked.

'I think I should take Amber and go and bring the car to the front of the bar.'

'Good idea,' she said.

I pulled up in front of the bar, left Amber in her car seat and went to help Shirley who was trying to get Phil onto his feet. We half carried him to the car, then tried to manoeuvre him into the back of the two-door BMW. The waiters from the Taverna had gathered and were enjoying the comedy show.

It was the same procedure with Albi. Getting him into the front seat was slightly easier, although as we drove up the hill to the flat he kept lolling against me, which interfered with my driving. By the time we got them into the apartment we were exhausted, and irritated when they both started snoring loudly on the sofa. We managed to drag them into the spare room and slung them on the bed. They cuddled up together. Then some devilment overtook us. We stripped them of their clothes and took Polaroids of them naked with their arms around each other. We arranged the photos on the dining room table to greet them when they awoke.

They reacted very differently. Phil laughed until he had tears rolling down his cheeks. Albi's face was tight with fury. When he got me on his own he started.

'How dare you? Supposing someone had come round and seen them. Supposing I had been busted in the night and the police had got hold of them. I want them all destroyed now.'

'Albi, it was only a joke.'

'Well, I'm not laughing.'

As usual, I did as he asked.

In April 1979 Jim got a message to Albi to meet him in Paris.

'Albi, are you sure you want to get involved with him again?' I asked.

'He'll have calmed down by now. Don't worry. And I won't give him the number here.'

He returned three days later.

'Jude, he wants me to send him a load of Thai sticks to Dublin.

This means I'll have to go to Thailand and Hong Kong but I'll only be gone seven to ten days maximum.'

'Not away again, Albi,' I said.

'Look, when I get back we'll go and spend some time in Ireland. You've never been and you'll love it.'

When he returned to Campione, he had plenty of tales of his trip to Hong Kong and Thailand, film reels to amuse us – we'd bought each other movie cameras that Christmas – and armfuls of presents for Amber and me. We packed up and flew to London.

Albi had remained out of the press for more than three years now, but we heard through the grapevine that an article was coming out about him in the *New Statesman*. Albi flew ahead of me to Dublin while I waited in London for a couple of days for the magazine to come out.

The article was written by crime reporter Duncan Campbell. Chief Inspector Fairweather's confidential report into Albi's disappearance while on bail in 1974 had been leaked. Campbell explained that Fairweather had been sent for by MI6's legal adviser, Bernard Shelton. Shelton had told him that 'a former Balliol College fellow undergraduate of Marks, who is now an MI6 officer, contacted Marks with a view to using his company "Anna Belinda", which also had a shop in Amsterdam, as a cover for his activities. He later realized that Marks was engaged in certain activities and requested him to obtain information concerning the Provisional IRA.'

Albi was rather pleased with the article. This was the first admission by any British government authority that he had worked for MI6 and been asked to spy on the IRA.

Amber and I flew to Dublin and took a taxi to the Shelbourne, a historic Georgian hotel overlooking St Stephen's Green in the city centre. The porter carried our cases up to the first floor where Albi had booked us a suite. As Amber and I arrived, Jim McCann was on his way out.

'Ah, Judy, good to see you.' He enveloped me in a hug. 'Let's have a look at the wee one now. I'm glad to see she looks like you and not your Welsh wanker,' he said, jerking a thumb at Albi. 'Sylvia and the kids are here as well, so we can all get together. I've got to go now. H'ard, I'll see you in the morning.'

Since I had last seen Jim he'd had another daughter. They named her Ashling.

'How was the flight, Jude?'

'Fine. I'm dying for a cup of tea, though.'

'I'll ring room service.'

'Can you order some sandwiches too, please?'

Amber was at the age where she banged her head on tables as she walked round rooms. In the centre of the room was a round wooden table and a couple of chairs; I moved them to the side so there was less chance of her hurting herself.

There was a knock on the door. I opened it to a man who looked like Jeeves. He had in his arms a large silver tray, with silver teapot and matching milk and sugar bowls, exquisitely cut sandwiches and delicate white china cups and plates. He walked into the centre of the room and said, 'Now,' in a lovely, gentle Irish accent. The tray landed on the floor, the contents spilling everywhere. The man had a look of total astonishment on his face. The table was not where he supposed it to be.

Unable to suppress my laughter I ran to the bathroom, while Albi, with Amber on his knee, hid his mouth behind his hand.

While we were waiting for the load to arrive from Thailand, we decided to tour Ireland. I phoned up a car hire company.

'Hi, I'd like to rent a car tomorrow, please.'

'And where would you like to be going in this car?' said a soft male Irish voice.

'To Limerick. Can you fit a baby seat in the back?'

'Aye, that'll be no problem whatever. I'll have it ready for you at midday tomorrow.'

'Brilliant, thank you.'

The following day I took a taxi with Amber to collect the car. I walked into the car hire garage and a ginger-haired man with a freckled face grinned at me.

'Ah, you must be Mrs Lane to collect the car with the baby seat.'

'That's right,' I said. 'Is it ready?'

'Aye, we got the baby seat in the back. But we've got one small problem: the car tyres are all flat, so's you won't be getting to Limerick in that car tonight.'

I was speechless.

'I'll be sure to have it all ready tomorrow,' he said.

Bemused, I returned to the hotel and related the story to Albi. He laughed and told me about years ago when, during one of the early Irish scams, he'd rented a small cottage and needed a phone line putting in. He called the local telephone company and asked them to install one. The man replied, 'Now why would you be wanting a phone? I write letters meself.'

'And another time,' continued Albi, 'I went to hire a van and the man in the office says, "Now, I can't be letting you have one today, it's raining."' We both laughed. I was falling in love with my motherland.

When Jim heard we were going touring he decided to join us for a while. He and Sylvia and their daughters Siobhan and Ashling, Albi, Amber and I all checked in to a hotel next to Bunratty Castle, not far from Shannon airport. We arranged for a babysitter for the children, then after dinner we went to a pub, Durty Nellie's, a ramshackle cottage with a thatched roof. It was a warren of small rooms and little bars with cosy inglenook seats. There were a few American tourists sitting around a bar.

Jim introduced himself. 'I'm James Kennedy. I'm with the boys in the North.'

The Americans were excited. They were going to have a story to tell their friends back home. Jim introduced Albi as Sean O'Connor, chief procurer of arms for the cause. Albi cringed. I was introduced as Bridie O'Connor, the head of the women's side of the IRA. Sylvia was introduced as Maggie O'Neil, the chief accountant of the struggle. None of us had to do any talking. Jim did it all for us.

'I'm a cultural incendiarist, Jude. I'm a fucking cultural incendiarist,' he whispered in my ear.

The evening ended with Jim and the Americans singing the latest emotional tearjerker to come from the North.

The following day we went out for a drive, our car following Jim and Sylvia's. On a small country lane we were met head on by a large herd of cows escorted by a farmer. Jim drove slowly through them, but after a while wound his window down and thumped a cow on the nose. This had the immediate effect of causing them to stampede. The poor farmer dived into the bushes lining the road while Albi, Amber and I sat rocked and battered in our car as crazed cows crashed wildly into us.

Two days later Jim, Sylvia and the children returned to Dublin, and Albi, Amber and I were left to finish our tour of Ireland in peace. We had a magical time. Albi took us to wonderful hotels and regaled us with the early stories of his, Graham's and Patrick's adventures in the early days of smuggling with McCann.

We returned to Dublin and rented an executive house near Fitzpatrick Castle in Killiney.

'Albi, can you please make sure no dope comes here. I really don't want any in the house with Amber,' I said.

'Of course, Jude. I've told Jim to rent somewhere to store it.'

Two days later, Albi, Amber and I were having lunch when we heard the doorbell ring. I opened the front door. On the step stood Jim with a box in his arms and a grin on his face.

'Colour television delivery,' he said in an exceptionally loud voice, which I presumed was for the benefit of our neighbours, as he pushed past me into the front room. He went back outside and brought another large box from a battered van parked in our drive-way. Altogether the boxes contained 750 kilos of Thai sticks. Albi looked pale.

'Pressies, pressies,' Amber sang, as she jumped excitedly about.

'Colour televisions, H'ard,' Jim said, placing another box in our front room. I was livid.

'Jim, stop what you're doing. I'm not having this in the house with Amber,' I said.

'Stop fussing. H'ard, tell her to stop fussing,' said Jim.

'Fuck you, Jim. Store it in your house with your kids,' I yelled. Memories of the fear I had felt in Ibiza came back.

'No one talks to me like that. H'ard, tell her. No one talks to the kid like that,' Jim said.

'I'm talking to you any way I want. Now get it out!' I glared at Jim and then at Albi.

'Jude, I promise you I didn't know he was going to bring it here,' Albi said.

'Albi, I cannot stay here with Amber unless it's gone,' I said.

'She's got spunk, H'ard, she's got spunk,' Jim said. 'I'll rent a garage, okay. But you'll pay for it, H'ard.'

'Whatever, Jim, let's just get it away from here,' said Albi.

McCann found a lock-up garage nearby and he and Albi removed all the 'televisions'.

Albi arranged for various friends to hire two-door Ford Capris and bring them on the ferry to Ireland. Capris, he told me, were able to conceal more than other cars. The first friends to come were a young couple, Jeff and Penny, who had some connection to Oxford. I liked them.

'Jude, pack a picnic and we'll drive to the woods,' Albi said.

We drove to a wood in the Wicklow mountains. Jeff and Penny followed in their Capri with a box of Thai marijuana in the boot. We found an isolated spot and parked the cars. While Penny and I were laying out the picnic, Albi and Jeff were taking off the door panels and removing the back seat, then filling the spaces with marijuana.

I started singing to Amber, 'If you go down to the woods today you're sure of a big surprise.'

Each car could hold only 50 kilos, so altogether fifteen runs were done. Two friends of Phil's did the last run. They were arrested at Liverpool by Her Majesty's Customs and Excise. It was the first time Albi had lost a load from an Irish scam, which he and Jim had been doing intermittently for over eight years.

Jim was furious and was straight round to the house, ranting and raving.

'Okay, you Welsh arsehole. That's it. I'll not be having any more of your fucking friends fucking things up. Next time I'll take care of it myself. You understand me?'

'How will you do that?' Albi asked.

'Our Gerard's got a fruit company. I'll take it as bananas,' Jim said.

During this time Pete phoned us in Dublin. He had some Colombians interested in moving into the UK market. He asked Albi if he could arrange the unloading of 50 tons of Colombian weed. It was discussed with Jim.

'I've got the perfect place to land it,' he said.

The following day we drove with Jim to a tiny little quay in an isolated estuary.

'Perfect spot, H'ard, isn't it?'

I looked at the water; it was about two foot deep. Back at the house Albi said, 'Jude, I'll think I'll ask Stuart if he can do it.'

'I think that would be better,' I said.

Albi, Amber and I returned to England. Stuart Prentiss came to see us in London and Albi put the proposal of the Colombian scam to him. There was no way, he said, that he could handle 50 tons, but he was willing to receive 15 tons. To do this, he said, he would need another yacht. Stuart also explained he could only store 5 tons at Bar nam boc. Alternative premises would also have to be found. The terms and conditions between all interested parties were thrashed out.

Meanwhile, Phil sent another load of Thai marijuana to Dublin. Jim successfully picked it up. An articulated truck left the docks at Cork with a load of South American bananas and pulled into a lay-by on the main road just south of Dublin. A rented van was parked in the darkness. A courting couple were in their car further up the lay-by. Jim, who had been experimenting with cocaine and was also slightly drunk, went up to the couple and threatened them. They drove off, stopped at the first phone box in the little town of Naas and reported to the Garda suspicious-looking men at a certain lay-by.

A patrol car went to investigate. Jim tottered around on unsteady legs waving a pistol, which was kicked out of his hands. He then jumped into a Hillman car, also parked in the lay-by, and roared off. He crashed into the first available hedge and was overpowered as he tried to scramble up a hill.

'I did it for Ireland,' he yelled as he was dragged off.

The Irish army bomb-disposal team was called. The truck doors were blown open. Instead of the expected IRA explosives, there were twenty-one tea chests full of Thai marijuana and a load of bananas.

The largest bust ever in Ireland.

We heard the news in our flat in Cathcart Road, Chelsea, which I had bought shortly after Amber was born. It was worrying. Albi was convinced they would connect him with Jim. One of Albi's oldest friends from Kenfig Hill was among those arrested in the lay-by with Jim. We packed up the London flat and moved back to Campione. The Mr Nice passport would have to be laid to rest. A new one in the name of Roy Green was procured. The Mr Nice passport was buried in the children's playground below our apartment building in Campione.

CHAPTER TWELVE
Cannabis Galore

The closeness of my involvement with the Irish load worried me. The whole business was beginning to worry me. I was a mother now. Would Albi ever stop smuggling?

McCann's arrest had unnerved us both.

'Jude, we'll just do this Colombian one and then we can knock it on the head. We ought to clear a million pounds,' Albi said.

The Colombian load needed careful planning. We moved back to London and rented a large house in Kennington. Mike, one of the financiers of the Colombian load, came and stayed with us. He was a New York vegan and wouldn't eat any of the food I cooked. Albi and Mike flew up to Scotland for meetings with Stuart. Mike explained that an ocean-going salvage tug called *Karob* would carry the 15 tons from Colombia to Scotland.

'Salvage boats are such a good front, Jude.'

'How come?'

'Well, they have an excuse for hanging around anywhere in an ocean so they don't attract suspicion.'

I wondered what it must be like floating about in heavy seas waiting for some vessel to fall into difficulties.

We got in touch with Peter Whitehead, whom Nik Douglas had introduced us to. He had blondish hair and a moustache and vaguely made me think of a Hollywood star from the 1940s. He was a film director who had reached fame in the 1960s with his short film

Wholly Communion, about the 1965 Beat Poetry conference at the Royal Albert Hall, and *Tonite Let's All Make Love in London*. He was now breeding falcons for the Saudi Arabian royal family in the tiny village of Pytchley in Northamptonshire.

'Peter, would you be willing to rent a stately home on the waterfront somewhere in Scotland? I'll make it worth your while,' Albi said.

Peter agreed.

Albi, on Worldwide Entertainments notepaper, wrote to the Lochaber Estate Agency, Fort William, Inverness-shire.

> Dear Sirs,
>
> During the winter period, our company will be producing a semi-documentary film located in the Western Isles, and set in the latter half of the last century. We intend to rent a large lochside property capable both of accommodating the staff (about 6 to 10 people) and of featuring in certain parts of the set.
>
> We would wish to resume tenancy by about December 1st of this year and stay for a minimum of three months. Adequate funds are available for the right property. If you have anything which you might consider suitable for our purposes, would you please let me know as soon as possible?
>
> Yours faithfully,

They wrote back to say they had a large property with a porter's lodge, Conaglen House, on the coast just by the entrance to the Caledonian Ship Canal at Fort William, which was available for £1,000 a week. Peter Whitehead, Stuart Prentiss and Albi went to suss it out.

Prentiss said it was ideal. Peter Whitehead negotiated the lease and rented it in his company's name, Lorrimer Films.

Albi got in touch with an old Oxford connection, James York, a tall skinny man with brown hair and eyes and an angelic face. He had recently come out of prison for a marijuana offence. His wife Sarah was the daughter of a high-ranking judge. James arranged the rental of a warehouse in Basildon, Essex, to store some more of the Colombian marijuana. He also agreed to wholesale it.

Cyril was worrying about the numbers of people involved. The frown rarely left his face. He was also going to wholesale, as were Johnny Martin, Old John and a few others I did not know.

'How much dope do you reckon gets smoked in England a week, Albi?' I asked.

'I reckon it's about three tons a day.'

I was shocked.

'Jude, in America it's twenty-eight tons.'

'Well, then it should sell quickly, shouldn't it?'

'You have to remember there's not just ours arriving in the country. And some people only like hash and others only like Thai. I reckon a ton a week is the best we can hope for,' he said.

Patrick agreed to move to London with Jude and their children to handle the accounts and finances. He hired a completely innocent schoolfriend, Hedley Morgan, to help him.

Patti's parents came to stay at the Kennington house, bringing messages from Pete. Amber had her second birthday in London, and then with everything set up we returned to Campione for peace, rest and relaxation.

The phone rang in the Campione flat. It was Pete.

'Okay, it's on its way.'

We hastily packed up the flat and flew back to London. I rented a bizarre serviced penthouse flat in Bayswater. It had a lift that came straight into our sitting room. Only we were supposed to have access to the penthouse. However, occasionally, entire Pakistani families or burka-wearing women would be beamed into our living room. I quickly found another duplex flat in the Colonnades building in Bayswater.

At the beginning of December 1979 the *Karob* picked up 15 tons of Colombian hash. The tug started its three-week journey through the Caribbean seas and then across the Atlantic Ocean towards the chilly rough northern seas of Scotland.

On 29 December, Stuart's two 40-foot yachts, *Bagheera* and *Salammbo*, left the island of Kerrera for the seas of the Inner Hebrides.

In the middle of the night the Colombian weed was transferred from the tug to the two yachts. Later that night, still under cover of darkness, *Salammbo* returned to Kerrera and unloaded 5 tons of Colombian weed to Bar nam boc, where it was unloaded by friends and family of Stuart's. Meanwhile, the *Bagheera*, captained by a friend of Stuart's, delivered 10 tons to the waterfront Conaglen House. Here Albi and Tom Sunde unloaded it with the help of a few vegan New Yorkers, who had been sent over specially. It was then transferred to four three-ton box-vans. James York and his friend Nick Cole took 5 tons to the stash in Essex. Cyril and a friend took another 5 tons to the falconry in Pytchley. The 5 tons at Bar nam boc stayed there.

I sat nervously at home waiting for Albi to phone. Late on the thirtieth he called.

'I'm on my way home, Jude. Chill the champagne.'

At the beginning of 1980, 15 tons of the finest Colombian marijuana was safely stored away. It was the largest importation ever into Europe.

We moved into a £500-a-week flat in Hans Court, Knightsbridge. Peter Whitehead's film company rented it for us. Patrick and Jude moved into a house by Orme Square, overlooking Hyde Park.

One morning in late January, closely entwined in our huge bed, Albi and I lay peacefully, tired and satisfied from an early morning of love.

'Will you marry me, Jude?'

I laughed. 'Who will I marry? Donald Nice, Albert Waylon Jennings or one of your other aliases?'

'You choose, love.'

I sat up and looked at him; he was serious.

'Albi, I would love to marry you, but only as you.'

'I want everyone to know I love you. Can we at least become officially engaged?'

'Of course. I love you so much I'd love that,' I said.

We turned to each other and sealed our engagement with a long lingering kiss, until we heard the sound of running small feet and felt the touch of another body. Our beautiful daughter Amber joined us in bed.

'I guess it's time to get up. I'll run to the corner shop and get something extra special for breakfast,' I said.

Albi grinned; his brilliant blue eyes sparkled. Amber sat on his chest.

'Get some champagne too. Dom Perignon,' he said.

The corner shop I referred to was Harrods. Podge constantly told me off for calling it that.

'But it is on a corner – four corners.' I liked to tease her.

It wasn't the most convenient store to have as your local because it was so often full of American and Japanese tourists. But you couldn't complain about the range of goods. I collected my purchases and returned home, by which time Albi and Amber were in the kitchen. As I cooked breakfast I heard Albi on the phone to my father in Brighton, making an appointment to go and see him.

'I want to do everything properly. I'll go and see your father and ask him formally for permission to marry you,' he said.

Touched by this gesture, I went and kissed him.

'I also want to throw an engagement party to celebrate. I'll take care of all the arrangements – I just want you to enjoy yourself.'

I felt happy and cared for. I loved Albi so much.

True to his word, Albi took care of all the preparations for the party. He arranged for the Caviar Bar in Knightsbridge to take care of the catering. He went to see my father and asked for his permission to marry me. My father gave his consent.

On the morning of the party, Howard was up early. He came into our room while I was still in bed, carrying a small box in his hand. He lowered himself onto his knee, opened the box, took out the most exquisite diamond and emerald ring from Asprey's and slipped it on to my finger.

'This is to show you how much I love you and always will.'

I made myself scarce for the rest of the day while Albi and Tom Sunde, who was living with us, finished the preparations. I went out and bought a Zandra Rhodes dress, and spent the rest of the day being pampered in beauty salons. When I returned to the flat I was amazed to see sculpted-ice swans positioned around the entrance hall and living room. Vases of red roses were everywhere. The food was limited to foie gras and caviar, the drink to Stolichnaya vodka and Dom Perignon.

All our friends who came were a fun and welcome presence, which only served to deepen our feeling of joy and love.

Peter Whitehead introduced us to his attractive fiancée Dido Goldsmith, with whom he had had a whirlwind romance. She and I hit it off straight away. She was the daughter of the ecologist Teddy Goldsmith and the niece of the millionaire Jimmy Goldsmith. Peter asked Albi to be his best man. The reception lunch was held at the Caviar Bar; among the guests was Bianca Jagger, a close friend of Dido's. After lunch we returned to Peter's apartment where Jade Jagger joined us straight from school and played with Amber and Maxime, Dido's daughter from a previous marriage. Albi tried to impress Bianca with his piano-playing skills but failed to astound.

Peter and Dido spent their honeymoon in the Conaglen house.

In March we learnt that James McCann had been acquitted. He had managed to separate his trial from that of the three others caught in the lay-by. The lorry driver and his mate were acquitted. Their defence was that they knew nothing about the contents of the metal containers mixed among the cases of South American bananas in their lorry. One of the men pleaded guilty and received twelve months. He told the Garda the operation had been planned by an Englishman. He refused to testify at McCann's trial, and when threatened with contempt of court merely shrugged his shoulders.

McCann had worked out an elaborate defence story. The tabloid press would have feasted for weeks on all the elements it contained. However, he did not need to use it. His defence team managed to tie the prosecution up in such knots, the judge ruled the prosecution did not have a strong enough case and acquitted him. He fled back to Sylvia, who was in Holland, before the prosecution had a chance to file an appeal.

* * *

In March the sales of the Colombian marijuana were going too slowly for the American investors. They started to put pressure on Pete.

'Jude, the American investors are really giving Pete a hard time,' Albi said one night as we were lying in bed. 'They don't understand why it's taking so long to sell. In the States the market is so much vaster; fifteen tons would be sold in a week.'

'But surely they must realize this is not a very big country,' I said.

'Pete's told them, but they're getting paranoid they're being ripped off or I'm not being efficient enough.'

'Did you not tell them at the beginning you thought it would be a ton a week?'

'Yeah, and that's what's been sold. But they've told Pete they want to send people over to check they're not being ripped off.'

'So what's going to happen?'

'Pete's going to try to talk them out of it.'

One of James York's dealers, another Oxford graduate, was arrested with LSD. He was also found with 50 pounds of Colombian grass in the boot of his car.

At the end of March I realized I was pregnant again. I went to see Dr Lee, who confirmed it and told me to expect the baby towards the end of November. Albi was ecstatic.

'Jude, this will all be over soon and we can go and live somewhere quietly,' he said. I couldn't wait; he was far too strained and short-tempered.

Pete phoned and told Albi he couldn't put the investors off any more. They were coming over to make an inventory and check on the accounts.

Albi was not happy about it. Nor was Tom Sunde, who now understood how things worked in England.

Meanwhile, another friend of Albi's had 200 kilos of Thai grass sitting in Heathrow airport. It was not known if the authorities were on to it. It was more than likely they were. Did Albi know anyone who would be willing to take the risk and go in and sign for it? It was discussed with Phil, who had recently bought a seafront Brighton flat with Shirley.

'Yeah, I know this poof friend of Shirley's who'll do it. He's called Sandy,' Phil said.

Albi, Phil and Sandy had a meeting. A plan was devised. Sandy was to hire a van and go to Heathrow with the relevant paperwork and pick the load up. He was then to break into the container to see if the Thai grass was still there. If it was, great. The likelihood would be it wasn't known about. If it wasn't, he was more than likely to be followed by Customs. It was reasoned that Customs would not arrest him, but follow him to find the Mr Big.

The container had been broken into. It was empty of any Thai grass. Sandy drove to Maidstone College, parked the van and ran up the steps and into a locker room. He opened locker 616, changed his clothes and put on thick-lensed glasses, removed a pile of text-books and joined the rest of the students making their way down the college steps as eight determined Customs officers ran up the steps past him.

Unfortunately, no one had thought to hire Sandy's van in a false name. A silly oversight. Shortly afterwards, his flat and his parents' house had their doors battered down. Phil and Shirley hid him for a couple of days; Albi suggested Sandy should remove himself to Thailand under false ID as soon as possible.

Meanwhile, two Americans arrived in London to do an inventory of the unsold Colombian marijuana. Albi did not invite them round to the flat. He was far from happy they were here. They booked into the Dorchester on Park Lane. They were Joel Magazine, a Miami defence lawyer, and Walter Nath, a Sicilian with a droopy black moustache.

Walter contacted an old friend of his, Ron, a yacht captain based in Devon. He wondered if perhaps he could move the Colombian faster. Unfortunately, Ron was under surveillance by UK Customs and Excise and his phones were tapped. They followed Ron up to London where he met Walter. Customs then kept Walter and Joel under surveillance. Customs were intrigued to see their old foe Howard Marks turn up for a meeting with Walter and Joel at the Dorchester. Albi, without us knowing it, was followed back to our flat; our telephones were also tapped. He was followed to a meeting with James York, to whom he introduced Walter. York and Nath were then followed to the Essex store.

The following day Albi drove Walter to the Pytchley store and introduced him to Ed Kennindale, who was looking after the store there and feeding mice to the falcons. Customs watched.

Albi took Walter and introduced him to Stuart at Heathrow. Walter and Stuart flew up to Glasgow for Walter to do an inventory of the remaining marijuana. As they were driving towards Oban, Stuart realized they were being followed. They abandoned the idea of doing an inventory check. They managed to lose their pursuers and they made their way back to Glasgow. Stuart phoned the Mount Pleasant house and told Dianne to pack up, destroy all paperwork and meet him in London. He phoned the Bar nam boc house and told them to get rid of the marijuana – by throwing it into the sea if necessary.

Five tons were reloaded onto *Bagheera*, taken out to sea and dumped overboard. For a few weeks afterwards bales of Colombian marijuana were being washed ashore on the Scottish coast. The press had a field day. The story of *Whisky Galore* was resurrected.

In England, sales continued.

The Americans were far from happy with Stuart's decision to dump the marijuana. Arguments arose about who would pay for it.

'Albi, shouldn't we just halt everything for a bit until things quieten down?' I asked.

'No, the sooner everything is sold the better,' he said.

Phil's girlfriend Shirley was picked up by Customs and questioned for three days about Sandy and Phil. Phil scarpered. Walter Nath and Joel Magazine returned to Miami. Patrick and Jude decided to take a break at their place in the Dordogne. Tom Sunde flew back to the States to give a report to Pete.

Natasha flew to the Caribbean to join a yacht there.

Stuart Prentiss hid with Dianne in London under the name Paul Morgan. Friends of his sailed the two yachts to Canada.

We went to Brighton for the weekend and took Podge and Amber to the fairground. Albi hallucinated the big wheel was chasing him. We decided to have a few days' break in Suffolk. We drove to Lavenham and booked into the Swan, a beautiful fourteenth-century Tudor hotel.

We spent the next day pottering about the village. In the evening Albi and I decided to have dinner on our own. The hotel had a baby listening service. While I tried to get Amber to sleep, Albi went down to the bar to wait for me.

Amber was on the verge of dropping off when there was a knock at the door. A voice called through the door: 'Hotel manager.' I opened it and there stood two men and a woman. One of the men held a badge out to me. 'Customs and Excise,' he said.

CHAPTER THIRTEEN
Brixton

They came into the room. Amber fully woke up and got out of bed. The woman officer asked her if she wanted a sweetie. She refused to accept any.

They searched the room; they found some hash and various bits of paper belonging to Howard. One of the men collected these items and disappeared downstairs.

'What's the name of the man you're sharing this room with?' the other man asked me.

'No comment,' I said.

He shrugged his shoulders. 'Well, pack the cases, you're coming to London with us,' he said.

While I packed the cases, the woman officer looked at Amber's picture books with her. When I had finished, Howard entered the room escorted by two more men. He looked strained and nervous.

'I guess this is it, Jude,' he said.

We hugged each other tightly.

'We'll pull through this. Somehow I just know it,' I said.

'I hope you're right, love. Be strong,' he said.

He picked up Amber, kissed her and held her close. Tears entered his eyes.

'Come along now, time to go,' said one of the men. Once downstairs, Howard, now handcuffed, went with two of the men outside to a car; I settled the hotel bill. Amber and I, escorted by our two officers, went outside and climbed into a car parked behind the car Howard was in. The journey to London was long and tense. Every time we stopped at a traffic light, Howard would turn round and look at me. I blew him kisses. I don't know if he saw them. Amber slept on my lap.

On entering London, the cars drew up outside a Kentucky Fried Chicken restaurant.

'Would you like anything to eat, Judith?' asked the man who'd been sitting next to me on the journey. His name was Terry Byrne.

'No, thank you,' I said, having lost any appetite I had earlier.

He returned to the car with food for the driver and the woman officer. The car stank of stale grease and dirty dead chicken afterwards. I felt nauseated. I didn't know if my sensitive stomach at this early stage of pregnancy would survive the rest of the journey without embarrassment.

On arrival at New Fetter Lane, the headquarters of Customs and Excise, I immediately asked to use the bathroom. Then Amber and I entered an interview room where questions were fired at me all night. Amber sat on my knee throughout. I would have been distraught, and so would she, if they had separated us. In fact, they went out of their way to make Amber comfortable and even brought up a camp bed for her. She, however, preferred to snuggle up on my lap. All night long, and it was a long night, a series of men came in to question me. To all questions I answered, 'No comment.'

In the morning they told me I could phone friends to come and pick Amber up. I called two good friends in Brighton and asked them to look after her. Amber knew them well. My friends arrived after a couple of hours; Amber was happy to see them and left. I had never spent any time apart from Amber and it saddened me. But I had a firm belief it would not be for long.

In the afternoon two Customs officers drove me to a police station. I found myself placed in an underground cell that had a glass-brick window high up at street level. I felt ill. I had had nothing except black coffee and cigarettes for nearly eighteen hours. Nor had I had any sleep. I asked the female jail warden if she could get me a doctor. A doctor came; he looked at me as if he thought me scum. He took my pulse and gave me a couple of aspirin and left. I thought of my pregnancy with Amber when I had been so healthy. No cigarettes, little wine and no coffee, healthy walks and plenty of tennis and a loving partner. I sat with my head in my hands looking at the floor. Sunlight from the small window just feet above my head cast shadows of the prison bars on the rough stone floor.

I heard Dianne Prentiss's voice speaking to the warden. I wondered who else they had arrested. Several memories came to mind. The feeling of people watching me as I shopped in Harrods food halls. My constant feeling of unease, coupled with Howard's paranoia. He had thought the big wheel was chasing him in Brighton. I wondered how long they had been watching us.

It was another long night. Saturday night in the cells of a London police station are not quiet. Throughout the night drunken women and prostitutes were shoved into the cells. A lot of screaming and swearing. Thankfully, the jail warden took a liking to me and throughout the day and evening handed me sweetened cups of tea and chattered through the small barred hole in the door about her children and new grandson.

I wondered how Howard was bearing up. I missed him. I missed Amber. I was convinced I would be released the following day.

The following morning I had a solicitor's visit. Bernard Simons, Howard's solicitor from his last arrest, sent David Walsh, one of his clerks, to see me.

'Judith, how are you bearing up?'

'Oh, I'm tired but okay. But please call me Judy. How is Howard?' I wasn't calling him Albi any longer, and it took some getting used to.

'Bernard Simons is with him now.'

'How soon can you get me out of here?'

'Well, Judy, I don't think it will be easy. You must realize you are involved in the biggest smuggling operation Europe has ever seen and you live with the mastermind behind it.'

'That doesn't make me the mastermind.'

'Judy, this is a serious operation. You should see the Sunday press. There is almost nothing but this story. You are in a serious predicament.

Obviously we will apply for bail for you as soon as possible. You have a two-year-old child and you're pregnant. You have no record of a criminal background, so I am confident we will be successful.'

I began to feel frightened.

'Look, I'll come and see you tomorrow afternoon and let you know how the case is progressing. We will do our best for you.'

He left and I returned to my cell. I still had the feeling I would be released. But I also had the fear I wouldn't.

Fewer than two hours later, my friendly warden from the night before unlocked my cell door.

'Okay, lovey, you can go. I knew you were all right.'

'What do you mean?' I asked.

'You're free to go. Now her –' she jerked her thumb at Dianne's cell door '– she's in it up to her neck.'

I felt compassion for Dianne and was vaguely suspicious about why I had been freed and not her. Two Customs officers picked me up from the police station. One of them introduced himself as Michael Stephenson. I recognized him from Harrods food halls.

'Where's Howard?' I asked.

'Snowhill police station.'

'Can I visit him?'

'If the police at the station let you, we have no objection.'

I was driven back to New Fetter Lane where officers Terry Byrne and Nick Baker greeted me. They gave me back my and Howard's possessions. A friend came and picked me up and drove me to Snowhill police station. I entered a room where Howard was sitting at a table. He looked tired and drawn. We hugged each other for a long time.

'Howard,' I said as I looked into his warm blue eyes, 'will you marry me?'

'You'll marry me in jail? I might remain locked up for years,' he said. Tears crept into his eyes.

'That doesn't stop me loving you. I'll wait. And I have the feeling it won't be that long.'

'You know I want you to marry me, Jude. You make me so happy and I love you so much.'

After the police station my friend drove me to Brighton, to the house Amber was staying in. It was a relief to hold her in my arms again.

The next day, Howard appeared in front of Judge Miskin at the Old Bailey, who remanded him to the custody of Brixton prison for the 1973 speaker scam. Amber and I returned to the Knightsbridge flat. The day after, Howard was due to appear at the Guildhall magistrates' court. Amber and I attended. Sitting in the reception area of the magistrates' court was Terry Byrne.

'Hello, Amber, how are you?' he said.

Two-year-old Amber, with a serious lawyer look on her face, replied, 'No comment.'

Appearing with Howard were Marty Langford and Bob Kennindale, who had both been arrested at Peter Whitehead's falconry. James York and Nick Cole had been arrested in London. Stuart Prentiss and a worker of his called Alan Grey had also been arrested in London, as had the utterly innocent Hedley Morgan, who had helped Patrick count the money. Dianne had been released.

They were all charged with conspiracy to import 15 tons of Colombian marijuana into Scotland and remanded to Brixton prison. Customs claimed it was the largest amount they had ever busted; it was more than the grand total of every piece of dope they had busted up to that day.

I enrolled Amber into a Montessori nursery school in Jerome House, Harrington Gardens SW7, run by a lovely woman called Karen. Amber adored her. I picked up Patrick's new Renault 14 from outside the Orme Square house. The following day, after dropping Amber off at school, I drove to visit Howard at Brixton prison. This was to be my daily routine nearly every day for eighteen months. Memories of the prison in Stafford shot into my head as I joined the long line of women queuing outside the massive iron gates in the towering Victorian walls.

After going through some formalities, I entered a drably painted waiting room, overcrowded with mainly women and children. I sat for at least an hour before a guard opened an iron door in the right-hand corner of the room and called out, 'Marks.' I followed the guard into a large room about the size of a school canteen, containing two trestle tables with wooden chairs on either side. Prisoners sat on one side, visitors on the other. Prison officers patrolled up and down the room. High up in the walls were barred windows. The room was painted as drably as the waiting room, an institutional dirty yellow.

Howard sat at the beginning of the trestle table on the left-hand side. Opposite, on the table on the other side of the room, sat the East End high roller Ronnie Knight and his wife Barbara Windsor. We were to learn shortly that these were the best visiting positions and afforded the longest visits.

'Jude, how are you?' he asked.

'I'm fine, love, how are you?'

'Not too bad. Have you spoken to my parents?'

'Yes, they're fine. They and Linda are going to come and visit you on Saturday,' I said.

'Jude, I've got a really nice cellmate called Jonathan Kern. He's a young Jewish kid. His girlfriend Alison lives near you. Could you give her a lift when you come to see me?'

'Yeah, sure.'

'I've given Jonathan your phone number, so she'll probably ring you tonight. Jude, you're allowed to bring me in a meal every day with half a bottle of wine.'

'Yes, I've got a list of the prison rules.'

'Perhaps you could bring in two meals then I can have another half-bottle of wine. If I find someone who doesn't have any visitors, could you do that for me?'

'Of course.'

'Could you set up a newspaper delivery for me? If I take the *Telegraph* and you take *The Times*, we'll be pretty much covered. There's apparently a shop behind the prison that delivers here.'

'Okay, I'll do that today. I've spoken to Rosie; she's going to bring Podge to see you in a couple of weeks.'

'Great.'

'I also got a message from Patrick. He's fine about me having their car. He, Jude and the kids are safe with Pete in California. Pete wants me to get a safe number he can phone me on.'

'That's great news. I've made an application for us to marry. The social worker says it should be no problem given your pregnancy.'

'Well, that's something to look forward to.' We smiled at each other and clutched and stroked each other's hands. Visits normally lasted no longer than fifteen minutes. Ours and Barbara Windsor's lasted an hour and ten minutes.

I found myself leaving the visiting room as Sarah York left. She, like me, was pregnant, just a few more weeks advanced.

'Hey, Judy, how are you?' she said.

'I'm okay, and you?'

'God, I can't believe I'm going through this shit again,' she said. It was not long ago that James had been released from jail for another bust. 'I'm on my way to organize a newspaper delivery.'

'I've got to do that too. I'll come with you,' I said.

We walked up Jebb Road in the shadows of the towering walls. Cockroaches scuttled across the pavement and disappeared into cracks in the walls. At the end of the street facing the rear prison wall was the most extraordinary paper shop I have ever seen in my life. The shop front, which was about seven foot high, was made from years and years of newspaper, hardened into a solid wall. A wizened man leant over the top with a black order book in his hands. You had to shout your order up to him, giving the surname and prison number of the inmate. Orders were allowed for only two weeks at a time and only cash was tendered.

I also sent Howard in some yoga books and bought him a gold medallion of Saint Jude from Asprey's. The patron saint of the hopeless and despairing.

John Denbigh's girlfriend Liz came to visit me that evening. She too was pregnant, but a month less than me. John was out of the country and had told Liz he would remain out until Howard was freed. I thought this was slightly unfair on Liz. But John was an odd man.

'Judy, John wants to talk to you. I have a friend round the corner who said we can use her flat to receive calls from him,' she said.

It was more than likely that Customs still had the tap on my phone. I went with Liz to her friend's place; shortly after we arrived the phone rang. It was John.

'How are you?'

'I'm fine. Congratulations to you for the baby,' I said.

'Yes, well, that's another thing. Now, how's the old man?'

'He's good. At the moment we have no idea of the evidence against him. He's going to try for bail but he thinks it's unlikely he'll get it.'

'Yes, well, the thing is I have a man with some carpets.'

'Excuse me?'

'I have a man with some carpets. Now tell the old man that my friend with the carpets could do many fine things with his life. Of course, it's all a question of timing. It doesn't want to be done when the moon is setting or the sun is rising. Like my good lady there, who is a Leo like your old man. I mean, they both like to roar.'

He had lost me. He had always talked in riddles but this was beyond me.

'Okay, thanks for calling. I'll put you back on to Liz,' I said.

'Don't forget my friend with the carpets. God bless now,' he said.

When Liz had finished talking to him I said, 'I didn't understand a word he said.'

She laughed. 'That's John.'

Back at the Knightsbridge flat the phone rang. A female voice said, 'Hello, is that Judy?'

'Yes,' I said.

'Hi, my name is Alison. My boyfriend is sharing a cell with your boyfriend.'

'Ah yes, Howard said you wanted a lift. That's fine but can you be here before nine as I have to drop our daughter off at school first.'

'Great. I'll be round at 8.30.'

The following morning the doorbell rang at 8.30. I opened the door to a tall slim young woman with short dark hair.

'Hi, come in,' I said as I shook her hand. 'Would you like a cup of tea before we go?'

'Ah, yes please,' she said, following me into the kitchen where Amber was eating her Coco Pops.

I made the tea and set it in front of her. I noticed that her foot was tapping and she was clutching her hands together. She seemed nervous.

'So do you and your daughter live here on your own?'

'Yes.'

'I thought your brother Patrick might live here with you,' she stammered.

I looked at her and she blushed.

'Jonathan told me you had a brother,' she said.

'I have three brothers.'

'Oh and where are they all?'

'One of them is at school, one of them is teaching in the Middle East and one is I believe in France.'

'And how are you coping for money?'

'My family and Howard's family are helping,' I said.

When I got to see Howard I told him of all the questions she'd asked me. 'Howard, I reckon she was put up to it by Customs. Be careful. I think your cellmate's a grass planted by Customs.'

'It certainly sounds like it.'

'I've told her I can't give her a lift any more.'

Two days later, as Howard was walking past a prison interview room, he spotted Jonathan Kern talking to Customs officer Nick Baker. A couple of East End villains also observed this interview and gave Kern a beating. He was transferred to another prison. Howard got himself a new cellmate, a bisexual named Jim Hobbs. He was in jail for having sex with underage boys.

I cancelled the Campione flat lease and arranged for the sale of the BMW through an English couple we had befriended there. The furniture and all our possessions were shipped back to England and put into storage.

My routine became established. Each morning I took Amber to school and then drove to Brixton where I handed in meals for Howard and Hobbs with two half-bottles of wine. Once a week I would take Amber with me and take Howard in clean clothes. On one occasion, as I sat in the waiting room with Amber on my knee, a middle-aged woman sitting opposite me with scarves wrapped round her head began meowing.

'Mummy, shall I tell her she's not a cat?' Amber said.

'I think maybe it's best to leave her,' I said.

Amber could not take her eyes off her. Right at the end of the visiting room were two isolated tables with glass screens. Intrigued we watched as the cat woman walked up to one of these tables, where the man sitting behind the glass woofed at her.

During Amber's visits with Howard she would sit on his knee while he told her stories and sang her songs. Her favourites were 'My Boomerang Won't Come Back' by Charlie Drake and 'Sparkie's Magic Voice'.

Howard had settled into the jail routine. He had been given the coveted position of tea boy on A wing. The position brought various perks, such as extra-long visits, and he was allowed out of his cell most of the day. He practised yoga and meditated.

The weekends Amber and I spent in Brighton, where we had a small house we had bought from Johnny Martin a couple of years earlier. I spent the weekends renovating it, which left Saturday visits free for Howard's family or friends. I arranged with a friend of Natasha's who lived in Brixton to deliver Howard's and Hobbs's meals on Sunday when there were no visiting hours.

The governor of Brixton gave us the go-ahead to marry. With the help of Howard's parents we found a minister to marry us at the Welsh Congregational Church in Southwark. I arranged the wedding as if it was a normal wedding. The reception was to take place at the Basil Street hotel in SW3, even though Howard had told me he would not be allowed to attend. I bought a beautiful long white wedding dress. For Podge and Amber, who were to be my bridesmaids, I had two matching blue dresses made. My father had not been too impressed with our arrest, so I thought there would be little point in asking him to give me away. I asked Arthur to perform the duty, as it had been his flat we'd met in. Howard asked Johnny Martin to be his best man.

On the morning of 22 July 1980, when I was five months' pregnant, a large white Cadillac drew up outside the Knightsbridge flat. Podge and Amber had already left for the church with my friend Frances, who was to be my maid of honour. Arthur escorted me to the church in the Cadillac. My feelings were mixed. I was happy to be marrying the man I loved but sad at the thought we would not be spending the night together, or even be able to enjoy the wedding reception together.

On drawing up in the limousine at the chapel, Frances, accompanied by Podge and Amber, came excitedly up to me.

'Judy, you'll never guess what. They're going to let Howard come to the reception.'

'Are you serious?' I could hardly believe it.

'Yes. One of the guards is going to travel in the Cadillac with you.'

My heart soared. I walked into the chapel on Arthur's arm with a big smile on my face, followed by Podge, Amber and Frances. Howard turned as I walked up the aisle. On his face was a smile to match mine.

After the ceremony, Howard, Amber, Podge and I climbed into the back of the Cadillac. The prison officer sat in the front with the chauffeur. Arthur handed us a bottle of champagne and a couple of glasses and we drove off through the London streets to Knightsbridge.

The reception was a very happy occasion, surrounded as we were with good friends and family. For just a little while we were able to forget Howard was a prisoner. We all drank copious amounts of champagne, including the prison guards. Howard and I were allowed to spend some time alone in a hotel bedroom while a guard stood outside the door.

After about three hours it was time for Howard to return to prison. I spent my wedding night on my own with Amber.

In August the lease was up at the Knightsbridge flat and Amber and I moved back to our Chelsea flat in Cathcart Road. Pete phoned me regularly and if the call needed discretion I would go to a phone box in the Bolton's, a leafy street with millionaire mansions a short walk from our flat, and call him back.

Pete felt guilty that Howard was in jail. He felt it was his fault for having allowed Joel Magazine and Walter Nath to come over and oversee the situation. He offered to pay all the defence costs, however high, and for me to have whatever I wanted or needed. His phone calls were a great comfort to me. Jim McCann also called regularly to find out how I was. 'Tell the Welsh wanker to play the green card, Jude. The green card – that's the way for him to go.'

'I'll tell him, Jim,' I said.

In October Victoria moved into Cathcart Road to help me with Amber and to be there when the new baby arrived. We noticed that the top floor of the house opposite was occupied by someone who liked taking photos of all my visitors.

On the evening of 23 November my beautiful little daughter Francesca Maria was born. Victoria attended her birth. Howard had applied to be allowed to attend, but his application had been refused. Francesca had much darker skin and hair than blonde Amber and I called her my little Golly Wog. It has since been shortened to Golly and is what most people still call her today. Amber adored her. While I was in hospital, Howard's parents visited him and took him his food and wine.

When she was just three days old, I took Golly to visit Howard. He instantly fell in love with her. He spent the visit cradling her in his arms and gazing tenderly at her beautiful little face.

Just before Christmas I had a phone call from Natasha.

'Judy, I won't be in touch for a while.'

'Why? You're not going to do anything silly, are you?' Something about her voice made me feel uneasy.

'No, I've just got a yacht delivery to do.'

'Well, be careful. We don't need any more problems at the moment.'

We spent Christmas in Brighton with Howard's parents and sister. Rosie and Podge, who were now living in Lewes, came for Boxing Day lunch. I sent Howard a Harrods food hamper.

In Brighton one weekend George's new girlfriend Yvonne came to visit. She and George had met the previous summer on a kibbutz in Israel. She was now studying geology at Queen's in Belfast, and George was working for the British council in Beirut, Lebanon. Patrick phoned me regularly, particularly to see if I had heard from Natasha. He was worried about her. So was I.

Slowly the evidence from the prosecution was being handed over to Bernard Simons. Howard asked me to go to Bernard's office and read all the depositions. There was a lot of it. It took days to go through. A key had been found in his pocket on the day of his arrest. It opened a door at the falconry in Pytchley, behind which lay a few tons of Colombian. Meticulous accounts in Howard's handwriting had been found. There were statements from Customs officers and photos to support meetings with co-defendants in Scotland and elsewhere. A suitcase containing £30,000 was found under our bed in Hans Court. Peter Whitehead was the chief prosecution witness, who was to testify that Howard was the prime organizer.

Howard made several appearances at Guildhall magistrates' court, mostly for administrative purposes or futile bail applications. Downstairs in the cell area Howard and I made good friends with the guard. He was a big jovial man who would let me in Howard's cell with him until the prison officers came to collect him.

One day while I was locked up with Howard, the guard called out to me, 'They want to see you upstairs.' He unlocked the door and I made my way upstairs to the reception area. There was no one there except the receptionist.

'I was told that people wanted to see me,' I said to her.

She shrugged her shoulders. 'No one's said anything to me.'

I felt eyes on the back of my head. I turned around and there were four heavy-looking men scrutinizing me through the plate-glass window. They had an American police vibe about them. I wondered if they listened to my and Pete's conversations. Having checked me out from head to foot with distinctly unfriendly looks in their eyes, they walked away. They frightened me. The memory of their look made me feel uneasy for years to come.

CHAPTER FOURTEEN
From Mexico to the CIA

I told Howard about the four men.

'Who do you think they were, Jude?'

'I don't know, certainly not friends. They reminded me of being in Miami – maybe Cubans.'

'How strange.'

I felt he wasn't taking the threat I felt from these four men seriously.

'When are you talking to Pete next?' he asked.

'He said he'd call by the end of the week.'

'Okay, good. I must seriously work on my defence.'

'Pete told me that since he's retired, Tom now works for the CIA.'

'You're kidding. If that's true, they might be able to help me.'

Pete had retired from smuggling. He was thirty-five years old and had, in the last six years, by his own estimate made well over $20 million.

Two days later Pete called me. I explained Howard's problems of having to justify large sums of money and the possibility that he was going to use some security or spy defence. He said he would get back to me within twenty-four hours. He did. He told me to go to the phone box. I made my way to the phone box in the Bolton's.

He filled me in on various possibilities.

'I also got my lawyer to check out Tom's boss, Karl. My lawyer used a naval intelligence contact he has to get in touch with the CIA. The response that came back was negative, said they'd never heard of a Karl. Then two hours later I had Karl on the phone yelling at me. Telling me word for word the enquiry my lawyer had made about him. It kinda convinced me he is CIA. Maybe they'll be able to do something to help,' Pete said.

I went to see Howard and repeated my conversation with Pete. He looked thoughtful.

'God, Pete's amazing, isn't he, Jude? I think I'll use an MI6 defence and then I can throw in loads of stuff about McCann and produce newspaper headlines about me working for MI6. It's a pity I haven't got a copy of the Fairweather report.'

'I think Jim said he could get it,' I said.

'Great.'

Pete phoned and told me that Tom Sunde and Karl were coming to visit me. He also promised me he would give us $250,000 to help with our retirement when Howard got out.

'Yeah, Tom and Karl want me to become involved with smuggling helicopter parts and sealed canisters from Vietnam for the CIA and the National Security Committee,' continued Pete. 'They said for an investment of $2,000,000, I'd get a return of $7,000,000. It's tempting.'

I made little comment. It was all a bit too incredible for me.

I phoned Jim and asked him if he could get hold of the 'confidential' Fairweather report. Two days later it arrived in an envelope addressed to Gladys, Jim's favourite name for Howard.

I posted it to Howard. A while later I recieved a letter from Mr A J Pearson, the Governor at Brixton at that time:

Dr Mrs Marks,

   I write to inform you that the undated letter you recently wrote to your husband containing a typewritten enclosure was opened in the course of routine censorship of mail.

   After perusal of the contents I have to advise you that the

issue of the letter and enclosure has been stopped for security reasons.

Yours sincerely,

Tom Sunde arrived in London. He booked into the Intercontinental on Park Lane. He was travelling under the name Major Ross Wood. He had credit cards and documents to support his new identity, of which he seemed proud. I met him for dinner; he looked very well. Karl, he told me, had an important meeting that night. He talked a bit about his new job.

'Yeah, the CIA pay me an annual salary of $65,000.'

'I see you've given up smoking,' I said.

'Yep, that's right, and Valium, cocaine and alcohol. I went to do this special training at this CIA college.' He took out his wallet and handed me a photo. 'Take a look at this, Judy.'

It was a newspaper photo of Tom with Ronald Reagan, walking and talking earnestly on what looked like a deserted Californian beach.

'Most impressive,' I said, wondering if it was a fake. 'But are you not nervous about being back in London? It's less than a year since you were personally involved in this whole deal. You must be in some of the surveillance photos.'

'No problem. I didn't even have to go through immigration or customs,' he claimed.

'How are Pete and Patti?'

'A pair of fat baboons – they're both huge. They made so much money last year and most of it's gone up their nose.'

'You're kidding. Pete sounds great to me.' I didn't like to hear Tom talk of Pete and Patti that way. What had happened to his devout loyalty to Pete?

'Well, they're not, mark my words,' he said.

I arranged to meet Tom the following day for a late breakfast after visiting Howard. He was waiting for me in the lobby of his hotel. We went to the lobby of the Dorchester and sat at a table; a man with cold steely eyes and salt and pepper hair, who looked super-fit, joined us. He was probably a couple of years older than Howard.

'Karl, this is Judy,' said Tom. I held out my hand. He ignored it and sat down. I took an instant dislike to him. All through breakfast he ignored me. Instead, he talked to Tom about various hookers he'd had. It was explicit and made me uncomfortable.

Finally, he turned to me. 'Judy, tell Howard we'll help him in return for James McCann.'

'How can we give you Jim?' I said. 'As far as I'm aware he lives fairly openly in Paris and isn't known for keeping a low profile. Why are you interested in him?'

'Just tell Howard what I said. We'll be in touch,' said Karl. He left the table.

Later that day when Pete called I told him I was far from impressed with Karl. I felt he wasn't playing me straight but Pete was convinced he had a connection to the CIA.

The following morning I told Howard the same thing. It was impossible for Howard to judge as he had only my impressions to go on. But he thought the message I brought from them was strange.

The next visitor Pete sent over was a likeable Mexican named Carlos, who spoke perfect English. He came with me to visit Howard in Brixton.

Early one evening near the beginning of June my phone rang.

'May I please talk to Judy?' asked an American woman's voice.

'Judy speaking.'

'Ah, Judy, my name is Sister Antonia, I'm calling for your sister Natasha. Now she doesn't want you to worry, she is fine. However, she is in La Mesa state penitentiary in Tijuana, Mexico.'

'Oh my God – what happened?' I asked.

'She was arrested by the Mexican navy on May twenty-fifth with two tons of marijuana onboard her boat. She has been charged with possession, introduction, and transportation and trafficking in marijuana. She will need some money. She says you mustn't worry about her.'

Easier said than done. I'd heard some horrific stories about Mexican jails. I got all the details I possibly could and a contact number for Sister Antonia.

I got a message to Pete through his lawyer. Pete called me back.

He knew the jail and told me she'd be fine, and that he would arrange for a lawyer immediately. He told me not to worry – they'd get her out. I asked him to let Patrick know what had happened.

'Are you guys trying to solve Mexican unemployment?' Pete joked.

I then had to let my father know about Natasha. Once again, he was unimpressed.

Howard's defence was coming together well. Bernard employed the barrister Lord Hutchinson QC, a socialist who had a record of defending spies and anti-establishment troublemakers. He had at one time been married to the actress Peggy Ashcroft, from whom he told me he had learnt his advocacy skills. He had defended Penguin Books when they had been prosecuted for publishing D.H. Lawrence's *Lady Chatterley's Lover*. He had also defended Russian espionage agents George Blake and John Vassal.

Howard's defence was that in 1972 he was recruited by MI6 to hunt down the IRA arms dealer James McCann by involving him in dope deals. Things were going very well until Her Majesty's Customs and Excise, not realizing Howard was working with MI6, arrested him in 1973. Bail was arranged and he skipped it, as instructed to by MI6. Somehow the media discovered that he was MI6 and blew his cover. MI6 then arranged for Howard to work for the Mexican Secret Service, who, coincidently enough, were also interested in McCann. The Mexicans believed that McCann was aiding the Mexican terrorist group the September 23rd League by supplying arms and fundraising through dope deals. The Mexicans supplied Howard with a passport in the name of Anthony Tunnicliffe and other supporting documentation. He managed to track McCann to Vancouver. He informed the Canadian authorities, who arrested McCann but then let him go. He next traced McCann to France, where he discovered McCann working with Colombian narco-terrorists as well as with heroin drug lords in the Golden Triangle area of Burma, Laos and Thailand. The British and Mexican security services gave Howard a complicated mission. Howard was to infiltrate the Colombian drug hierarchy and find out where they were banking their money and how it was getting into the hands of the September 23rd League. He was also to make sure that McCann was caught red-handed in Ireland or Europe.

Howard's disguise was as a hippie marijuana dealer and smuggler. He claimed he had arranged for Thai sticks to be sent to Ireland and informed MI6 how they could catch McCann. However, an Irish court let him go. To infiltrate the Colombian drug lords he arranged the delivery of Colombian weed to Scotland. Customs and Excise, not realizing it was an international security operation, ruined it all by arresting Howard.

'Jude,' said Howard looking rather morose, during the visit after he first met Hutchinson, 'Hutchinson thinks it's one of the most ludicrous defences he's ever heard.'

'Well, that's not surprising, is it? It is.' I laughed, and was pleased that he also saw the humour. 'The important thing is – will Hutchinson defend you?'

'Yes. I think he's rather looking forward to it.'

'I wish I was. I feel exhausted.'

'Jude, the trial's not starting until September. Why don't you and the kids go for a holiday somewhere warm? Take Rosie and Podge with you. You've worked so hard for me and the trial will be exhausting. You deserve a break.'

The idea was appealing. 'Are you sure you won't mind? I can make a visiting rota and make sure everything you need is brought in.'

'It would make me happy thinking of you in the sun. But perhaps you should make sure Pete can always get hold of you,' he said.

I phoned Rosie. Was she up for a holiday with all the kids? She didn't need much persuading. We booked a wonderful villa in Corfu for the first three weeks of August. It was called the House on the Rocks, and it was high on a cliff situated at the end of a beautiful sandy beach. It had a phone to receive incoming calls and a maid who provided breakfast and lunch.

Pete phoned me weekly and always cheered me up with his silly jokes.

Rosie, Muffin, Podge, Amber, Golly and I had a wonderful time and I returned renewed for the battle ahead.

'We'll all go there after the trial,' I told Howard when I next saw him. I felt strongly he would be acquitted.

My sister Masha returned from the Caribbean island of Bequia where she had been working on a yacht with friends of Natasha's. She came to help me with Amber and Golly.

Tom Sunde popped in and out of London. 'To see how things are going,' he said. I showed him a copy of the Fairweather report. He took a photocopy of it. He then told me he'd taken the copy and shown it to his 'friends' at Scotland Yard. I was perplexed as to why he would show them a report that had originated from them. He took Masha out for dinner and got her very drunk. My distrust of him grew.

Karl arrived in London during one of Tom's visits, again staying at the Dorchester. He told me he had a meeting later that morning with Lord Hutchinson. While Tom and I sat at a table drinking coffee, Karl, within earshot, picked up a phone and spoke as if he was talking to Hutchinson. He addressed him constantly as his lordship, and arranged for them to meet. I had my suspicions. Ten minutes after saying goodbye to Tom and Karl, I slipped into the lobby and picked up the phone Karl had been speaking on – it was only an internal hotel phone. What was he up to?

What the hell was going on? There was no one I could talk to. I could only talk to Howard. He told me to listen to Pete and asserted that Tom would never do anything to harm him. I wished I could be so sure.

I repeated my feelings of unease to Pete about Tom and Karl. Pete admitted he had doubts at times, but said they would then produce some kind of evidence that convinced him. Tom and Karl were able to access extremely useful information, which must mean they had powerful connections, said Pete. He had also observed that whenever Reagan was out of the country, so were Tom and Karl, and usually in the same part of the world.

I repeated all these conversations to Howard. He was isolated, locked up, worrying about his duties as tea boy. The last time he had seen him, Tom had been a regular dope smuggler like him. He'd been Pete's Doberman. The stories I brought to Howard, about people he thought he had known well and people he hadn't met, must have seemed like stories from another planet, one he could not know.

The trial was due to begin on 28 September. Carlos the Mexican came over for another visit. He brought with him Jorge del Rio, the Mexican Secret Service man. I took them to visit Howard in Brixton. Jorge del Rio assured Howard that he would testify in court for Howard's defence.

After the prison, we went to Bernard Simon's office; I introduced Jorge to Bernard. Jorge produced his credentials and was able to satisfy Bernard that he was bona fide.

Carlos and I went for lunch in La Famiglia, an Italian restaurant just off the New King's Road, while Jorge went to the Mexican embassy.

'I went to visit your sister Natasha with her lawyer last week,' he said.

'How is she?'

'She's good, she asked me to give you these.' He handed over some photographs. They were photos of Natasha looking better than I had seen her in years. She was sitting in a well-furnished comfortable living/dining room with a television; behind her was a balcony. There was one of her standing in a smart kitchen with wooden units, and another one of her and her boyfriend Stuart lying on a double bed with a flowery bedspread.

'Where were these taken, Carlos?'

'That's the apartment we've bought for her. She gets to lock her own front door, not the guards.'

'What, these are taken in prison?'

'That's right,' he said with a proud smile. 'Beats where your husband is, doesn't it?'

'But what kind of prison is it?' I found it hard to imagine having your own luxury apartment in jail.

'It's run like a little village, a village you can't leave. No one wears a uniform. Everything is done by the prisoners. It has its own bakery. There are restaurants serving Mexican food and others where you can have chicken or steak. There are shops selling tins of food; there's a butcher's and even an ice-cream parlour.'

'That's incredible,' I said, thinking of Brixton.

'Yeah, and Stuart has got into teaching some of the kids football.'

'There are kids in jail?'

'Yes. There's a school and a church as well. They are in there with their mothers or fathers. In Mexico we don't believe in breaking up families. A prisoner can have his whole family come in and stay for a while. This is not only beneficial for the prisoner, but for all the family, so often the innocent victims. A prisoner can work and help support the family.'

What a humane system. 'Does everyone have their own apartment?'

'Only those who can afford it. But everyone has a bed and a roof over their head.'

This new concept of prison took a while to digest. It certainly stopped me worrying so much about Natasha. I thought of Howard's stories of slopping out in the mornings.

'The government gets much of the cost of running the jail from the percentage they make from the shops and restaurants and the sale of apartments,' said Carlos. 'They all belong to the prison administration, which sells them to an inmate for the duration of his stay, after which the prison resells them.'

It was a way of getting back criminal profits without the expense of court cases and lining the pockets of lawyers. 'Are all the apartments the same?'

'No, they're all different. Most of the bigger houses were built when the prison held a lot of drug kingpins. They lived in luxury and carried on their operations from the prison. In the late seventies there was a big shoot-out and so then they were moved to different jails all over Mexico. Anyhow, her lawyer reckons he'll have her out soon.'

Carlos and Jorge left the following day, promising to be back in time to take the witness stand.

* * *

Howard and I enjoyed one last long visit before the trial began. Our routine of seeing each other nearly every day was over. We didn't know if we would be able to see each other at the Old Bailey, and had no idea how long the trial would last.

'Do you know, Jude, how many times you have visited me here?'

'Lots.'

'Three hundred and thirty-eight times,' Howard said.

'God, that makes six hundred and seventy-six lunches I've brought you, and probably somewhere close to seven hundred half-bottles of red wine.'

It was hard saying goodbye. We were both nervous, and apprehensive about the results of the trial.

CHAPTER FIFTEEN
Judgement Day

The Old Bailey, the most famous criminal court in the world, stands on the site of the infamous Newgate prison. The impressive dome of the court carries a statue of Justice, a blindfolded figure holding sword and scales. I was nervous walking in the main door that first day, 28 September 1981. People were racing all over the place: barristers and judges in wigs, solicitors in suits, clerks struggling under mountains of paperwork, turnkeys and police officers. I saw Bernard Simons standing outside court number six deep in conversation with a tall, skinny man wearing a lawyer's wig, who looked to be in his sixties.

'Judy.' Bernard called me over. 'Allow me to introduce you to Lord Hutchinson.'

I looked up into intelligent, kind eyes framed by laughter lines that contradicted the lines of concern on his brow. His face was thin, gentle. We shook hands. The night before I had lain in bed tossing and turning, dreading today. I felt strangely reassured by him.

'It's a pleasure to meet you, Judy. Please do call me Jeremy.'

The day before the trial began, my brother Patrick sent me a poem to give to Howard. The poem touched us both deeply. It contained these lines:

Dear Brother: Five hundred days stand between us, and
All the distance I have managed to create.

No word has passed, no smile exchanged, no touch of hand,
And yet, as Dawn intrudes, we still relate ...
In one brief span, as the world turns, the sun's warm kiss
Touches many loving hearts that beat with yours: you will
*   get this.*

James York, Marty Langford, Nick Cole, Alan Grey and Bob
Kennindale had all pleaded guilty, and some had made long statements implicating Howard as the mastermind. Luckily, these
statements were inadmissible as evidence. Sentencing of those who
had pleaded guilty would take place when the trial was over. Only
Howard, Stuart Prentiss and Hedley Morgan pleaded not guilty.
Hedley's defence was to be that he didn't know the vast sums of
money he had counted came from drugs. I believed him – Patrick
had always told me that Hedley knew nothing. Stuart's defence was
one of duress. This defence works if the jury believe that a more serious offence is avoided by the act of the offence charged. Stuart was
to claim that if he didn't import the 15 tons of Colombian marijuana, the mafia were going to kill him.

Twelve jurors were sworn in. I studied them closely. My
husband's fate was in their hands, and therefore my fate too. The
press benches below the jury were full. The public gallery was full.
As the wife of a defendant, I sat in the main body of the court. I
felt vulnerable in such a prominent position, as if I too was on trial.
The eyes of the press and jury were often on me, as mine were
on them.

The Director of Public Prosecutions counsel, John Rogers QC,
began to lay out the case in front of Judge Peter Mason, aka 'Penal
Pete'. Incriminating evidence was piled up on Rogers's table:
accounts, address books, witness statements, passports and sealed
plastic bags containing samples of the Colombian marijuana.

'This was crime on the grand scale,' began Rogers. 'It was no
surprise that a man of Marks's background and intelligence set up
the UK side of the organization just like a high-powered business's.

Howard, Stuart and Hedley all looked solemn. The jury looked
solemn.

Rogers warmed to his task. 'Mind-boggling quantities of cannabis and money ... The whole of this operation was run like a military operation ... An intricate web of bluff and counterbluff and false names. It was the largest seizure of cannabis ever in the United Kingdom. Marks had so many identities one wonders how on earth he remembered who he was.

'The organization had to be very slick, very smooth and carefully planned to succeed, and it will not surprise you to learn that those involved are extremely intelligent people.'

The next day the front pages were full of it. 'Eggheads Ran £20m Drugs Ring' said the *Sun*. 'The Graduation Connection' was on the front of the *Daily Telegraph*.

Day after day the trial continued. The prosecution took six weeks to present their case. A long stream of witnesses took the stand in front of the jury, testifying to having followed this car, seized this piece of paper, followed this person, and watched such-and-such premises. One such witness was Customs officer Michael Stephenson. He claimed he had seen Howard visiting Walter Nath and Joel Magazine at the Dorchester.

After he'd given his evidence, Lord Hutchinson, cross-examining, tore into him.

'How did you know it was Mr Marks in Mr Nath's hotel room?'

'I viewed him through the keyhole,' replied Stephenson.

'Ah, you recognized him by his knees, Mr Stephenson.'

The court exploded into laughter. One of the women jurors laughed so much she began choking and a five-minute recess was called. I hid my merriment behind my hand.

When Lord Hutchinson had finished his cross-examination of Michael Stephenson, his evidence had been torn apart. I doubted if even Stephenson himself was now sure he had been to the Dorchester. It was a brilliant act of advocacy. I started to hero-worship Lord Hutchinson.

One day the judge entered the courtroom carrying a bouquet of flowers. 'Ladies and gentlemen of the jury,' he began. 'I expect you are wondering why I am carrying this bouquet. It is a practice that was originally developed in an attempt to mask the stench from the dock, and to mask the smell of the Newgate cells.' He raised the bouquet in the air. There settled across the court an air of embarrassment.

Days in the courtroom were draining. Much of the evidence was monotonous. I left home every day at 8.30 after having attached myself to the electric milking machine, which made me feel like a cow but made sure Golly had enough breast milk to last her during my absence. I dropped Amber off at school and drove straight to the Old Bailey. My visits with Howard in the dungeons of the old courthouse after a day in court were far from satisfactory. They took place through glass and were five minutes long if we were lucky. Sometimes I'd wait for over an hour for these few minutes. I collected Amber from school and arrived home exhausted. I fed and bathed Amber and Golly, telephoned Howard's parents and sister to give them a general view of the day's proceedings, then collapsed into bed. It was the same thing day after day. I felt so grateful to Masha for her physical help and emotional support. The girls adored her.

Saturday morning visits at Brixton were not much better, but at least Howard and I could hold hands. Saturdays were the busiest visiting days at Brixton and our visits were never longer than fifteen minutes.

When Howard asked me one Saturday morning if I'd heard from Pete yet, I realized I'd been dreading the question. The trial had been on for three weeks by this stage and I had not heard from Pete in over four.

'No, but I'm sure he'll be in touch soon.'

'Bernard wants to know when the Mexican is coming over.' Howard looked worried.

'Pete's never let us down yet. Why should he now?' I tried to keep my tone light. The thought of what Tom had said about Pete and Patti's drug habits often crossed my mind. I had decided not to tell Howard this, as I saw little point in us both worrying.

'Jude, don't be cross. I asked Hutchinson to talk to the judge.'

'What about?'

'I told Hutchinson that I would plead guilty if I didn't receive a sentence of more than seven years.'

'And?'

'Mason said no way, he wanted to give me much longer than that.'

Howard looked sad and vulnerable. I wanted to take him in my arms and tell him it would be all right. 'Listen, Howard – please don't try to make any more deals. You might think I am mad but my intuition tells me you will be acquitted.'

All throughout the trial, whenever Howard entered the courtroom he gave me a warm smile, which I returned. Whenever we caught each other's eye through those long days, we'd smile at each other again. These loving exchanges gave me great comfort. I believe they did Howard too.

One day Judge Mason addressed Howard. 'Mr Marks, this is a serious courtroom. What you find so much to smile about is beyond me.' His dislike of Howard was palpable.

Howard asked for permission to address the court. It was granted and he took the stand.

'My lord, I am fully aware I must establish my innocence, or I face many years' imprisonment, with considerable distress to myself and my family. But I still try to smile, although I have spent the last eighteen months in prison. It is the only way of dealing with adversity, and is in no way smugness or contempt.' The judge grunted and Howard was escorted back to the dock. It was a clever speech.

The next witness called by the prosecution was Peter Whitehead.

Dido and I had travelled to court together and sat next to each other as Peter was called to the stand. Peter did not relish being a prosecution witness. But it was either that or be in the dock himself.

Rogers took him through his first meeting with 'Donald Nice'.

'Did you ever know him by a different name?' asked prosecutor Rogers.

'I knew him as Donald Albertson, and then as Howard Marks.'

Rogers had Peter explain his relationship with Howard. Peter, of course, denied he had any idea that he was involved in a drug deal. He came across as confident and as someone who had been grossly misled and used.

'A very large sum of money was found in the red filing cabinet by Customs officers who found it at the porter's lodge at Conaglen House ... Has that anything to do with you?'

'Nothing whatever.'

By the close of the day Peter had finished giving his evidence. Nick Baker and Terry Byrne looked happy. I visited Howard in the dungeons, then on my way to the car park I saw Baker and Byrne in a pub with the junior counsel, having what looked to me like celebratory drinks.

I went home feeling depressed and worried about the lack of communication from Pete. I had tried leaving messages with him through his lawyer but to no avail. I wanted to give Howard some good news before he had to take the stand.

The day after, Dido and I drove to the court together again. Dido had been sweet to me throughout this period. She often took Amber out for treats with her daughter Maxime. She was a special woman.

Hutchinson was to begin his cross-examination of Peter. I felt nervous for Peter. One thing I was certain of was that I would not want to be cross-examined by Hutchinson. I saw Jeremy outside the court. He seemed in a buoyant mood, almost rubbing his hands in glee.

'I'm looking forward to today's proceedings,' he said to Bernard Simons and me.

Inside the court Peter took the stand. Lord Hutchinson stood up and inspected Peter gravely.

'Well, Mr Whitehead, it is perfectly clear from what you were saying to the jury yesterday that, as far as you are concerned, the taking of this estate at Conaglen was purely for the purpose of film-making,' said Hutchinson.

'That's what I understood.'

'Is that right?' enquired Hutchinson in a sarcastic-sounding voice.

'That's right.'

'You are quite an experienced person in business?'

'I would like to think so.'

'You have got your head screwed on?'

'I don't like that phrase, but it is clear that it is on my

shoulders.' Peter, I thought, looked rather pleased with himself for that.

'You are not an innocent abroad?'

'I am certainly not.'

'You went up to Scotland, you negotiated the lease, you agreed the figure ... Your company rented Hans Court ... Premises where the cannabis was found, you had a tenancy of that cottage?' Hutchinson ground on relentlessly. 'Were you arrested by Customs?'

'I don't know if arrest is the word. I was taken away for questioning.'

'For about how long?'

'Eight or nine hours.'

'Did you agree to give evidence for the prosecution?'

'I agreed to make a statement.'

'Yes, I know that ... there was quite a lot of explaining to be done by you.'

'Yes, the statement is quite long ... What I did for Howard Marks is entirely consistent with the fact that I considered him to be a successful film-maker.'

'And that is your explanation, of course, of being associated with all these things which are of importance in this case.'

'It is.'

'In July 1979 you saw these newspaper reports bearing his photograph, indicating that he had been involved in drug smuggling in 1971 while working for British Intelligence?' Hutchinson waved the papers in front of the jury before they were introduced as evidence.

The court became tense. The jury sat up straighter and looked more alert. The press began scribbling frantically in their notebooks. I was impressed at how skilfully Hutchinson had managed to introduce the MI6 defence.

'Obtaining information was the suggestion,' continued Hutchinson. 'That the money got by people involved in drug smuggling was going to the IRA for the purpose of buying arms, and that he was giving this information to MI6, the Intelligence Service ... he was Howard Marks, and he had been involved in this way with the British Intelligence, drug running and the IRA ... and furthermore, he was, according to these articles, involved with an Irishman called James McCann, who had been arrested as a result of the information he had given?'

The jury looked at Howard.

'I believe that this is what we might call the Howard Marks political story,' said Peter in a voice that dripped with sarcasm.

Hutchinson continued to tear into Peter for the rest of the day. He suggested that Peter's falcon business might be ethically and legally dodgy; that the falcon eggs were obtained illegally and sold at a substantial profit.

The judge interrupted at one point. 'This case is about cannabis, not falcons.'

'I agree, my lord,' replied Hutchinson and then continued, now bringing up Peter's relationship with the Saudi royal family.

Hutchinson went through the flat leases, Conaglen rental, bank payments and film contracts Peter had signed. When Hutchinson had finished with Peter, most of Peter's earlier confidence, if not all of it, had ebbed away. It was Peter Whitehead who looked like the organizer behind the drugs operation. I was immensely amused; even Dido was. Peter wasn't.

The case for the prosecution rested.

Hedley's defence was the first to be heard. I was relieved. I still had no news from Pete. Hedley's defence was followed by Stuart's. In the middle of the night just before Howard's defence started, the phone rang.

'Jude, it's Pete.'

It was the squeaky Californian voice I had so been longing to hear. 'Thank God.'

'Yeah, you can thank him if you want. How's it all going?'

I filled him in on the proceedings.

'Look, Tom will be with you in a couple of days and the Mexicans are on the way over,' he said.

'Thanks so much, Pete.'

'Hey, girl, you didn't think I'd run out on you, did you?'

'No, but I was getting worried something had happened to you.'

'Hey, talk to you in a couple of days.' He hung up.

Many mornings at the Old Bailey, as Howard was brought up from the dungeons, the guards would let me kiss him and have a few words with him. The following morning there was a new guard we didn't know. He wouldn't let me near Howard. There was no way for me to let him know Pete had been in touch.

I saw Bernard. 'Are you going to be talking to Howard today?'

'Possibly. Why?'

'Could you tell him everything's fine,' I said.

'Everything's fine. You want me to tell him everything's fine?' He looked at me quizzically, slightly suspiciously.

'Please.'

Howard's first defence witness was a boyfriend of Rosie's known as Leaf. He was Welsh and owned a pub called the Oranges and Lemons at St Clements in Oxford. He swore that Howard had been with him on 15 March 1980, watching a Welsh–Irish rugby match. The day Michael Stephenson claimed Howard was at the Dorchester. I'm sure Leaf thought he was telling the truth. Howard had watched many Welsh rugby games with Leaf. Leaf would often be drunk and wouldn't remember which games they had watched together. But because Howard had told him they had watched that one together, Leaf believed him.

Next to take the stand was Howard. He took the oath promising to tell the truth, the whole truth and nothing but the truth.

Judge Peter Mason, the jury and the press listened intently as Lord Hutchinson extracted Howard's ludicrous story from him. In the absence of Patrick and Natasha, Howard ascribed to them many of the roles he himself had played. I worried about what harm this might do to them.

Howard got his revenge on Anthony Woodhead for having ripped him off years earlier by naming him as the MI6 agent who had recruited him for the Mexicans.

Rumours had started among Customs, the prosecution and Howard's defence team that one of the young women jurors had been spotted doodling a heart on her notebook with hers and

Howard's initials on it. I had noticed her. She was a young woman who rarely took her eyes off him. Bets were beginning to be made that Howard would be acquitted.

I was feeling daily more confident that he would be. Not just because of the young woman, but more from a general feeling in the court. In terms of personalities, Hutchinson was immensely likeable and humorous, and Rogers seemed ungainly and rather bad-tempered.

During this week, Tom arrived. He stayed at the Intercontinental on Park Lane. He introduced me to Henry McNeil, a tall, slim, slightly greying Englishman in his late forties or early fifties. Tom told me he was 'our man in Hong Kong'. He looked to me like he'd walked off the pages of a John le Carré novel. He was old-school British.

He walked tall and dressed in nondescript clothes under a dark-coloured trench coat and a trilby. His voice was quiet, his accent public school. His eyes were grey and unreadable. He had an aura about him of intrigue and mystery. He wore a gold ring with the initials HM engraved on it causing me to wonder 'What the hell was going on

He accompanied me to the Old Bailey where I introduced him to Bernard Simons, Lord Hutchinson and Howard's junior barrister, Stephen Solley; Tom declined to come. McNeil asked Lord Hutchinson if he could have a private word. They disappeared into a room and closed the door.

'Who is he, Judy?' asked Bernard and Solley.

'Our man in Hong Kong,' I replied. 'Secret Service.'

After half an hour Hutchinson and McNeil reappeared. They shook hands.

Hutchinson told me later that it was one of the most intriguing meetings of his career, and that when he came to write his memoirs it was one he would most definitely include. Unfortunately, Hutchinson has not written his memoirs yet, so I am still in the dark about what transpired behind those locked doors. I would love to know.

It was the lunch recess. McNeil invited me for a drink. As we walked down the street to a small wine bar near the court, I asked

ABOVE: *Smile for the camera: 3-year-old me with brothers George and Patrick, and sister Natasha*

LEFT: *Christmas 1962, posing with my new doll*

ABOVE: *A young Masha wondered what exactly had made Mother laugh so much as George, Natasha and I looked on*

ABOVE: *My father looking every bit the dashing movie star*

LEFT: *Patrick Murphy, my grandfather, who had been murdered by the IRA on Easter Sunday 1942*

ABOVE: Marcus and the imaginiatively named Dog play at Le Moulin while Masha and George's girlfriend Pam sit in the sun with me

RIGHT: Patrick blending into French life at Le Moulin, 1974

LEFT: *George and a 16-year-old me, caught on candid tourist camera in Barcelona*

BELOW: *Masha, George and I with Golly and Amber, in the garden at Cathcart Road 1981*

ABOVE: Amber and I in Keerera, Scotland, where the Moroccan hash came in

RIGHT: Howard and Podge in Brighton 1973

ABOVE: *Howard relaxing during our wine tour of France*

ABOVE: *Outside the Swiss Bank in Lugano where*
I set up one of many bank accounts

ABOVE: *Podge is captivated by her feet as Howard and a pregnant me get a family picture taken in Lugano, 1977*

ABOVE: *Amber and I enjoying a day of sightseeing, 1980. Just hours later Amber, Howard and I were arrested*

Peter Whitehead's wedding. Dido's daughter Maxime was flower girl and Howard was best man. A great day was had by all

ABOVE: *Howard, out of prison for a few hours for our wedding at the Welsh Congregation Church, 23 July 1980. Marcus stood by me while Amber and Podge looked pretty in their white dresses. Howard's parents stood proudly by*

RIGHT: *Another family outing to the Bull Ring in Majorca, 1983*

ABOVE: *Looking every bit the 70s family, Amber and Golly enjoy a roadtrip with their Mum*

ABOVE: *Howard's Mother holds a newly born Patrick, while Golly gives him a helping hand. Podge, Amber, Howard and I look on*

The Asian Adventures:
ABOVE: *Edith Moynihan, Lord Moynihan and Marie Tess with me in a bar in Manila*
BELOW: *Howard with his business partner Orca and his friend Julian*

DAILY Mirror

Wednesday, September 26, 1990 **COLOUR NEWSPAPER OF THE YEAR** Sale w/e September 15: 3,941,542 (INCORPORATING THE DAILY RECORD) 22p CHANNEL ISLANDS 23p

EXCLUSIVE TODAY
Why I fell for the Pimpernel
BY THE WIFE OF BRITAIN'S MOST WANTED MAN ● Pages 12 & 13

INTERNATIONAL police agencies were claiming last night they had smashed the world's biggest ever marijuana ring ever uncovered. Among a group of people arrested in Spain in connection with the massive drugs bust were James "The Fox" McCann, a suspected IRA gun-runner, also known as the "Emerald Pimpernel".

The 200 million dollar ring had been operating for more than 20 years and its network spanned three continents. Police in Britain, Spain, France, Taiwan and Morocco co-operated with U.S. detectives in a complicated, long-running plan to smash "Operation Cobra".

● James "The Fox" McCann . . . arrested in yesterday's big drugs round-up.

Some of the haul of drugs and guns police found in a cave in Spain

MY WIFE IS INNOCENT, SAYS Mr BIG

Howard Marks

EX MI6 man Howard Marks, branded the world's biggest drugs godfather, made a desperate plea from his Majorca prison cell yesterday.

Near tears, he begged Spanish police: "Please let my wife go. Judy is innocent."

His emotional "hands off" message came in an interview behind bars in Palma Prison on the holiday island.

SHAKEN

Marks, dishevelled and shaken after three days in jail, hit out angrily at the tactics of Miami Drugs Squad officers who swooped on the couple this week after a year-long undercover operation involving half a dozen police forces across the world, including Scotland Yard.

Judy Marks

RIGHT: To look at us modelling knitwear in 1989 you'd never know we were imprisoned in Yeserias. My fellow models were Bahia and Bernie

BELOW: Howard enjoys another delicious prison meal in Terre Haute, 1994

LEFT: *Patrick gets a phone call from Howard on his eighth birthday*

BELOW: *Amber and Golly on a visit to Terra Haute to see Howard*

BELOW: *Howard and I enjoy the effects of magic mushrooms on the Millenium*

*Amber, shortly after qualifying as a barrister, jokes that she
is not impressed by my adventures with Howard*

McNeil, 'What would your MI6 bosses think of you walking down the street with Howard Marks's wife?'

'Lucky chap, I should think.'

I wondered who and what he was. Sometimes I felt way out of my depth. Although I had many good friends, there was no one I could talk to about this particular madness. I had tried talking to Masha, but it went way over her head. Pete phoned that night. I told him about McNeil and asked him who he was. He said he had no idea but that Tom had told him McNeil was someone who could help.

In the afternoon Rogers began his cross-examination of Howard. Unfortunately for the Crown, he started with a dangerous admission.

'It is conceded that you worked for the Secret Service until March 1973. But then, after your arrest for drug offences, you were immediately dismissed.'

The press pens scribbled furiously. The Fairweather report had been leaked to the world and Rogers was in a difficult position.

'No, that is not true. I carried on working for them,' countered Howard.

The rest of the afternoon continued in much the same vein.

'You fanned the legend, didn't you? You encouraged the Marks religion to grow that you were a secret agent on the run from the police, and made as many smokescreens as you could, while indulging in very high-level drug-trafficking?'

'I deny that most strongly,' replied Howard.

That evening the Mexicans flew in. They booked into the Grosvenor House on Park Lane and I met them for dinner. I was relieved they were finally here. They were on fine form and we had a pleasant evening.

'Did you know Natasha is pregnant?' Carlos asked me.

'No I didn't. I haven't heard from her for a while. Is she okay?' With everything that was going on with Howard, I had barely given her a thought.

'She's doing fine. Eating well and keeping strong. Her lawyer hopes to have her out before the baby's born.'

'If you speak to her, give her my love and congratulations. I've been so busy I haven't had time to write.'

The following morning I told Hutchinson, Stephen and Bernard that the Mexicans had arrived. I was unable to let Howard know. While he was on the stand I was not allowed to visit him. I missed the visits, even though they were only for a couple of minutes. They were better than nothing.

'We must meet them this evening. Where are they staying, Judy?' Hutchinson asked.

'Grosvenor House, Park Lane.'

'Okay, let's meet in the hotel bar at seven thirty,' said Hutchinson, looking at Stephen, Bernard and me in turn. McNeil was standing nearby; he was going to watch the court proceedings from the public gallery.

When I arrived at the hotel that evening, I was surprised to see McNeil talking to Jorge and Carlos. Tom, I learnt, had left thirty minutes earlier. Hutchinson, Stephen and Bernard arrived. I introduced where necessary.

Jorge showed Hutchinson his credentials and badge.

McNeil suggested that the hearing, because of its sensitivity, should be held in closed court. Jorge agreed. Hutchinson said he thought there would be no problem with that and he'd speak to the judge in the morning.

We adjourned to a nearby restaurant. We made for a strange collection of dinner guests: three eminent members of the legal profession, a Mexican fix-it man, a Mexican Secret Serviceman, the young wife of a drug smuggler and the mysterious Henry McNeil. For me it was slightly unnerving.

In court the next day, Hutchinson prevailed on the judge to hold the Mexican's testimony in closed court. While the arguments were taking place, neither the public nor the jury were allowed in the courtroom. I waited nervously outside. Carlos and Jorge turned up. They looked worried.

'What's wrong?' I asked.

'Jorge got summoned to the Mexican embassy this morning. They have stripped him of his badge and taken his credentials away,' said Carlos.

I wondered if this meant he wouldn't be able to give evidence.

When Hutchinson, Stephen and Bernard emerged, Carlos told them what had happened.

'Not to worry. I've seen your credentials,' said Hutchinson. Bernard frowned; Stephen looked bemused.

The court resumed, cleared of all public. Carlos and I stood outside. I wondered where McNeil was and if he had something to do with the recall of Jorge's documentation and badge.

Later I read the transcripts of the secret hearing.

'Do you understand English, sir?' enquired Judge Mason.

'The court has been cleared of the public and the press, do you understand?' Hutchinson said as he handed Jorge a piece of paper. 'Is what is written on that piece of paper, as regards your name, correct?'

'Shouldn't the jury see it as well, as the court has been closed?' asked Mason.

'He would rather not,' said Hutchinson.

Jorge confirmed that he knew Howard as Anthony Tunnicliffe, that Howard was introduced to him by Anthony Woodhead, that Howard was employed by the Mexican Secret Service, and that they had paid him large amounts of money to infiltrate Colombian drug organizations.

John Rogers then began to cross-examine.

'What was the purpose of advancing the money?'

'I'm sorry, sir, I'm not allowed to answer that for security reasons.'

Several other questions were asked and a similar response given.

'So what opportunity will you afford me to check your credentials?'

'None,' replied Jorge.

'Well, how am I to determine that you are who you claim to be?'

'You have no way to do it,' replied Jorge.

'He is saying you might be anyone – you follow that?' interrupted the judge.

'I know that,' said Jorge.

'Can I ask you, in view of that – are you ever allowed to show your credentials?' asked Hutchinson.

'No, sir.'

'Thank you very much,' said Hutchinson. 'You are free to go.'

Lord Hutchinson then discussed with the judge as to how the Mexican should be referred to by counsel.

'Mr "X", I suppose,' said Judge Mason.

'I always think Mr. "A" sounds less sinister,' said Hutchinson.

'Mr "A" it shall be,' replied the judge.

Jorge and Carlos didn't hang around. They flew out of the country that evening. Carlos promised to phone me when he had any more news of Natasha.

The following day in court the closing arguments began. Rogers went first.

'Marks is the biggest-ever trafficker apprehended with a single consignment. His claims of being a secret agent are utter rubbish. It is conceded that Marks was recruited for three months in 1973 by someone who was indiscreet enough to ask for his assistance. The rest is a myth mounted by Marks in order to conceal his real activities. His cover story is that he was an Intelligence agent. I invite you to treat that as a load of rubbish.'

It was then Hutchinson's turn. 'Howard Marks was used by MI6 to infiltrate the IRA. Three times he traced James McCann, but three times he managed to slip away. But British Intelligence would not come into this court and admit, as the prosecution did, that Howard Marks was working for them. They just sit up in the public gallery here. You can see them, members of the jury, I'm sure.'

I wondered if Henry McNeil was up there. I had not seen him since the night before. The jury would notice him if he was, I thought.

Hutchinson continued, 'Howard Marks was left as the "spy out in the cold". It is the code of the Intelligence services. They say, "You are on your own, old boy." You may remember the cases of those Russian spies, not only Kim Philby, but also Anthony Blunt. It appears that British Intelligence can grant immunity from prosecution to spies who have acted against this country. But not so, it would seem, when they have actually been acting on behalf of this country.'

Judge Peter Mason summed up: 'You have seen Mr Marks, ladies and gentlemen of the jury. He has extraordinary charisma and an encyclopaedic knowledge of the evidence, enabling him to come up with an answer to every question. As with the other defendants, you must decide whether he participated in this conspiracy or not. Either he had nothing to do with it, or he was into it up to his neck.'

The jury retired. I went for a coffee and a walk. I felt nervous, frightened. Sometimes I wished I was a million miles away or had married a man who had a normal nine-to-five existence. But then I thought I wouldn't have Amber and Golly and I might have been bored. I couldn't ever claim to be bored with Howard.

I returned to the court and sat outside the courtroom. I saw Baker and Byrne pacing up and down. At the end of the afternoon, the jury came back in. The tension in the court was high. The jury announced they couldn't agree. They were sent to a hotel for a night.

I returned home. My shoulders and back ached from tension. I phoned Tom's hotel and was told he'd checked out. Pete called to see if there was any news. I told him of my suspicions of Tom and McNeil and said I thought they had something to do with the documentation being recalled. Pete listened and said that Tom did his head in as well. I went to bed after drinking too much wine in a futile attempt to unwind.

I returned to the court the following morning. It was not until after lunchtime that the jury came back into the courtroom to announce a verdict. They found Hedley, Stuart and Howard 'not guilty of conspiracy to import marijuana'. The press stampeded out of the courtroom.

I felt all tension seep out of my body as warmth replaced it. A smile that contained all my joy swept over my face as I caught Howard's relieved, stunned eyes.

Howard was, however, found guilty of two charges of having false passports. For this he received a two-year sentence. With the time already served, this meant he would be home in five days. It was hard for me to believe.

Leaving the court I came face to face with Baker and Byrne. The look they gave me was far from friendly.

* * *

Customs pressed ahead with the 1973 speaker scam prosecution. This did not surprise us. A date for the trial was set for February 1982. It was back to the routine of daily visits to Brixton.

Hutchinson advised Howard that he would be unlikely to get a second acquittal and advised him to plead guilty. I also felt this to be the case. Hutchinson went to see the new trial judge, Judge Miskin, the Recorder of London. Miskin agreed to give Howard a sentence of three years if he pleaded guilty.

For the sentencing, Howard's parents accompanied me to court.

In court Miskin said Howard had shown 'greed and insensitivity to the misfortunes of the ultimate buyers'. He elaborated: 'I work on the basis that you were then young, and were full of remorse, and that you are even more full of it now; that you were a first offender ... you spoke the truth. You agreed to come to England, and waive any rights you may have had to deportation ... If I thought you had disappeared without any understandable reason in an attempt just to avoid your trial, I would ignore the passage of those years and the evidence I have that during them, save for the passport offences, you have led an honest and industrious life—'

I wondered if I was hearing right. I couldn't bring myself to look at Howard in case I started laughing.

'—that your adoption of an alias in England, and elsewhere, once you had escaped, was perhaps not so much the consequences of fear of trial, as of fear of those who might wish you ill ... I can and do take into account, in reduction, the evidence I have of your blameless life over these years.'

I looked at Howard's parents. His mother was smiling proudly as the judge uttered the last few words.

As Howard was arrested first for the 1973 scam, all the time he had done in custody would count towards that offence and for the passport offence. With remission he would be home in ninety days.

I could handle that.

What I found hard to handle was that Inspector Fairweather had committed suicide. He had gone to his bosses and confessed that he had leaked his report to the press about Howard's work for MI6, and he knew that Howard's acquittal had partially been won by that leak. They threatened to prosecute him in public under the

Official Secrets Act. The 58-year-old Second World War veteran and distinguished police detective committed hara-kiri in his back garden with an eight-inch kitchen knife. His reasons for doing so were kept secret at the inquest into his death. I was interviewed by the police as to how I had come into possession of the confidential report. I explained it had come anonymously in the post.

Nobody in all this madness should have died.

CHAPTER SIXTEEN
Forgotton Banks

Howard served his sentence in Wandsworth prison. To visit him I had to wait for him to send me a visiting order. The visiting room at Wandsworth had a more relaxed air than the one in Brixton. It was a setting more akin to a café, with crisps, sweets, coffee and tea available from the counter. Now Howard was a convicted prisoner, he was no longer allowed food or wine from the outside.

The children, Masha and I moved to Brighton while I had the London flat refurbished. I spent my nights dreaming of having him home in my arms. These days it was Golly and Amber who shared my bed, crawling in at various hours during the night.

Three weeks before his release, Howard had five days' home leave. He had to report to the probation officer at Brighton police station every day. It was strange having him home after two years' absence. Golly didn't like it at all. She cringed and cried if he went near her, and she resented any signs of affection from him to me. His presence in my bed particularly irked her. I could see this was a problem I had to sort out.

The five days gave us a chance to adapt to one another again. We took the children out on excursions and visited friends. It was sad driving him back to prison, but knowing it was only for two weeks helped.

I was looking forward to living a normal life, to having friends round for dinner without worrying they would tell the authorities where we lived. No more lying and hiding. No more dope deals. Howard had promised.

'What will he do when he comes out?' Dr Lee asked me one day.

'Oh, he's so clever I'm sure he'll be good at whatever he does,' I replied happily.

Money was not an urgent issue. Johnny Martin was still holding a fair amount in Brighton from the Colombian deal and Pete had promised us a large sum on Howard's release. We had discussed it in jail and Howard thought he would like to open his own business. We decided to postpone any decision until we returned from the month's holiday I'd booked in Corfu. Masha was coming too, to help with Podge, Amber and Golly.

I went to the passport office in Petty France with all the necessary forms and photos to get Howard a passport. After much time and many surreptitious looks from the office staff, a Mr Appleton introduced himself to me.

'Mrs Marks,' he said. 'We really cannot give your husband another passport until he has returned all his false ones to us. Her Majesty's Customs have returned passports in the names of Cox, Goddard, Green and McKenna, and our records show there are at least two more in the names Tunnicliffe and Nice.'

'But I've booked us a holiday four days after his release.' My heart sank at the thought of having to cancel it.

'Well, I will probably issue him a temporary one, but not until I have interviewed him.'

We arranged a time and a date for the interview to take place.

On the morning of his release, 6 May 1982, I woke up early. I could scarcely believe the nightmare was finally ending.

'It is today, isn't it, Masha?' I asked constantly, seeking assurance even though I had visited him only the day before.

She laughed. 'You'd better get going or you'll be late.'

I set off from Brighton praying that nothing would go wrong and they would let him out. There was a long tailback on the A23. I realized I was going to be late. It began raining. I had been due at Wandsworth prison at 8 a.m. I drew up outside at 9 a.m. It was still raining. There was no Howard. He didn't even have a coat. I looked for a phone box. There wasn't one in sight. Where would he go? Perhaps they hadn't let him out after all. I began to panic. I drove to a phone box, phoned Masha and asked if she'd heard from him.

'No. Why?'

'The traffic was awful and I was late. I'm frightened something's gone wrong and they haven't let him out. If he phones, can you tell him to go to Cathcart Road? And tell him I'm so sorry.'

I drove as fast as possible to our Chelsea flat, which was crawling with builders but no Howard. There was no phone in the flat. I didn't want to go to the box in the Bolton's in case Howard arrived and I missed him. Then I saw him coming round the corner. I ran across the road and straight into his arms, almost knocking him over. He staggered slightly with the force at which I'd run to him, before slipping his arms round me and burying his face in my hair.

We began the drive to Brighton and the sun came out. We stopped at the Gatwick Hilton for sausage, bacon, eggs and champagne.

'Our wedding breakfast, better late than never,' said Howard as he smiled and raised his glass to mine.

Four days later, with the temporary passport Mr Appleton had issued to Howard, we were flying to Corfu for a month-long holiday. The girls were excited to be going back, even though we didn't have the same house as last year. This house was, however, equally good, perched high on a cliff on the north-east of the island near the resort town of Kasiopi and surrounded by sandy beaches and lush vegetation. It looked towards Albania.

'Why's it our bania?' asked Amber. Howard picked her up and hugged her.

The first morning, Howard decided to go jogging. He'd had dreams in jail of getting super fit when he came out. He limped back twenty minutes later. His right knee had given in. He was so disappointed.

Sunbathing and swimming began to remove the prison pallor from his skin. I loved seeing him laughing and playing with the children. We explored the island in our rented car. Many times it was just Howard and me, while Masha looked after the children.

We made good friends with our neighbours, who were long-time residents of Corfu. Through them, we met John Fort, who had been the British consul on the island, and many other expatriates, including the writer Gerald Durrell.

The Falklands War was at its height and dominated most of the conversations. Howard and I were not ardent supporters of Margaret Thatcher and refrained from taking part in many of the discussions.

Our neighbours were keen golfers and invited us to join them for a game. Never having played before we booked ourselves a few lessons, but soon realized it was not the game for us.

'The only part of this game I like, Jude, is the nineteenth hole,' Howard said.

The nineteenth hole was the bar where the golfers enjoyed a plate of fried eggs, washed down by large glasses of cheap Greek gin. Howard enjoyed the eggs and gin; I enjoyed the fried eggs alone.

One day in the nineteenth hole a crowd of us sat round a table and John Fort turned to Howard and asked him, 'What's your line of country, dear boy?'

'Borderline,' was Howard's rapid response. A few heads turned in his direction. I hoped he would say no more. 'Well, to tell you the truth, John, I'm a convicted marijuana smuggler that's just come out of the nick.'

Silence descended on the bar, as all looks now concentrated on Howard and me. I felt a blush begin to spread across my face. Why couldn't he just keep quiet, I thought. I had been enjoying all the socializing. I had been enjoying being with straight people with no mention of dope or prisons. I knew we'd be dropped like hot cakes.

'How fascinating. I'm Ronnie,' said a tall man as he held his hand out to Howard. 'Ex-arms dealer. Aren't you that Balliol chap that was all over the papers? Some connection, wasn't there, with MI6, IRA and Mexicans? Do tell us all.'

Now Howard looked like he wished he had kept his mouth closed. He stammered and said it was all a long time ago. I went to the ladies' before I could be drawn into the conversation. To my relief, by the time I got back conversation had returned to the latest news from the Falklands.

When we returned to the UK, we spent a fair amount of time in Wales. It was the first time we had travelled to Howard's parents' house as a family. His parents were delighted to welcome their son back home and made a great fuss of us all. Howard took me to his old haunts. In the pubs, he was well known, but no one referred to his long absence from the town of his birth or to any of his other activities. There also was no mention of Marty, who was still in jail, having been convicted of working for Howard.

That first trip home after an absence of nine years was a nostalgic one for Howard. He was like an excited little boy. For me it was interesting to meet the people and go to the places he'd described over the years. I felt foreign among the Welsh accents; Howard's own accent became much more pronounced.

His father had a smallholding in the Black Mountains. We went there for a few days and walked and picked blackberries, while Amber tried to count the number of sheep with an 'M' on their back that belonged to her grandfather.

Back home in Brighton there were messages from Bernard Simons. Several authors had been in touch with Bernard, wanting to write a book about Howard.

'Jude,' said Howard coming off the phone, 'Bernard says there could be a lot of money in it, and that maybe even a film could come out of it.' Howard's eyes lit up with excitement at the thought of a book and a film about him.

'Would there be no legal problems?' I asked.

'Bernard said I would have to be careful or there could be legal complications. Also, those bastards at the tax office have been in touch. They want me to pay them tax since 1973.'

'But you haven't had a proper job,' I said.

'They want to tax any money I made from dope.'

'But that's crazy, you were acquitted.'

'They don't care what the jury said. They told Bernard they want their cut.'

'But wouldn't that mean they were profiting from crime?'

'You'd think so, wouldn't you.'

A few days later Howard and I travelled to London. In the afternoon, we had a meeting with Bernard Simons.

'Bernard, what about that £30,000 Customs took from under our bed? Shouldn't it be given back?' Howard asked.

Bernard shot Howard a look of pure astonishment. I giggled at Howard's cheek.

'Howard, you were extremely lucky to get acquitted. This would be pushing your luck a bit, don't you think?'

'But they nicked it,' said Howard. 'I proved to them it had been given to me by the Mexican government. They should have given it back.'

'Bernard,' I said, 'surely an innocent person would sue them? Otherwise it's like admitting you're guilty.'

Bernard shook his head. 'Are you, Howard, asking me to sue them?'

'Yes, Bernard, I am.'

After the meeting in his office, Bernard took us to a building just off Marble Arch. Here he introduced us to an accountant called Shelton Black. He was about the same age as Howard. The tax situation with the Inland Revenue was discussed, as well as the setting up of a company, Stepside Ltd, to deal with any possible earnings from book or film deals. This is something I most wanted to happen. I felt sure that with a book or film deal, Howard would not be tempted to return to his old ways.

For most of the time that Howard talked to Shelton and answered his questions, Shelton's face wore a wide grin. This grin increased in size dramatically when Bernard told him of Howard's plans to sue Her Majesty's Customs.

I liked Shelton.

In June, Howard went up to London to attend a meeting with Bernard, Shelton and the Inland Revenue. He came back in a foul mood.

'What happened?'

'There were two guys, a Welsh guy called Price, who seemed

okay, and this obnoxious English specimen called Spencer. Basically they don't believe a word I'm saying and told me I'd be hearing from them.'

There were times I was astounded at Howard's indignation that people didn't believe him. Why on earth should they?

Leaving the children in Brighton with Masha, Howard and I went for a long overdue honeymoon to a hotel called Chewton Glen in the New Forest.

Old John got in touch. Would we join him and Liz in Lyon for Howard and Liz's birthdays? Howard and Liz shared 13 August as their birthday. We agreed. John and Liz's son Charlie got on well with Golly, and Amber adored them both. Mr Appleton from the passport office gave Howard an extension to his temporary passport. We flew to Lyon. John did not look much changed since the last time we had seen him, over two years previously. He had spent much of this time in Kathmandu. It was good to see Liz happy; she had found John's self-imposed exile hard.

We spent our evenings childless, having discovered a wonderful babysitter, and enjoyed the gastronomic delights for which Lyon is famous. During the day we took the children to parks and zoos. Golly was a little toughie and bashed Charlie to bits, much to John's mortification and my and Howard's amusement.

One night over dinner and a few good bottles of red wine, John put a suggestion to Howard.

'The thing is, Howard, what we should do now is bring this in,' he said, picking up a bottle of wine and waving it over the tablecloth. 'We should forget all the other kinds of madness.'

'You want us to become wine importers?' said Howard.

'That's right, forget the madness.'

Liz started giggling.

'John,' I said. 'We don't know enough about wine, except for drinking it.'

'That's true, but I know a man who does, the Mad Major. I sold him a stove.'

Liz at this point began clutching her sides in pain from laughter.

'Liz,' I said. 'What's the joke?'

'The man's a lunatic.'

'But he knows his wine, Liz, don't knock him for that,' replied John, looking gravely at her.

This did not stop her laughing.

Howard and John decided they would become wine importers with this Mad Major, whom Howard and I were yet to meet.

Howard, Amber, Golly and I left John, Charlie and Liz and drove to Zurich. We then drove to Campione to relive some good times and enjoy the views.

Not having the money of old, we decided against staying in the Splendide and opted instead for an apartment-style hotel on the border of Campione. We spent that evening eating in the Taverna and drinking in Tonino's bar. We received a warm welcome from all, who seemed unaware of Howard's recent imprisonment. The next morning we took the ferry from the little pier in Campione across the lake to Lugano.

We made our way to our normal café in the main square of Piazza Reforma. Near the café were two wooden rocking horses and a small climbing frame, which Amber and Golly immediately clambered upon. Howard and I ordered two cappuccinos and fresh orange juice for the girls. I thought back to all the times I had sat in this bar watching Amber on the wooden horse, waiting for Howard while he made strings of phone calls from the PTT around the corner. This triggered the memory of him also waiting in this café for me. Why did he wait for me?

Because I was in the bank. I sat bolt upright and looked at the Union Banco on the corner of the square. I grabbed hold of Howard's arm.

'Howard, we've forgotten the bank over there.'

A look of a memory returning swept across his face. 'God, of course, do you think there's still anything in it?'

'There was when we left and I asked John and Sarah to pay the money from the sale of the BMW into it, and any money owing us from the deposit on the apartment.'

I left Howard in the café watching the children as I went across the square and into the bank. I showed my passport and asked for my balance. It was better than I had hoped: well in excess of £20,000. I closed the account and collected the money in Swiss francs. Because of the large-denomination notes, it was not too bulky an amount to carry.

I made my way back across the square, furiously wondering if there were any other banks that might be holding our money. The frown on my face led Howard to believe I had had no joy.

'No luck, love?'

I laughed. 'Only £20,000 or so.'

'This calls for a celebration. Let's book into the Splendide tonight.'

Back in England there was still no word from Pete. He hadn't once been in touch since Howard's release. I worried about him and missed his voice.

We moved back up to London to our flat in Cathcart Road. Amber started school at Queensgate, a ten-minute drive from our house. Golly started at Victoria nursery, which was conveniently directly opposite.

John and Liz came for dinner, accompanied by the Mad Major. His real name was Major Michael Pocock. He was a tall, thin, well-spoken, pleasant man. Earlier in the day, he had phoned me to find out what was on the menu so he could bring the appropriate wines. He arrived with enough for twenty people.

He agreed to go into partnership with John and Howard. Howard took over offices at 18 Carlisle Street, Soho, premises that had previously been Peter Whitehead's, who was now living with Dido in Saudi Arabia. Shelton set up a company called Drinkbridge to handle the wine importation.

'Howard, now you have those premises, why not open a secretarial and business service?' I said.

'Yeah, that's a good idea. Then if I get a package from Karachi, it can be Joe Bloggs's package, not mine.'

I was alarmed – that wasn't what I had in mind – and he laughed. But he did as I suggested. He set up a company by the name of Moontape, which traded as West End Secretarial Services. He employed a girl called Kathy to run it and much to my relief it seemed perfectly legitimate.

David Leigh, the head of the *Observer*'s investigative team and author of books on government secrecy, wanted to write a book on Howard. Howard consented, and he and David agreed to split any profits. The advance offered was disappointingly low, only £15,000, quite a bit less than I had found in my forgotten bank account. But at least it would be entirely straight.

The hearing for our attempt to recover the £30,000 confiscated by Customs was held at the Royal Courts of Justice on the Strand in the autumn of 1982. The same legal counsels who had represented Howard and Customs at the Old Bailey were once again locked in battle. I was thankful this time to be arriving with, sitting next to and leaving with Howard.

The hearing was held in front of Master Bickstall-Smith. The Crown's QC argued that despite Howard's acquittal, the money had most certainly arisen from drug dealing of some kind. He was a notorious drug smuggler and had no other profession.

Howard's legal team argued he had been cleared of drug smuggling and that the Crown had failed to prove their case.

Master Bickstall-Smith summed up in the most extraordinary speech I have ever heard.

'Mr Marks might be the biggest smug druggler [sic] in the world, but money is money, and we have to stop somewhere. He has been acquitted. The money is his. But before I finish, I want to say a few words about kif. Last summer my wife and I went to Morocco, to the Kasbah and the Rif. We were driving through the kif plantation when we came across a man sitting in the road blocking our course. My wife told him in no uncertain terms to move. She threatened him with our gun. Do you know he just stayed there? He wouldn't budge. He was stoned. That's how strong that stuff is. Well, good luck, Mr Marks. The money is yours.'

The court sat in an almost stunned silence at the end of this speech until the good master left the court. Howard and I left with smiles on our faces and had a glass of champagne in the Savoy on the way home.

I prayed that was the end of our court cases.

Customs were not happy and told Bernard that Howard would never see a penny of it. They finally relented but would only hand the money over to the Inland Revenue as part of Howard's debt to the taxman.

We met Lord Hutchinson, Stephen Solley and Bernard for a celebratory dinner at the Dorchester. Hutchinson thought dinner there was a grand idea 'as Howard has never set foot in the place before'.

Patrick phoned me one night with the good news that Natasha had been freed on 23 September and deported to Belize. I was amused at the date of her release from Mexico, remembering the September 23rd League and their part in Howard's defence. I wondered if a Mexican official had a sense of humour. Patrick also spoke to Howard, and said that Pete wanted to meet with him in Vancouver. Howard's passport had now been extended to one year and he readily agreed.

He returned from Vancouver depressed. Only Patrick had shown up, and although it was good to see Patrick he said the conversations he'd had with Pete on the phone had saddened him.

'He was incoherent, Jude, totally lost it. Patrick says he is addicted to Demerol and his cocaine use has quadrupled. I don't know if we can depend on any money coming our way from Pete. And Patrick says to stay well clear of Tom. I can't work out what the hell is going on there.'

'Don't tell me about it,' I said.

Patrick phoned a couple of days later from Amsterdam. The Americans had refused him entry back into the States, and the Canadians had put him on the first available flight to Europe. Luckily, for him, it had not been one to London, where he would almost certainly have been arrested. He asked me to fly over to meet him.

I flew over with Amber and Golly. It felt good to be back in Amsterdam. I hadn't been back there since my holiday with Julia and the stuffing of the rucksack straps. I had certainly learnt a lot since those early innocent days only ten years before.

I spent one night with Patrick. It was a pleasure to be in his company again. He told me they were living in a town called Santa Cruz, just south of San Francisco. I asked him about Pete. He told me that Pete and Patti had become reclusive and he hadn't seen them for over six months, and that Pete was in a bad way.

Patrick left to fly to Mexico where he was going to use contacts of Natasha's in Tijuana to help him over the border and back into the States. He was nervous and worried. I wished him luck and promised to fly over soon and visit them.

Back in London things seemed to be going well. The secretarial services were busy and had many clients. David Leigh's writing of the book was coming along.

Howard and the Mad Major made trips to Paris and Dieppe, and Drinkbridge imported thousands of bottles of wine and spirits. These were stored at premises of the Mad Major in Twickenham.

Howard embarked on a self-taught wine education. This involved me cooking menus specified by him to accompany whatever wine he had selected for that evening. At first he would choose a couple of courses, then we progressed to four with a different bottle to go with each. Looking back, I am amazed either of us managed to get up in the morning and function normally. However, I was happy. I had a normal life. Friends would come for dinner and at weekends we'd go away to Wales or Brighton.

One morning Howard was upstairs having a bath. The post arrived, landing on the mat. Along with the normal household bills was an envelope addressed to Howard from the Inland Revenue. I opened it. It was a tax demand for a quarter of a million pounds. I laughed. It had to be a joke. I ran upstairs and into the bathroom.

'Howard, guess what?'

'What, love?' he said, without turning round.

'The taxman wants you to give him a quarter of a million pounds.'

Quick as a flash he leapt to his feet, sending a wave of water slopping over the side. He held out his wet hand for the letter.

Judging from his face, maybe it wasn't someone's idea of a joke.

A quarter of a million pounds was a hell of a lot of money in 1982.

CHAPTER SEVENTEEN
Lake Tahoe

Howard hastily arranged a meeting with Shelton and Bernard, who in turn arranged another meeting with the Inland Revenue.

Howard, unable to travel to the US himself, asked me if I would go to the States and try to see Pete, and while I was there find out all I could about Californian wine. He was worrying about money, especially with the Inland Revenue case hanging over him. He wanted me to find out if the offer from Pete was still on, and whether he seemed to be in a position to fulfil it. I desperately hoped he was.

I was happy to go. I was looking forward to seeing Patrick and Jude, and Natasha, who was now living in San Diego with her husband Stuart and son Albi, named after Howard, and who had entered the world in jail in Tijuana in June 1982. It was also Amber's dream to visit Disneyland. We decided to go over Easter.

Howard drove us to Heathrow. Amber, Golly and I flew to New York, where we booked into the Plaza hotel. I enjoyed being back in New York, taking Amber and Golly on a nostalgic trip to cafés and restaurants Howard and I had enjoyed six years ago.

The last time I had spoken to Pete he had given me a new number to call him on. An electronics expert called Flash had built him a telephone-switching machine like the one Denys Irving had been working on when he died. I dialled the number from the public phone in the lobby of the hotel. A voice answered, 'LAPD.'

It was, of course, not the Los Angeles Police Department, but a joke of Pete's.

'Is Pete there, please.'

'Who is it?'

'Judy.'

'Hang on and I'll check for you.'

I hung for on a couple of minutes until the voice came back.

'I'm putting you through.'

'Judy, what's up?' Pete's voice was slurred.

'Hey, Pete, good to hear you, how are you?'

'Good.'

'I'm in New York on my way to stay with Patrick. I was hoping I could see you while I was over here.'

'Yeah, that would be cool. I'll give you a call at Patrick's in a few days and tell you how to get here.'

'Okay, great. Look forward to seeing you soon.'

I was glad to have spoken to him, but the sound of his voice concerned me. I phoned Howard at home; he was relieved I had spoken to Pete. He said he was lonely at home on his own. It made me feel like flying straight back.

The children and I flew to Los Angeles. Because it was the Easter holidays, the plane was full of badly behaved children on their way to Disneyland. It was nightmarish, even for Amber and Golly.

We booked into the Holiday Inn in Hollywood. The area surprised me, how rundown it was and how tacky the hotel was. Still, it was cheap and only for a couple of nights. The following day I took the children to Disneyland. When Amber's eyes caught sight of Sleeping Beauty's Castle, she gasped as if for air and I heard her say to herself, 'Now all my dreams have come true.' Tears of happiness sprang to my eyes. It made up for the endless queuing for the attractions.

Natasha, Stuart and Albi arrived the following day. It was wonderful to see Natasha. By her radiant complexion and large smile, motherhood clearly suited her. Her husband was a Scottish man, blond and blue-eyed with a heavy accent I found hard to understand. Albi, Howard's first nephew, and mine, was blond like his father. The girls adored him.

They had arrived in a clapped-out blue Chevrolet. It didn't look like it would make it to Santa Cruz. They weren't sure it would either. They were clearly short of money. I offered to pay their fare to San Jose, the nearest airport to Santa Cruz. Natasha gratefully accepted and Stuart decided he would risk driving if he didn't have the worry of breaking down with Natasha and Albi as passengers.

Natasha and I stayed up late that night talking. We had a lot to catch up on. I wanted to hear about her Mexican adventure. When Natasha had left England in early 1980, she had flown to the Caribbean. On the tiny island of Bequia, she had bought a small yacht. Masha and Victoria eventually joined her on the boat.

After Victoria left to come back to the UK, an American friend of Stuart Prentiss approached Natasha. He asked her if she would sail a boat of marijuana from South America to a rendezvous point off the coast of San Diego. She agreed, and while she was away arranged for Masha to get a job on a luxurious charter yacht as a stewardess.

Natasha flew to the Pacific coast, where she picked up the boat and its cargo. She had sailed solo up the coast as far as Costa Rica when she discovered she wasn't alone but sharing her cabin with a poisonous snake. She sailed into a small harbour on the coast of Costa Rica where she knew some people. There she saw her old friend Stuart and asked him to join her for the rest of the trip.

They headed up the coast towards the rendezvous point, where they made radio contact with the landing party and gave their location. For three weeks they fought to stay in one spot as day after day the landing boat failed to appear.

With food supplies gone and water on impossible rations, they had little choice but to find some supplies. They chose the Isle of Guadalupe, about 140 miles off Baja California in Mexican waters. Here they thought they could find some drinking water and hide the marijuana. They made their way towards the island, which, unfortunately for them, was far from deserted – it was a base for the Mexican navy. When they saw the Mexican navy steaming towards them in a gunboat they attempted to scuttle the yacht, but it was too shallow where they had anchored and the boat would not sink.

I listened in wide-eyed awe to this story, imagining how frightening it must have been.

'Natasha, you must write a book about this, and your experiences in jail,' I said.

'One day, Judy. One day.'

'But how did you get into the States?'

'Well, because I gave birth to Albi in Mexico, he has a Mexican passport. So after two weeks in Belize, we went back into Mexico. We even went back into the jail to visit friends.'

'That jail sounds too extraordinary for words,' I said.

'It is. Then we crossed over to the US before our names were put on any "undesirable" list.'

Stuart left at dawn the following morning. The rest of us took a lunchtime flight to San Jose. Patrick was waiting for us at the airport when we arrived.

Patrick and Jude's wood-built bungalow was on the outskirts of the hippie town of Santa Cruz. It had views over a golf course and a huge garden for the children to play in. When we drove up, Jude, Peggy and Bridie were standing by the front door ready to greet us. They all looked healthy, happy and tanned. Patrick had restarted his tax consultancy business, Overseas United Investors. He had worked hard and his client basis was growing daily.

They were not flush but managing to survive. The two girls went to local schools and Jude kept herself busy either helping Patrick or helping at the school. They had a large circle of friends.

It rained nearly every day we were there. The Queen was visiting California at the time and the weather was much covered in the press. On the occasional days it didn't rain, we managed to get some sights in. One place fascinated me and the children: the Mystery Spot, an area about 150 foot across in the redwood forests just outside Santa Cruz, where the laws of physics and gravity cease to exist. As you enter the area you feel yourself leaning towards the south-west. This becomes more acute as you advance towards the centre of the spot, where people lean over so far they can't see their shoes, yet they don't fall down. A golf ball rolls up a board rather than down, compasses don't work correctly and trees don't grow straight.

Patrick drove me round a few of the vineyards in Napa valley and a few of the wineries scattered round the Santa Cruz mountains south of San Francisco Bay from Saratoga down. Although California has produced wine for about 170 years, it has only challenged the world in the last thirty years or so. Patrick was friendly with a man called Bob who owned a wine shop in Santa Cruz. He gave me a few bottles and some wholesale price lists to take back to Howard; Bob was keen to export to Europe.

I had been at Patrick's for almost two weeks before I heard anything of Pete, despite leaving messages with Flash. It was Patti who called. She suggested the children and I flew to Carson City in a week's time. She asked me to phone and let her know my flight details so she could arrange for a car to pick me up and bring me to the house.

Patrick warned me that Pete and Patti's appearance had changed. He told me that Tom had encouraged Patti to take cocaine. I couldn't imagine this. The last time I'd seen her she was a pure marijuana smoker: no tobacco and little alcohol. She used to get annoyed with Tom and Pete doing too much cocaine. Patrick said her intake had become so bad that Pete had put her into a rehabilitation clinic. She got clean. Tom moved back into their house and at the same time she became hooked again. It was hard for me to take in. I hoped Patrick was exaggerating.

Before going to Carson City, the girls and I flew down to San Diego with Natasha. She very much wanted me to see the trimaran they had bought, which they intended to do up and sail through the Panama Canal to the Caribbean. It was in need of a great deal of work.

We arrived at Carson City airport late one afternoon. A limousine was waiting for us. Amber and Golly squealed with delight to see the television in the back. It was about an hour before we turned up at a large isolated house on the shore of Lake Tahoe. It was still cold up there and the ground was partially snow-covered.

I rang the doorbell. When the door eventually opened, my mouth dropped open. Shock at the sight of Patti must have shown all over my face, as she turned pink. Patrick hadn't been exaggerating.

She was very overweight in an unhealthy, blubbery way. She looked tired and unhappy.

I pulled myself together and hugged her.

The children and I entered a large hall that had a sunken jacuzzi in it. The limousine driver deposited our cases in the hall and drove off. Patti asked if he had taken us to the supermarket because she had given him $400 to buy food. When I replied that he hadn't, Patti shrugged resignedly.

She showed us into two massive suites with king-sized beds off the main hall and asked if they would be comfortable enough for us. They reminded me of luxurious hotel rooms. Both suites had large televisions and video players. Then Patti shocked me by saying she had better remove the guns from beneath the beds in case the children should accidentally play with them. With the children occupied watching the television, Patti proceeded to pull out guns from under the bed, explaining, in response to my terrified expression, that Pete was nervous these days.

These were not the sort of guns I'd seen when we visited Pete and Patti back in 1976. In those days, Pete and Tom Sunde went horseback riding and hunting. They took Howard with them once. Pete lent him his gun to practise shooting at tin cans with. Howard had never handled a gun in his life, and when he pulled the trigger the force of the explosion sent him flying. Pete thought the story hilarious and loved to tell it often, much to Howard's embarrassment.

But these guns were not hunting weapons. They were a different ball game altogether. I was happy when Patti put them well away and started to show me round the house.

Downstairs was the galleried hall with the jacuzzi and our rooms. Off the hall was an enormous racquetball court and gym, neither of which, I felt, got much use. Upstairs was a large kitchen, a huge living room with delightful views across Lake Tahoe, and the gallery overlooking the hall below. Off this was a dining room and a pool room with a full-size table. At the end of the gallery were three more bedroom suites, one of them Pete and Patti's. Another was occupied by Patti's cousin Spencer, whom I had yet to meet. Patti's parents had used the third suite but her mother had died and her father had moved out.

It was a lovely house but I couldn't help feeling it had a sad, neglected air, an almost tangible sense of melancholy and decay.

We didn't see Pete that first night. Patti said he was too ill with laryngitis. He was disappointed, she said, because he'd been looking forward to playing with the children. Amber and Golly contented themselves with playing games with Patti's dog Heidi. Patti's sister and her husband called by and we sat around the blazing log fire drinking wine. It amazed me to see Patti chain-smoking cigarettes. When we'd stayed with them before, Pete had not tolerated tobacco smoke in his house. Howard and I always had to go outside if we wanted to smoke.

Patti retired to her room about eight o'clock. I went to the kitchen to fix the children some dinner. I found the fridge and cupboards almost bare and the kitchen equipment almost unusable. In 1976, Patti had been the most house-proud person I knew. She was constantly cleaning. Her homes were always spotless. She was a gourmet cook and very much into health foods and organically grown vegetables. I wondered where Spencer was. I hoped he could take me to the store.

The phone rang often but it got answered in the bedroom. Sitting in front of the fire that evening after I'd put the children to bed, I looked out the window as the snow fell gently outside and the expanse of water shimmied in the moonlight. I felt sad. I was fond of these two people and I could see that they were destroying themselves.

Amber and Golly woke early the next day. I found some eggs and mouldy bread. I cooked the eggs, and cut the mould off the bread and toasted it. We found Heidi's lead and took her for a walk along the lake's edge and built a snowman. On the way back to the house, we stopped to have a snowball fight. When we got back about two hours later, we were happy and relaxed, giggling and dusting the snow off each other.

Back at the house an extremely agitated Patti met us. She asked me never to go out walking again and never to allow the children or the dog out. She said that Rick Brown's dog had been shot dead four days earlier outside his home and that an attempt had been made on Pete's life only two weeks previously. Rick Brown was Pete's oldest schoolfriend; he'd also been indicted in the 1973 speaker scam.

I was beginning to understand why the house was like an armed fortress. I was relieved we were only staying a couple of days.

'Patti, why would anyone want to kill Pete?'

She told me a bizarre story involving their crooked lawyer. A tale of lawyers, guns, money and murder. It was all too heavy for me. I wanted to be a million miles away.

Later as we sat in front of the fire I heard Pete coming out of his room. He moved ponderously and wheezed like a monster. I willed the children not to scream, and stood up ready to greet him. Once again, I was shocked. He was enormous. He looked dreadful.

He gave me a huge hug, apologized for not having seen us earlier and introduced himself to the children. They took a liking to him even though he could hardly talk because of the laryngitis. He asked if I liked the house and was obviously proud of it. After about an hour of casual chitchat, he returned to his bed.

Spencer returned home. He struck me as a sponger. Pete and Patti were giving him board and lodging in return for him carrying out caretaker duties, such as paying the bills and seeing to repairs. But from what I could see, he just took the money and had a good time.

I asked him if he could drive me to the store to buy some groceries. He said, 'Yeah, yeah, yeah,' but never did.

Patti said I could borrow any of the cars I wanted. There was a Porsche and a couple of jeeps in the garage. The Porsche had been Pete's present to Patti as a welcome home after coming out of the drugs clinic. I had never driven in the States and none of the cars were taxed or insured. I declined the offer.

Later that same day, a young woman came round. She was the wife of Pete's man in Thailand, who was sending monthly consignments to Pete. Patti and the young woman snorted large amounts of cocaine as they attempted to do accounts. It seemed that Patti was running things because of Pete's illness. The two women were so out of it I couldn't see how they could possibly run anything. I was so glad Howard was no longer involved. I could only see disaster.

In the evening Patti left the house to go to a call box to phone Thailand. I didn't see her again that night.

The following day, while the girls were watching television, I visited Pete and Patti in their bedroom. Empty junk-food containers covered every surface. Pete was lying in bed snorting coke. I had taken over a video about Howard's Old Bailey trial, which we watched.

At one point Pete fell out of bed and couldn't lift himself up. Patti and I struggled to pick him up and put him back in bed. He weighed a ton.

While I was talking to him, I asked if the offer of £250,000 was still on. It wasn't. He'd almost been cleared out, which is why he'd had to come out of retirement.

The following day we left. Spencer drove us to Carson City where we caught a flight to LA and our connection to London. I was relieved to be going home, but not happy with the news I was taking back to Howard.

CHAPTER EIGHTEEN
Suspicion

The children and I arrived back home exhausted. Old John and Liz were throwing an all-night party that night and Howard had arranged a babysitter for the girls. Within a couple of hours of being home, despite my jet lag and exhaustion, I was dragged out. The party was fun and Howard and I danced for hours and drank far too much.

We staggered out of the party in the early hours of the morning, climbed into the car and put on our seat belts. Howard started the car and promptly wrapped it round the nearest object. I stared jet-lagged and drunkenly out of the windscreen. The bonnet now had a lamp post rising majestically out of it.

'My car, my car,' I cried.

A minicab driver stopped and told us to jump in.

'Come on, Jude, quick, before the police get here,' said Howard.

'But my car.'

'Jude, quick.' Howard opened my door and pulled me out and into the minicab. The minicab tore off and dropped us at home. A few hours later, a police officer arrived at the door. Howard answered it while I was still lying in bed nursing a sore head, thankful that the girls were asleep. I heard his voice downstairs. Yes, he had been driving. No, he had not been drinking. No, he did not mind going to the station and making a statement.

He came back an hour later grinning. 'When they realized who I was they gave up asking me any more questions.'

We settled once more into life in London. I told Howard all about my visit with Pete. Like me he found it depressing and we resigned ourselves to the fact that no money would be forthcoming from Pete.

'I'll just have to make Moontape and Drinkbridge work,' he said.

'Any more news on the tax situation?'

'It looks like the English twat is off the case and now Shelton is in talks with just the Welshman, Price, who is a lot more reasonable.'

'Well, that's good.'

'It's certainly more promising. But Shelton thinks we should become ex-resident otherwise I'll forever have the taxman on my back.'

'Sell this flat?'

'No. I would still have to come back here to keep an eye on the office. However, if we lived outside the UK and I physically spent only two months a year in this country, I wouldn't incur any tax liability, and the Revenue would have no business being on my back in the future.'

'Where do you think we should move to?'

'Somewhere that's only a couple of hours' flying time from here.'

'What about the children's school?'

'We'll find somewhere with an international school.'

'It's a lot to think about. Where do we start?'

'How about Tuscany?' he said.

The offices at 18 Carlisle Street were getting busier and busier. While I had been in the States, Howard had sold the house in Brighton and invested the money into the office. There were now several phone lines installed, a £10,000 word processor, a large photocopying machine and a telex. West End Secretarial Services had more than fifty clients who paid well for message-taking and mail-holding. Parcels and letters arrived from all over the world and some of the strangest-looking people came to pick them up. Office accommodation could be hired at hourly rates and people queued to use the photocopier.

Kathy typed out wine lists and letters from strangers to strangers, as well as the rough drafts for David Leigh's biography. Heinemann had paid the advance and we bought a red Mercedes estate, which Howard, much to the girls' delight, nicknamed Rudolf.

Howard's friend from prison, Jim Hobbs, was released. He came round to the flat. I didn't like him; he gave me the creeps.

'Howard, I really don't want him coming round.'

'Why not?'

'Well, first he gives me the creeps and secondly he's a paedophile. I'd rather he wasn't anywhere near the children.'

'He's not a paedophile.'

'What was he in jail for then, if it wasn't for having sex with underage boys?'

'They were under twenty-one but over eighteen.'

'How do you know?'

'He told me.'

'Anyway, if you have to see him, and God knows why, can you not see him in the pub, or in the gutter?'

'Yeah, okay, I won't bring him round again.'

A couple of days later the phone rang. I answered it.

'Judy, it's me. Is the Welsh wanker there?'

'No, he'll be back in a couple of hours.'

'Okay, I'll try him at the office. Bye now.'

I put the phone down uneasily. What did Jim want? I hoped all the nonsense wasn't going to start up again. The faces of the four men who had eyed me up at the Guildhall came into my mind.

Howard arrived home early evening.

'Howard, did Jim call you?'

'Uh yes. Why, did he call here too?'

'Yes. What does he want?'

'Oh, he just wants us to meet for old times' sake. I said I'd go and see him in Paris at the beginning of next week.'

'Howard, Jim doesn't get in touch except for a reason.'

'Well, that's the only reason he gave me. I promise, Jude, I won't do anything.'

He left for Paris. I worried and prayed he wouldn't be pulled into any deals with Jim. I couldn't bear the thought of going through all the shit of the past two years again.

He returned from Paris with perfume and a dark-red leather dress for me.

'So what did he want?'

'Oh, like he said, just a drink and to catch up on things. He's straight now, Jude, into art dealing.'

I found the idea of a straight Jim McCann hard to believe, but maybe the last arrest in Ireland had scared him. And surely by now Sylvia would have had enough.

With my friend Frances and her partner Patrick and baby daughter Bridie (Howard's goddaughter), we rented a house for a month in the Tuscan countryside, near the town of Lucca. At the beginning of August 1983, we flew with Podge, Amber and Golly to Pisa. Waiting for us at the airport were two hire cars. We followed Patrick and Frances to a large old house standing on a small hill surrounded by beautiful lush green Tuscan countryside. Yet again, the country, language and people seduced us.

After a week, Podge flew home. We decided to visit Campione and have lunch in our favourite restaurant, the Taverna. As always it was wonderful to be back. There was an American international school in Lugano, but we ruled it out as a place to live because it was so exorbitantly expensive. A fact we had not appreciated before.

We sped back along the autostradas to the villa in Lucca. The villa was old and I was sure it was haunted. I heard barking on the locked top floor and occasionally thought I saw a dog walking through a room. Over wine and dinner, it turned out that Howard, Frances and Patrick had experienced similar sensations.

I was also having uneasy feelings about Howard continually making phone-box calls. Admittedly, there was no phone at the villa so he had to go to a phone box, but the number of calls he was making from the towns and villages of Tuscany seemed excessive.

'Who are you calling all the time, Howard?'

'Kathy – she's been having a few problems in the office, and you know what the Italian phone system is like, always breaking down, cutting out and bad lines.'

Was he lying? I hoped not. I wanted to believe him.

Howard had an autostrada addiction, so we decided to drive down to the Amalfi coast. I hadn't been there since I was thirteen when my parents had taken me to Rome for the audience with the Pope. I excitedly told Howard how beautiful it was. We hired a bigger car, rose early one morning and set off. We drove straight down the autostrada until we hit Castellammare di Stabia.

Castellammare di Stabia was ill equipped to deal with an autostrada finishing in the middle of the town. Cars that had been travelling at 120 kilometres an hour were suddenly faced with traffic lights, traffic jams, traffic police blowing bad temperedly on their whistles, cars tooting endlessly, mopeds going in all directions and irate drivers yelling out of windows. It was so chaotic as to be amusing, if you weren't the driver. Eventually, Howard managed to negotiate his way through the madness and we found ourselves driving along a precarious coast road, with volcanic cliffs descending steeply to the limpid and crystalline sea. Blind hairpin bends greeted us every few minutes, and occasionally the cliffs gave way to the silver-green of cultivated olive terraces. On the land-side of the road olive trees also grew but were interspersed with vineyards and orange and lemon groves. Rustic fishing villages could be glimpsed far below, reached by the steep meandering cart tracks.

As the sun was setting we reached the picturesque town of Sorrento perched high on a cliff. Our hotel was in the centre, a large turn-of-the-century Italian villa, insulated from the noise and the bustle by extensive grounds. After a few days here, on the spur of the moment, we decided to fly to Sicily. We checked the car in at Naples airport and flew to Palermo. Inside the airport terminal, we were forced to walk in a single file through a door into the baggage and customs hall. Just inside the door were a policeman and his dog. The dog barked at Howard. Two heavily armed policemen walked over to Howard and asked him to follow them. I was told to wait.

'Why did that dog bark at Daddy and where are they taking him?' asked Amber. She looked with alarm at the large Alsatian.

'It's a sniffer dog and I don't think the dog liked his aftershave. He won't be long, love, they just want a few words with him.' They took Howard into a room. I also wondered why the dog had barked at him. I hoped there were no lumps of hash in his trouser pockets he'd forgotten about. He hadn't smoked any hash since leaving England nearly two weeks before.

After ten minutes, the door opened and a smiling Howard and a grinning Sicilian policeman emerged. Howard rejoined us at the baggage carousel.

'What was that all about, Howard?'

'The dog just picked up on me being a dope smoker. They searched me and then did a check on my passport and then they started laughing,' he said, looking amused.

'The girls and I were worried.'

We had booked into the Villa Igiea, Palermo's most luxurious hotel and an old haunt of the mafia boss, Lucky Luciano. The hotel sent a limousine to collect us from the airport. Spotlessly groomed in a Versace suit was the driver, Mario.

Our suite overlooked the jasmine-scented gardens and the Bay of Palermo. We ate on the hotel restaurant terrace. To our disappointment, the restaurant hosted no recognizable mafia chieftains. In fact, no Sicilian guests of any description. On the table next to us sat David Frost and his new wife. The menu had no prices. The hotel was seriously expensive.

'Howard, how can we afford this place?'

'Let's not worry about that now and just enjoy ourselves. We're only here for three nights.'

The next day we went into the city centre, which was dominated by its prison. At that time a mafia trial involving several hundred defendants was in progress.

In 1974, there had been eight deaths resulting from drug-use in the whole of Italy. Less than a decade later, there were some 250,000 heroin addicts in the country and the death toll had topped 400 a year. As investigators in Sicily turned up more and more data on the drug trade, the Cosa Nostra responded. Police officers, prosecutors, journalists and politicians were murdered.

In 1981, Palermo saw the outbreak of the most vicious mafia war in its history. A new dominant group within the mafia, headed by Salvatore 'Tot' Riina of Corleone, killed off the traditional bosses of Palermo and hunted down and exterminated hundreds of their associates, friends and relations. The explosion of drugs and violence made the mafia a major national issue. Most public figures who dared to stand up to the mafia were assassinated, one after the other. The mayor of Palma was forced to resign.

A major crackdown was called for. A new courthouse was built at a cost of $19 million; a specially constructed tunnel connected the L'Ucciardone prison with the courthouse. Armed police snipers stood on roofs and patrolled the perimeter of the court. Two blue tanks guarded the gates. I raised my camera to take a photograph but before my finger could press the shutter, a policeman shouted at me to stop.

Witnesses from within the mafia began to give evidence. This was unheard of in Italy before 1983. More than half a dozen witnesses testified to Cosa Nostra's ties to the Christian Democrats, pointing the finger at senior politicians and the then prime minister Giulio Andreotti. It was the largest and most important mafia trial in history.

We explored the city, constantly looking out for mafia men. One evening we asked Mario to recommend us a restaurant. It was slightly out of town on the seashore and famed for its seafood. We left the children with a babysitter. As we sat on the restaurant terrace, a large black car drew up. Two large men climbed out and walked into the restaurant. They checked it out before returning to the car and opening the back door to allow an elderly, distinguished-looking gentleman to emerge. The restaurant staff treated him with reverence and the manager personally escorted him to a table. The two men stood guard by the restaurant door. It was like a scene from *The Godfather*.

'I would really love to come back here again one day, Jude,' said Howard.

The following day we flew back to Naples and tore up the autostrada back to the villa. A week later, we were at Pisa airport to catch the flight home.

I left Howard in the duty-free shop while I took the girls to the bathroom. When I came out, I saw Howard talking to a screw from

Brixton prison. He was one who'd often made things difficult for me when I wanted to hand over food or clothes. I had no wish to talk to him or ever see him again. I didn't want to be reminded about those days. What was Howard thinking?

'Howard,' I called. They both turned to look at me.

'Howard, can you come here please,' I called again.

Howard came over to me. The screw walked away.

'Howard, what were you doing talking to that horrid little screw? I thought you'd have had enough of talking to people like that.'

Howard started laughing.

'What's so funny?'

'You silly girl – that was Neil Kinnock.'

Kinnock had recently been elected leader of the Labour Party. I felt the blood rushing to my face. I buried my head in his chest in mortification. He hugged me and warmed my cheeks further with kisses and we both laughed. Later, on the plane, the children saved my face slightly by asking Mr Kinnock for his autograph.

Back in London, the girls returned to school and Howard returned to the office. The Mad Major was causing concern. Howard and John had done an inventory of the stores in Twickenham and many bottles were missing. The conclusion Howard and John came to was that the Major had drunk them, although, that said, we used to help ourselves to a bottle or two.

Another of Howard's prison mates was released from Brixton for lack of evidence. He was from the East End and had been in and out of jail for armed robbery. His name was Ricky Hawkins. He called round one day with his attractive tall blonde wife, Sharon. They had just returned from a prison-pallor cure in Mallorca.

'Wonderful place it is, H, and only two hours' flying time from here.'

'I've only spent one night there, but I must say I found the city very attractive,' Howard said. He must have been thinking of his first meeting with Prentiss. I'd also spent one night there, on a boat with Victoria. I hadn't even left the marina.

'I've got a pad out there, H, if you and the missus want to use it,' said Ricky.

Coincidentally, a couple of days later I was talking on the phone to Frances, who had just come back from Mallorca.

'What's it like there, Frances?' I had an image of package holidays and lager louts in my head.

'It's beautiful, Judy. The mass holiday market is contained to a few resorts. It's easy to stay away from that.'

'Where did you stay?'

'With friends of ours at La Mola club in Andratx. I highly recommend Palma – it might be your solution about where to live.'

At the end of October, during half-term, we left the grey skies of London and flew to Palma de Mallorca. We climbed off the plane into bright sunshine under blue skies.

Although I wasn't keen on cultivating Howard's relationships with East End villains, we took up Ricky's offer. The flat was on the border of Torrenova and Magalluf: the epicentre of the mass tourist market. It fulfilled all our nightmares about package holidays. The area around Ricky's flat abounded with pubs called Benny Hill's, Rovers Return, London Pride and Princess Di. In one pub a notice-board was littered with messages. 'Two girls in need of sex, room 707 Hotel Sol.' 'Two hunky Glaswegians willing to give service all night.' In the early hours of each morning we'd hear through the paper-thin walls of the apartment four Scottish lads retiring for the night next door, crashing about and retching in the bathroom.

Ricky had suggested we looked up a friend of his, Claude, who owned a bar called Baraca on the beach in Palma Nova. As far as I can remember, he was a French Corsican. Many of the clientele were East Enders dripping with gold. We introduced ourselves to Claude as friends of Ricky's, and before long we had been introduced to other people. There was a Doctor Clark from the north of England who was hoping to open a GP practice on the island. I met Debbie, an attractive blonde woman with a cockney accent, who had two daughters, Laura and Kristi, of similar age to Amber and Golly. She was able to fill me in on the international schools on the island. We also met a Mallorcan travel agent called Justo, who also seemed to be a Mr Fix-it for the non-Spanish-speaking expats.

Unable to face the thought of another night in Ricky's apartment, we booked into an apartment hotel in Palma Nova, where we celebrated Amber's sixth birthday. We hired a car and began to explore the island. What we found delighted us. Then, most of the island was deserted and enjoyably tranquil. The smell of vomit and alcohol, which pervaded Magalluf, was replaced with the scent of pine forests and cherry and almond blossoms. Villages perched on the sides of mountains. In the small town of Deia, it was easily possible to see why so many artists, writers and musicians had made this island their home. We decided we could too, and planned to visit again soon to check out the schools and look for a house.

When we returned home, there were several messages on the answer machine from Pete. He sounded remarkably coherent and together. He wanted Howard to call him.

'Jude, perhaps he's going to give us the money after all.'

'Wouldn't that be wonderful? It would make up for the Mad Major and ourselves drinking all the profits.'

'We won't be doing that any more. John has put some heavy-duty padlocks on the storeroom door.'

While I bathed the girls and put them to bed, Howard went to the phone box in the Bolton's to call Pete. He was gone a long time. Eventually he phoned and said he was in the pub with John. He sounded drunk. I was very curious to know what Pete had said, but I couldn't ask him on the phone.

He eventually arrived home at 1 a.m.

'You like him, don't you, Jude? He was good to you,' he slurred.

'Who?'

'Pete,' he said as he passed out on the sofa.

I was cooking breakfast in the kitchen the next morning when he finally surfaced.

'Why did Daddy sleep on the sofa last night, Mummy?' asked Amber.

'He'd had a bit too much to drink and fell asleep.'

'Morning, all,' he said rather sheepishly.

I handed him fresh orange juice and then asked what news Pete had.

223

'Why don't we have a talk, love, when you come back from taking the kids to school?'

'Okay,' I said.

When I got back, he'd gone out. He'd left a note saying he had to meet John because of a crisis with the Major. He phoned at lunchtime. 'Sorry about that, Jude. Look, book a babysitter and we'll go out for dinner. Your favourite, La Famiglia, if you want.'

Sitting in my favourite Italian restaurant in London that evening, I said, 'So, tell me what Pete said.'

He looked down at the table for a while, and then looked me in the eyes. 'He wants me to send him five tons of hash from Pakistan. I have Durrani's friend Malik out there who can do it.'

'But you're not going to do it, are you, Howard?'

'I owe him, Jude.'

'What do you mean, you owe him? A few months ago, he thought he owed us.'

'Look at everything he's done for us. He didn't have to spring Natasha out of jail, but he did.' Howard knew that was a weak spot and capitalized on it. 'She could have been languishing in filthy conditions for years, not living in a fancy apartment while they sorted the legal side out. And he took care of your brother and his family for months.'

'Howard, I can't stop you deciding what to do. But I have two children. I don't want to be involved. If they catch you again, because of that Old Bailey trial I know they'll go for me. And honestly, after what I witnessed with Pete a few months ago, he and Patti have completely lost it.'

'Oh, he's totally straightened out now, Jude. Very together.'

'But what about all the heaviness going on over there? All those guns, for Christ's sake. Spooks and murders, dogs being shot, attempts on Pete's life.'

'Everything's fine now.'

'That's not what it looked like to me,' I said.

'Jude, I'll just do this one and then stop. I promise.'

He left for Hong Kong the following week to meet Malik,

whom he'd met years ago when Durrani was in hospital. I felt acutely depressed and disappointed.

Howard phoned at least twice a day and always made sure I had his hotel phone number. Five days after he had left, he phoned in the early morning my time, before I had taken the children to school.

'Jude, I thought while I was out here I'd fly to Bangkok and say hi to Phil.'

'Oh God, Howard.' Now he's really going to be dragged back into it.

'Look, Phil's a really straight businessman now. Seriously, Jude.'

I couldn't imagine Phil Sparrowhawk being straight about anything. Much as I was fond of him, I doubted if he'd managed to be straight for the first five minutes he'd entered the world.

After ten days, Howard arrived back home laden down with Christmas presents, talking excitedly about how much Hong Kong and Bangkok had changed since he'd last been there. He also talked about some wild scheme he had of exporting Welsh water to Saudi Arabia in the ballast tanks of oil containers. I was glad he didn't discuss dope deals with me. I still hadn't managed to accept that he was so irresponsible as to even consider doing one, especially after what I had told him about Pete and Patti. I was sure this was exactly what Customs were waiting for him to do; indeed, expecting him to do.

I had nothing against marijuana, or anyone being a swashbuckling marijuana smuggler who was single and had no responsibilities. However, smuggling dope was against the law. However much we thought its illegality was wrong, long sentences could be and often were imposed. We had become parents. We had taken on a responsibility that I did not feel we were fulfilling properly by breaking the law. Howard had parents who were ageing, and whom he had already put through so much. Given that Howard had made such fools out of Customs, I knew they would watch him like a hawk. They would be in no hurry, either. But they'd make sure that next time they got him for good. I was also afraid that they would go for me. I repeatedly voiced this concern to Howard.

'Judy, I'll have to go back out there in the New Year. Will you and the children come with me?'

'What about Amber's schooling?' I asked.

'It'll be a fantastic education for them both, Judy. Please say yes.' His blue twinkled eyes at me. I found it impossible to resist.

'Okay, I'll go and have a word with the school.'

At the start of 1984, we spent a few days in Kenfig Hill with his parents. Howard went to see the Welsh water board. He returned to his parents' house with a stack of laboratory test reports and impressive multicoloured multilingual brochures, and talked excitedly to his father about his latest scheme. I wondered if he was serious about this or if it was a front to cover his real business interests in the Far East. His parents fell for it.

In London I went to see Amber's head teacher, Angela Hollyoak, and asked for permission to take Amber out of school for four weeks. Mrs Hollyoak did not feel it would do undue harm and that travel was an education in itself. She arranged for me to take some schoolwork with us and asked Amber to keep a diary of her trip.

Howard left. The following week I went to see the travel agents he'd recommended, Hong Kong International Travel Centre, who had offices on the first floor of a building in Beak Street. A young couple owned it, a man with a heavily birthmarked face, who introduced himself to me as Balando, and his older girlfriend Orca Liew. He was from Hong Kong and she was from Malaysia. They booked our flights and put them on Howard's account.

Two days later Amber, Golly and I were flying on Cathay Pacific to Hong Kong. By the time we had cleared immigration at Kai Tak airport, we were exhausted. Howard was waiting for us. He had ordered a large white Mercedes limousine to take us to the Shangri-La hotel in Tsim Tsa Shui East. It was a newly built five-star luxury hotel on the waterfront near the Star Ferry terminal. It overlooked the magnificent Hong Kong harbour with its non-stop traffic.

Howard had booked us the penthouse suite, which had wall-to-wall windows overlooking the skyline of Hong Kong Island with its erratic stretches of skyscrapers, hotels and apartments. The room had vases of fresh orchids placed on nearly every surface and bowls of exotic-looking fruits on the table. A knock came at the door and a Chinese man in a gleaming white uniform wheeled in a table of ice-cold champagne and two dozen oysters. I felt immeasurably touched by the trouble Howard had taken to make us feel welcome. Howard grinned at our happy faces. He raised his glass. 'Welcome to Hong Kong, my lovely family.'

After the girls and I had had a sleep, Howard took us all out for a romantic dinner on a boat touring Hong Kong harbour, with junks and sampans plying up and down and glittering skyscrapers in the background. The next day he took us on a whirlwind sightseeing tour.

In the evening, with the girls settled in with their first Chinese babysitter, Howard and I joined Bruce Aitken for dinner. Bruce was a straight friend of my brother Patrick's. He was a likeable American who ran a finance company called First Financial Services. I wondered if he was doing business with Howard. Was Patrick involved again? I didn't want to know. But it was hard not to be curious, and I had to discipline myself not to ask questions.

Talk over dinner was about the return of Hong Kong to China and the ending of British rule.

'I don't understand why Thatcher is doing it,' I said. I had read in the papers that it was a case of the hundred-year lease running out, but Howard had told me that this was untrue. The lease only applied to part of the Kowloon peninsula and the so-called New Territories. The remaining part of the Kowloon peninsula (Tsim Sha Tsui), Hong Kong Island and a few hundred other islands, the British had simply stolen.

'It's simple really,' said Bruce. 'The Chinese want it back. There are five million Chinese here, twenty thousand Americans and seventeen thousand British. Who do you think really runs the place? Jude, the Chinese are fantastic business people and long-term planners. They really are a race I admire. It took them over a hundred and fifty years to build the Chinese wall and it's taken them only a hundred years to gain control of the largest shopping, banking and shipping centre in the world. They're very astute.'

I thought about the Chinese, and all the China towns I had visited in Canada and the US and even in London. It seemed to me that, unlike other races, the Chinese had an uncanny knack of just moving in and getting on with whatever, without really integrating, but without upsetting anyone either. They got what they wanted.

Howard introduced me to Sam the Tailor. He was a good-looking Indian man of medium height. He had a tiny little shop in a large warren-like building, the Burlington Arcade, just off the Nathan Road in Kowloon. In the shop he had photos of himself with Dennis Thatcher, David Bowie, Prince Philip and many more celebrities. He had the reputation of being able to copy exactly any garment you took in. He could even make a replica of an outfit from a photo in a magazine. Howard had told me to bring with me all my favourite clothes so I could have them copied. Sam and I talked about what materials would be the most sensible to use for the replicas of my Armani, Versace and Kenzo originals.

The results did not disappoint me.

The girls and I spent much time exploring Hong Kong on our own, while Howard was doing whatever he did and meeting whomever he did. Sometimes he met us for lunch. One day he took us to a snake shop and a snake restaurant. The shop was overflowing with bags and cages of writhing snakes. Amber and Golly held onto each other in the doorway. Howard ordered two shots of snake's gall bladder.

'It's an aphrodisiac, Jude. You've got to try it.'

The shop owner pulled three different snakes out of their cages. He expertly ran his hands down their bodies until he reached their gall bladders and then, with a sharp knife, removed them. He pushed the mutilated snakes through a hatch into the restaurant next door. The gall bladders he then slit open. He squeezed thick, dark-green blood into a brandy glass. On top, he poured a shot of expensive Armagnac and mixed it with a cocktail stick.

'Howard, I'll pass,' I said.

Howard took the glass and swigged it in one, trying to keep the look of distaste off his face. The girls didn't try to hide their grimaces. This shot set him back 3,000 HK dollars.

'Howard, I think I'll just stick to Dom Perignon and oysters. It's cheaper, and by the look on your face considerably pleasanter.'

In the restaurant next door the girls happily tucked into their snake soup. Again, I declined.

'Mummy, it tastes just like chicken,' said Amber, trying to reassure me.

We spent time shopping and the girls quickly built up their already considerable collection of Barbie dolls and accessories. These they would play with in the evenings with their babysitter while Howard and I went out. Some evenings after dinner, we went to the basement of the New World Centre near our hotel where there was a complex of bars with different themes. Howard's favourite was the country bar, where they often played Waylon Jennings. Mine was the blues bar. Another of his haunts was Bottoms Up, a seedy topless bar that had opened in 1971 and featured in the 1974 James Bond film *The Man with the Golden Gun*. We walked in there one evening, and to my horror I saw Jim Hobbs sitting at the bar.

'You didn't tell me he was here.'

'Well, you said you didn't want to know what was going on. I needed someone to run some errands for me and he was available to come out immediately.'

He had a way of saying it that made me feel guilty I was no longer the one running errands.

Two of the bar girls who had been talking to Jim came over.

'Ah, Marks, we not see you for a while,' said one of the girls.

'I have my family here. This is my wife, Judy. Judy, this is April and this is Selena.'

I held out my hand and shook theirs, thinking as I did that they had unlikely names.

'Ah, Judy, welcome to Hong Kong. We leave you enjoy drink with husband.' They moved away.

'They are another reason Hobbs is here,' said Howard.

'What does someone of Hobbs's orientation want with two hookers?'

'He's going to marry one of them. They are all frightened of the Chinese taking over and they desperately want British husbands. They'll pay good money too. So Jim is going to get as many as he can of his persuasion to come over and marry as many that will pay.'

I felt slightly sorry for the poor young woman who was so desperate to have a British passport she would take Jim Hobbs as her husband. I also wondered about the legality of arranging such marriages.

Howard asked us if we wanted to visit Bangkok on our way home. I had heard so much about Bangkok I was very curious to see it, and one of Amber and Golly's favourite films was *The King and I*. We flew first class on Thai Airlines into Bangkok's Don Muang international airport. We sailed through customs and immigration controls to a waiting limousine. It took us through busy streets where the traffic lights seemed to be permanently on red. Children as young as Amber banged on the air-conditioned car's windows trying to sell us flower chains. The traffic jams consisted of cars, taxis, elephants and tuk-tuks, all honking madly. We eventually arrived at the serenity of the Oriental hotel where Balando had booked us into a VIP suite.

Howard must have received a fair amount of money in Hong Kong – the Oriental was one of the world's top hotels. It had won awards year after year and been a favourite among writers such as Joseph Conrad, Somerset Maugham and Evelyn Waugh.

I liked Bangkok. I liked the people. I liked their quiet serenity, their genuine warmth and smiling politeness. I liked the way they bowed and held their hands in a praying position, which Golly soon copied. Golly had an affinity with Thailand. She'd inherited her father's double-jointedness and could bend her fingers like the Thai traditional dancers in the hotel, who invited her up to dance with them.

We wandered the bustling streets and watched young children at work, many tending their parents' stalls or selling goods up and down the endless traffic jams. Hygienic food kiosks with wonderful aromas lined the exhaust-filled streets. In the wonderful temples Golly copied the Thais in prayer and lit incense sticks.

Phil called round to the hotel with his new Thai wife Pao and baby daughter Marisa. We had afternoon tea in the authors' lounge, seated on white rattan furniture with cane fans spinning above our heads. He hadn't changed. He still managed to blend into the background. And, despite my fears of what he might involve Howard in, I was pleased to see him, and he seemed genuinely delighted to see Amber, Golly and me.

One night Howard and I went out drinking. I wanted to see the famous sex area of Patpong, which had started out as an R&R spot for US troops in the Vietnam War. It now catered mainly to foreign tourists and was at the centre of Bangkok's sex industry. The touristy surface masked much of what went on behind closed doors. The area consisted of two narrow streets, each crammed with bars where young girls danced or posed on stage wearing numbered badges. The girls were available to customers, who would pay a bar fine to take them out. Some clubs employed kathoeys, or lady boys. Everything was available in Patpong. Touts accosted the pedestrians in the street. 'Want see live sex show?' 'Want see ping pong show, razor blade show, sex with live chicken, want see fucky-fucky?' It was hard to believe that prostitution was illegal in Thailand.

We went to a bar called the Superstar. It was full of middle-aged, sweaty, pot-bellied European men fondling young girls while the girls tried to keep the famous Thai smile in place. It was where it is said lust and raw wallet power meet a culture of grace and politeness. There were a few couples like us. Howard seemed known to some of the girls. They came up to say hello and were happy when Howard introduced me. They seemed far more interested in talking to me than attracting any male attention. After one drink, we left.

Two days later Howard left for a four-day trip to Karachi while he was away. I took the girls to Pattaya Beach, about a two-hour drive from Bangkok. It was Thailand's equivalent to Magalluf on Mallorca, but with nicer beaches and far better food. We all returned to Bangkok and the Oriental at the same time.

One evening Howard was late joining me for dinner. I knew he was meeting Phil for a drink so I took my chances they would be in the Superstar. They were. So too seemed to be about half of Brixton prison. Jim Hobbs was there with a kathoey on each knee. A half-Irish half-Jamaican Londoner called Mickey Williams, an armed bank robber, was too busy to notice me as he jiggled two girls on his lap. Ricky Hawkins, with young girls draped all over him as he flashed money around, did notice me and choked on his orange juice. Howard and Phil seemed amused.

'Judy! H, you never told me you had your missus out here.'

'Haven't had a chance to, Ricky, you've been so occupied since you've arrived,' Howard replied.

'Thing is, Jude, I don't drink and I don't smoke but I do like the odd bird,' Ricky said, having by now shaken the girls off. 'You won't say nothing to our Sharon, will you, Jude?'

'It's none of my business what you do, Ricky,' I said.

Howard and I left the bar and took a tuk-tuk to a seafood restaurant.

'What are that lot of villains doing out here, Howard?'

'Just having a holiday.'

'Do you expect me to believe that? You're really asking for trouble getting mixed up with that lot.'

'I'm not, Jude. I simply introduced them to Phil.'

'That's what I mean, that's getting mixed up.'

The four of us flew a couple of days later to Bombay. Howard stayed one night with us in Bombay and then flew to Karachi. The girls and I tried to explore Bombay. It became impossible. Word went out that a young Englishwoman with two small children was walking around on her own. Beggars and street urchins crowded round us.

I was feeling very low. From what I had witnessed in Bangkok, Howard had been smitten with the smuggling bug again. And this time round I wasn't sure I liked the players.

CHAPTER NINETEEN
Fish Fingers

Back in London, the girls and I settled back into a routine. Howard settled back into his routine of no routine at all. Shelton told us that progress towards a sensible settlement with the taxman was imminent and we should consider moving abroad soon.

The wine business in London had dwindled almost to nothing. The secretarial services were still going, but with Howard's frequent absences Kathy was becoming demotivated.

For the Easter holidays, we flew out to Palma to research the schools and do some serious house hunting. There were four international schools on the island. We viewed them all, and settled on the one we felt was nearest in atmosphere and teaching methods to Queensgate, where Amber was so happy. We paid the deposit and enrolled Amber and Golly. They would begin in September 1984.

We looked at several properties. Many of the places we liked were too far away from the school we had selected or too expensive. Neither we nor Howard's parents wanted to sell the London flat; they kindly said they would help with any purchase, within reason, that we made.

A young blonde American estate agent called Linda showed us a large old house on the outskirts of Palma. An American woman and her three children lived in it. It needed a lot of work, but it fitted our budget. We agreed a purchase date and the price.

Back home, Amber was enjoying her last term at her school.

Golly was still enjoying her nursery and Howard was forever running around. Phone boxes were back on the agenda, as were large bags of coins. He often went to the Far East but was never gone for more than seven to ten days.

One day, just before Howard was due back in London from Karachi, I got a phone call.

'Hi, Judy, how're you doing?'

'Hey, Pete, I'm fine. How are you and Patti?'

'Not too good. Is he back yet?'

'No, he's due any minute. What's up?'

'The champagne's gone flat.' Although I had known nothing of the details of this deal, I knew enough of the codes to know a load had gone down. 'I think it's Tom and Karl's fault. They say it's his,' continued Pete.

'Well, I know who I'd believe.'

'Yeah, I know. Get him to give me a call as soon as he can.'

So Pete was back dealing with Tom and Karl. Why? I also realized I had involved myself again. I decided that when we moved to Mallorca I would install two lines in the house. I would keep one for domestic calls, family and friends; Howard could have the other line for business calls. Much as I enjoyed chatting to Pete, he would have to be on the business line.

Howard arrived back. He had as usual bought me several bottles of perfume and presents for the girls.

'Everything all right, Jude?' He put his case down and kissed me.

'Pete called.' I repeated our conversation. Howard turned grey.

'I better go and call him right away,' he said, reopening the front door.

He returned about forty-five minutes later looking even greyer.

'Jude, you met this Karl bloke, didn't you?'

'Yes, a couple of times. Why?'

'Well, Malik and I sent a five-ton load to New York through a CIA connection of Pete's to the AT&T. When I arrived in Zurich yesterday morning from Karachi, Pete phoned me and said he had it. Now Pete says it never arrived. He puts Karl on to me, who first off tells me he did me a big favour and got me out of jail.'

'Bullshit.'

'I said, I heard you got well paid. That, he says, is irrelevant and asks me if I physically saw the plane being loaded. When I said no, he says, right, your man in Pakistan owes us $1,500,000 plus expenses. I asked to talk to Pete again and he said he was asleep. Jude, did you tell me once that Karl had a brother in Germany?'

'Yes, he claims his brother is a German Intelligence officer based in Düsseldorf. I have no idea if that's true. Why?'

'Because the flight with the load on stopped in Düsseldorf and maybe Karl arranged to have it taken off there. What the hell do I tell Malik?'

'The truth.'

'It's not a call I'm looking forward to. Best get it over with.' He opened the front door and left again.

As it was, Malik was surprisingly philosophical about it all.

Our friendship with Balando and Orca grew. Howard was beginning to take an interest in the travel business, an interest I was happy to encourage.

'Jude, Malik's got a travel agency in Karachi and can get cheap PIA air tickets to China. Maybe I can somehow merge the two travel agencies and get some deals together there. Malik also wants me to become involved in his papermill business.'

'Any straight business I'm for. Why don't you talk to Balando about the travel business in Pakistan?'

He returned from having lunch with Balando the following day in a buoyant mood. Balando and Orca had asked him if he would be their official Far East representative and said they would pay him commission for any new business he put their way. I was delighted; maybe this was a straight business that would work. I hoped so.

Cooking the children's supper one night and fetching some frozen steaks from the deep-freeze, I realized that with all the travelling I had not cleared out the freezer for over a year. I decided to do it there and then. Any packets with dates over six months old I put in the bin.

Two days later, we were entertaining some friends when Howard got up and went to the kitchen. He came back into the living room.

'Jude, where are the fish fingers that were in the deep-freeze?'

I looked at him puzzled. I had never known Howard express an interest in the contents of the freezer.

'I cleaned it out a couple of days ago. Why?' I noticed he went pale in response to this.

'Did you throw fish fingers out?'

'If the date was over six months, yes.'

'Oh God, Jude – I'd hidden a kilo and a half of good Afghani and Nepalese in there.' He rushed out the front door to the dustbin area. The dustbin men had been the night before. He came back in looking depressed.

'Howard, why didn't you tell me?'

'I thought you'd be pissed off having so much dope in the house.'

'Not as pissed off as I am at thinking of all that beautiful dope wasted.'

In June, Tom Sunde came to visit at Pete's behest to try to work out where the AT&T scam had gone wrong. Howard supported Malik and Tom supported Karl. They had many discussions in the sitting room. I stayed in the playroom with the children. I avoided Tom as much as possible. I just did not feel good around him. Howard took him to Amber's sports day and he took Howard's place in the fathers' race, competing with, among others, Nigel Havers, who had recently filmed *Chariots of Fire* and was fit from hours of training. Tom won.

In July, we were going to drive the Mercedes down to Mallorca, packed with bedding and whatever else we could cram in. Howard managed to fit in another trip to the Far East. Pete, he told me, had decided to do another deal, using Malik and not using Tom and Karl. He had another CIA agent whom he claimed could smuggle the dope through a naval base in Alameda, California.

'I don't want to know, Howard. I do not ever want to be questioned and to have to choose between being taken away from my children or giving information about you. I just want you to stop dealing, but if you won't, do not involve me. Please.'

On 16 July we caught the ferry from Plymouth to Santander. We drove across Spain to Barcelona and caught the ferry to Palma. We excitedly moved into the house in La Vileta, much in a camping fashion. It was a three-storey, 150-year-old house with thick stone walls. In the garden were five enormous palm trees and a well.

We drew up plans for the changes we wanted to make to the house to return it to its former glory but with modern plumbing and electrics. We employed Justo, the Mallorquin Mr Fix-it, to engage builders and take general charge of the project.

We drove back to London and arrived on 15 August. My brother George was marrying Yvonne and the wedding was to take place on the outskirts of Belfast. Amber and Golly were going to be bridesmaids along with Yvonne's little sister Bridget, all in matching pink dresses. I had not been to Belfast since I was twelve. Now tanks, barbed wire, police checks and British soldiers invaded the streets. It was a war zone. There were serious riots in Protestant areas following protests against a 'supergrass' trial, and Loyalist paramilitaries had opened fire on RUC officers on the Shankhill Road.

To George and Yvonne, who had just returned from Beirut, it must have seemed home from home. George had been almost continually out in the Middle East since the early 1970s working as an English teacher and as a freelance journalist, and had a whole host of adventures behind him. He had spent time in Afghanistan, where the Russian-backed Afghan army held him for a short time when they invaded the country. He had written for *Kayhan International* and taught English in Iran to the Imperial air force until the fall of the Shah, when he was one of the last to leave the country. He had been on the Doshen Tappeh airbase in east Tehran on 11 February 1979, the day his air force cadet students had finally risen in revolt against the king. During a lull in the ensuing bloody battle he had made his escape from the besieged airbase on his faithful CZ 250 Enduro motorbike. His interpretations of events in Tehran over those chaotic post-revolutionary months were published in the *Jordan Times* after he arrived in Amman on his bike. The Jordanian army were the next grateful recipients of his teaching skills, a job he kept for a year.

He moved to Beirut in 1980 where he worked for the British Council. A KGB agent by the name of Valery tried to recruit him to the KGB. He employed George to give him English lessons but as he spoke perfect English George suspected that more was at stake than grammar exercises. Valery would turn up at George's flat over-looking Beirut's seafront cornice late at night with a bottle of Scotch and the conversation soon veered sharply away from Fowler's *English Usage*. Other times George would be summoned to the heavily guarded fortress-like Soviet embassy but within minutes the inevitable bottle of Scotch appeared with which to lace the lemon tea a dour-faced secretary provided. George secretly delighted in inviting Valery to parties thrown by the dwindling expatriate community and introducing him to British embassy friends who, of course, were well aware of Valery's identity. He has one memorable photograph of a bemused Valery with the wife of the British embassy's second secretary, both of them cradling AK47 Kalashnikov machine-guns, which George had posed them with.

Unfortunately George had no secrets to sell, but Valery contin-ued the lessons anyway. After George had left Beirut, Valery hit the international headlines when he and three other Soviet diplomats were kidnapped and their Lebanese driver shot dead. Within hours the Russians had arranged for their own contacts within the Druze militia in Beirut to seize a family member of the kidnappers'. A message was sent to the kidnappers along with an appendage sliced from the victim's body. Some reports said it was a finger, others a toe, and some claimed it was the hapless victim's penis. Whatever the body part, Valery and his fellow Soviet abductees were released immediately.

In 1982 George himself was kidnapped by George Habash's PFLP, a radical branch of the PLO, on suspicion of been an Israeli spy. He was held for sixteen days. This was before kidnapping by Islamic militants had become fashionable and the incident attracted little attention. His British Council boss, Mike Ward, had left when the situation in the city had become untenable with the Israelis advancing north after their invasion of Lebanon on 6 June 1982.

Before leaving, he informed the British embassy that, as far as he was aware, all British Council staff had left West Beirut for the comparative safety of East Beirut and were safe and accounted for. This is what the embassy told Yvonne, who was frantically trying to get news of George's whereabouts. They stuck to this story despite Yvonne's desperate insistence that this was impossible because he had not contacted her or his family.

In fact, he was in a dungeon deep beneath the headquarters of Fatah's interrogation centre in the Fakhani area of West Beirut, adjacent to the Sabra refugee camp. He remained there under Israel's heaviest bombardment of the camps. When he emerged he was to find that despite the use to which it was put, the building under which he had been held was the only undamaged structure in the area. The only possible explanation for the building not being bombed, and therefore his life being spared, was that it housed at least one Israeli prisoner, whom George had glimpsed. Eventually, satisfied that George was who he said he was, namely an English teacher and part-time journalist for Beirut's *Daily Star*, the Palestinians let him go. They returned all his possessions including some $2,000, his passport and his motorbike, and shaking hands and exchanging kisses and body hugs, they took him home and dropped him outside his seafront apartment block.

Sixteen days before, Beirut was a bustling albeit besieged capital city. Now it was bombed and devastated, every street sandbagged and barricaded. George decided it was time to leave. Finally getting through to his girlfriend, he arranged to meet her in Cyprus. They had an emotional reunion in Nicosia and then took the ferry back to Jounieh, in Israeli-occupied Lebanon. From here they could watch the daily bombardment of Beirut and wait until the situation had calmed enough for them to return to the city they had both grown to love.

When the British Council reopened in October 1982, they were welcomed back. Both soon had jobs as the Lebanese clamoured to return to normality.

During this period I was tearing my hair out about Marcus, who was now a troublesome teenager of seventeen. He had left home and seemed to have no direction. Howard and I foresaw him getting into trouble with the law. I decided to send him out to stay with George, and bought him a one-way ticket to Beirut. Many questioned me about sending him out to a war zone, but I felt it was better for him to be with George than fall into a life of petty crime.

George and Yvonne, returning exhausted from work every day, found the sounds of punk rock echoing around their apartment tiring to deal with. After two weeks of Marcus, George sent him to stay with friends of his in the Bekaa Valley. Marcus got himself a job working on a hash farm in Baalbek, where an estimated 150,000 acres of cannabis grew.

In 1984, the international peacekeeping forces left Lebanon. The ensuing battle for Beirut was bloody and complicated. I tried to follow George's letters and understand the different factions of Shiite, PLO, Druze and Maronite. The British Council again closed down their operations in Beirut, and George and Yvonne returned to Ireland. Marcus went and briefly worked on a kibbutz where he met a beautiful English-Pakistani girl called Kieran. They returned to Europe and went to live in Patrick's old mill in France.

Thankfully, Yvonne's family home was out of the city of Belfast. The wedding took place in a small church in the village close to the farm where she had grown up. It was wonderful for me to catch up with aunts and uncles I had not seen for years, and for Howard, who had not met my mother, to meet her close family.

Howard read a speech at the church service. At the end of the ceremony, as all the Catholics filed up for Holy Communion, Howard joined in. However, when the priest gave Howard the bread representing Christ, instead of swallowing it, much to the bemusement of the congregation he stuck it in his pocket.

The reception took place in County Antrim, in a beautiful seventeenth-century hotel not far from the Giant's Causeway. Dancing carried on long into the night. The Irish know how to give a wedding. It was a night to remember.

The next day Howard and I had lunch with George and Yvonne. They were unsure what they were going to do with themselves now they had had to leave Beirut. They loved the Middle East. George was fluent in Persian, written and spoken.

'George, would you consider living in Karachi?' Howard asked.

'Yes … what do you have in mind, Howard?'

'I have a couple of businesses I am involved in there: a paper mill and a travel agency, which ties in with my agency in London. I was wondering if you and Yvonne would be interested in running an English language school for me out there. There isn't one there with native speakers and I can see it being a big success.'

It was the first I had heard of this idea. 'When did you think of this?'

'Well, just now, from talking to George and Yvonne,' he said to me. He turned back to George and Yvonne. 'You don't have to decide now, but if I pay all your expenses perhaps you could go out there and do a feasibility report.'

'I can see no harm in that, George,' said Yvonne.

George's eyes brightened. 'Well, yes. We'll at least go and check it out.'

I felt slightly uneasy and wasn't sure why.

George and Yvonne left for their honeymoon touring Ireland. We went back to Belfast, stopping off at the Giant's Causeway on our way. We had arranged to meet my mother's sister Joan and her eldest brother Martin in Belfast. Martin, because of his position in the Northern Irish police force, had been unable to attend the wedding. As one of the few high-ranking Catholics in the force, his life was constantly under threat and there were concerns for his safety.

Joan's husband Michael owned a well-known IRA-frequented pub, the White Fort, in the Anderstown area of Belfast. McCann's brothers were regulars. Martin and Michael had a pact to avoid political discussions. They were both amused to meet Howard; leaving Joan, Mika (Martin's wife) and me they disappeared to the pub and were gone for hours. Howard said later it was one of the most enjoyable drinking sessions of his life and that he loved my mother's family. It made me happy to hear him say that.

* * *

We returned to Mallorca and started the girls in their new school. We rented a flat as work on the house started. Howard enrolled on a Spanish course and, while the girls were at school, we explored the island. One lunchtime we were sipping Pimm's in Tim's bar in Puerto Andratx when we came across Linda, the estate agent who'd found us our home.

'It's so odd, guys. I went to see an astrologer this morning and she told me my future chart was blank.'

I had never had much time for astrology, but two days later we heard she was dead. Her husband had discovered she was having an affair and had stabbed and killed her. Her death and the violence of it shocked me; I hoped it was not a bad omen for our house.

Howard went out to Karachi to introduce George and Yvonne to Malik and do whatever else he had to do. George and Yvonne liked Malik and his wife and children. Malik felt the same towards them. He immediately employed them to teach English to his two daughters and son.

In England, the taxman finally came to an agreement with Howard and Shelton. They would settle for £60,000. Clearly unable to take a plastic bag full of cash to pay them, I took out a mortgage on the London flat and sent them a cheque.

I worried about Amber. She was far from happy in her new school. She'd always enjoyed school so much – it seemed such a shame. She'd return from school with a red mark on her chest where the teacher had prodded her with a pencil. Our second choice of a school didn't have a place available until the following September.

'Jude, I don't like seeing her unhappy like this. Why don't you teach her yourself? The house won't be ready for another couple of months, so you can travel with me more,' said Howard.

It was tempting. I looked into it. In London, I contacted an organization that advised on the home-taught child. They were able to provide me with the textbooks and guidelines on what Amber should be learning that year. At half-term, I took the girls out of school.

We flew with Howard to Karachi the week that *High Time* by David Leigh was published. The reviews were not favourable. It was dark when we arrived at Jinnah international airport, and there were very few streetlights so it was difficult to get a feel of the place. We took the complimentary hotel car straight to the Sheraton. It was Amber's seventh birthday the next day. Howard and I had bought all her presents in Europe before we'd left. She and Golly spent most of the day in the hotel swimming pool where they were assigned their own lifeguard.

George and Yvonne joined us for breakfast. They had a small flat in town but Malik was in the process of renting them a larger house with a swimming pool in an area known as DHA. They had settled in well and already had a fair number of students. Malik and Howard were both investing in the school. The old American consulate had been rented and was in the process of being refurbished. It would shortly open as the International Language Centre, Karachi, or ILCK.

After three nights in Karachi, we wanted to fly to Bangkok. All the flights were full. Howard flew out first and the girls and I followed the next day. On the flight, in the upstairs bar of the jumbo, I got talking to an American. He told me he had been in Pakistan for six months, mainly in Baluchistan, and was now on his way to Bangkok for some R&R. He had been drinking heavily, which liberated his tongue. He expressed the view that Pakistan, and various other places he described as 'rag-headed' countries, should be nuked off the face of the earth.

We arrived in Bangkok on my birthday. Howard had arranged a lavish display of flowers, oysters and champagne to greet me. Returning to the Oriental was like returning home. We spent four days here, then it was back to Hong Kong and the Shangri-La, where we felt equally at home.

'Jude, I've finished what I have to do here. Do you fancy spending a few days in Tokyo?'

'I'd love to.'

At the time we flew to Tokyo it was the most expensive city in the world. The taxi from the airport to our hotel, the Keo Plaza, cost well over £150; a considerable amount in 1984. The city seemed to be a mass of modern-day confusion: high-rises jostling for space, giant video screens on the sides of buildings, neon lights hanging over bumper-to-bumper traffic jams, incessant noise. Webs of tangled overhead cables stretched from building to building above the masses of pedestrians and cars.

We started to explore the city the following day by subway. There was a network of twelve lines, a plethora of tunnels and passageways in the stations, and signs only in Japanese. People pointed at us and openly laughed, especially at Amber with her long blonde hair and blue eyes.

'Mummy, why do they keep pointing and laughing at me?'

'They're not used to seeing such a beautiful little girl and they're not used to seeing blonde hair,' I said. It was rather disconcerting and we felt a bit like a freak show. We gave up on the subways and took to taxis.

What surprised me most about Japan was the drinking. I had always thought of the Japanese as hard-working and serious, rushing to work in their suits, working all hours and then going home. Howard and I were unprepared for seeing Japanese men completely addled at six in the evening, sitting on the pavement in their suits with bottles of Scotch. Not only did they work hard, they played hard.

We went to Roppongi to explore the nightlife, and stumbled across a twelve-storey high-rise with a differently themed discotheque on each floor. There was one called the Cavern, which we could not miss. It was done out to be an exact replica of the Liverpool club. However, what astounded us was that the four musicians had had plastic surgery to look exactly like the Beatles. Not only did they look like the Beatles, they sounded like the Beatles too. It was eerie.

Japan we decided was somewhere we wanted to visit again.

The rest of the year, we yo-yoed between Hong Kong and Bangkok. I had established a routine of teaching Amber and she was responding well. Golly's reading and number work as well as her Thai dancing and appreciation of Thai culture had also taken great leaps forward.

* * *

At the beginning of December, on our way back to Europe, we stopped off in Karachi. George met us at the airport in a yellow Toyota Starlight with Karachi plates and the ILCK logo emblazoned all over. He drove us up to the newly rented house in the area of Gulshan-e-Iqbal. It was a four-bedroomed house in a newly built estate. There was a swimming pool at the back and a lawned garden at the front. A chokidor, or watchman, lived in a hut by the gate.

They had made it homely in the short space of time they'd been there. We settled into the two bedrooms assigned for us.

The last time we had been here, I had hardly ventured from the hotel. On this visit I wanted to get to know this large cosmopolitan port city, the commercial hub of Pakistan and home to eight million people. From what I had seen out of the car windows, nothing struck me as particularly attractive. It seemed to sprawl and have few obvious landmarks. It was hot, humid and dusty. Beggars appeared everywhere. Legless people ingeniously wheeled themselves around on skateboards. Few women were to be seen. The men, except for policemen, wore salwar kameez: loose pants and knee-length shirts. The roadside food kiosks looked far from clean. Howard warned me not to eat at them. Tied to carts were skeletal cows; scrawny chickens wandered the streets eating spit off the roads. There were no pavements.

The roads were chaotic; hand-decorated buses weaved around the streets with people hanging out of doors and from the roof. Handcarts, mechanized rickshaws, bicycles, scooters, motorbikes, mopeds, all competed for road space. Many of the cars darting in and out of the chaos dated from the 1950s; graffiti-painted trucks with Urdu lettering snorted diesel fumes into the air. Amid it all were laden camels plodding slowly down the streets, their arrogant noses held high in the air.

George and Yvonne took me to the Empress Market – named after Queen Victoria, Empress of India. The Victorian buildings dotted around the city centre were visible reminders of the British Raj. A Gothic-Mughal style clock-tower more than 50 metres high dominated the market. Inside it was teeming with humanity and food stalls, with flies buzzing everywhere. Amber and Golly didn't like it and wanted to go back to the house.

'We'll take you to Clifton Beach, it's the most exclusive part of Karachi,' George said to the girls. We drove along looking out at the Arabian Sea until we arrived at a sandy beach. The girls jumped and swam in the sea and then I took them for a camel ride.

Pakistan was not the place to go out drinking. However, although it had been alcohol-free since 1977, it was possible as a foreigner to purchase a certain amount of alcohol per month from a government-bonded warehouse. To do this you had to apply for a permit for the purchase, possession, transport or consumption of intoxicating liquor. A form available from the excise department had to be filled in declaring that you were an addict, and passports produced. The top half of the form was for opium addicts. The bottom half was for alcoholics. George, Yvonne and I filled in the bottom half, as did nearly all expats.

George took the forms and our passports into the appropriate office. We did not realize until he got back to the house that he had lost my passport. I did not rate the chances of my passport being found on the streets of Karachi and handed in to the police very highly. We drove back to the office and searched the pavements and roads immediately outside; we emptied the car and searched that. All to no avail. We drove back to the house, and arrived at the same time as a policeman on a moped.

'Judith Margaret Marks,' the policeman said as he looked directly at me.

'Yes.'

'We have your passport at the central police station; you may come and pick it up in twenty-four hours.'

'That's fantastic. But why can't I pick it up now?'

'Tomorrow. Ask for Lieutenant Salim Khan.' He rode off.

'That's crazy, George. Why can't I get it now?' I felt insecure without my passport.

'Let's have lunch and then I'll drive you to the station,' he said.

After lunch, we drove back into town to the central police station, an old colonial building on Chundigar Road. It was surprisingly empty and quiet inside. I asked for Lieutenant Khan. George and I were escorted up a wide sweeping staircase to the first floor and then along a passageway to an office that was bare apart from a wooden desk with a policeman behind it. He jumped to his feet as we entered the room.

'Ah, Judith Marks. I ask you to come tomorrow.'

'We were passing by so we thought we would call in,' said George as he held out his hand and shook the policeman's.

'I see. I see,' he said. He opened an otherwise empty drawer, removed my passport and handed it to me. He looked very proud, as if he had solved the crime of the century. Maybe he wanted to hold onto it for another twenty-four hours to show off to his colleagues. It was most bizarre.

The following morning Golly woke up very ill. Malik and his nephew Aftab, who looked like a young Omar Sharif, called round to see how she was. Malik had his driver take Golly and me to his doctor. She had acute dysentery. The doctor thought she had probably caught it in the sea. While she recovered, we delayed our return to Europe for two weeks. We were to meet Howard's parents and sister in Switzerland for Christmas.

Howard divided his time between Karachi and Bangkok while I concentrated on teaching Amber and making Golly strong again. One evening Yvonne babysat and George took me for a drink at the American Club, the only establishment in Karachi where you could buy an alcoholic drink. The son of the manager was one of his students at the ILCK.

We walked in. I stopped in my tracks. Sitting at a table by the window was one of the faces I least expected to see. It was Michael Stephenson. I had not seen him since Hutchinson had humiliated him on the witness stand, and I did not want to see him now. He was deep in conversation with a white man in glasses with receding hair.

I turned my back to them before they could see me and faced George.

'George, do you see those two guys sitting by the window?'

'Yes.'

'Do you know them?'

'No, not to talk to, but they are often in here. The one with glasses is DEA. I think his name is Harlan,' he said.

'Harlan Bowe?'

'That's right, and the other one is English Customs, something Stephenson. All the embassies out here have a drugs liaison officer attached. One of Yvonne's students is the wife of the Dutch drugs guy.'

'Can we leave?' I asked. I was feeling faint.

On the drive back, I explained to George who Bowe and Stephenson were. George was unperturbed; he was running a respectable language school. Howard's past had nothing to do with him.

Harlan Lee Bowe was the DEA agent case officer in charge of the 1973 speaker scam. Pete had told me stories of Bowe's obsession with him. Both Bowe and Stephenson would love to bust Howard and Pete. I wondered if they knew Howard was a frequent visitor here. They were bound to, I thought. It was their job. Was that, I now wondered, why the policeman had wanted to hold onto my passport for twenty-four hours?

Did Howard know that Bowe and Stephenson were based here? I would now have to wait until we met up in Switzerland to ask him. If he did, why hadn't he told me?

CHAPTER TWENTY
Busted

Just before Christmas we heard from Pete that the load Howard had sent to the naval base in Alameda had been busted. Howard was not looking forward to telling Malik, but once again Malik was understanding.

We spent Christmas at the ski resort town of Davos. We were glad to be back in Europe, but disappointed with the service at our five-star hotel after having become used to the faultless Far East. Howard's parents and sister arrived the day after us and booked into a hotel close to ours.

'Howard,' I asked at the earliest opportunity, 'did you know that Michael Stephenson and Harlan Bowe were in Karachi?'

'No, I didn't. Malik said he would find out for me which drugs officers were there. How do you know?'

'I saw them at the American Club.'

'Did they see you?'

'No, I don't think so. I left.'

'You've nothing to worry about, Jude. You were just visiting your brother, who runs a respectable school.'

'But they're bound to know you're always there. Doesn't that worry you?'

'Not particularly. Malik and I have legitimate businesses. Malik has just made me a director of Mehar Paper Mills and the language school is doing well,' he said. I noticed a crease appear on his forehead.

'They are hardly going to think that's your reason for going to Karachi, Howard.'

'Maybe not. However, unless they catch me doing something, which they won't, they can speculate all they like. The whole thing is about avoiding mistakes and knowing the opponent.'

'Howard, with that load that's just been busted they are sure to be investigating thoroughly. And they're bound to be unhappy that one of their naval bases was being used.'

'It will probably be an internal investigation. I didn't tell you but the man who was supposed to be getting it out died of a heart attack. So he won't be able to tell them much. Don't worry, Jude.'

The next few days we concentrated on Howard's parents and sister. We took horse-drawn sleigh rides and enjoyed a white Christmas. The girls and I had ski lessons and bought a toboggan. For New Year, Howard, the girls and I returned to the Splendide in Lugano and had dinner at the Taverna.

From here we returned to Palma to check on the work on the house. It was still far from finished, but beginning to look good. We flew to London.

'Jude, what do you say I go into partnership with Balando and Orca?'

'I think it would be a wonderful idea. How do they feel?'

'Well, what they want are street-front premises in London. It's hard for them to expand from their present location. I thought if I offered them investment in return for becoming a co-director of the company they might go for it.'

'How much investment were you thinking of?'

'I thought somewhere around £100,000.'

'That's a lot of money. I thought with all these deals going down you'd be short.'

'Well, the deals I've done with Phil have been successful.'

It was as I suspected. There were a bunch more deals going on.

'Would you want active involvement in the travel company?'

'I'd love to. I find it an interesting business.'

'Well, I think it's a great idea. Why don't we take them out for dinner and talk about it,' I said.

Balando and Orca leapt at the chance of expanding their business and made Howard a partner. Howard closed down the offices at Carlisle Street, which were now losing money, and a search began for new offices for Hong Kong International Travel Centre. A large shop front and offices were eventually found and rented on Denman Street, just off Piccadilly Circus.

Howard threw himself into his new business with enthusiasm. He and Balando went on a visit to China for talks with CACC, the Chinese national airline. On the way back, he stopped off to see Phil in Bangkok. He arrived back in London with tales of his visit to China and photos of the Great Wall and Ming tombs.

'How's Phil?' I asked.

'He's opening a massage parlour in the Hyatt Hotel, Bangkok. Look what he's given me.' He handed me a business card.

Howard Marks
Procurement Manager

'Don't you think that's funny, Jude?' he said, with a wide grin.

'No, I think it's sick.'

'But, Jude, it's a lot more interesting than most business cards.'

'I don't think so. It just says you're a dirty old man. You know I hate all that sleazy shit.' Since my visit to Bangkok, I had learnt a lot more about the sex industry there, and what I had learnt had sickened me.

Howard returned from the travel offices the next day looking worried. 'Pete's been busted,' he said.

'How, when and what for?'

'I'm not sure. He's still in the nick. Flash wasn't sure of all the details. He thinks it's for the 1973 speaker scam. He'll phone again when he has more news.'

The speaker scam was over twelve years ago. Pete had the best lawyers, police, politicians, CIA agents and more on his payroll. Pete had always told me that the US law enforcement rarely went after drug-smuggling fugitives because they didn't have the money or manpower necessary. How had this happened?

Flash phoned a week later to let us know Pete was out on bail and that it was for the 1973 speaker scam. Patrick phoned and wanted to know if the girls and I were going to visit this Easter. Howard said he had to go to Australia for the travel agency, and if I went to California we could then all meet in Sydney. I liked this idea.

'Jude, maybe when you're in California you could meet Pete for a drink and see how he is.'

'Do you think that's a good idea if he's just been busted?'

'He'd love to see you, and you can take over a copy of *High Time* for him.'

I applied for Australian visas for the children and me. My friend Frances was also on her way to Sydney with her young daughter Bridie and had decided to have a stopover in LA. Her partner Patrick was currently working in Sydney. Frances and I arranged to meet in Los Angeles and take the children to Disneyland and Universal Studios.

Orca booked our round-the-world tickets. We were to fly London–New York–Los Angeles–Hawaii–Sydney–Hong Kong–Bangkok–London.

Howard drove us to Heathrow on 31 March. After dropping us off he was on his way to apply for his Australian visa. We spent a couple of days in New York, where I took the children on a helicopter tour of the city.

We arrived in Los Angeles early evening. We took a taxi straight to the hotel where rooms adjoining Frances and Bridie's had been booked for us by HKIT. We expected them to have already checked in, but reception told me they had not done so.

The porter carried our bags to our room. When he had left, I noticed there were dirty glasses from the last occupants. The mini-bar was empty and I noticed traces of white powder on the dressing table and remnants of a joint in the ashtray. It looked like a bunch of drug dealers had just checked out. I phoned the reception desk and complained the room was dirty. They were offhand and suggested I sat in the coffee shop while they sent the housekeeper up. I wondered where Frances was.

When we returned to our room, I unlocked the connecting door to the room Frances was booked into. Frances and Bridie were there asleep.

'Oh hi, Judy,' said Frances sleepily.

'Sorry, I didn't mean to disturb you. Reception told me you hadn't arrived yet.'

'They're odd down there. They disappeared for over half an hour with my passport and kept giving me suspicious looks and were so unfriendly,' Frances said.

The following morning after breakfast we returned to our rooms.

'Judy, someone has gone through my luggage,' said Frances.

'Are you sure?' I asked, walking into her room.

'Absolutely. I had all Bridie's clothes neatly packed on top – now look.'

'Is anything missing?'

'Not that I can see.'

'I'm going to check mine,' I said.

I walked into my room and opened my case. Like Frances's it had been tampered with. Amber's neatly piled textbooks were in disarray, as were our clothes. What were they looking for, and who were they?

'Judy, I don't like this hotel. I don't like the way they behave towards me at reception.'

'Let's check out. Last year I stayed in the Hollywood Holiday Inn. It's okay and convenient for Disneyland,' I said.

I rented a car and we checked out.

Three days later Frances flew to Sydney and the children and I flew up to Santa Cruz. The cousins were delighted to be together again and we had a great time. Howard phoned me. The Australians had refused his visa request because of his conviction on the 1973 speaker scam. He said he would meet us in Hong Kong instead.

Pete phoned while I was at Patrick's. He had bail set at $100,000 on condition he stayed at his father's house in Long Beach, California. He gave me the phone number. I said I would see him after visiting Natasha in San Diego. Howard suggested I met Pete at the Newporter Inn in Newport Beach, the hotel he'd been staying in when he first heard of the 1973 speaker bust on the television.

I drove from San Diego and phoned Pete when I had booked into the hotel. He asked me to book him and Patti an adjoining room. They arrived the following day. Patti seemed healthier than the last time I had seen her, still tired-looking but her weight was down. Pete was a bit the worse for drink and his appearance once again shocked me. His right nostril had almost disappeared.

'Mummy, what's happened to Uncle Pete's nose?' Amber asked.

'He's been silly and naughty. He's been taking a drug called cocaine, which is making him ill. It eats your nose if you take a lot,' I said.

'Why does he do it?' she asked.

'Because it makes him feel nice for a little while,' I said, feeling unsure how much to say. Amber was a bright child and I saw little point in not telling her the truth. I also thought it might scare her from dabbling in it herself when she was older. I had played around with drugs at a young age but I didn't want my children to. I had by now seen too many people hurt.

I later found her in his room wagging her finger at him and telling him about the misuse of drugs. He looked rather taken aback at being lectured by a seven-year-old. He promised her he would do his best.

Howard phoned my room and asked me to fetch Pete. The two of them spent well over an hour talking while Patti and I played with the girls in the pool. Patti told me she thought she had finally kicked the cocaine habit and was hoping she could get Pete to do the same. I asked her what she felt about Tom and Karl at the moment.

'Those guys do my head in. One minute I think they're good friends, and then I think they're just trying to fleece us,' she said. 'They phoned Pete's dad and said for $500,000 they could get the charge dropped.'

'Do you think they could?'

'I don't know what to think. Pete is having a meeting with them next week.'

'What's happened to your house on Lake Tahoe?'

'They confiscated it and all the contents and all our cars and bikes.'

'I'm so sorry, Patti. I wish there was something I could do.'

'Get that husband of yours to send a load that doesn't get caught or found,' she replied.

Two days later we said goodbye to Pete and Patti. Pete promised Amber he'd be good. Patti came out to the car to see us off. I handed her a copy of *High Time*.

It was the last time we ever saw Pete.

In the middle of the night we flew into Honolulu. All I could see from the hotel window the next morning was concrete. The children had been looking forward to coming to Hawaii. I had shown them photographs of deserted sandy beaches. From where I stood I could not even see the sea. I rang for room service and was told there was a two-hour wait. I went down to the lobby and bought a guidebook. Hawaii couldn't possibly all be like this. I read about a resort on the north side of the island called Turtle Bay. We checked out and took a taxi. Our new hotel was on a peninsula with miles of pristine beaches. This was the Hawaii I had imagined. We spent five days here. Close by was a Polynesian Cultural Centre where we learnt the history and customs of the Polynesian people. I bought the girls grass skirts and they learnt the traditional hula dance.

We arrived in Sydney early in the morning and took a taxi to our hotel in Double Bay. It was close to the house Frances was staying in. I was sad not to be meeting Howard here.

On the way over we had read the in-flight magazine and discovered that Australia is home to some of the most dangerous creatures in the world, including deadly snakes, spiders as well as some curious sea creatures – and sharks. We decided not to do any swimming while we were there.

Once we had settled in and unpacked, I phoned Frances. She and Patrick invited us for lunch to a seafood restaurant in one of Sydney's many bays. Afterwards, Frances and I left the children with Patrick and went for a walk on the beach.

'Judy, when I was lining up to board the aircraft to leave LA, Bridie and I were suddenly hauled out of the queue by some grotesquely fat marshals, real bastards. They got hold of all my hand luggage and just fucking emptied everything onto the ground and rummaged through it as if I was a common criminal. It was awful.'

'What did they want?' A knot of tension formed in my stomach.

'I don't know. I was absolutely furious and Bridie started screaming her head off. Then they searched me, which was disgustingly horrid. They then told me to pick everything up and just stood there watching me. I asked them why they couldn't pick it up and they said it wasn't their job.'

'What do you think it was about?'

'I've no idea. They said it was a random search and they didn't so much as apologize. It was an experience I wouldn't wish on my worst enemy.'

I could not help but feel that this incident and our cases being searched in the LA hotel were linked. And then there was Pete's bust. Things were not right.

The ten days we spent in Sydney were great fun. It was I thought the most attractive city I had visited in the world. Frances and Bridie accompanied us as we did all the tourist activities. I enjoyed it, despite my unease over recent events. On Bondi beach we sat in a café and watched the surfers, and I had the strongest feeling that I, the watcher, was being watched.

We were sad to leave Sydney, but excited to be meeting Howard in Hong Kong. While we were in Australia, he had been in the Philippines. I wondered what he had been doing there.

On 10 May 1985 Howard met us at the airport. His face lit up when he saw us. The girls ran excitedly into his arms and he enveloped us all in a huge hug.

Once again we were in our suite at the Shangri-La. The girls showered him with the small gifts they had bought and showed him photos of our trip. They put their grass skirts on and danced around him. Howard sat and watched them with a joint in his hand and a contented grin on his face.

Later, after a rest and a long hot bath and with the girls tucked up in bed, Howard and I ordered dinner in our room. I told him about our luggage being tampered with and Frances being hauled off the queue to board the plane.

'What do you make of it?' I asked.

'Well, you obviously didn't have anything incriminating on you and neither did Frances, so I wouldn't worry about it.'

'But, Howard, don't you find Pete's bust, Harlan Bowe and Stephenson both in Karachi, and mine and Frances's cases being searched and Frances hauled off a plane just a bit too much?'

'I agree it doesn't look good.'

'It doesn't look good at all. Please, just stop before it's too late.'

'Jude, I'm trying to build up the travel agency and I'm enjoying that side of things more and more. I have a perfectly legitimate reason for travelling now and Malik is far more interested in his straight businesses than the mother business.' The 'mother business' was Malik's code for drug smuggling.

'Howard, I just don't want you getting arrested again. The children and I need you. It frightens me. I'm terrified they'll arrest me too. Then what will happen to the children?'

'Yeah, I know, love, but stop being silly. You're not doing anything wrong. No one is going to arrest you.'

CHAPTER TWENTY-ONE
Elephants and Ecstasy

Over breakfast in our room, Howard told me about his trip to the Philippines.

'It's a fascinating place, Jude.'

'What made you go there?'

'Phil wanted to introduce me to his partner in the massage parlour.'

'Another slime bag?'

'No, Jude. Actually he's a British lord. Lord Anthony Patrick Cairns Berkley Moynihan, to be precise. His half-brother is Colin Moynihan, the minister for sport in Thatcher's government. He seems to have a hand in everything. He's very in with the Marcos family and government and seems to be able to arrange anything in the Philippines. I wanted to meet him to see if he could introduce me to the people in charge of Philippine Airlines. They have just started flying from Manila to Beijing. As Philippine Airlines also flies from Manila to London, I was thinking it could be an alternative route for our customers flying to China.'

'Was the lord able to help?' I asked.

'He's going to arrange a meeting some time in the next week. Would you and the kids like to come? I'm sure you'll like Moynihan – he went to Oxford.'

'Yes, I'd love to.' I was pleased Howard was devoting more time and energy to the travel business.

Five days after arriving in Hong Kong, Howard, Amber, Golly

and I caught a Philippine Airlines flight to Manila. Moynihan had sent a stretch limousine to the airport to pick us up and drive us to the Mandarin hotel, where he had booked us into VIP accommodation.

'Jude, Phil is already here in Manila. He's staying with his girl-friend and they want to have dinner with us tonight.'

'What about his wife?'

'Jude, you know what Phil's like.'

'Yeah, I know, but it just makes me feel so awkward when I'm with Pao.'

'Well, do the best you can. And Michael Heatara, the king of the Maori kingdom of Tetiti, will be joining us for dinner.'

'Where the hell is Tetiti?'

'It's a small group of islands off the coast of New Zealand. He's going to give Phil and me Tetiti diplomatic passports. He has appointed Phil as consul general to the kingdom of Thailand and I'm going to be the minister for transport and consul general in the UK.'

I started laughing. 'Can you actually travel on these passports?'

Howard grinned back. 'I don't know. We haven't got them yet.'

'How did you meet this king, Howard?'

'At that lunch party I told you about at Moynihan's.'

Later, with the children in bed and their Filipino babysitter watching over them, we went down to the bar to await Phil and his girlfriend. They arrived shortly after we had sat down.

'Jude, this is Marie-Tess. Marie-Tess, this is Howard's wife, Judy,' said Phil.

Phil's girlfriend bore an uncanny likeness to his ex-girlfriend Shirley, despite been a Filipina. During the evening I learnt that he had bought her a flat in Manila, which is where he stayed when visiting the Philippines.

A tall, burly, dark-haired and dark-skinned man came over to join us. He shook hands with Phil and Howard and kissed Marie-Tess.

'Michael, I would like you to meet my wife, Judy.'

'Enchanted,' he said as he bowed and kissed my hand.

After a couple of drinks at the bar we made our way to the hotel restaurant.

Over dinner Michael complained that his race was speeding to oblivion. This was why he had made a declaration of independence, establishing the Maori kingdom in the South Pacific 'so my people can have a place to call their own, their rightful place in the sun'. His worries were how to finance this new kingdom. Howard had suggested to him that he accepted people's nuclear waste for a fee. Phil and Howard said they would supply him with a list of the companies wanting to dispose of nuclear waste. Michael was up for it, which is why he was giving Phil and Howard diplomatic passports. Phil later claimed it was the contracts they negotiated that led eventually to the storm over nuclear waste when Greenpeace's *Rainbow Warrior* was despatched to New Zealand.

Phil by now had several successful straight businesses. He owned and managed with a Chinese partner Topp Food, an export food business sending tuna and pineapple slices, instead of Thai sticks, around the world. He also had a manpower business, Sarco Siam, with two Englishmen called Kevin and Dennis. They supplied cheap labour to the Saudis. The Philippines was one of their sources. It sounded to me a bit like modern-day slave trading. There was also the massage parlour in Bangkok he co-owned with Moynihan. Despite all these 'straight' concerns, he was still heavily involved in marijuana smuggling, mainly, as far as I knew, supplying Australia. He was a wealthy man, though you wouldn't know it by looking at him. He still dressed the same as he had always done.

Marie-Tess offered to be my guide while we were in Manila. I gratefully accepted.

The following day Balando flew in from London. Lord Moynihan had set up a meeting between Balando and Howard and Martin Bonoan and Roman Cruz, president and chairman respectively of Philippine Airlines.

The Philippines has many different languages and dialects but most Filipinos speak tolerably good American-influenced English. Marcos was elected president in 1965. By 1970 widespread poverty, rising inflation, pitiful public funding and widespread corruption had triggered a string of protests. When several demonstrators were killed by the police outside the presidential palace of Malacañang,

Marcos's image as a political saviour was shot to bits. In 1972 he imposed martial law to keep himself in power and to protect his foreign business friends. He raised money by handing over prime land to foreign investors and imposing taxes on those who could least afford them.

Thousands of anti-government suspects were jailed, exiled or killed. In 1981 he let the country vote again but rigged the elections. He claimed to have won over 80 per cent of the vote. American Vice-President George Bush Snr travelled to Manila to congratulate Marcos on 'the preservation of democratic principles'.

In 1983 Marcos's exiled political rival, Benigno Aquino, returned to the Philippines. Thugs gunned him down and he became a martyr. The thugs, it was commonly believed, belonged to Marcos.

While Howard and Balando were at their meeting with the Philippine Airlines executives, Marie-Tess took the children and I around the city. Shops ranged from simple street markets to ritzy boutiques. Everywhere were milling crowds, noise and traffic jams, and dirt in the gutters and pollution in the air. Jeepneys, gaily painted jeeps with two lengthways benches in the back, acted as buses and taxis. They were decorated with horns, badges, crucifixes, images of the Virgin Mary, aerials and mirrors, and sometimes had a padded interior. In the front a tape deck blared out rock or pop music. Another form of taxi was the tricycle, the Philippine answer to the rickshaw: a little roofed sidecar bolted to a motorbike or bicycle. Horse-drawn two-wheeled carts known as kalesa were also used as taxis. And among all this madness would be the occasional stretch limo, and several expensive Mercedes and BMWs with bulletproof windows. In the streets you could feel tension in the air. If I had known the political situation beforehand, I probably wouldn't have come to Manila.

Lord Moynihan arranged a large dinner to take place at the restaurant in our hotel one evening. I was yet to meet the lord and his third wife Editha and I was curious to do so after all I had heard about him from Howard and Phil.

Lord Moynihan, the 3rd Baron Moynihan of Leeds, had fled Britain and his seat in the House of Lords in 1969, just as Scotland Yard was about to charge him for some complex fraud. He had been the Liberal Party spokesman for African affairs. He had scandalized society by marrying an Pakistani fire-eating dancer in the 1960s. She had performed in nightclubs around the world as Princess Amina. For a while Moynihan sought refuge in Franco's Spain, then made his way to Australia where he took to playing the bongos in a Sydney nightclub. He finally ended up in the Philippines. The British tabloids described him as the Barmy Baron.

His second wife was at one time a secretary at the Philippine embassy in Pakistan. After her marriage to Moynihan ended, she went on to own and manage massage parlours. She also remarried. Her new husband was called Robert Walden; he and Moynihan disliked each other but still had dealings together. The wife he had now was in her early twenties, twenty-seven years his junior. She was an ex-lingerie model he had met when she was sixteen.

Howard and I settled the children and went down to the bar, where a few of Moynihan's guests had already assembled. Howard introduced me to the two Philippine Airline executives, Ramon Cruz and Martin Bonoan. He also introduced me to a London solicitor called Jimmy Newton and his Australian wife Helen, and an armed tattooed Australian called Joe Smith, who I later learnt was the first person to smuggle marijuana into Australia. Phil and Marie-Tess arrived with the king, and Balando joined us.

Presently I heard a booming voice.

'I'll be over to you all in a minute.'

I turned to look at the owner of the plummy accent. I could see a man in his early fifties, about six foot tall, greyish-haired and dressed in a short-sleeved white shirt that covered an enormous belly. He was with an exquisite young Filipino woman, and a tallish, brown-haired man, who I later learnt was the Frederick, of the 1960s singing duo Nina and Frederick. His real name was Baron Frederick von Pallandt; he used to have a house on Ibiza.

Eventually Moynihan came over to us.

'Tony, I'd like you to meet my wife, Judy. Judy, this is Tony,' said Howard.

'Delighted to meet you, my dear,' he said, as he took my hand and kissed it.

He turned round and in his booming voice called out, 'Editha, Editha, over here.'

His exquisite young wife scuttled over. 'Editha, this is Howard's wife, Judy. Judy, this is my wife, Editha.'

'Judy, welcome to Manila. I hope you enjoy your stay here,' she said in a Filipino American accent.

We sat down for dinner. Throughout, Lord Moynihan dominated the conversation, his voice drowning out the rest.

'Judy, have you met Jimmy? We went to Stowe public school together and then up to Oxford. Jimmy got first-class honours in history.'

'Yes, Howard introduced us,' I said, and smiled at Jimmy.

I later learnt that Jimmy was a supplier of fake British passports.

'I tell you, old boy,' he boomed to Jimmy Newton, 'everyone in the higher echelons of British society is a homosexual, a pervert or a spy.'

'So, Tony, talking of the higher echelons of British society,' I asked, 'what happened to Lord Lucan?'

'Lucan – he's lying at the bottom of the English Channel.'

'What about the sightings of him all over the place?'

'A load of old rubbish. I'm telling you he's in the Channel. Now on Sunday, Judy, before you leave, I want you, Howard and the children to come for lunch. After lunch we'll play Trivial Pursuits.'

'That sounds good. I'll look forward to it.'

'It'll be me and Editha against you and Howard.'

'Sounds like a challenge, Tony.'

After the dinner, Tony and Editha wanted us to go for drinks in a few Manila bars. His chauffeur dropped us off at one seedy bar after another. Lord and Lady Moynihan were well known in them all. I subsequently found out that many of these bars Moynihan owned.

The following evening Howard and I spent with Amber and Golly. Balando had returned to England and Phil to Bangkok. Howard and Balando were pleased with their talks with the Philippine Airline executives and further meetings had been scheduled. We took the children to a touristy dinner show and then to an extraordinary folk-music club called the Hobbit House, where all the waiters were dwarfs. Four-year-old Golly was delighted to be, for the first time in her life, taller than some adults.

On Sunday at one, Moynihan sent his car to pick us up. It was a tired-looking American Cadillac. Sunday lunches at Lord Moynihan's were well known in Manila society. While I was in Sydney Howard had met Elizabeth Marcos, the president's sister, at one of them. Many other high-ranking government officials had been there as well, and also the self-proclaimed king of the Maoris. Today it was to be just Tony, Editha, Amber, Golly, Howard and me.

The car drove us to the Alabang area of Manila. We passed several embassies and large houses with beautifully tended tropical gardens before drawing up in front of security gates manned by armed guards. We drove in through the gates and up a sweeping drive to an impos-ing house surrounded by sweetly smelling tropical plants and palm trees. It had been the home of the Peruvian ambassador.

A servant dressed in white ran down the steps and opened the car doors for us. Another similarly dressed servant ushered us up the steps and into the house. Here a beaming Moynihan stood, wearing white linen trousers and a blue silk smoking jacket tied with a belt over his large belly, a fat Havana cigar in his chubby hand. He looked like a lord.

'Welcome, welcome. Ah, what beautiful children you have, Howard, Judy,' he boomed. 'I want you pretty girls to call me Uncle Tony.' He took their hands and kissed them, then ushered us all into a comfortable living room full of African paintings, wooden statues and tusks. A stuffed lion's head hung on the wall.

'It looks like you're fond of Africa,' I said.

'Well, dear girl, I used to be the minister of African affairs. Now come out on to the veranda and have some champagne,' he said. He clicked his fingers at one of the servants.

Editha joined us and spent her time playing with Amber and Golly. She seemed to take as much delight in dressing their Barbie dolls as they did.

'How long have you lived here, Tony?' I asked, as I spread foie gras on thinly sliced toast for the children.

'Seventeen years now, and I know everyone who matters. My only complaint about the Philippines is the cuisine, which has combined the worst elements of Chinese with the worst elements of Spanish, creating an inedible gruel. It's so hard to get decent quality caviar out here, even with my back door connections. Any decent food has to be imported. You do know, don't you, that I'm the man who introduced asparagus to the Philippines?'

I found Moynihan at times uncomfortably pompous.

Over lunch I could see that Howard, because of his education, appealed to the intellectual snob in Moynihan, and vice versa. It also became apparent that Moynihan worshipped people with 'serious money', which is what he thought Howard had; an illusion Howard did nothing to dispel. He also revelled in his own criminality and his relationships with criminals. He described the hated slum landlord Rachman, who he claimed was the nearest he had to a father, as a kind and gentle man.

Over coffee Moynihan brought out the Trivial Pursuits. Much to Howard's and my delight, and to Moynihan's embarrassment and Editha's amusement, we thrashed them.

'Too many science questions,' said Moynihan.

After coffee his driver took us to the airport, where we caught an early flight back to Hong Kong.

The following morning, back in our suite at the Shangri-La, the phone rang and Howard answered it.

'Hello … Yes, this is Howard … Oh hi, Gerry, Pete told me to expect your call … You're checked into this hotel? Okay, what's your room number? … I'll be up within the hour.'

'Who was that?' I asked.

'Gerry Wills, a friend of Pete's. Did Pete not mention him to you?' said Howard.

'No,' I said. 'Tell me.'

'The meeting was arranged when you were staying with him at the Newporter Inn. He wants to buy ten tons of hash.'

'I thought you were going to stop, Howard.'

'Pete asked me if I would introduce Gerry to Malik. I said I would. Now there's no harm in that, is there, Jude?'

'I'm not going to say any more, Howard. You're obviously not going to listen to me.'

Shortly afterwards Howard left the room to go and visit Gerry. I thought about leaving Howard, but I couldn't see what that would achieve beyond making us all unhappy, and I loved him too much to leave anyway. The phone rang again.

'Jude, Gerry has his wife Wyvonna with him. Do you want to book a babysitter and we'll all have dinner together?'

'Okay. Does eight o'clock sound good?'

At eight o'clock there was a knock on our door. Howard opened it. In walked in a very tall man, blond and blue-eyed, in his mid to late thirties, dressed in light grey trousers with a blue and white shirt that wasn't tucked in and covered a paunch.

'Jude, this is Gerry. Gerry, this is my wife, Judy,' Howard said.

'Hi, Judy, nice to meet you. My wife Wyvonna will be down in a few minutes,' he said in a laid-back Californian accent.

A few minutes later there was another knock on the door. Howard opened it to an attractive Faye Dunaway lookalike about four years older than me, clutching a bottle of Evian water.

'Hi, guys,' she said.

'Wyvonna, this is my wife, Judy. Judy, Wyvonna,' said Howard.

'Hey, great to meet you and you've got your kids here. That's so cool. I can't wait to meet them. Are they in bed? We've got two little girls too, Isis and Mimmi. I'm so excited to be here. I can't wait to go shopping. Will you show me around, Judy?'

'Okay, honey, just calm down a bit,' Gerry said to her.

'Yeah, okay, hon. Do either of you guys want an E?' Wyvonna asked.

We weren't familiar with E. Gerry gave a rather technical explanation, looking a little embarrassed by his wife.

'Love-making is just divine on it, isn't it, hon?' said Wyvonna.

'Yeah,' said Gerry, his pale complexion turning slightly pinkish.

'I'll think we'll pass for now. I only ever smoke marijuana or hash. That's enough for me,' said Howard. He proceeded to roll a joint.

'Well, let me know if you change your mind. I brought plenty with me and it's not illegal.' Wyvonna popped a pill into her mouth.

We ate dinner in a Japanese sushi bar.

'Do you ever smuggle cocaine, Howard?' asked Gerry.

'No. I think it's the devil's drug, along with heroin,' said Howard.

'There's bloody good money in it though, Howard. I used to fly planes from Colombia up to California; you get such a buzz from those runs. You have to fly real low to avoid the AWACS planes. I once employed a member of the US skydiving team to parachute a load of cocaine into the US – that was a real laugh.'

'Have you ever smuggled from Asia to the US before, Gerry?' Howard asked.

'No, this is a first. They're gasping for good hash in California at the moment,' said Gerry.

'Oh, I'll make sure it's the best,' said Howard.

'I forgot to ask you earlier – can each slab have a slogan stamped on it?'

'I should think so. What were you thinking of?'

'I hate those commie bastards out in Afghanistan. I was thinking of a drawing: a pair of Kalashnikov rifles, underlining the legend "Smoke Russia Away".'

'You're a real American boy at heart, aren't you, Gerry?' I was amused at the idea of a political slogan on a slab of dope.

Gerry and Wyvonna, whom Howard and I nicknamed Mr and Mrs E, loved Hong Kong. They decided to accompany us to Bangkok, too. Howard wanted Gerry to meet Phil. We flew together on Thai Airways and booked into the Peninsula, a fairly new luxury hotel. It was close by to the Erawan buddhist shrine, one of Golly's favourite places to pray.

I wanted to take Wyvonna and the children to the floating market, where boats were piled high with tropical fruit and vegetables and where floating kitchens served steaming hot soup, heated by a stove improbably and precariously balanced in the stern. We climbed into a long-tailed boat powered by a diesel engine for the journey to the market along the canals. The canals in and around Bangkok are an important part of the city. People live alongside them in houses built of teak and use boats as a method of transport.

The canals themselves are used for bathing and laundry. The boat trip offered an intimate glimpse into local life. Wyvonna, however, kept up an incessant chatter.

'Look at that cute child! I'll take that one home, ooh, and that one there,' she said as if she was in a shopping mall in California. Every hour or so she popped another pill into her mouth.

In the evening after settling the children, Wyvonna and I made our way to the Superstar bar. As we walked in the door we spotted Gerry watching a young girl writhing up and down a pole. Wyvonna walked up to him and slapped him round the face.

'I know that look,' she screamed at him.

The following day they left Bangkok. They were going back to the States to buy a boat to pick up the hashish from Pakistan. Before Wyvonna left she pressed her few remaining Es into my hand.

'Although they're not illegal, Gerry says it's best I don't fly back to the States with them,' she said.

Howard left for Karachi to see Malik about Gerry's 10 tons. We arranged to meet in a few days back in London. That evening Sandy, who had fled from England all those years ago after being followed by Customs to Maidstone College and never gone back, called round to see me at the hotel. George and Yvonne, who were having a week's holiday in Bangkok, came round too. Howard had by this time installed Jim Hobbs as caretaker of the school and general dogsbody to George and Yvonne.

Sandy and I decided to try Wyvonna's Es. George and Yvonne declined.

After about an hour my body began to feel cushioned and I felt myself turning into a laid-back Californian. A knock came at the door and a waiter brought in a bottle of Dom Perignon we had ordered earlier. I looked at the champagne and felt nauseous. I couldn't stand the thought of any alcohol. Sandy felt like me and declined. George and Yvonne drank the champagne. I also went off the taste of cigarettes. Amber got out of bed and wandered in; she must have picked up a vibe in the room.

'Mummy, you're so naughty.'

'What's up, Amber?' I asked as I reached out to give her a hug.

'You're like Mrs E,' she said, and marched back to bed leaving me feeling guilty.

The following morning the effects of the E had still not worn off. I didn't want to fly back to London so instead booked seats for the girls and me to fly to Chiang Mai in northern Thailand. It was a spur-of-the-moment decision, and because I was feeling so relaxed I failed to let anyone know where I was going.

From Chiang Mai we found ourselves on a two-day elephant trek through the hills and forests of northern Thailand with only a young boy as our guide, visiting remote villagers. It was a fascinating glimpse into a different life. Although the villagers were used to seeing Western adults, judging by their curiosity in Amber and Golly they were less used to Western children.

Back in Bangkok, the hotel reception informed me there were a number of messages from my husband in London. I phoned him.

'Jude, where have you been? Why are you still there? You're meant to be back here.'

'Oh, Howard, we had a really cool time. We went up to Chiang Mai and got an elephant up through the jungle. We went to visit these hill tribes who live so quietly and peacefully. Such simple lives. No alcohol, no cigarettes. You should try it,' I said, still feeling slightly laid-back.

'Jude, just get the next plane back. Sandy told me what you took. Just come home now.'

I could almost hear him tearing his hair out in exasperation.

CHAPTER TWENTY-TWO
A Son and No Pope

When I arrived back in London, the E had completely worn off.

Beyond teasing me for a bit, Howard said no more about it. We left London and moved into our new house in La Vileta, Mallorca. Masha, who spoke good Spanish, moved with us.

Patrick, Jude, Peggy and Bridie came to stay, as well as Podge and a friend of hers. It was a busy summer for visitors. Howard turned forty and I baked him a large hash cake.

At the end of August we returned to London for the official opening of the offices of Hong Kong International Travel. The People's Republic of China's ambassador to London His Excellency Hu Ding-Yi and his wife Madame Xie Heng had agreed to open them. Golly was presenting the ambassador's wife with a bouquet. Over a hundred people from the travel industry were present. Other guests were the local MP Peter Brooke, the Right Honourable Lord Bethell, MEP, senior members of foreign embassies and Hong Kong government officials. We had also invited all our friends and family, including Phil, who had flown in specially from Bangkok. Hong Kong International was now the tenth largest travel agency in Britain and was the one doing most of the ticketing to China and Hong Kong. Howard's parents looked proud and happy. It looked like Howard was successful and straight. I thought how devastated they would be if they knew the truth.

We returned to Palma in time for Amber and Golly to start their new school: Queens College, Palma. Within two weeks they were both put up a class. My teaching had clearly been a success. But Golly came home from school one day cross with me.

'Mummy, why have you never told me what a runt is,' she said with her little hands on her hips.

'Sorry, Golls, but that's why you go to school. To learn new things. Mummy can't teach you everything.'

Masha got herself a job crewing on a luxury yacht and was busy pampering the likes of Paul McCartney and his family. She was away for weeks at a time.

'Howard, I've had two phone lines put in. Can you just give one number out and we keep the other for family and straight friends?'

'It's okay, Jude; I've installed Hobbs in Amsterdam. Everyone will call that number and he'll reroute them here.'

We settled into our new life in Palma, gradually making new friends among the expat community – mainly through meeting the parents of the children's friends. Howard introduced himself to our new acquaintances as a travel agent and paper mill owner. It was unique for us to have no one knowing our past and I enjoyed it for the short time it lasted.

For half-term we returned to London and Howard took us all to see *The Mousetrap* in the West End before he flew out to Karachi and loaded Gerry's boat up with 10 tons of 'Smoke Russia Away' slabs.

We spent Christmas in the flat in London.

'Jude, I'm moving Hobbs to Portugal, to Lisbon,' Howard said.

'Why? I thought you said he liked Amsterdam.'

'He's had a funny feeling the phones were being tapped.'

'That's a bit worrying, isn't it?'

'Well, he's got no definite proof they were so they might not have been. But just in case he thought it best he moved somewhere else.'

When we got back to Palma the telephone began ringing at all hours of the day and night. I answered calls from Gerry, Phil, Pete, Old John, Hobbs, Malik and others.

'Howard, you said this wouldn't happen.'

'Jude, Hobbs said he would have the phones working in Lisbon by the end of next week.'

'But that's not going to stop them calling here. They've all got this number now.'

Malik phoned early in the mornings. Howard was avoiding talking to him.

'Jude, tell him I'm driving the kids to school or I'm away in Paris.'

One Saturday morning it was Malik again. 'Morning. Is D.H. Marks there?'

'No, sorry, Malik. He had to go to Barcelona last night.'

'Please tell him that your brother Mr George's home was burgled yesterday and many things disappeared. It is of the utmost importance that I talk to him.'

I repeated the conversation to Howard who was lying next to me.

'He's probably just saying it to get me to talk to him. He wants money and until Gerry gives me some I don't have anything to give him,' Howard said.

'Howard, I like Malik and I hate lying to him all the time. Please talk to him soon. By the way, I got a letter from Patrick telling me they've moved from Santa Cruz to Coral Gables in Miami and would I bring the girls over soon to visit them there.'

'That will be nice for you, and make a change for Amber and Golly from California. Jude, I spoke to Gerry yesterday and he and Wyvonna are separating.'

'Well, that hardly surprises me giving the way he was in Bangkok,' I said.

'Do you know, Jude, he told me he spends well over $200,000 a year on hookers?'

Much as Wyvonna had driven me mad, I was fond of her and hoped she was all right.

Later that evening, watching the news on satellite TV, we saw that Marcos's regime had fallen. It was February 1986.

'What effect do you think this will have on Moynihan?' I asked.

'I was just wondering that myself. Phil's coming here in a couple of days and might well have some news.'

A couple of days later Phil arrived. He booked into a hotel in central Palma but spent most of his time at our house. He felt that Moynihan would be feeling insecure with the fall of Marcos because he had so ingratiated himself with the Marcos regime.

One evening after dinner, when the children had gone to bed and Howard and Phil had gone out drinking, the doorbell went. I picked up the intercom.

'Hey, Judy, it's Ricky, will you let me in a minute?'

'Howard's not here,' I said, hoping he'd go away. I was not keen on the East End villains or Howard's involvement with them.

'Okay. Well, can I just come in and leave you a message to give him.'

'Okay,' I said and buzzed the gate open.

It was winter and the double wooden doors to the veranda were locked. I unlocked them as I heard Ricky Hawkins approaching. As I was opening them, they were knocked wide, sending me sprawling backwards, hitting my shoulder on the marble floor. I looked up in surprise into Ricky's face; his brown eyes were hard and expressionless.

'Where are they? Where's H and that scumbag Phil?'

I understood now why one of his nicknames was the Screamer. 'I don't know – they've gone out drinking.'

He pulled a knife from his pocket. The eight-inch blade glinted in the light from a lamp.

'Where?'

'I don't know, Ricky, they could be anywhere,' I said.

'Get up and sit in that chair and don't move,' he yelled, indicating a nearby rattan armchair. He sat opposite me on an identical chair and picked up the telephone. From the number of digits dialled I could tell it was an international call.

'I've got her,' he said. 'Right ... Right ... Okay, I'll call you in an hour and give you a report.' Ricky put the phone down and glared at me.

'You surprise me, Ricky. I wouldn't have expected such behaviour of you.' My comment was met with an angry glare.

'May I at least offer you a drink?' I said.

'I don't drink.'

'Oh, that's right. You don't drink, you don't smoke but you do like the odd bird,' I said. 'Well, I would like a glass of wine. Would you like a glass of orange juice, or water?'

'Orange juice will do.'

We were in the seating area of the kitchen, so he was able to watch me as I rose from my chair and went to the fridge. I poured him a glass of orange juice and opened myself a bottle of white Rioja before returning to my chair.

'So how is Sharon?' I asked.

'Fine.'

'So how would she feel about you holding me at knifepoint?'

'Just shut up and drink your wine,' he screamed.

We sat in silence that hung in the air like smoke for a good hour. Then he made another call to someone I could only imagine was his boss. Less than charitable thoughts towards Howard and Phil went through my mind.

'Situation the same, nothing to report yet. I'll phone again in an hour.'

The doorbell rang. Ricky jumped to his feet.

'Who's that?'

'I'm not expecting anyone. Maybe it's Howard and he's forgotten or lost his keys.'

The doors to the veranda still stood ajar and in the distance I could hear my name being called.

'It's Justo. You can buzz him in,' said Ricky.

Ricky and Justo were close friends and Justo looked after Ricky's properties on the island. I was relieved. I couldn't imagine Justo condoning Ricky's behaviour. He rushed in. From his dishevelled look and worried expression, it seemed to me that he had been expecting to find Ricky up to no good.

'Now, Ricky, this is no way to solve a problem,' Justo said in a quiet voice.

'It's my way and I'm going to hold her until I get my hands on that scumbag. He's been avoiding me for weeks. He better not

avoid me any more or he'll have to answer the consequences.' Ricky
was still screaming, his body quivering with anger. Justo was no
match for Ricky. Ricky was six foot four with a large frame and had
spent many years keeping physically fit while a guest of Her Majesty
the Queen. Justo was my height, five foot seven, and slight.

Justo tried to reason with Ricky. 'Look, why don't we go into
Palma and look for them in the bars?'

'No way, we wait here until the scumbag or H gets here,' Ricky
screamed.

'Would you like a glass of wine, Justo?' I asked.

Justo looked at me in surprise. 'Are you all right, Judy?'

'Fine, beginning to feel a bit tipsy though.' I had almost finished
the entire bottle of wine. Still what else could you do when held at
knifepoint by a madman. 'There's another bottle in the fridge,' I said.

'You sit there and I'll get it,' Justo said.

He opened the bottle, poured himself a glass, then came and
joined us in the seating area.

A winter storm had started outside. In February heavy rain often
came on unexpectedly. The poorly drained streets in the village
would flood and sometimes, depending on the direction of the wind,
a couple of inches of rain came into our kitchen. The sound of thunder and the incessant downpour filled the conversational void in the
room, and it was because of these that all of us failed to hear the creak
of the front gate or Howard and Phil running across the courtyard.

They burst through the door, hair and clothes soaking wet,
and smiled drunkenly at me, before they registered Justo, and
then Ricky.

I ran out of the room, up the stairs and locked myself in the
bedroom.

I could hear much shouting downstairs, mainly Ricky screaming. This would be interspersed with Howard, Phil or Justo trying
to talk in reasonable tones. I was frightened and worried that the
loud voices would waken the children, although I had heard
Howard closing all the doors downstairs. Finally it quietened down
and I must have fallen asleep. The next I heard was Howard knocking on the bedroom door asking to be let in. I was so angry I

thought twice about it, but I was also too tired to have an argument. I opened the door to him. He looked as drained as I felt.

'Let's talk in the morning, Jude,' he said.

In the morning when I awoke I could hear Howard and the girls talking in the kitchen. We were meant to be having Sunday lunch at the parents' house of Amber's friend Rachel. I lay on the bed and let the events of the night before play in my mind.

I heard him coming upstairs. He came warily into the bedroom and sat by me on the bed.

'Jude, I'm really sorry about what happened last night. Ricky was totally out of order behaving like that. It won't happen again.'

'How do you know it won't when you involve yourself with people like that?'

'Tell me what happened, Jude.'

I told him.

'I'm so sorry, love,' he said as he took me into his arms. 'Neither Phil nor I will have any more to do with him. That's a promise.'

'What the hell had Phil done to him?'

'A load of Thai sticks got busted as it was being put on the plane out of Thailand. Ricky got it into his head that Phil had arranged for this to happen because Ricky had arranged the shipment independently of Phil and cut Phil out.'

'Did Phil do that?'

'No, Jude. Phil would never do anything like that. Basically Ricky and his partner got too greedy and stopped greasing the right palms. They just don't like to admit it's their fault. Anyhow it's all over now. I promise nothing like that will ever happen again.'

'I hope you'll make it plain to Ricky that he's never welcome round here again.'

'I will, love. I don't want to have any more to do with him either.'

I later learnt that Ricky boasted about this night and claimed he had tied me up.

A few days later we were in the kitchen when the phone went. Howard answered it in the living room. He came back in to the kitchen and I looked at his face.

'What's wrong?' I said.

'That was Mick McCarthy, a friend of Hobbs's. Jim's been arrested in Lisbon.'

'What for?'

'Apparently he's been charged with kidnapping a boy and homosexuality with minors.'

'What are you doing, Howard, surrounding yourself with the likes of Hobbs and Ricky Hawkins?'

'Don't start now, Jude. This puts the whole communication thing into disarray.'

The next call to come in was from Pete, telling us that Gerry's boat had arrived in Mexico and the dope had been unloaded and would shortly be transferred to California.

Howard seemed to relax and get into life on Mallorca. Ricky Hawkins disappeared from our life. Howard restarted Spanish lessons and we took up tennis again. Howard and I made good friends with the father and mother of Golly's friend Lucinda, David and Jules Embley. He was a retired Birmingham business-man. They introduced us to their friend Geoffrey Kenion, a retired theatre and film actor who at one time had a lead role in *The Mousetrap* and had been a policeman in *Dixon of Dock Green*. Geoffrey was in the process of opening a bar and restaurant in a new marina being built at Puerto Portals. Howard had now confessed to several of our new friends about his nefarious past. No one held it against us.

I discovered I was pregnant again. Howard, Amber and Golly were delighted. They were even more delighted when I learnt it was to be a boy. Howard and I immediately decided on the name Patrick as both our grandfathers had been called Patrick.

The dope had arrived in Los Angeles and Pete was selling it. We went to London for the Easter holidays where Wyvonna met us to give us $70,000, a fragment of the thousands owed to us. She then came and spent a few days with us in Palma; this time she did not bring a supply of E with her and was calmer and easier to spend time with. While she was staying with us we received a phone call from Gerry with the news that Pete and Patti had been busted. They had been arrested in the Beverly Pavilion hotel in Los Angeles. The DEA had found $50,000 cash and 576 grams of hashish in their room. Gerry was unsure whether the DEA knew about the 10 tons. It was decided that until more was known about the arrest, sales of the hash should be suspended.

Patti was let out on bail. She assured everyone that she and Pete were only being done for the hash and money found in their room. So Patti took over the sales, and people took advantage of Pete being in jail and started ripping her off big time.

Howard and Gerry decided that Gerry should take over. Howard sent Old John over to LA to take care of his money from the sales. He also phoned my brother Patrick in Miami to help with transferring the money out of the States. Shortly after Old John arrived in LA, he phoned and told Howard that 'our dog was sick'. This meant our phone was tapped.

'How does John know this?' I asked.

'Apparently, during Pete's pre-trial court hearings, the prosecution accidentally let slip that the DEA and Spanish police had installed wire taps on our phone.'

'The phone is in my name. Howard, does this not freak you out?'

'Well, I'm obviously not happy about it. The name of the game now is to make sure they don't bust me or any more money or dope. Jude, I'll have to find other places to receive calls. I'm sure the Taj Mahal will let me receive calls from Pakistan, and the Thai restaurant in Santa Ponsa will be a good place to receive calls from Phil. Justo says I can use his office any time I like and I could use David Embley's phone too, he'd be none the wiser.'

Howard now spent most of his time out at phone boxes or in bars waiting for calls. Occasionally he got lazy and called from the home phone. I couldn't eat, which added to my anxiety as I was pregnant. I started drinking milk to make up for my poor appetite. By the end of my pregnancy I was drinking over six litres a day.

Howard approached Geoffrey Kenion and asked him if he would fly to the States and pick up some money. He said he would pay Geoffrey 10 per cent of whatever he picked up. Geoffrey, who was running short of money to invest in his new bar and restaurant, immediately agreed.

George and Yvonne came and stayed with us for a holiday.

'Judy, you know I think Howard behaves like a real idiot sometimes,' Yvonne said.

'Why, what's he done?'

'Well, the last time he came to Karachi, George and I drove to the airport to pick him up. He comes over to us, and George points out to him this car with the American and Dutch drug agents in it. So he stumbles drunkenly over to them and starts asking them if they were waiting for him. I just wouldn't have thought with his history that it was a sensible way to behave. And then a few nights later we were having drinks at the American Club when Bowe walked in and gave us all filthy looks. When he sat down at his table, Howard started making anti-American comments. Bowe complained to the waiter that we weren't American and tried to have us thrown out. Why does he try to antagonize them so much?'

Yvonne and George were trying to make a success of the school and gain acceptance in the expatriate community and they didn't feel that Howard's cheek would help them. They were right. Before long Stephenson and the Dutch drug man had made their names dirt.

At the end of May Howard told me he had to go and see Phil in Bangkok. David Embley said he would like to go with him if he was going to Hong Kong as he hadn't been there for twenty years.

'Howard, do you think with all this heat on you should go? Can't you just give it a rest?'

'It'll be all right, love. I'll be with David and he's completely straight.'

I couldn't see what difference flying with David would make except to make David look suspicious.

Howard flew first to Bangkok to see Phil, then to Manila, where he met Malik. David Embley joined him there. Just before Howard and David left Manila, Howard phoned me and said he would phone me as soon as he got to Hong Kong.

I didn't hear anything for nearly twenty-four hours. Then the phone went.

'Jude, you can't believe what a relief it is to talk to you,' Howard said, sounding as if he was almost in tears. 'They totally tore me apart here and held me for nearly fifteen hours. I can't say too much because I know they're bound to be listening at both ends of this. But I'll call again soon. I'm at the Shangri-La if you need to phone me. Love you.'

He was clearly worried, which worried me even more.

When Howard returned to Palma he decided not to do any more travelling for a while.

'If anyone one wants to see me they'll have to come here, Jude.'

The Hong Kong pull had scared him. It scared me.

Two days after Howard got home in the middle of June, George and Yvonne returned to Karachi. By the middle of July, the 10 tons in California had finally all been sold. Geoffrey Kenion had successfully completed two money-courier missions and was now in a position to finish building his restaurant, Wellies.

At the beginning of August, Gerry Wills, his new Peruvian girl-friend, Flash and Gerry's partner Ronald Allen all flew by private Learjet from Monaco to Palma. It was time to celebrate. We were all very rich.

I hoped this would now be it and that Pete and Patti's arrest, the phone taps and all the other signs that something was strongly amiss would be a wake-up call for Howard. It was not to be. They all wanted to be much richer and do another scam. This time Gerry wanted to do 20 tons from Pakistan. He had his boat, the *Axel D*, ready and waiting in Darwin, Australia.

Gerry brought with him to Palma a stocky, balding friend of his with a deep southern Georgian accent, called Roger Reaves. He had been one of the top pilots for Colombia's Medellín cartel and was suspected of flying tons of cocaine into the United States before his arrest in 1982. He was convicted of running a 'continuing criminal enterprise'. He served two years in prison before being released on twenty-five years' probation. He fled the country, living first in Brazil and then the south of France. In 1985 he was indicted in

Miami for cocaine trafficking. He was near the top of the DEA's most wanted list. His glamorous wife Mari and their two daughters and a son accompanied him.

Howard threw a lavish birthday party for himself at the local restaurant in the village, complete with flamenco dancers and deliciously cooked lobster. Old John and Liz, Podge and various other friends from London flew in for it.

After they all left, Howard, Amber, Golly and a pregnant me went on a quiet family holiday to Interlaken in Switzerland. When we returned to Palma, Lord Moynihan and his wife were on the island. They were staying with friends of theirs in the small village of Esporlas; we joined them for dinner on a number of occasions. Tony appointed himself Amber's godfather.

Howard flew out to Karachi to organize the 20 tons for Gerry. When he returned at the beginning of October, we all went to London. I wanted Dr Basil Lee to deliver my baby. Patrick was born on 16 November, a beautiful, blond, blue-eyed boy. Howard helped deliver him and cut the umbilical cord. We all fell in love with him. Unlike at the time of Golly's birth, I was able to rest instead of charging off on prison visits.

'So, Howard, now you have a son will I get to see you change a nappy?' I asked.

'You must be joking. That's women's work.'

'This is your fourth child and you've never changed a nappy.'

'I've far more important things to do.' He looked irritated.

We decided to stay in London for Christmas and the New Year. I went back to teaching Amber and Golly, this time with work supplied by their teachers.

Shortly before Christmas 1986 the doorbell sounded in our flat in Cathcart Road. I went to open the door. There to my great surprise was Tom Sunde.

'Judy, let me in. I have some very important news for you and Howard.' He pushed his way past me.

Amber and Golly were in the playroom and Patrick was sleeping.

We went into the living room. Howard stood up, surprised to see Tom.

'Hey, Tom, this is a surprise.' He held out his hand to shake Tom's. Tom took it as his brown eyes looked intensely at Howard.

'Look, I'll get straight to the point. The DEA are going to indict you both,' said Tom.

A feeling of sickness filled me.

'They are so pissed with you, Howard, it's untrue.'

'Slow down, Tom. They can't indict Jude, she's done nothing,' said Howard.

'They've got photos of her handing a package to Patti at the Newporter Inn over a year ago,' said Tom.

'That was a copy of *High Time*, hardly an indictable offence,' I said.

'Believe me, Judy, they're serious. They had your phone tapped in Palma for the first eight months of this year, and your friends' and the phones in the bars and restaurants you use. They're going for you both.'

'Can you prove this, Tom?' Howard asked. He slipped his arm protectively round my shoulders.

'I can't stop now, I just wanted to check you were here. I'll stop by this evening and tell you more. I have a load of paperwork to show you both, then you'll believe me.'

Tom left. I felt sick and scared.

CHAPTER TWENTY-THREE
Twilight

A few hours later Tom returned with a briefcase under his arm. I had spent the day since Tom's earlier visit in auto-mode. I'd cleaned the house, played with the children, shopped and cooked. Now the children were tucked up in bed sleeping peacefully. Howard had spent most of the day in his office, chain-smoking joints and sorting out paperwork. He let Tom into the house and we went into the living room. I had closed the curtains tightly and the gas log fire warmed the room. Howard sat on the sofa next to me, joint in hand. Tom sat in the high-backed dusty- pink wing-chair. He opened his briefcase and pulled out official-looking papers.

'Now, Howard, the DEA have you as the head of a worldwide drug-smuggling organization. This is a list of all known acquaintances and associates of yours,' Tom said. He handed official-looking sheets of paper to us. My eyes scanned the pages: they named almost everyone we knew, even complete innocents like my friend Frances and Dr Lee.

I noticed there were asterisks by some names. I asked Tom what they meant.

'They mean that person has a Naddis number. It's the Narcotics And Dangerous Drug Information System. The numbers are issued to drug trafficking and money-laundering suspects. But every name on that list is in the computer as known to you.'

I noticed there was an asterisk by my name. Beside Phil's name was written: 'Major supplier of marijuana from Thailand to the dope dealers of both Britain and Australia. Known associate of Dennis Howard Marks.'

'Where have you got all this information from, Tom?' Howard asked.

'From Karl. Now, the DEA agent out to get your arse is Craig Lovato and he has agents all round the world watching your every move. They are determined to get you, Howard. They have even done a psychological profile of you. What has really pissed them off is you getting that ten tons into the States right under their noses, and the Alameda scam because it was government territory.'

I scanned a typewritten document about Howard: 'He enjoys having several deals in operation at the same time. Gets a kick out of it. Needs to fill in his time and mental space. He is a Machiavellian-type character.'

Looking at all the documents Tom showed us, I realized for the first time the sheer scale of the DEA operation against Howard. It wasn't just the DEA but, unsurprisingly, British Customs and, from what I could see, just about every other law enforcement agency in the world. I thought back to the American Club in Karachi where I had seen Customs officer Michael Stephenson and DEA agent Harlan Bowe sitting together.

'Tom, are they really going to go for me?' I asked. I was terrified.

'Yeah, they are,' said Tom.

'How can they, Tom? Giving a copy of a book written about me even to the biggest criminal in the world is hardly an offence,' said Howard.

'I'm just passing on what I know,' said Tom.

'So what do you suggest I do?' Howard asked.

'Well, number one, watch out for Pete. He's telling everything he knows.'

'I find that hard to believe,' said Howard.

I also found it hard to believe.

'Believe me, it's true,' replied Tom. 'Meanwhile, I'll keep you informed of the DEA investigation.'

'Thanks, Tom.' Howard lit up yet another joint.

'This does, of course, cost, and I have one very important piece of information I should tell you, but Karl wants $50,000 for it,' said Tom.

'If I think it's worth it I'll pay,' said Howard.

'The DEA have put a radio transmitter on Gerry Wills's boat, the *Axel D.* They know it has left Australia and is on its way to Pakistan to pick up twenty tons. They are out to get this one, Howard, and you with it.'

'Can you tell me where on the boat, Tom?' asked Howard.

'Sure, as soon as I get the $50,000.'

'Tom, I'll pay.'

I still didn't trust Tom, but there was no mistaking the information he was giving us was for real.

After he and Howard had arranged to meet the following day and Tom had left, Howard and I discussed his revelations.

'Jude, there is no way anyone can possibly arrest you.'

'Howard, you heard Tom, he said they were going to indict me. They have Frances down on that paper, which means that pull she had was because she was with me.'

'Yes, but neither you nor Frances were doing anything wrong. Jude, I bet Tom was just saying that so I would pay more money for information. You will not be in trouble.'

'Howard, can't you just please stop.'

'I will, Jude. I promise. Just let me sort out what's happening now. Come on, it's late. Let's go to bed.'

That night Howard took a sleeping pill and I lay by his side tossing and turning.

Tom's news put a dampener on our Christmas celebrations. We spent the holiday quietly in Cathcart Road with Marcus and his girl-friend, Kieran. Howard met Gerry in Denmark and told him the news from Tom.

'Jude, Gerry knew about the tracker device. He had heard from Pete, to whom Tom had already tried to sell the information. Pete apparently told him to fuck off. Pete warned Gerry that Tom is working with the DEA and US Customs,' said Howard.

'So Pete's not cooperating with them?'

'Not according to Gerry.'

'I really don't trust Tom. Do you think he is working for the DEA?'

'I don't think so. But he's obviously got someone who is, or at least has access to their information.'

'What's Gerry going to do about the tracking device?'

'He's going to fly Flash down at some point to remove it. But he reckons we shouldn't go ahead with the twenty tons from Pakistan even though we've put down a $1,000,000 non-returnable deposit.'

'Thank God for that.'

'Gerry wants to go with Phil instead and send thirty tons to Canada,' he said.

The relief I had felt was short-lived.

'Howard, this is madness. You have every drug agency in the world watching you. We've got three children to think about. Tom said they were going to go for me – what will happen to the children then?'

'Jude, I keep telling you nothing will happen to you, and if I have my way nothing will happen to me either.'

We returned to Palma in early January 1987. A sense of unease was never far away from me. Drinking one evening in Geoffrey's new bar, which had now become the trendy bar to hang out in, we befriended Rafael Llofriu, a chief inspector of Palma's Policía Nacional and head of security at Palma's San Juan airport. He knew nothing of Howard's past. He had heard from regulars in the bar that Howard was a wealthy entrepreneur and was looking for a business to invest in on the island. This was partly true; Howard and I often talked about opening something. When we first moved to the island we had thought about opening an Indian restaurant. Justo talked us out of this. He said Indian food was not popular with the Spanish.

Howard and Rafael got on well and we continued to meet for drinks. One Sunday lunch he took us to his favourite restaurant in Valdemossa. We met up with him outside Palma prison before driving up into the hills. At first I was suspicious of him, but I learnt to relax in his company. It gave me a sense of comfort that he didn't appear to know of Howard's past or present business activities.

Surely if the DEA were so on top of us, Rafael would know. Wouldn't he?

Frederick, half of the Nina and Frederick duo, was visiting friends in Mallorca. He had stopped singing years before and now spent his time sailing boatloads of marijuana around. He and Howard met for many discussions.

In February Howard took off on a tour of the Far East, visiting Karachi, Bangkok, Hong Kong and Manila. Roger Reaves went with him to the Philippines – he thought it might be a good place to live and grow marijuana. Howard introduced him to Lord Moynihan.

About this time a series of newspaper articles about Moynihan began to appear in the Manila paper the *Inquirer*.

The first article alleged that he had taken over the multi-million-dollar drug-smuggling operation of a jailed trafficker named as 'Fat Cat' Smith. The second article ran under the headline 'Fugitive Lord Travels On False Papers'. It gave one of his aliases as William Kerr. Phil confirmed to us that Moynihan did have a false passport in this name. The third article's headline read: 'Lord M's Feud With British Businessman Probed'. It alleged that Lord M was suspected of ordering the killing of Robert Walden in November 1986, the husband of his former wife. Phil claims to have been with Robert when he was shot.

Another six articles appeared in the newspaper alleging fraud, drug pushing, smuggling heroin to Australia, prostitution and involvement in the sex trade, involving exporting 2,500 Filipino women to brothels in Japan and Australia. The articles put Roger off moving to the Philippines or ever meeting Moynihan again.

'Boy, Judy, your husband sure knows some weird folk,' he said the next time I saw him.

Howard, meanwhile, much to my distress, seemed to be involving himself in more and more deals. Jim Hobbs had got out of jail in Lisbon, the charges against him dropped. He moved to Palma where he rented a flat behind the cathedral and opened a seedy basement bar in the old town. I was far from happy with Jim moving to the island and gave his bar a wide berth. I complained to Howard.

'It just makes it so much easier for me, Jude, if he's close by.'

Howard went to Canada for a week to meet an old acquaintance named Bob Light. Bob had the facilities to unload Gerry's boat. Here Howard and the other investors in the 30-ton scam met up to discuss the details. While there, Howard also arranged to have one of Frederick's boats filled up with Vietnamese marijuana, which was also to be taken to Canada.

While he was away, Patti phoned. She told me to tell Howard not to have anything to do with Tom. 'He and Karl are dangerous, Judy.'

Howard returned from Canada with a beautiful hand-crafted bronze statue of a mother holding aloft a baby.

'This is for giving me a son, Jude,' he said.

Roger Reaves visited us again in Palma and decided to move his family to the island. They rented a huge luxury house in Puerto Andratx overlooking the sea, complete with tennis court and swimming pool. He enrolled his children in the British international school. I liked Roger; he was an amusing, larger-than life-character. What I found hard to deal with was his inability to talk about anything except dope deals (which was the last thing I wanted to know about). If we were sitting on the terrace at Wellies, he would continually speculate about the dope-holding capacity of each yacht berthed in the marina and ponder whether to approach any of the yachts' captains. If it wasn't dope deals, he was quoting from the Bible.

In early May articles about Moynihan began to appear in the British press. *The Times* carried a story headlined 'Peer Is Detained In Manila'. It began: 'The fugitive British aristocrat, Lord Moynihan of Leeds, has been prevented from leaving the Philippines pending investigation of drug trafficking and prostitution syndicates.'

The *Today* newspaper also ran an article. It said that 'Lord Moynihan had been called before immigration officials and was likely to be deported in a week ... The authorities were acting on a request of Interpol, who have a standing warrant for his arrest over alleged offences in London ... Police in Manila claim he runs a chain of "escort" girls and massage parlours. They are also concerned about the murder last year of a nightclub owner said to have been feuding with Moynihan.'

It looked like Moynihan was suffering from the fall of the Marcos regime, and to me he was emerging as an ugly character.

I had repeated to Howard my conversation with Patti about Tom.

'Jude, I'm confident enough to think Tom wouldn't do anything to harm me,' he said.

I wished I could be sure. Whenever Tom came to stay he gave me the impression of snooping and eavesdropping. My intuition told me he was bad. Tom flew in and out of the island with more snippets of information and Howard paid him more money. Moynihan telephoned Howard and said he needed to see him urgently about Howard's security.

'What do you think that's about, Howard?' I asked.

'I don't know. I think what I'll do is have Tom go over and see him and find out what's going on.'

Tom went, and came back with the news that Moynihan was helping the DEA in their investigation of Howard. They'd asked him to help in a sting operation. Moynihan had told Tom that the DEA had approached him, but he didn't say that he had agreed to cooperate. Tom found out that through his sources.

We assumed he had agreed in return for having various charges against him dropped and to prevent his expulsion from the Philippines.

'Don't worry, Jude, there's nothing he can tell them,' Howard said.

I tried desperately not to think about it all. I immersed myself in taking care of the children. Amber and Golly were both doing extremely well at school and consistently won the end-of-year prizes. Patrick was a happy and contented baby. I couldn't bear the thought of anything happening to them.

Gerry flew into Palma in the early summer.

'Well, they've jettisoned the tracking device. Flash, the genius, has made it so it will float. They threw it overboard at the northern end of the Arabian Sea. That will keep them busy chasing for a while.' He and Howard both laughed. If I hadn't been so worried I might have laughed as well.

With the tracking device removed, the *Axel D* made its way to the Gulf of Thailand, where it was loaded up with 30 tons of Thai weed. Several weeks later, the Thai weed was sitting in a warehouse on Vancouver Island, and the empty *Axel D* made its way to Lima, Peru.

The phone rang.

'It's me, Judy. Is the Welsh wanker there?'

'Hey, Jim, it's been a long time,' I said.

'How's you and the kids? Marty tells me you have a little boy now, is that right?'

'Yes, he's adorable. How's Sylvia and the kids?'

'They're all grand. So is the wanker there?'

'He's out playing tennis; he'll be back within the hour.'

'Well, tell him I called and I'll call back shortly.'

Jim called back and Howard arranged to go and meet him in the south of France. No doubt, I thought despairingly, to arrange another deal.

I later learnt from Roger that he had bought a ton of Moroccan hash off Jim. Roger was going to have it delivered to England on a German boat he had just bought. I hadn't even realized Jim and Roger had met.

'Jude, you're looking tired,' Howard said one morning.

'I'm just so worried all the time, Howard. Can we go away somewhere for a while? Away from telephones and have a relaxing holiday.'

'Yeah, I'm way up for that. Old John is handling all the money for me from the sale of the Thai grass. Balando's handling moving the money out of the country with his Chinese connections in Vancouver, so I'm free. Where shall we go?'

I thought back to what a good time we'd had in Sicily and how we had always promised ourselves to go back.

'Brilliant idea. I'll have Balando book the tickets. Let's call in to Campione on the way and then we could get the train down to Rome and fly from there,' suggested Howard.

There were no direct flights from Palma to Italy so we flew to Zurich and from there took the train to Lugano, one of our favourite journeys. We had our normal nostalgic dinner in Campione and once again enjoyed the comfort of the Splendide. An overnight train took us to Rome; the girls, who had never slept on a train before, loved it. We, of course, had the best cabin money could buy.

We stayed in Rome a couple of days and took the girls round all the tourist sights. We flew to Taormina and stayed at a wonderful clifftop hotel, the Santa Domenico. Masha had travelled with us to help with the children. I was slowly beginning to unwind and I noticed Howard was, too. We spent the days lazing on the beach and one day took a rowing boat around the bay while the oarsman serenaded us. We visited Greek amphitheatres and the surprisingly active Mount Etna, then one day we drove to Corleone. We planned to have lunch there but there were no welcoming little bars or pizzerias, and the houses were all heavily shuttered.

'You'd think some enterprising kid would have opened a bar called the Godfather, wouldn't you? There must be loads of tourists who come here out of curiosity,' I said. The place disappointed us.

In the evenings we spent our time strolling around the cobbled streets of Taormina, where the shops stayed open late. One evening we walked into a tourist shop that printed T-shirts. Howard had been fascinated by a young kid he'd met during his time in Brixton who had 'FUCK YOU' tattooed on his forehead. Obviously thinking of this kid, he bought a bright orange T-shirt and had the words 'FUCK YOU' emblazoned across it in bright green letters.

We had dinner and then Masha took the children back to the hotel.

Howard and I hit the bars. Sitting outside a bar in a picturesque little square, we got into a humdinger of an argument. Howard has highly polished debating skills. He can tie you up in knots, get you to say things you don't mean, make you contradict yourself and make you want to scream. My solution was normally to ignore the wind-up or agree with him. This particular night, probably because of the drink I'd had, I got caught up in the argument. Once I was well tied up in knots, rather than scream in frustration, I pulled the orange T-shirt with the garish 'FUCK YOU' lettering out of the bag and slipped it over my head.

'Right then,' he said. And he stood up and stormed off.

I sat there for a few minutes in a kind of blurred haze before it dawned on me that we had run up a bar bill of over £100 and I had no wallet, no credit cards and no ID, and I was wearing a bright orange T-shirt with the words 'FUCK YOU' —blazoned across it.

Feeling rather foolish, I peeled off the T-shirt and ordered another drink while I tried to figure out what to do.

What I didn't know was that Howard was hiding round the corner, watching me and giggling. He let me suffer for twenty minutes, then he came back.

'What were we arguing about anyway?' I said.

'Jude, I really don't remember.' We both laughed.

We flew back to Palma in time for the children to return to school. Chief Inspector Rafael Llofriu met us at the airport and whisked us through immigration and customs. He asked us if we knew anyone who wanted to buy a seafront flat in Palma Nova. Howard said he would buy it.

'It'll be useful to put people up in and I think a good investment. What do you think, Jude?'

I thought it a very good idea, and we went ahead and bought it. Moynihan and Editha were among the first people to stay in it – this I thought was a less good idea.

'But he's working for the DEA,' I pointed out.

'There's nothing he can tell them. He's never been involved with anything and I can feed him a load of bullshit instead. Remember that old saying: keep your enemies close.'

While Howard was at the airport meeting Lord and Lady Moynihan, I got a phone call from Gerry's Peruvian girlfriend.

'Hi, Judy, it's Esther.'

'Hi, Esther. How are you?'

'Not good. Gerry, John and a bunch of others have been arrested in Vancouver. That's all I know at the moment.'

'Esther, Howard's not here – he'll be back in about an hour.'

'Tell him I'll call back at ten your time this evening. I'll try to find out all I can before I ring again.'

Howard returned to the house, having left the Moynihans at the flat to settle in. I greeted him at the gate with the bad news from Esther. He looked shaken.

'I'd better go out, Jude, and make some calls, see if I can find out any more. Maybe Liz will know something. Don't leave the house in case someone else calls. I'll be back as soon as I can.'

He was unable to find out much. He asked Liz to get hold of all the Canadian papers she could. She had so far heard nothing from John and was anxiously awaiting news.

The following morning we dropped the children off at school and then went to the Palma Nova flat to see the Moynihans. Tony opened the door.

'Morning, morning. Come in and I'll get the coffee going. Judy, Editha gives her apologies, she had a couple of errands to run, but will join us for lunch if you can make it. Howard, dear boy, you look shattered.'

'I had a bit of bad news last night,' said Howard.

'Oh dear, I'm sorry. Nothing too tragic, I hope,' replied Moynihan.

'Some friends of mine got busted in Vancouver with some dope,' Howard said.

'Was it yours, dear boy?'

'No, it was my friend Gerry's. He came to Manila with me one time. Tall, blond.'

Moynihan then proceeded to give Howard the third degree. He was painfully obvious in his interrogation and could barely look either of us in the eye. I couldn't understand what we were doing here. I made an excuse to leave and told Howard I'd pick him up in a couple of hours.

'Howard, I really don't feel comfortable being in Moynihan's company,' I said later.

'Jude, they're not here for long. Try not to let on you suspect anything.'

The Canadian bust was a disaster. The dope that was busted was the Vietnamese load of Frederick's. It had been organized by Howard and Bob Light. It had nothing to do with Gerry or his partners or Old John and Phil. Phil had managed to leave Vancouver and get back to Thailand. Gerry Wills, Ron Allen and John Denbigh could not really tell the Royal Canadian Mounted Police that the millions of confiscated dollars were actually the proceeds of a Thai importation and had nothing to do with the Vietnamese grass they had found.

Howard summoned Tom Sunde to Palma and asked him to find out all he could about the Canadian bust. Tom agreed for a price. He phoned back later to say there was no suspicion of Howard being involved in the busted Canadian load. This at least was some relief.

John Denbigh was released on bail in Vancouver on condition he remain in Canada. Liz went over with their son Charlie to stay with him. Gerry Wills and Ron Allen were also released on bail but allowed to return to Los Angeles.

Lord and Lady Moynihan left Palma for Miami.

'Jude, I've given them Patrick's number. Moynihan says he has some money to launder,' Howard said.

'You've done what?'

'Oh, it's probably just his bullshit, but I thought Patrick would get a kick out of meeting him.'

'But I don't understand. Surely given what we know about him the fewer people he meets the better. Did you ask Patrick if you could give him his number?'

'Yes, of course I did.'

'Did you tell him we think he's working for the DEA?'

'No, I told him not to totally trust him and he would probably just have a laugh.'

I was far from happy with this news. There were times when I couldn't work Howard out at all. It seemed total madness to be introducing Moynihan to my brother. I considered phoning Patrick and warning him. If only I had.

CHAPTER TWENTY-FOUR
Promise

We returned to London for the children's half-term. Amber was in her last year of junior school and for the sake of her education we had decided to move back to London the following September. I started to research schools.

George and Yvonne called around to the flat in London. They felt let down by Howard. Since the cancelled deal with Gerry from Pakistan, Howard had not put any more money or interest into the school. This made George and Yvonne feel as if Howard had used them. Customs officer Michael Stephenson had spread stories among the Karachi expatriate community that the school was a front for a drugs operation, and many of their students had left. All George and Yvonne's hard work looked like it had been in vain. They wanted $20,000 compensation. An almighty row broke out between Howard and George and Yvonne on the doorstep of our London flat. Howard refused to give them anything.

They flew back to Karachi and with Malik's help and sympathy managed to sell the schoolbooks and furniture before leaving for Bangkok and getting teaching jobs there. I at this stage was only privy to Howard's side of the story. I decided not to get involved.

On the morning of my birthday, Howard had filled the house with flowers and he and the children showered me with presents. That evening he ordered a stretch limousine (an unusual sight in London in those days) to take us to the theatre to see *Phantom of the Opera.* I was always immeasurably touched by Howard's romantic gestures. Amber and Golly joined us for the ride to the theatre. When we were dropped off, the driver gave them a sightseeing tour of London. They sat in the back finishing our champagne and pretending to be royalty or celebrities before they were taken back to the flat to join Patrick and his babysitter.

Howard had finally decided not to do any more dope deals. The Canadian bust had shaken him and he had decided to concentrate on straight business. I hoped he had not made this decision too late.

Back in Palma I put the house on the market. The children were sad to be leaving, but as well as for the benefit of their education, living in England would also make it easier for Howard to work in the travel agency.

For Christmas and New Year we were in London. We spent New Year's Eve with Julian and Helen Peto and a couple of other friends. There was no talk of dope deals and no phone calls about them. It seemed like a good omen.

January 1988 saw us back in Palma. The phone rang one evening while Howard was out. I answered it.

'Hello, is that Judith?' said a man with an American accent. Nobody ever called me Judith, except my mother when she had been cross with me, and the British Customs officers back in 1980.

'Who is this?'

'Call me Top Cat. Is your husband in?'

'No, he'll be back in about an hour. Can you tell me what it's about?'

'No, just tell him it's important I talk to him. I'll call back.' He hung up.

I paced the kitchen, causing Amber to ask me what was wrong.

'Nothing, lovely girl,' I said as I looked into her beautiful blue eyes.

Howard came home. I asked him to come into the living room and gave him an account of the phone call. He looked worried. I felt worried. I went back into the kitchen.

The phone rang and Howard answered it. He called me back

into the living room when he had finished. He looked close to tears.

'What did he want, Howard?'

'He said a grand jury was about to indict me in Miami and that our phones here and in London are tapped. He said that within a couple of months they would seek my extradition and that Gerry, John, Phil and others would be arrested. He said if I wanted more information I would have to pay him $250,000.'

'Howard, what are we going to do?' I asked.

'I'm going to make an appointment to see Bernard Simons in London. Find out more about extradition and American law. I'll also phone Tom and see if he knows any more.'

'He didn't say there was anything against me?'

'No, love, what could they possibly have against you?'

'I don't know, Howard. Tom was so adamant last year.'

'But he hasn't mentioned anything about you since, Jude.'

Howard left for London a couple of days later. He went to see Bernard, who didn't know a lot about extradition law. However, he was able to tell Howard there was no extradition between Taiwan and the United States. Howard also befriended an American lawyer, Michael Katz, who was licensed to practise law in the United Kingdom and the United States.

Meanwhile I had real estate agents trawling through the house in Palma. My first choice of agents put a sign up on the outside of the house. This attracted more real estate agents than potential buyers. One afternoon the doorbell went; it was three Spanish men who wanted to take the house on to sell. I showed them round, after which they gave me a long complicated form in Spanish to sign. I couldn't understand it, so I refused to sign it. They became aggressive, telling me it was standard practice.

I got a bad feeling from them. I wondered who they were and what it really was they wanted me to sign.

Howard returned and was as nervous as a cat. He jumped at the smallest sound, slept restlessly and chain-smoked joints. He was distracted and much of the time lost in his own thoughts. He also was drinking more than usual. One night after dinner in the Taj Mahal he drove far too fast and knocked a man off his motorbike.

Rather than stop, Howard drove faster. Amber and Golly both stared out the back window. They were distraught.

'Daddy, that poor man might be hurt,' said Golly.

'Howard, don't you think we should check he's okay?' I said.

'Look, I'll drop you and the kids off and then I'll take the other car and go back.'

When we got home he drove off in the Fiesta. He arrived home twenty minutes later to say there was no sign of any man or motorbike.

In April we went to London. Howard had heard no more from Tom and thought it would be a good idea to go and check out Taiwan.

'I'll check the schools out while I'm there, Jude. It might be a sensible place to live.'

I prayed it would not be necessary to go on the run again, this time with three children.

I took Amber and Golly for an interview at Faulkner House, South Kensington. As Amber was a year ahead I thought she could repeat her last year at junior school, get used to being at an English school and sit her entrance exams. They were both accepted, and invited to spend the last two weeks of the summer term at the school to acclimatize themselves.

I felt nervous the whole time I was in London. My appetite had decreased again and I had difficulty in swallowing. I felt like I was being watched.

I phoned Howard in Taipei. 'Hi, love. Any news?'

'I've met some really nice New Zealand guys living out here. I can see quite a lot of businesses I could get involved in. I like it here. I haven't checked out the schools yet.'

'Anything from Tom or Katz?'

'I'll let you know as soon as I hear. How are the children?'

'Amber and Golly both got accepted at the school and Patrick's as jolly as ever. We're flying back to Palma tomorrow so call me there.'

Although Amber, now ten, had known by listening to conversations that Howard had been in jail because of his 'special tobacco', and even remembered visiting him, seven-year-old Golly had no idea. I decided to tell her in case something awful did happen. I explained to her that the police did not like Daddy's 'special tobacco' and that before she was born he had spent time in jail for it. She was shocked and upset. I told her that she could talk to Daddy about it when he got home.

We flew back to Palma and the girls settled into their last term at Queen's.

Howard called. 'Tom says nothing is going on at the moment. So I'm coming home.'

This didn't do much to relieve my anxiety.

Roger kept phoning for Howard.

'What does Roger want so urgently?' I asked after Howard had come back from meeting him.

'Roger got pulled in Amsterdam last week and thinks the passport I gave him was dud.'

'What happened?'

'He didn't wait to find out – he just ran. Said he ran across a runway and then jumped over two barbed-wire fences.'

'And he got away?'

'Well, he's here to tell the tale. Albeit rather scratched.'

The phone went. 'Judy, what's up with that damned husband of yours?'

'How do you mean, Roger?'

'Well, straight after I met him this afternoon, four plainclothes guys got out of a car and tried to arrest me. I escaped through a bakery and down an alley.'

'I'll put you on to him.' I handed Howard the phone.

Afterwards he said to me, 'Jude, he thinks I'm hot but if that's the case why haven't they arrested me?'

'I don't know.'

We both took sleeping pills that night, which I didn't like doing in case Patrick woke up.

The following afternoon, as I was leaving the house with Patrick to pick up the girls from school, Mari, Roger's wife, jumped out of a taxi. Armed police had finally succeeded in arresting Roger the day before, outside the school where he and Mari had been collecting their children. He'd spent the night in Palma prison and that morning had been taken to the Palacio de Justicia to see the magistrate. Once he'd been taken into the magistrate's room on the second floor, Roger had leapt over the desk, through the open window and onto the roof of a parked car. It was bad luck for him that the car he dented belonged to the police, and the startled occupants were quick to grab him. Traffic ground to a halt as drivers stopped to watch the spectacle. It made the front page of all the local papers.

We collected the children from school then took Mari down for a drink in Puerto Portals. Howard thought it would be safer than having her in the house. The whole time we sat on the café terrace, I felt again like I was being watched.

It turned out that Roger had been arrested for extradition to West Germany for the Moroccan scam he and Jim had done. They had sailed the dope to England, but in a German vessel. Under German law it is an offence to use a German boat to transfer dope anywhere. The crew of the boat had confessed all they knew to the German authorities, which didn't include any details of McCann.

'Were you involved in that, Howard?' I asked.

'Not really, except for introducing Jim and Roger.'

'So the Germans aren't going to arrest you?'

'I think it's unlikely, Jude.'

We heard from Tom. He needed to see Howard urgently. He turned up at the house early one evening in the middle of June.

'What's going on, Tom?' Howard asked.

'They are definitely going to indict you in Miami.'

'So what's happened?'

'Craig Lovato has got a hotshot Prosecutor Robert O'Neill who is determined to get you for the 1986 Los Angeles load.'

'But I don't understand why Miami.'

'They're really keeping a tight lid on this, Howard. Something must have happened in Miami for it to go before a grand jury there,' said Tom.

'There's absolutely nothing that I can think of, Tom.'

'And what about me?' I asked.

'Jude, your name hasn't come up since last year,' said Tom.

'So can anything be done to stop this indictment?' asked Howard.

'Well, we can stall it. We can't make it go away, but with Karl's contacts and money it could be delayed indefinitely.'

'How much money?'

'We would need $50 to 100,000 immediately and then more later.'

'I can't do it, Tom. I'm not dealing any more.'

'Give us what you can and we will at least try to warn you if you are about to be arrested.'

Tom left and said he would call in a couple of days from Düsseldorf, where he was meeting Karl.

I was about to take the girls for their two weeks at the new school in London before coming back to Palma for the rest of the holidays.

'Jude, I really don't believe anything will happen to you. What I suggest we do is pay Tom a bit more; you go ahead and take the children to London. I'll go back to Taiwan and check out schools. If the news gets worse, then you and the children join me in Taiwan, otherwise we meet back here mid-July.'

'Do you think you could get Tom and Karl to stop anything?'

'I just don't know, Jude. I'm sceptical, like you.'

'Podge is booked to come out here on the twenty-sixth and Masha and her new boyfriend want to come for a visit.'

'Don't change any of those plans. If Masha and her boyfriend want to come out before you're back from England, let them. It might be a good idea to have someone in the house while we're away.'

It was with heavy hearts that we went to bed that night.

We all flew to London together and then Howard flew on to Taiwan. He had tears in his eyes as he walked out the front door to the waiting taxi. I was sad and afraid.

The girls started school. Amber became ill; her glands were swollen and she was listless. Dr Lee could find no cause despite a series of blood tests. Was she noticing the worry I continually felt and suffering from it too? She got better and managed to join Golly for the last two days at Faulkner House. As I walked down the road to the school with Patrick in his pushchair and Amber and Golly on either side of me, I felt a profound feeling of loneliness I could not fully understand.

We flew back to Palma. Masha was waiting at home for us. I hadn't seen her for several months because she'd been living and working on a yacht in Malaga. The children and I were delighted to see her.

'Where's your boyfriend, Masha?' I asked.

'Oh, Nigel – he's gone out. He'll be back later.'

I thought she looked embarrassed and I wondered why. I hadn't met this boyfriend before. I hoped he wasn't another of her disasters. He finally showed up at midnight, drunk. Masha was upset. I didn't think this was how she wanted to present her new boyfriend to me.

The following day, however, he seemed fine. He spent the day playing with the children in the pool. I was standing on the terrace watching them when suddenly I had a terrible sense that I wouldn't see them grow up; that I might get cancer like my mother. I had to try hard to shake off this feeling.

Howard phoned. Michael Katz, the lawyer, had been to see him in Taipei, having flown there from Los Angeles where he had been investigating possible charges against him. Howard sounded happier than he had in a long time. He told me that in Michael's opinion there was no indictment against him and that no extradition had been requested.

'Jude, I'm coming home.'

He arrived home and showered us with presents from Taiwan. Two days later, 22 July, it was our wedding anniversary. I awoke to a house full of flowers. Howard gave me a beautiful jade cross. Masha and the children made us a champagne breakfast, which we ate out on the terrace.

That evening Howard took me out for dinner to Tristan's in Puerto Portals, a fashionable and extremely expensive restaurant.

We discussed the future. Howard said once we were back in

London he was going to work nine to five at Hong Kong International, developing the new opportunities and contacts he had made in Taiwan.

'No more dope deals ever, Jude.'

We ordered a bottle of champagne. The future was looking brighter.

CHAPTER TWENTY-FIVE
The End my Friend

Sun slid through the curtains and woke me. I was still smiling peacefully from the gentle love of the night before. It was about 9.30, a beautiful morning. All the windows in our bedroom were wide open; the five palm trees in our garden stood motionless in the heat. Noises drifted up from downstairs. I could hear the voices of Howard, Golly and our friends David Embley and Mari Reaves. I stayed lazily in bed and thought about phoning Howard on the internal house phone to let him know I was awake. I was longing for a cup of tea. I heard David saying goodbye and the distinct sound of our big iron security gates open and close. Almost immediately, the gate bell buzzed. I assumed that David must have left something behind and was returning to collect it. I heard the creak of the gate open and suddenly the peace of the morning was shattered by a major commotion of shouting and banging.

I leapt out of bed naked. In the courtyard below I saw David with his wrists handcuffed behind his back. Several men stood in the courtyard. A single anguished howl – like the cry of a wounded animal, something caught in a trap – rose from downstairs. It was Golly. Trying to stifle my rising panic, I called for Howard at the top of my voice. There was no reply.

I threw on my pink silk dressing gown and dashed into the hall, calling for Golly. Amber came stumbling bleary-eyed out of her room, woken by her sister's scream. I hugged her to me just as Golly reached the top of the stairs. Her eyes were terrified, great orbs in a deathly pale face. She ran and collapsed into our arms. Two men came after her: a tall, thin man, and a large fat man with a full, down-curved moustache.

'Are you Judith Marks?' the tall man asked me in a middle-class English accent.

'Yes,' I replied.

'Is there anyone on the top floor?'

'Possibly my sister and her boyfriend.' I had no idea that in fact they had left the house.

He continued with a couple of Spanish-looking men, who had followed him, to the top floor where Howard's office was.

At that moment Patrick began to cry. I rushed into his room with Golly still clutching on to me and Amber close behind. He was standing in his cot looking petrified, his arms stretched up to me. I picked him up and held him close.

I took all the children into my bedroom. The large ugly man followed us.

'I want you all to sit on the bed and don't move,' he said. He had an American accent.

Golly was sobbing and shaking violently. Amber was shivering, and eighteen-month-old Patrick was strangely silent. My mind was in a whirl. My dressing gown was falling off me. The belt had come off in my flight from the room and the children clutching at me had left my nakedness exposed. I felt the man's glare.

'Please may I put on some clothes?'

'This is an arrest situation; the wardrobes need searching for weapons.'

Weapons? Why would there be weapons in the cupboard or in the house? I thought. I must have looked at him as if he was mad.

'Are you American?' I asked, wondering if the nightmare we had feared was finally happening.

'What are you doing? What's happening?' Amber cried.

'I'm from the American Drug Enforcement Agency and we're arresting your parents and taking them to Miami, Florida, for conspiracy to smuggle drugs,' he told my ten-year-old daughter, a gleam in his eyes.

I felt nauseous, paralysed with fear. Tom had warned us they were going to go for me, but Howard had constantly reassured me they had no reason to. I had done nothing wrong.

'You can't do that.' I could hear my voice rising in hysteria. 'I've done nothing wrong. I can't leave my children.'

'We'll have to see what the Spanish judge says about that, won't we,' he sneered.

Golly threw herself into the bedcovers, her small shoulders heaving. I kept repeating, 'You can't do that.' One part of my mind kept saying he's not serious, but his manner told me he was.

For the sake of the children I tried to pull myself together. As calmly and casually as I could, I said to Amber as I stroked Golly, 'I won't let them do this, they cannot. I won't leave you.'

Amber's reply stunned everyone in the room.

'Mummy,' she said. 'Last week they shot down an aeroplane and killed everyone on it. Americans think they can do what they like.'

Two weeks earlier, on 3 July 1988, a US warship had shot down an Iranian commercial airliner after supposedly mistaking it for an F14 fighter jet. All 290 people on board died. Why and how the warship mistook the bulky, wide-bodied airbus for a sleek, super-sonic F14 fighter plane barely a third of the size was a mystery. President Reagan had promised a 'full investigation'. Iran had accused the United States of a 'barbaric massacre' and 'vowed to avenge the blood of their martyrs'.

As Amber spoke, the American's expression became more grotesque. He directed a look at my daughter which shocked me. It occurred to me that if Amber had been older he would also have had her under arrest. In later interviews with the press, he would say he had been shocked by 'the vulgarity of the children and the anti-Americanism that had come from such young mouths'.

At that moment another man came into the room, a Spaniard. He looked horrified at my state of attire and told me to dress. I went to my wardrobe and stared blankly at my clothes.

'You're not getting dressed for no cocktail party,' the American spat. I got a skirt and T-shirt and headed for the bathroom. Golly still clung to me while Amber stayed with Patrick on the bed. I paused by a drawer to get some underwear. 'Leave that alone until I've searched it,' the American yelled.

He went through my underwear drawer, sweat dripping from his forehead. The armpits of his shirt, which stretched tightly across his torso, were wet. As he handled my underwear, I felt unclean. When he had finished, I went into the bathroom with Golly and dressed. I was ordered not to close the door. All the time I was dressing Golly held me; she was still shaking and her eyes were wide, full of fear and disbelief.

When I had finished dressing we returned to the bed. Patrick did not understand what was going on but I'm sure he knew it was not something good. He looked sombre – usually he was laughing, crawling or walking round on his podgy little legs. He sat on the bed silently sucking his bottle, watching.

It seemed hours that we sat there. Occasionally other men came in and whispered to the American. The tall man who had asked my name came in at one point.

'Are you English?' I asked.

'Yes, Scotland Yard,' he replied.

The American eventually ordered us downstairs; it seemed to me that there were men all over the place. I asked the American where my sister was.

'She left the house early this morning with her boyfriend on a moped.'

Howard was gone. Mari Reaves was there.

'Mari, are they arresting you too?'

'No,' she said.

'Please may I use your phone, Judith?' the Scotland Yard man asked.

They were in my house, searching all the cupboards, walking where they pleased, and yet he asked if he could use the phone. The American lacked any such etiquette. The phone also rang several times – all the calls were for and answered by the American. Finally, my sister called.

'Ah, Marsha,' he said casually. 'My name is Craig Lovato from the DEA. I am arresting your sister and extraditing her to the US. Could you come back here and look after the children?'

Masha told me later that she thought it was Howard playing a practical joke so she had replied, 'Come on, Howard, stop fooling around.' It took several minutes for her to realize the seriousness of our plight.

So this was Craig Lovato. He was the DEA agent who had made it a personal crusade to hunt Howard down. I had never stopped to picture what he might be like. I felt sick. Amber fetched me a bucket and I vomited.

Like all Americans who meet abroad, Mari and Lovato chatted away like old friends about where in the States they came from and what schools they had been to. I found it strange, considering that a mere two weeks before, her husband Roger had been arrested.

Eventually Masha arrived and the girls ran to her. She came to hug me but Lovato told her not to touch me as I was under arrest. He told Mari she could now leave. We sat in the kitchen for a long time, about an hour or so. At one point Amber went out to sit on the terrace and was told by Lovato to stay put in the kitchen because she was in an 'arrest situation'. I sat in a chair with the girls and Patrick. Lovato sat next to us complaining about the heat, sweat beading on his gleaming forehead as he fanned himself with the local English newspaper, the *Daily Bulletin*. Masha sat close to me on a stool constantly telling me not to worry. She was convinced the whole scene was a ghastly mistake.

'Mummy, Mummy, this is the worst day of my life and I hope it's a nightmare and I'll wake up soon,' Golly whimpered.

'I hope it will be over soon too,' I said, not knowing how to comfort her. I did not know then that she had seen her father arrested violently with a gun.

She got up to go to the bathroom and Lovato barked, 'Where are you going?'

'To the bathroom,' she answered.

He rolled his eyes and muttered, 'Ask me before you go anywhere.'

'May I take my niece to the bathroom?' asked Masha.

Lovato grunted.

'Peter, doesn't Patrick look the splitting image of his father?' Lovato remarked to the Scotland Yard man before turning to me. 'Did you name him after your brother Patrick?'

'No, after my grandfather and Howard's grandfather.' I did not want him talking to me and I was unnerved by his referring so casually to my eldest brother.

Eventually a Spanish official showed an inventory in Spanish of all the items they were removing from the house.

'Sign this, Judit',' he said. I didn't know whether to sign it or not. Lovato said he didn't care if I did or didn't. Masha advised me to sign it, which I did with a very shaky hand.

There was hash in the house that Masha and Nigel had bought for Howard the night before – I thought it odd the police didn't touch it. Lovato asked for the car keys and I told him they were in my handbag. My bag then became an exhibit and was added to the list of articles to be removed from the house. When the time came to leave, I was shaking almost uncontrollably. I heard Lovato telling someone that I was hyperventilating. I couldn't bear leaving the children. They wouldn't let go of me.

Lovato told them I was going to see the judge and I would be home later in the day. Masha said she would arrange a lawyer for me.

I suddenly remembered Podge, Howard's eldest daughter, who was due to arrive the following day to spend the summer with us. I asked Masha to phone Rosie, and said that she had better tell Howard's parents.

I was led out of the gate by Lovato and put into the back of a police car. The Scotland Yard man got in beside me, and a Spanish policeman drove. As we pulled away I saw Lovato and another man I had spotted in a bar a few weeks earlier walking up the road in the direction of our local restaurant. Many little coincidences began to fall into place, and I now knew for sure I'd been under surveillance – for months or possibly even years. All those times I had felt I was being watched, I was.

I was driven to the police station on the Paseo Mallorca in Palma. As I walked up the station steps, crying, bewildered, freaked, I saw Jules walking down the steps with Lucinda, her daughter by David Embley. At the time Jules had left David and was living with Geoffrey Kenion, a situation that had created great drama on the island. She looked stunned when she spotted me but I was too distraught to acknowledge them or even wonder what they were doing there. Inside the police station a blonde woman greeted me in English. She said I had committed no crime in Spain but I was to be held awaiting extradition to the US.

This really was the nightmare we had been dreading.

I saw our policeman friend Rafael and begged him to do something. He looked embarrassed and upset. He explained there was nothing he could do. The initiative had come from the Americans and it was their show. The woman said something to two uniformed officers about fetching a doctor for me but they led me off. We went down three flights of stairs. When we reached the bottom, all I could see were cell doors. It was like going into medieval dungeons. The air-conditioning was full on and it was freezing cold.

I realized they were going to put me in one of the dungeon rooms. Apart from being cold down there, it was also dark. I flipped. I grabbed hold of the men and pleaded with them not to put me in a cell. They walked me back upstairs and out to a police car, and we drove to a doctor's surgery. He spoke no English and, such was my state, I think he thought I was a junkie. I babbled on about my children and protested my innocence but all it got me was a large injection of Valium and a ride in the police car back to the dungeon.

My wedding ring and watch were taken from me. While they were filling in details of my possessions, I spotted the names of David Embley and Geoffrey Kenion. I wondered who else they had arrested.

I was then shoved unceremoniously into a cell. It was almost pitch-black, the only light coming from a barred six-inch square cut high in the door. When I stood on tiptoe, I could see through into the dimly lit corridor. The only sound was dripping water from the air-conditioning unit. I felt tired and frightened.

At the back of the cell was a cold concrete bench, no cushion, no blanket – just a damp dark cell. I lay down on the cold slab and slept. The injection had knocked me out. Doors banging awakened me. I had no idea of how long I had slept – no idea of time at all.

I stood on tiptoe and peered through the bars of the door. Opposite I could see two toilets. Men from neighbouring cells were being allowed out two at a time to make use of the facilities. I spotted David Embley and Geoffrey Kenion. I noticed that as they were led back to their cells they were each given a blanket from a pile on the dirty floor. I was freezing cold and the overpowering smell of urine was making me feel ill. I wondered where Howard was and if he knew where I was.

Finally it was my turn to be let out. A policeman pointed to the toilet. It was a stand-up latrine, filthy with a swing-door falling off its hinges; when I had finished, they handed me a filthy, tatty blanket from off the floor. It stank of urine but it was so cold I flung it over my shoulders anyway. Once again, I was locked in.

I looked out of the door again hoping to catch a glimpse of Howard. Several minutes passed before I saw him. He didn't see me. He looked shattered. I called his name. He didn't hear me.

I waited until he came out of the toilet and as he passed by my cell I yelled again. He spun round, disbelief on his face at seeing mine peering through the tiny window.

'Jude, what are you doing here?'

'They're going to extradite me.'

He looked as if he had been punched. He stumbled backwards. 'They can't do that, you've done nothing wrong,' he said.

At that point a policeman shoved him. '*Silencio, silencio, no hable!*'

'*Pero es mi esposa,*' he pleaded.

'*Más tarde, más tarde,*' yelled the guard.

Howard was bustled away.

About half an hour later, my cell door opened and I was handed a bread roll. It was rock-hard, at least a week old. It was so dark in the cell I couldn't see if there was mould on it or not, but I did notice there was a small mound of bread rolls in the corner of the cell. I tossed my roll on to the heap, crawled back on the concrete slab and cried.

After what seemed an eternity I was summoned out of the cell and led upstairs. I was taken to an office where I recognized one of the men who had searched the house. I was introduced to a man who I was told was my lawyer. He spoke hardly a word of English and was exceedingly unfriendly. I was shown a piece of paper that declared I was being extradited to the United States because of my involvement in a series of cannabis importations totalling 700 tons and dating back to 1970. I was flabbergasted. In 1970 I was only fifteen years old. When asked if I would accept extradition, I replied no way. My lawyer shrugged and looked bored.

Lovato stuck his head round the door. I asked him about the magistrate and about going home to the children. He giggled. 'It's a fiesta and no magistrates work on fiestas – you should know that.'

I had forgotten that today was one of many Spanish fiestas. The Spanish man said I could telephone the children. I was in such a state I couldn't remember my own phone number. One of the Americans gave it to me. They all found my memory lapse amusing. I spoke to the children and told them I would not be seeing the magistrate that day. I tried to sound upbeat but it was a heart-rending call. Masha reassured me that everything was fine and a lawyer was being arranged for us. As I rang off, Howard was shown into the office. He looked pale and tired.

'Where are the children, Jude?'

'Masha has them. I've just spoken to them. Look at this, Howard, look what they are trying to do to me. I can't leave the children.'

Howard read the paper. 'They're nuts, Judy, absolutely nuts. Don't worry, we'll have a good lawyer soon who will sort this mess out.'

He was handed a sheet of paper more or less identical to mine. I was then led out and returned to the cells. Later I heard Howard coming back down. He called out to me not to worry, that if he went voluntarily to the States I would be released. That night was cold, dark, lonely and seemingly endless.

Early in the morning, I was fingerprinted, photographed and asked my details. I was then taken to a reception area, where Geoffrey Kenion already was. There was no sign of David.

'He's gone,' said Geoffrey. 'It's all his doing, you mark my words.'

Howard joined us. The guards came in and started to hand-cuff me.

'*Hombre, es mi esposa,*' Howard protested. '*No necesitan estos.*'

The guards argued back. They were laughing. I was crying.

We were all put into the same prison van and driven to the Palacio de Justicia.

As we emerged from the prison van, what felt like thousands of cameras flashed in our faces and thousands of journalists swarmed around us. I couldn't stand it. I wanted to hide. Howard kept apologizing to me. We were quickly taken through the throng to the Palacio's cells, where we were separated. One by one, we were taken up to see the magistrate. He was about my age with a kind face; the blonde woman from the police station the day before was there as an interpreter. She explained that because of a United States government request, I was to be held by the Audiencia Nacional in Madrid. I could volunteer for extradition at any time. I also had the right to fight the extradition, and I would have the backing of Spanish law if I did so. I was asked if I would accept extradition. I said no.

I begged the magistrate to let me go home to my children. I pleaded and pleaded. I had never left the children. The man looked sympathetic but said it was not his decision, that it was up to the Audiencia National in Madrid. The translator, also sympathetic, explained that I could have Patrick in jail with me. In Spain, children under the age of seven are allowed in jail to stay with their mothers. I was horrified at the thought of my little Patrick in jail. The magistrate told me I could use his phone to call the children.

Outside the magistrate's room a crowd of friends had gathered, and as I was led past them they called out that the children were fine and I shouldn't worry. I was too distraught to say anything. I was returned to the holding cells for several hours. As the three of us emerged from the Palacio, handcuffed again, the media circus was still there. Howard and I looked at each other as we were driven up to the Centro Penitenciario de Palma.

'Do you remember when we stood outside here with Rafael, and he told us they had chosen the location carefully as one in which there was no escape from the sun?'

'Yes,' he said quietly. 'I was just thinking the same thing.'

We got out of the van and were greeted by friendly, smiling wardens.

'Can I have the same cell as my husband?' I asked a warden and winked at Howard.

The wardens roared with laughter.

'*Posible, más tarde.*' They allowed me to give Howard a kiss before I was led off to the women's section.

It had been thirty hours since I had woken relaxed and happy in my own bed with the sun streaming through the windows. One and half days in which my whole world had been turned upside down.

CHAPTER TWENTY-SIX
Behind the Bars

The women's section of the jail in Palma was small. After preliminary form-filling, I followed the warden into a canteen-like dark room that led onto a concrete patio surrounded by high brick walls. Behind the brick walls were even higher brick walls with razor wire on top and armed-guard towers every 200 metres. A group of gypsies dressed in black sat out in the sweltering heat, watching their children play on the dusty concrete.

A large television placed high on a wall in the canteen was blaring out a South American soap opera. The room was full of about thirty women of all shapes, sizes and ages, all of whom took their eyes momentarily away from the television to stare at me. Looking down at a table, I could see why. Photographs of Howard and me filled the front page of the local newspapers and national press.

The warden, who had led me into this room, introduced me to a tall, long-haired blonde in her mid-twenties.

'This is Chantal, who you will share a room with.' She left and returned to the warden's office. Chantal was French but spoke English as well as Spanish, and was awaiting trial for having in her possession a couple of kilos of hashish. Although I was in shock from the events of the last thirty-odd hours, I was relieved to meet her. I'd been frightened about who I might find myself locked up with.

Within an hour of being there, I had a lawyer's visit. This took place in a small sitting room between the women's and men's sections of the jail.

He introduced himself as Luis Morrell and said he would be representing Howard and me in Palma. He was in his late forties, grey-haired and softly spoken. I immediately liked him. He explained that he had spoken to Masha and that she would be visiting me the following day. He said he had seen the children and they were being well taken care of. He gave me a bag of clean clothes that Masha had put together, all the newspaper cuttings of the last two days, a carton of cigarettes, some money and some handmade cards from Amber and Golly with photos of them all. He said he was about to go and see Howard and would try to arrange a visit between us. I asked him if it was possible for the Americans to extradite us. He explained that until he had seen all the paperwork it was impossible for him to say. He assured me, however, that he would do his damnedest to see that they didn't. Meanwhile, he asked me to write a statement describing the arrest.

It was with a heavy heart that I returned to the women's section. I had hoped to hear that it was all a terrible mistake. When I got back, it was siesta time and all the women were upstairs locked in their rooms. The warden escorted me up to mine. My legs were shaking almost as much as the large bunch of keys dangling from the warden's hand.

'*Tranquilo, tranquilo*, Judit',' she said as she patted me on the arm.

She unlocked the door, I walked in, then she closed and locked it from the outside. The sound of the keys disappeared back down the stairs.

There were two sets of bunk beds in this long narrow room. One set faced you as you walked in. It was opposite the door and to the right of the barred window. The other set was to the left of the door. In the far left corner was a sectioned-off area with a toilet bowl and a small sink. After the horror of my accommodation the night before I was glad to see it was at least clean.

Chantal was lying on the top bunk of the set facing the door, listening to her Walkman. She indicated that I should take one of the beds on the other set.

I climbed wearily onto the top bunk and gazed out of the

window at a view that was so similar to my view from home. I was locked up in prison just two kilometres from my children. What was going to happen to them? I curled up into a ball and wept until I felt as though there was no moisture left in my body.

The doors were unlocked at 6 p.m., when everyone had to exit their rooms and go back to the miserable canteen-like room downstairs. I took the bag of newspaper cuttings outside on to the patio, sat on the rough concrete ground and proceeded to read.

The media coverage was awesome. We were front-page headlines on all the tabloids and broadsheets in the UK. The competition in exaggeration was extraordinary. The *Daily Mirror* described Howard as 'the evil genius behind the world's biggest marijuana and hashish racket'. *The Times* claimed he was 'one of the top four drug barons in the world'. They all reported quotes from the Florida US attorney's office that they had just busted the 'biggest marijuana operation the world has ever seen'. Jack Hook, then the DEA spokesman in Miami, said: 'After Marks was acquitted at the Old Bailey, he is quoted as saying he was too smart, too sophisticated for any law enforcement agency to catch him. We are very pleased to have had the chance to make him eat his words.' *The Times* ran a story on how, according to Scotland Yard, the US had plotted the kidnapping of Howard but the authorities in Britain could not condone the kidnapping of one of its citizens. The papers had photos of Howard, Geoffrey and me all looking distinctly dishevelled as we were led into the Palma courthouse. Lord Moynihan was elevated to almost superhero status. 'Lord Supergrass', read a headline in the *People*.

Chantal called me into the canteen and there on the television were pictures of Howard and me. They were showing pictures of our house. This was followed by a film of a cave on the Costa Brava where 15 tons of Lebanese hash had just been discovered along with fast boats and a cache of machine-guns. This supposedly belonged to us, along with a fleet of freighters, finance houses and homes all over the world. It was all unreal. Howard described it to me later as 'a senseless Hollywood comedy'.

Before the newscast had finished, a warden called me. I was

shown into the sitting room where I had earlier met Luis Morrell. This time Howard sat there. As soon as I entered the room, he stood up and embraced me. I rested my head against his chest before uncontrollable sobbing rattled my exhausted body. He led me to a sofa at the far end of the room, keeping his arms wrapped tightly around me. We sat wordlessly for several minutes with our tears mingling together.

'Jude, I've only managed to arrange this visit by agreeing with the director of the prison that we would give a press interview.'

'Howard, I can't. Have you seen what they've been saying about us?' The idea of being interviewed appalled me.

'Jude, I think it's important that the world knows what the Americans are doing to you. Public sympathy can only help.'

'I just don't think I could answer any questions.' I felt my body shaking.

'I'll do that, Jude. At least this way we get some time together. I reckon the director of the jail gets a kickback when he lets them interview people.'

There was a knock at the door. About thirty journalists burst into the room. Flashbulbs went off and microphones were pointed at us as the journalists jostled for position. A couple of them placed packets of cigarettes on the coffee table in front of us before barraging us with questions.

Howard proclaimed that we were both innocent and pleaded to the Spanish authorities to let me go. The incessant questioning and bulbs flashing made my head feel as if it was going to explode. Eventually they left. We were given twenty minutes alone together but we were too exhausted to do anything other than sit with our arms around each other, drawing what comfort we could.

I arrived back in the women's section as dinner was being served. I sat down at a trestle table. A plastic bowl of unrecognizable meat in congealed fat was placed in front of me. Any tiny bit of appetite I might have had rapidly vanished. A big fat gypsy woman sitting opposite me laughed at the expression on my face and said, '*Es rata.*' It's rat. I could believe her.

Chantal told me to take no notice of her. 'The food is cooked in the men's section so it is always cold when it reaches here. You must eat to keep up your strength. If you have money, you can order food from outside, fresh fruit and juice and cold snacks. You can place an order this evening and it will arrive tomorrow.'

Later that evening I placed an order for some food and much-needed toiletries.

The following morning, after a restless night of tossing and turning, I had my first shower since my arrest. It made me feel marginally better physically but did nothing to dispel the ache in my heart or the fear I felt. Later in the morning I had another lawyer's meeting. I approached the meeting room at the same time as Howard. He looked grey, shattered; dark circles rimmed the blue eyes that had lost their fire and his shoulders drooped dejectedly.

In the room sat Luis Morrell and a balding, bearded, fattish man dressed in Howard's clothes. I was confused. Why was he wearing Howard's clothes?

'Judy, this is Michael Katz,' said Howard. This was the lawyer Howard had met in London and had asked to find out if there was an indictment against him. He'd said no. He clearly had it wrong. I shook his hand.

'Judy, do you have a statement about what happened at your house when you were arrested?' Katz asked me.

'Yes,' I said and handed it to him. He quickly scanned it.

'This is brilliant. I have Amber and Francesca's statements here which back Judy's up. Lovato has screwed up badly,' said Katz.

'In what way, Michael?' Howard asked.

'There is an act called the Mansfield Amendment. It forbids United States law enforcement agents from participating in a foreign arrest. You can beat your extradition on this,' Katz said gleefully. Luis raised his eyebrows sceptically; I got the impression from the way Luis looked at Katz that he was unimpressed by him. Katz had beside him Howard's briefcase; he picked it up and withdrew some papers. He handed us Amber and Golly's statements.

I read Golly's statement while Howard read Amber's.

Francesca Marks age seven

It was very early in the morning and me and Daddy were the only ones of the family up. Mummy and my sister and little brother were still asleep. The doorbell rang. I was in the mess room making a card. It was an American friend of ours. It was only five minutes until the doorbell rang again. I thought 'what a lucky day. We don't usually have so many visitors'. A dozen men barged in through the gate led by a fat, nasty look-ing man with a gun. I didn't know what was happening. I ran into the kitchen and saw Daddy with handcuffs behind his back. I started crying as the fat man was pointing a gun at my Daddy. He told our American friend Mari to get out but she said she wasn't Daddy's wife and just sat down. My Daddy told me to go upstairs and see Mummy. The fat, nasty man who I found out later was called Craig Lovato went upstairs first. I asked him what he was doing to my parents. He said 'your parents have been drug smuggling in the United States and I'm going to try to arrest them and take them there'. Upstairs I went into Mummy's bedroom. She was crying and cuddling Amber. She started to cuddle me. Lovato told Mummy he was going to take her and Daddy to the US. Mummy clutched onto us and said 'I'm not going to leave these children'. Lovato looked up and down Mummy who was wearing her silky dressing gown that was open and said 'I'll search the wardrobe for weapons then you can get dressed'. After he searched the wardrobe, he allowed Mummy to go into the bathroom and get dressed. We all went downstairs and Daddy was nowhere to be seen. The phone rang and Lovato answered it. 'Ah, Masha, just who I wanted to talk to. Can you come over here?' Masha is my aunt who was staying with us at the time. Masha arrived and Lovato wouldn't let her cuddle Mummy. He told her Mummy was under arrest. Men were searching the house and Mummy saw an English looking man walk past. She asked him where he was from. He said he could not answer. After a while he said 'I'm from Scotland Yard'. He went into the sitting room and I followed and I heard him telling someone about the phones and things in our house. Craig Lovato took Mummy to the police station. She was crying and trying to get back to Amber and I. Amber and I were crying. Lovato looked at us and said not to worry, as Mummy would be back that afternoon or tomorrow as it was a holiday but it was all lies.

When I'd finished reading her statement I had tears streaming down my face. I could not bear thinking of the horror she had witnessed. My poor sweet little Golly. I wished I could take the pain away.

'What will happen next, Luis?' Howard asked.

'All extradition cases are heard at the Audiencia Nacional in Madrid, so at some point you will both be taken there. The courts are all closed now until the beginning of September. I will try to keep you both here as long as possible so the children can visit you.'

'What about at least getting Judy bail?' Howard asked.

'As I say, the courts are closed now, and so far we don't know precisely what you are being charged with.'

The idea of being sent to Madrid appalled me and September seemed such a long way away. How could I possibly be separated from my children that long?

In the afternoon Masha came to visit me; she had visited Howard the day before. Men's and women's visits took place on alternate days. It was such a relief for me to see her face and sweet smile. The visit took place in a corridor of little cubicles. Prisoners were separated from their visitors by a sheet of almost opaque glass that was covered in smudgy handprints; at the bottom of the glass were a few pencil-sized holes through which conversation was meant to take place. With the noise of all the other prisoners and their visitors and screaming children, hearing Masha was difficult. She was able to reassure me that the children were fine. She had spoken to the prison director Joaquin Mejuto, who was going to let me have a visit with them in a few days in the small sitting room. She also gave me the depressing news that Patrick had been arrested in Miami, and our two cars had been confiscated. She told me that Marcus and Kieran were on their way down from France to visit me.

She was unhappy with Michael Katz. He was staying in our house, behaving as if it was his, and using the phone relentlessly. He was helping himself to all Howard's clothes, drinking his way through our wine collection and eating all the food. She had little money to run the house or pay the bills and supporting Katz was putting an added strain on her. On top of which she did not like him. His behaviour certainly sounded a bit odd.

All too soon the visit was over. She said she would visit Howard tomorrow and me the following day.

On the way back to the women's section, I was called into the little sitting room. Howard, Luis and Katz, now wearing a shirt I had bought for Howard the previous Christmas, were all sat in there.

'Howard, did you know they've arrested Patrick?'

'Yes, Michael has just told me. I'm sorry, Jude.'

'Who else have they arrested?' I asked.

'Balando and Moynihan's friend Jimmy Newton in London, Phil in Bangkok, Jim Hobbs in Amsterdam and a guy you don't know called Robb, John Denbigh in Vancouver, Pete, Patti, Wyvonna and Rick Brown in Los Angeles, some guy called John Francis in New York, some woman called Teresita Caballero in Miami and Malik in Karachi,' said Howard, sounding and looking glum.

I was shocked at the worldwide scale of the arrests.

'They've also charged Roger Reaves, so he's now up for extradition to America as well as Germany,' said Howard.

'There are also arrest warrants out for Gerry Wills, Ronald Allen, Bradley Weller and George Lane,' said Katz.

'George – why George?' I asked, surprised and fearful.

'I don't know, Jude. It's all madness,' said Howard.

I wondered if George and Yvonne were still in Thailand.

I thought about my father. In March, he had been invited to Buckingham Palace to be presented with an OBE from the Queen. I wondered how he felt now with two children in jail and one being hunted for allegedly being the biggest drug smugglers in the world.

At the end of the legal visit, the director wanted us to give an interview to some television companies; in return, he would give us time alone.

The interview was a rerun of the previous day. Howard again made impassioned pleas for my release, stressing my complete innocence and the suffering of the children. Four lots of TV crews interviewed us, one after the other. I felt too drained to say anything and let Howard answer all the questions.

When the interviews were over, we were allowed forty minutes together.

'Jude, why don't you have Patrick in with you?'

'I couldn't do that, Howard. The conditions are too rough for a child. The only women with children in here are the gypsies and they are all crowded into one small room together.'

'I was just thinking if you had Patrick with you it would make it harder for them to shunt you around.'

'I'm not using Patrick for my convenience. He is much better with his sisters and in the house he's used to. It would be horrible for him in here. What do you think they are charging us with, Howard?'

'I would imagine some kind of conspiracy; Katz keeps mentioning something called RICO but he doesn't seem to know what it is.'

'I don't think I like Katz, and what's he doing wearing all your clothes and using your briefcase?'

'It's very odd behaviour, isn't it?'

'It's extraordinary,' I said. 'But why do you think it's a conspiracy charge?'

'Because American conspiracy law is the most powerful weapon they have. It makes every member of a criminal conspiracy guilty of the criminal acts of every other member of the conspiracy. The members don't even have to know each other to be members. Even legal acts become criminal if they are in furtherance of the conspiracy. It's a scary law, Jude.'

We both lapsed into silence and spent most of the rest of the visit as we had the day before, arms wrapped tightly around each other trying to give each other comfort.

At the end of the visit, we kissed goodbye.

'I'll see you tomorrow, love. Try and get some rest,' Howard said.

'See you tomorrow, Howard.'

Early the next morning I was told to go to the main door of the women's section. Through the barred six-inch hole in the door Howard's face peered.

'Jude, they're taking me, I'm being moved.' His voice sounded slightly hysterical and tears glinted in the dark rings of his eyes.

'Where to?'

'They won't say but probably Madrid.'

'But we've got a lawyer's visit later,' I said.

'Jude, I've got to go. Take care and, Jude, don't forget no matter what – I love you.'

He was led away.

'I love you too,' I said to the now faceless six-inch square.

I felt empty with Howard gone. When would I see him again? I spent the morning sitting listlessly in the one tiny piece of shade on the patio. Sadness, in which I could neither think nor feel, shrouded me like a thick fog.

Marcus and Kieran came to visit. Marcus broke down in tears to see me behind bars. He promised me that if I were moved to Madrid he would visit me as often as he could.

Luis Morrell came to visit me, without Katz, who had left the island for the mainland to try to find where they had moved Howard.

'Where's Howard, Luis?'

'He'll be on his way to Madrid. It often takes a week or so to transfer prisoners there. He may well stay a few days in Barcelona or Valencia depending on which route they take.'

'And me?'

'I have applied to the courts to keep you here as long as possible. The director is going to allow you an hour-long visit with the children. Now, I have power-of-attorney forms for you to sign to allow your sister to take care of your affairs while you are in here. I would like to tell you, Judy, that I think what the Americans are doing to you is a disgrace.'

I signed the forms and returned to the women's section.

Two days later, I was called for the visit from my children. I felt nervous. It had been ten days since that dreadful day, ten days since I had seen them. It felt much longer. I was beginning to feel terrifyingly used to the dull ache in my heart. My life, which had been so full and purposeful and had centred entirely on Howard and the children, had lost all its clarity.

As I walked in the door, Amber and Golly ran into my arms. I held them closely to me, drew in their smell, felt the silkiness of their hair and revelled in the sound of their voices as they cried Mummy, Mummy.

They sat with me on the sofa. I looked at Patrick. His long blond curls circled his little face. He was sitting on Masha's knee watching me warily.

'Patrick, are you going to come and give Mummy a kiss?' I asked as I held my arms out to him. He buried his face in Masha's chest. Tears sprang into my eyes. Amber noticed. She got up and went over to him.

'Patrick, come to Amber.'

He turned to her and held out his little arms; she picked him up and came and sat down beside me. It took about ten minutes before I could coax him onto my lap. I finally had all three of my precious children in my arms again.

We sat, chatted, cuddled and hugged. Then the visit was over. I handed Patrick to Masha and he again hid his face in her chest. We all put on brave faces and tried not to cry.

'We can come and see you again soon, Mummy,' said Amber, who seemed to have matured very much in the ten days since I had last seen her.

'Oh, I do hope so, my lovely children,' I said as I struggled to hold back the tears.

They left. I watched them disappear out of the massive iron gate. And once again the feeling of desolation swamped me.

The days in Palma prison were monotonous. I wondered how the prisoners who had been there a few years survived. Apart from the canteen room and the patio, there was nowhere else to go. And apart from a few board games, a few books and the television, there was nothing else to do. Once a week the Salvation Army came with clothes and books to give to the women. For some of the women, this was the only visit from the outside they got. I learnt to have a great deal of respect for this organization as I realized how awful these women's lives would be without it. I spent my time waiting for my visits from Masha, eagerly waiting to hear news of Howard and the children. Since Howard had left Palma, no one had heard from him. I worried about him and missed him so much. I felt so much more insecure now he was gone.

Queen's College had been in touch with Masha and had offered Amber and Golly their places back at the school. It seemed the best option. It didn't seem right to move them now when they so needed the support of their friends and their friends' parents. Life was hard enough for them without uprooting them to a new school. Also the school in London was double the cost of the school in Palma, and money was going to be a big issue. Before his departure, Howard had arranged for money to be sent to a friend to support Masha and the children.

As the hot August days passed by, I became more and more terrified at the thought of moving to Madrid. Luis Morrell had no idea when the move would take place but suspected it would be before the start of September.

He said the director had promised I would have another private visit with the children before this happened.

Late one afternoon I was told that my children were here to visit me. I realized this meant my move to Madrid was imminent. My heart felt like a fist was gripping it. I didn't know if I would cope with saying goodbye to them.

It was a heart-rending visit. Patrick behaved even more distantly to me. Amber and Golly also realized this signalled my move to Madrid and clutched me tightly. We had no idea when or where we would see each other again.

'You will be home for Christmas, won't you, Mummy?' asked Golly.

'Of course she will be, silly,' said Masha, tousling Golly's hair.

Christmas – that was four months away. They had to let me out by then, hadn't they?

CHAPTER TWENTY-SEVEN
Yeserias

I arrived in the Centro Penitenciario de Yeserias on 23 August. I spent two days in *Ingresos* before entering the main body of the prison. I felt scared.

A couple of German women who had been with me in *Ingresos* moved into the main prison the day before me. They had returned a few hours later white and shaken, with tales of having been physically attacked and mugged with knives by Spanish junkies. They had described it as a jungle.

They had made complaints, filed a report and were now to be kept in isolation cells in the *Ingresos* section of the prison for their own protection.

It was my turn to join the jungle. I had done what the Dutch woman in Valencia had suggested I did, which was to tell the wardens that I had a friend called Lillian in department two. The contents of my case were removed and the case deposited in a room stacked to the ceiling with them, then I had the briefest of medical inspections. This consisted of no more than a couple of questions. I was given my possessions in a black rubbish bag and went with a warden out into the main prison. It was siesta, so all was quiet. I followed her out into a narrow street with narrow pavements; it had on either side what I had thought were two-storey derelict buildings. The street, which was one hundred and ten paces long, had brick walls at either end with even higher brick walls behind them covered in razor wire, among the wire the now ominously familiar heavily armed guard towers.

We entered the building on the opposite side of the street and climbed a wide staircase before coming to double iron doors that had glassed barred windows in the upper half. Above the door was a sign with '*Dept Dos*' written on it. With her large bundle of keys, the warden opened the door. To the right was a bathroom area with cubicles of showers and lavatories. To the left was a kitchen area. We then walked into what struck me as a large chaotic hospital ward. Thirty bunk beds lined the walls; large barred windows with washing lines strung across them separated every two beds. A mixture of black and white faces watched me. Women were in bed sleeping or reading, or sitting on each other's beds chatting and knitting. Different radio stations were on throughout the room, which made for a discordant medley of noise. I walked up the centre isle towards the end of the room where the warden pointed out an empty bunk bed. It seemed I had the choice between the bottom and the top. I chose the bottom. The warden deposited some clean sheets on the bed and left.

Two young women lying on the bottom bed next to mine, arms round each other, smiled warmly.

'*Hola*,' they said.

'Do you speak English?' I asked.

One of them answered. 'Yes, a little. I am Raisa and this is Jessica. I'm from Colombia and Jessica is from Venezuela. Are you from England?'

'Yes, but I have been living in Spain for a few years. How long have you been here?' I asked.

'Twenty months and Jessica eighteen. We should learn our sentences soon.'

'What are you charged with?' I asked.

'Oh, I had six kilos of cocaine and Jessica had seven – we're expecting six to eight years.'

I was surprised by the casual way she admitted their crimes and the casual way they seemed to accept years in jail.

A small attractive French Algerian woman with a kerchief tied round her head came up to me.

'Hi, I'm Bahia. I've seen you in the newspapers. My husband is in Alcala-Meco prison as well. Maybe our husbands know each other.'

I had not heard from Howard since he had left Palma. The only communication Masha had from him was a telegram telling her he had arrived at a prison in Madrid.

'Do you hear from him at all?' I asked.

'Yes, we're allowed a phone call once a week; you will be allowed one too.'

'Are you allowed only one phone call a week?'

'One phone call to your husband if he's in jail and one phone call to your family – you need to put in an application. I'll help you.'

She and her husband were in for extradition to Germany and Yugoslavia. She was cagey about the exact crimes but I got the impression that her husband had committed armed robbery in Germany and smuggled weapons into Yugoslavia. I could never work out what the charges against her were.

Yeserias was originally a plaster factory. During the Spanish Civil War it became a military hospital. It was now Madrid's only women's prison with an official capacity of 369. When I was there it held over 640, and fifty children up to the age of six.

Bahia offered to show me around. She warned me not to walk round by myself, certainly not for the first couple of weeks until my face became known.

'Is it really that bad?'

'It's the Spanish junkies – they'll attack and steal from you and they always go for a new face.'

'Where are they?'

'The Spanish and the foreigners are locked up separately. There are three foreign departments, this one, department one next door and the morgue.'

'The morgue?'

'Yes, from when it used to be a hospital. It still feels like a morgue – it has white tiles on the walls and feels spooky. You're lucky they didn't put you in there. It's where they usually put newcomers.'

'How many Spanish departments are there?'

'There are three, and there is another department for the under-eighteens. We never see them. They're kept separately. There's a separate department for mothers and children too. It's mainly the gypsies who have children in here, but there are two Nigerians with kids too.'

Just then, a tall young woman with a long mane of dark blonde hair and a pleasant face joined us.

'Would I be right in thinking you're English?' she asked in a lovely soft Irish brogue. It was the most welcome sound I had heard in a long while.

'Yes, I'm Judy,' I said, and felt the first flicker of a smile for weeks. 'Dee,' she said.

Dee was from Dublin and had been in Yeserias for nine months. She had flown from Venezuela into Madrid's Barajas airport with 6 kilos of cocaine. She was expecting an eight-year sentence. She was one of the most balanced, bright, straightforward people I have ever met.

'It was a moment of utter madness, Judy. What could I have been thinking?' she said when she reflected on what she had done.

The doors were unlocked at eight o'clock and I followed Bahia and Dee down the stairs to the canteen, which was underneath our department. There were masses of women everywhere. We joined a long line of women queuing for their dinner.

When I arrived at Yeserias, there were about three hundred foreigners in the prison and all except for four were in for smuggling drugs. The largest nationality groups were the Nigerians, who had smuggled heroin, and the Colombians, who had smuggled cocaine. There were also a few Lebanese who had smuggled heroin. The four women who were not in for drugs were Bahia, a German woman called Andrea, a Frenchwoman called Lawrence and my supposed friend Lillian.

Andrea faced extradition to Germany for the murder of her husband. She looked like Morticia from *The Addams Family*. She had straight dark waist-length hair and swanned around in designer gear as if she was in a five-star hotel. She smoked her cigarettes in a long ebony cigarette-holder. Dee informed me that she came from a very wealthy German family.

Lillian was a small chubby Belgian in her mid-forties who was facing extradition to France for fraud.

Lawrence was a bubbly French prostitute who was in for murder. Her trick was to lace her clients' drinks before robbing them. Unfortunately for her, one of her clients was a priest with a weak heart, and another client was a judge. Sentencing did not bode well for her. She approached me one day.

'I met your husband a few months ago,' she said.

'Really?' I dreaded what she might be about to tell me.

'Yes, in a bar in the centre of town with two Americans, Gerry and Flash. I had a good time with Gerry, nice guy.'

Given Gerry's liking for prostitutes, it was not surprising they had met. I wondered how long it would be before I could ask Howard about it.

The Spanish prisoners, as far as I could tell, were mostly in for drug-related crimes, mainly robbery and mugging. They were nearly all junkies. They looked emaciated; scabs, open sores and puncture marks covered their skin. There were no treatment programmes for them. Twenty-five per cent of the prison population was HIV positive, and they were nearly all Spanish. Dee told me she had heard there were only three needles in the entire prison.

The other large ethnic group were the gypsies, otherwise known as the Roma. This group makes up 25 per cent of female prisoners in Spain's jails. In Spanish society, the Roma community suffers from long-established discrimination and negative stereotyping. They are looked down on as dirty, suspicious foreigners, entrepreneurs in thievery, con games, drug dealing and extorting money from tourists and elderly citizens. They kept themselves to themselves and always dressed in black.

Unlike Palma, prison life in Yeserias was far from monotonous. On the first street between *Ingresos* and the building holding my department were the visiting cubicles, similar to the ones in Palma. Next to them was the telephone room, which was kept locked except for a few hours when each department was allocated a time to make or receive calls. In the walls of the crumbly old buildings were bullet holes left over from the Civil War. It added to the feel of being in a ghetto. Next to the telephones was the 'bank', which opened for an hour twice a week in the morning. If you were lucky enough to have someone on the outside to give you money, this is where you collected it. Care would need to be taken on leaving here, as this is where the junkies hung round waiting to grab a victim. Opposite here were various classrooms. Once a day, at two o'clock, one of the classroom windows turned into a poste restante. It led to scenes of total chaos.

Walking through my building, passing the canteen on the right, you came out on to another street. This street housed the mother and child department, the library, the factory where work was sent in from outside for the prisoners, and the supermarket that was open in the morning for three hours. A tall attractive woman ran it; she was in her late twenties. She had been a member of the Basque terrorist group ETA and had a twenty-year sentence for blowing up a judge. Most women terrorists were kept apart from the general prison population and housed in the men's Madrid jail, Carabanchel. She had apologized for her crime, denounced ETA and been moved to Yeserias.

Above the factory and library were the Spanish departments and the morgue. On the other side of the building were a small court-yard and the sports area. The sports area was mainly kept locked. It included a volleyball court, built on the old cemetery from the time this had been a military hospital.

Your bed was provided, but other items of furniture had to be purchased. I was lucky to inherit a bedside table from the previous occupant of my bed. Bahia managed to secure me a locker. Dee decided to move into the bunk above me, and between us we bought a table and chairs to put at the end of our bunks.

About five or six Nigerians ran the jail. They were the ones who smuggled in the largest amounts of heroin. This occurred during face-to-face visits. Once a month each inmate was allowed a visit in a small sitting room that also contained a bed in case the visit was conjugal. They would have their friends on the outside bring in the heroin on these visits, and they would insert the package into their vagina. The wardens were powerless to stop it as they were forbidden to do internal searches.

In the bed opposite me a small buxom Nigerian woman with a huge smile who was known as Mama ran a shop out of her locker. In the morning she would go down to the supermarket and stock up on packets of cigarettes, cartons of milk, biscuits and anything else she thought might sell later in the day when the supermarket closed. She marked up by 50 per cent.

The Spanish made their money either by stealing it or selling clothes their relatives on the outside had handed in for them. Many of the items were of a high quality – 'Morticia' was one of their top customers.

My first day in department two had been exhausting. There was a lot to assimilate. There were about four couples in the dormitory, including Raisa and Jessica. Dee had told me that many of the Colombians and a few of the Nigerians were lesbians. This made me nervous – I thought of American prison scenes I had seen in movies. Both Bahia and Dee reassured me it was not like that and that they had never had any problem.

I went to sleep quickly the first night and managed a few hours' sleep. I woke about six o'clock in the morning to find a cockroach staring at me from the bedside table. It was a sight I was to get used to; the place was crawling with them. The hardest to accept was the fact they lived in the frames of the beds.

At eight o'clock in the morning, the wardens opened the doors and shouted for everyone to be up. One warden would address us as 'narco-trafficantes'. We had to stand at the side of our beds and be counted. There were between fifty-four and sixty women in my department. The doors were left open until ten, during which time there was a mad rush to the supermarket. From ten onwards the doors were opened every hour in case you wanted to go out or come in. The factory and classes started at ten o'clock. At half past one, the doors were opened until three in the afternoon, when there was another count. The whole prison was then locked up until four thirty. The doors would again be opened on the hour until eight in the evening, then left unlocked until ten o'clock before the final count and lock-in for the night. The lights were turned off at midnight.

The following day I heard my name being called over the tannoy. I had a lawyer's visit. Bahia showed me where to go and said she and Dee would keep an eye out for me to walk me back to the department after the visit had finished.

I was shown into the lawyer's cubicle and met a distinguished-looking man in a bow tie who introduced himself as Gustavo López-Muñoz y Larraz. He said that Bernard Simons had asked him to come and see Howard and me. He had seen Howard the previous day; Howard had retained him for our defence against extradition. He was Cuban, and one of Spain's top criminal extradition lawyers. His family practised law in Florida and his English was fluent. I asked him how Howard was. He said he was bearing up; he was in Alcala-Meco, Madrid's top security jail, but had been put under a very austere regime known as article ten. He was going to apply for Howard to be removed from this and then we would be allowed conjugal visits.

I asked him about the extradition process. He explained that the precise charges and accompanying documents had to be submitted by the Americans to the Spanish authorities within forty days of arrest. The Audiencia Nacional then had a further forty days to make a decision. Both time periods were extendable in certain circumstances. An absolutely final decision had to be made within two years.

I asked him about my chances of getting bail. He reassured me that he was confident of getting me bail before Christmas and that he would be applying as soon as Howard and I had made our first appearance at the court, which would take place shortly. This appearance would be a formality, in which we would be asked whether we accepted extradition. I left the interview feeling a lot lighter than I had in a long time.

Dee and Bahia were waiting for me in the street outside. I repeated my conversation with my lawyer.

'That's fantastic news, Judy. You'll be home with your kids for their birthdays,' said Dee, smiling happily at me. Bahia kept quiet.

Every evening after dinner, Dee, Bahia and I walked endlessly up and down the street. It was the only form of exercise we got. The Spanish pestered us for cigarettes or money. The gypsies stood in groups and often performed impromptu flamenco dancing accompanied by clapping and singing. At half past nine a quiet descended on the prison as lists of those inmates due to go to court, hospital or allowed conjugal visits with their husbands in other jails were read out over the tannoy. One evening in September my name was called for the Audiencia Nacional. I felt excited. I would see Howard.

The following morning I went to the reception and joined the other four women due in court that day. After being processed out of the jail and handcuffed, we were herded into the back of a police van. The van took off into the streets of Madrid. With its siren blaring, it careered round corners, throwing us off our seats and tossing us from one side of the van to the other. It was a terrifying journey.

I was locked up in the dungeons of the court. I called out Howard's name.

I heard his voice call back from a distance. I immediately felt better just to have him close by. The walls, stained in time and crime, were covered in scratched messages. I added, 'I love you, Howard.'

After an hour we were led out of our cells. Our eyes met and the guards allowed us a short hug, a hug that was so comforting in its familiarity with his warm smell and touch, and so frustrating in its duration. He was dressed in a Giorgio Armani jacket I had bought him the year before in Rome. His hair was longer than usual and he looked tired and had lost weight. We were led holding hands to a waiting room outside the court. Geoffrey Kenion joined us.

The court appearance was brief. We were each asked if we would accept extradition to the United States. We each said no.

Saying goodbye was as hard as ever. We both smiled and tried to keep the tears from our eyes. The only comfort was that we were allowed a three-minute phone call to each other on Saturdays. I loved hearing his voice.

The first bail application failed. I was devastated. I had felt sure I would be home for Amber's eleventh birthday at the end of October. This prompted my brother Marcus and his girlfriend Kieran to leave the mill in the Dordogne and move to Madrid. In return for their keep, they had agreed to visit Howard and I as often as permitted, and liaise between our lawyers, our co-defendants' lawyers, our friends, our families and us. For me it was a lifeline – the three-minute phone call to the children was inadequate to find out how they were and the post was unreliable.

Masha brought the children to Madrid to see me as a birthday treat. All our birthdays are in November, except Amber, who was born at the end of October. I couldn't face seeing them through glass and couldn't understand how Howard was able to. I was due a two-hour face-to-face visit and put in an application for the children to see me then. It was approved. I applied for an interview to see the governor of the jail. It was granted. Dee came with me to translate. Normally children lived either in the jail with their mothers or with relatives who brought them to visit. I asked the woman governor if Patrick, who was only to be in Madrid for four days, could spend the days with me and go back to Masha in the evening. Everyone advised me it was unheard of and my request would be refused. The governor, much to my delight, agreed.

For four days, Masha brought Patrick to the prison and handed him over to a warden who after the briefest search handed him to me. Amber and Golly filled his pockets with loving little notes and poems to me. I filled his pockets with notes to them. We nicknamed him Postman Pat. I was moved during the daytime to the mother and children's department. It was in an even worse condition and far filthier than the department I was normally in. Luckily, Patrick and I only needed to be in here during the afternoon lock-up hours of three to four thirty.

I was distressed by Patrick's behaviour; he would thump my face, scratch my eyes, pull my hair and bite me. There was much anger in him towards me and I was riddled with guilt. What had happened to my placid, happy little boy? Those four days reinforced my decision that to have Patrick living with me in jail would have been wrong. He was an extremely cute baby with large blue eyes and tumbling golden curls. He attracted much attention and I lived in fear that every time someone touched him he would catch a disease. I found the visits stressful. There was very little I could offer him in entertainment and he disliked the fuss that was made of him by the other prisoners.

Masha came to visit me in the glass cubicle. She looked tired and complained of having a burst eardrum. She said she didn't know how it had happened. My elder sister Natasha, who now lived in Key West in Miami, constantly wrote to me offering to come and help Masha with the children.

Masha said she was fine and having Natasha and her two boys would be added work and more strain on the finances. Natasha had had another son the year before I had Patrick.

The face-to-face with the children was wonderful. Amber and Golly seemed to be happy back at Queen's College and said the teachers were been wonderful to them and academically they were both doing very well. They had met Muñoz and liked him. He had told them he was confident I would have bail by Christmas. Saying goodbye to them all was no easier than at any other time. We had all just learnt to hide our tears better.

Marcus and Kieran took it in turns to visit Howard and me. One day Kieran would visit me, and Marcus would visit Howard; the next day Marcus would visit me, and Kieran would visit Howard. They sent us in wonderful food packages from El Corte Inglés. I no longer went down to the canteen in the evening but ate dinner of smoked salmon, avocados and assortments of cheeses upstairs in the department. I still went to the canteen at lunchtime, not for the food but for my glass of beer. Each inmate was allowed one glass of beer with their lunch. Dee and I bribed some Spanish girls with cigarettes to give us their allotted beers too. We saved them to have with our dinner in the evenings. It seemed to make life more civilized, even if the beer was flat. I had also managed to purchase an electric cooking ring. If chicken was served in the canteen, I would bring it upstairs and make a curry. I also kept a saucepan of Jamaican coffee Marcus and Kieran had sent in on the go.

During the day, the department was quiet. Most of the women were at work or at classes. Working or going to classes counted towards their sentences.

I enjoyed the quietness when they were all out. I had time to shower in peace and answer all my letters. Marcus and Kieran had sent me wool and I kept busy knitting the children birthday and Christmas presents.

The evenings between eight and ten were the busiest times. Women wandered in and out of the different departments. The Spanish came round hawking their wares or trying to steal. The Lebanese came round offering to tell your fortune from coffee grinds or from your cigarettes or, for a higher price, your palm. Mama was at her busiest with her locker shop, arguing loudly with her customers over prices.

Dee, Bahia and I sat at our table and watched the goings-on, bemused.

Marcus, Kieran and Muñoz were all confident I would get bail and be home with the children for Christmas. It made me feel stronger. Muñoz strongly believed that bail would be granted this time because all our female co-defendants had been granted bail in the States' and my brother Patrick had been offered release on bail for a $1,000,000 bond. In London another defendant, Jimmy Newton, was out on bail.

Friends in London, the children's teachers, Dr Lee, psychiatrists and residents and friends from Mallorca all wrote compelling letters to the court supporting Muñoz's application for my bail.

Muñoz came to see me; he had tears in his eyes. The court had denied my bail application. I had missed my children's birthdays and I was now to miss spending Christmas with them. I saw in my mind the disappointment on their faces and felt their pain sear through me.

Fears span in my pounding head; I was drowning in blackness.

CHAPTER TWENTY-EIGHT
Racketeering Influenced Corrupt Organization

Marcus got hold of the American indictment against us from Patrick's wife Jude. There were in total twenty-two people indicted, including Howard and me. Among them were my two brothers Patrick and George. I and almost all the other co-defendants had been charged with conspiring to import 15,500 kilos of hashish into the United States during 1986. George had not been apprehended. It was thought he was still in Thailand.

Howard, Ernie and Patrick had all been charged with RICO: the Racketeering Influenced Corrupt Organization law, which had originally been passed by Congress to attack the mafia, but was now frequently used against drug smugglers. It was depressing reading.

Howard was charged with running, from 1970 until 1987, an enterprise devoted to cannabis dealing and money laundering. He had separately been charged with conspiracy to run such an enterprise along with a whole host of other acts and conspiracies ending with money laundering in 1987. The 1987 money-laundering charge was because of Patrick and Lord Moynihan's meeting, which had been taped by Moynihan and filmed by the DEA. This meeting allowed Lovato to go before a Miami grand jury and procure the indictment. Without this meeting, using Miami as a venue would have been near impossible. The LA US attorney's office had refused to prosecute the case for lack of evidence: there was no money and no dope save for the meagre amount found in Ernie's (Pete's) room. With the telephone taps, the Nevada 1973 speaker scam, the 1986 LA load and the money-laundering 1987 Miami meeting, they had enough to go after Howard, Ernie and Patrick with the formidable RICO.

Christmas in jail was miserable. Shortly before Christmas, as the weather became colder, the number of Spanish inmates increased dramatically. This apparently happened every winter. By being in jail destitute or drug-addicted Spanish women at least had a roof over their heads, even though the prison itself was freezing. The hot-water system constantly broke down and fights broke out more often, especially if there was a shortage of heroin in the prison. Then windows were smashed in the Spanish departments and the more desperate junkies slashed themselves, apparently to create a better high. We could see them in their department across the street from our windows.

The prison wardens made an effort to cheer the place up for Christmas. Fairy lights were strung up, tinsel was hung on the bars, a large Christmas tree was placed in the canteen and Christmas carol concerts were organized. An extra special meal was served and glasses of Spanish champagne were handed out. This all had the effect on me of increasing the isolation I felt at being apart from my family. I thought of the fun the girls and I had decorating the tree each year, and this year Patrick could join in. I thought of the fun of Christmas shopping and of their school Christmas carol concert. I felt terribly alone, and I thought they must too.

That night in the department all the women dressed up: jewellery was worn, hair was piled up, stockings and high-heeled shoes were put on, eyeshadow, lipstick and mascara applied. The shabby clothes, the unmade-up faces, the curlers were all gone. Dee hid under her covers suffering from a severe migraine which had had her bedridden all day.

Raisa, who was a talented musician and singer, got out her guitar and played. She sang some popular Colombian songs and some of the women danced. Within this small barred-in world, they were all there for each other, physically and emotionally. I felt apart

340

from them. I couldn't enjoy Raisa's songs when my children were suffering. The music intensified my pain. I was glad when Christmas was over.

In the New Year, Muñoz came to see me. He had managed to have Howard taken off article ten and moved back into the normal prison. This meant we could now apply to the court for a conjugal visit. The Audiencia Nacional had received all the paperwork from the Americans and a date for the extradition hearing would be given shortly. In the supporting document for my extradition request, Lovato said I had: 'instructed members of the organization in the furtherance of their illegal activities. These instructions included money transfers, coordinating travel and communications between the members of the organization. JUDITH MARKS has full knowledge of all alias' [sic] and codes utilized by the organization and such [sic] can pass instructions in the absence of her husband DENNIS HOWARD MARKS, with the same proficiency as he.'

Muñoz felt that in my case the fight against extradition could be won. He explained to me that there were a number of ways in which it was possible to fight extradition. 1) Being of Spanish nationality. 2) Being charged with an offence not recognizable in Spanish law. 3) Being arrested for an offence committed so long ago that it lay outside the Spanish statutes of time limitations. 4) Showing that there wasn't a shred of evidence admissible in a Spanish court to support the charge. 5) Showing that one had already been tried somewhere for the same offence. 6) Showing that the offence was a political one. 7) Showing that the resulting sentence could be one of death. 8) Showing that the resulting sentence could be more than thirty years, the maximum sentence allowed under Spanish law. 9) Showing that another country had a stronger extradition claim.

'Now, Judy, you've been charged with conspiracy. There is no offence of conspiracy recognizable in Spanish law. You can't be extradited from Spain to America unless what the Americans allege you did is recognizable under Spanish law. Howard's case is a lot more complicated. However, as most of his alleged crimes took place in Spain he should be tried here. To make sure this happens I am going to have a lawyer friend of mine launch an *acción popular*.

This is when a group of outraged citizens launch a private prosecution against any criminal the authorities have failed to deal with.'

'What sentence would he get in Spain?' I asked.

'The very worse he would face is twelve years. He would be eligible for *permisos* after serving two. *Permisos* allow you home once a month for a week. If the case was tried in Spain, you would be released immediately.'

I knew about *permisos*: quite a few of the women I knew had them. It was another way drugs got into the prison.

Marcus came to see me in the New Year. He and Kieran had spent the Christmas holidays in Palma with Masha and the children. He reported that all was well. He told me that Jude had sent copies of over ten thousand papers of evidence against us, two thousand of which were transcripts of telephone conversations, and that Howard was studying it all.

Marcus said the news from Miami was good. The only evidence they had against us were the telephone taps and they were illegal, and all the American lawyers were confident at having them thrown out of court. They also thought that Moynihan could easily be discredited as any kind of reliable witness. Marcus also told me that if the worst came to the worst, the charge against me carried a maximum sentence of five years.

The days dragged by. Survival, I discovered, was a skill that required dulling the mind and the senses. Howard was keeping busy talking to the press. He boasted about the number of Spanish laws he had broken, gave detailed accounts of how much hashish he had smuggled into Spain. The Spanish authorities ignored it all. The *acción popular* was rejected by the lower court, without saying why, and the high court rejected the appeal.

In early January 1989, Amber went to London to stay with Julian and Helen Peto, who were going to coach her through her common entrance exams. We still held out the hope I would be free soon and the girls could continue their education in England.

After years of not smoking dope, I started smoking again.

Bahia, Dee and I spent the evenings until the lights were switched off getting stoned and playing Scrabble. One evening when I was particularly stoned, Dee and I went into department one. Dee, to earn money, made beautiful birthday cards and greeting cards for women to send to their friends and relatives. Georgina, a middle-aged Belgian woman, had ordered a few. As we walked in we were astounded to see Georgina and Andrea (Morticia) dressed to the nines, sitting down to dinner at an immaculate white-linen-covered table, sipping Ribena out of cut glass. All around them was the normal madness: Spanish haggling, radio sets blaring and two Nigerians having a particularly heavy fight with chairs over drug money sparred at each other. Georgina and Andrea appeared oblivious to it all. If you ignored the surroundings, it looked as if they were enjoying dinner in a five-star restaurant. The thought occurred to me that people were being kind to me when they said I was in prison. I wasn't. I was in a lunatic asylum. I started feeling paranoid.

At the beginning of February, I heard that the Audiencia Nacional had given permission for Howard and me to have a conjugal visit. I was driven to his prison with nine other women. The police cracked ribald jokes during the journey and the Spanish women responded with equally bawdy remarks.

Upon arrival at the prison, I was shown into a double bedroom. Five minutes later Howard walked in, clutching sheets and looking rather sheepish. We had an amazing, breathtaking two hours together. Maybe things were going to get better.

I started having nightmares about the children. I would wake hearing Golly and Patrick crying. I continually sought assurance from Marcus and Kieran that they were okay. They said they were fine but maybe Nigel was drinking a bit much. About the same time, I received some photos from Masha of Golly and Patrick. Golly looked haunted; she was pale and her cheekbones jutted out. Patrick looked pale and unhappy.

I cried.

'Dee, what's happening to my children, what's happening to my children?'

She also thought the photos were disturbing but there was little she could do to comfort me.

'Look, Judy, if they weren't all right someone or the school would let you know.'

Golly's class teacher, Mrs Ramonell, frequently wrote to me and I tried to convince myself that Dee was right. But every night the nightmares persisted.

I suggested to Marcus that Golly should join Amber in London for half-term. While Golly was in London, she became ill. Liz Denbigh, John's wife, took her to see Dr Lee.

I received a telegram. The contents chilled me.

Judy, sorry about the circumstances. You must remove the children from your sister's and her 'amour's' care immediately or I will have no choice but to have them put in care.
    Dr Basil Lee

I stood holding it, shaking, wanting only to disappear from this vast factory of women. I needed to be with my poor hurt children.

After a sleepless night, in which images of my children scream-ing haunted me, Marcus came to see me. I showed him the telegram.

'What's going on, Marcus?' I asked.

'Nigel's become a junkie and he spends his time beating up Masha.'

'Is that why she had burst eardrums?'

'Yes, I suspect so, but she won't admit it. She throws him out and then lets him back in.'

'Why, did no one tell me?'

'We didn't want to worry you. Di, Debbie and Terry are all keeping an eye on things.'

'Marcus, little Patrick is there on his own. I want him taken to Liz in London tonight. I want Masha and Nigel out of the house now. Can you arrange that?'

'Yes, I'm sorry. I'll get on to it as soon as I leave here.'

'Will you send me a telegram as soon as Patrick is safe with Liz? Is Natasha still willing to come over?'

'I'll phone her and let you know tomorrow.'

I left the visit and felt such anger. I felt angry with Howard for putting us in this situation. I felt angry with the Americans for taking me away from the children. I felt anger and loathing at myself for not being there to protect my children. I felt the full frustration of been imprisoned.

I received a telegram the following morning advising me that Patrick was safe with Liz, Golly and Amber. I felt a huge relief. Masha and Nigel had left Palma. Natasha agreed to come over from Florida with her two boys to look after the children. Howard's parents said they could hire a nanny and they could all stay with them. I thought Amber and Golly should decide. They came over from London to see me with Marcus in a face-to-face visit. They wanted to stay in Palma; it was where all their friends were.

Golly seemed happy and greatly relieved the nightmare of Nigel was over. She was looking forward to having her cousins Albi and Thomas to stay. It was not for a long time that I realized just how awful hers and Patrick's lives had been.

Because of the children, I considered accepting the extradition. I talked it over with Marcus and Kieran, who talked it over with Howard. Marcus told Jude I was considering it. I got an urgent appeal from Patrick not to go over until his trial was finished. He was afraid I would be forced to testify against him.

Our extradition trial was set for the end of March. Patrick's and our other co-defendants' trial was due to begin in West Palm Beach, Miami on 3 April.

For Howard's defence, Muñoz had engaged a RICO expert to attend the trial to explain what RICO was and to show there was no equivalent in Spanish law. He had also asked Bernard Simons to testify that Howard had already been tried for the 1973 offence. The Audiencia Nacional refused to let either witness attend. They also refused to allow a stenographer, paid for by us, to transcribe the proceedings.

Muñoz was furious. He said the Americans were corrupting the

MR NICE & MRS MARKS

Spanish justice system and he had never known anything like it; that we were being denied our constitutional rights by not being allowed to present evidence.

Howard, Geoffrey Kenion and I stood in a bulletproof-glass box fitted with microphones, situated in the middle of the court. The court was jam-packed with the world's press. Three judges glared at us. Geoffrey had told us in the waiting room that his lawyers had struck a deal with Lovato and that he had agreed to be voluntarily extradited. He had agreed to plead guilty and be a prosecution witness in return for time served.

Geoffrey spoke to the court first and told them he accepted extradition. I then spoke and said I did not accept extradition and that I wished my lawyer to explain to the court why. Howard then spoke to the judges and on Muñoz's advice denounced each of the three judges by name and said they had denied him his constitutional rights and he was bringing an *antejuicio* against them.

The judges were furious.

They looked barely awake to me as Muñoz proceeded through his arguments as to the illegality of the extradition request. The proceedings were a farce. The court translator told me later that 95 per cent of the court was against my extradition but the Americans were putting on too much pressure for them to refuse.

Apart from the pleasure Howard and I had from being able to briefly touch and talk, it was a thoroughly depressing day.

Marcus kept us up to date with events in Miami. The case was entitled 'United States of America vs. Patrick Alexander Lane, et al'. Jimmy Newton, Geoffrey Kenion, Wyvonna Wills and John Francis did deals with the government and pleaded guilty for immediate release. All except John Francis agreed to be prosecution witnesses.

The United States government's case hinged on the telephone taps. All the lawyers of the remaining defendants were confident in having the telephone taps thrown out of court as they failed to meet the standards laid down under American law for a lawful telephone tap. If the telephone taps were thrown out, the case against us all would collapse. The original tapes of the recorded conversations no longer existed. All that existed were copies that Craig Lovato had edited and put together into an audio-collage.

We waited anxiously to hear the judge's decision. To everyone's bewilderment, the judge allowed them to be admitted.

The tapes lasted for well over twenty hours and were to the uninitiated far from understandable as much of the conversation was in code. It was unlikely a Florida jury would understand the variety of accents or what they were talking about. The prosecution asked if Lovato could interpret them for the jury. The judge said no. The jury could listen to the tapes and draw their own conclusions.

The prosecution argued and eventually won. Craig Lovato was allowed to tell the jury his interpretation of his illegal tapes.

Patrick, Ernie and Patti were found guilty. Rick Brown (Ernie's dope mover) and Teresita Caballero, who turned out to be a friend of Patrick's, were acquitted. The trial had lasted five weeks. Sentencing was to take place in July. Patrick was predicted to get anything from twenty to a hundred and twenty years.

During the course of Patrick's trial, we learnt that the Audiençia Nacional had granted Howard's and my extraditions to the US on condition that the US government gave assurances that we would not serve more than thirty years in prison, minus the time we had already served in Spain.

We appealed.

One of the lawyers for John Denbigh, who was still being held in Canada as he fought the extradition to Florida, came to see me. We discussed the recent trial in Miami. He thought the defence lawyers hadn't argued hard enough to have the tapes thrown out of court. We talked about the charges against me and the evidence against me, which was that I had answered my phone, in my house in Spain.

'Well, you do understand, Judy, that under the new sentencing reform act, you're facing a minimum fifteen years with no parole.'

'You've got it wrong. Marcus and Howard told me it would be a maximum of five.' I noticed the smoke from my cigarette rising upwards and curling round the bare light bulb.

'Under the old laws that would be correct, but this conspiracy runs into November 1987. That brings it under the new sentencing guidelines. Sorry to be the one to break it to you, Judy.'

My ears blocked up. I felt an intense pain creep into my brain. I thought my head was going to shatter into fragments, that chips of skull would fly round the tiny room and ricochet off the metal bars. Fifteen years no parole. Fifteen years no parole. Fifteen years no parole.

After a disturbed night in which I dreamt I was being chased, I saw Marcus. I asked him if it was true. He said no one was sure if we were to be sentenced under the old or the new laws. If it was the new laws, it was unlikely Howard would ever get out of prison. Things were getting worse and worse. I fell into a deep depression. I would never enjoy seeing my kids grow up because I had answered my home phone.

Finally, Marcus came with some excellent news. Patrick had been sentenced to three years. We grinned insane smiles at each other through the dirty glass. If Patrick had received only three years, I would surely get only three seconds. I decided immediately to accept the extradition. I asked Marcus to engage me an American lawyer and to let Muñoz and Howard know of my decision.

Between us all, after studying Patrick's trial transcripts, it looked like Rick Brown's lawyer, Don Re, had been the best. It seemed to make sense to have a lawyer who was already familiar with the case. He had excellent credentials. In 1984 he had succesfully represented John DeLorean, the Belfast car manufacturer who had been set up in a cocaine sting.

Marcus contacted him. For the sum of $25,000, he agreed to fly from LA and visit me in Madrid.

Don was a tall Californian, blond and blue-eyed. I liked him. He was appalled at the state of Yeserias. He agreed that the best thing I could do was to get to Miami as soon as possible and that I would be a lot more comfortable. For another $25,000, he said he would look after me on arrival and get me home again as soon as possible.

When Don got back to the States, he made contact with the

prosecutor Robert ('Bobby') O'Neill, who had told Don he was happy for me to plead guilty to a telephone count (a relatively minor charge) in return for time served.

Muñoz arranged for me to go to the Audiencia Nacional and accept the extradition. This was the first time I had made an appearance there without Howard. I missed him.

Natasha brought the children to see me. They seemed a lot happier. Patrick remained shy and suspicious of me. It hurt. The poor little boy was only two and a half and had three different mother figures. It was hard saying goodbye, knowing I was about to go to another continent thousands of miles away from them. But I felt it was the quickest way to get home.

On 10 August 1989 I packed my bags and left Yeserias. It had been my home for a year. Several of the women came down to see me off and wish me luck. A group of wardens stood by the main door to wish me *buen viaje* and *buena suerte*. They looked nervous for me.

I was taken to a police station and kept overnight in a cell. In the morning, I was collected by three US marshals, two men and one woman, and taken to the airport. I was on my way to face my fate in Miami, Florida.

CHAPTER TWENTY-NINE
No Civilization

After over a year in jail it was strange to be boarding an aircraft. The US marshals sat either side of me and thankfully ignored me the entire journey, on which I chain-smoked. The reassurance from Don Re that he would be in touch as soon as I got to Miami gave me comfort. Marcus had reassured me that Jude, Peggy and Bridie would visit me. I wouldn't be completely on my own.

On arrival at Miami international airport I was handcuffed and led through the airport to immigration. The immigration officer wanted to see my passport and visa. I did not have either.

'How can we let her in without a passport or visa?' a fat burly immigration officer asked the US marshals.

'We've extradited her here from Spain for crimes against America,' drawled the female marshal.

'If she's never been to America I don't see how she can have committed a crime here,' said the immigration officer, a puzzled frown on his face.

I was enjoying this and wasn't going to let on I'd been to the States before. 'I couldn't agree with you more. Can I go home now?' I chimed in rather cheekily. All three marshals glared at me. The immigration officer continued to look puzzled and shook his head.

The marshals took me to another room. One of them stayed with me while the other two went to sort out how to get me into a country I didn't want to enter and whose immigration officers didn't seem to want me to enter either.

They must have sorted it out. An hour later we were driven by another marshal in a limousine to North Dade detention centre. It looked a fairly attractive place, situated among what I thought might have been the Everglades. Once inside the building it didn't matter where it was situated because it was impossible to see out.

The marshals escorted me into the reception area. My handcuffs were removed. I was taken into a room and, with the door left open to the reception area, was told to strip. I stood there naked, embarrassed, while my clothes were minutely examined in case I had hidden anything in the seams. My hair was ruffled to see if anything fell out. I was asked to open my mouth, lift my tongue up and put my tongue out. Pull my lip up, pull my lip down. Then I was told to turn round, bend down and pull apart my buttocks, or cheeks as the American said. A female prison guard peered up my anus. Finally I was told to turn round, move my legs apart, bend with my knees outwards, straighten, bend and straighten again as the guard looked down to see if anything fell out of my vagina. I had never in my life felt so humiliated.

I was told to dress and was then led up a corridor; ahead of me I could see three barred cages like in a zoo. They were full of male prisoners. In the centre of the cages was a small patio with a table-tennis table. We entered the women's section, an identical set-up to the men's. At the second cage the guard stopped. With her huge bunch of keys she opened the cage door and signalled for me to go in before locking it behind me.

I stood inside not knowing what to do. There were ten smaller cages within the bigger cage, their doors padlocked open, each containing a bunk bed and a toilet. A television blared.

'There's a spare bunk in there,' a woman said, pointing to a cage. I wandered over to it. On the top bunk a white woman with long frizzy strawberry blonde hair was asleep. I lay down on the bottom bed, and slept.

The following day I was woken by breakfast trays being handed through a special compartment. It was 4.30 in the morning. The orange of the trays clashed with the dull orange of the bars of the cage. I ate some cereal, crawled back into my bunk and went back to sleep.

Then the sound of my name woke me. I was told to get dressed as I was wanted in reception. It must be Don Re, I thought.

I followed the guard to the reception area. There to my shock sat not Don Re but Craig Lovato, smirking.

'Did you have a good journey, Judith?' he asked.

'Fine,' I replied coldly. I switched all my feelings off, using the skill I had learnt in Yeserias. Two women DEA agents set about fingerprinting me and taking my photo. They asked me how much I weighed. I said I had no idea. Lovato looked at me and gave his opinion. They wrote his guess on a form. Various other questions were asked before I was taken back to my cage.

I later learnt that after this encounter I became known among the DEA as the Ice Maiden.

I phoned the number Don Re had given me when I saw him in Madrid, using the coin-box in the cage. I got an answer machine. I tried him repeatedly during the day with no luck.

The woman with the strawberry blonde hair was called Melissa. She was the only white American in my cage. All the other women were Hispanic and were in for smuggling cocaine. Melissa was in for smuggling marijuana from Jamaica. The impression she gave me was that she was from a fairly well-educated middle-class family.

I finally got hold of Don Re, who told me to expect to be taken to court within a couple of days for an arraignment hearing, and that I was not to worry, it was only a formality. He told me that Malik, the first Pakistani national ever to be extradited from Pakistan, had pleaded guilty to the same conspiracy charge as me four days previously and had been sentenced to four years

A couple of days later I was called to court. US marshals came to pick me up early in the morning. They handcuffed me and put shackles on my legs. The steel bracelets on my wrists and ankles chafed and hurt. I was driven to court in an air-conditioned transit van, the radio blasting out music from a local Miami radio station. I and several other women were placed in a filthy and cramped holding cell with a foul-smelling toilet stuck in the middle. After several hours in this cell, we were taken out and our wrists and ankles were once more encased in steel bracelets. A heavy chain, linking us to one another, was fixed around our waists. About twenty male prisoners were joined to this chain.

We were led stumbling through an underground car park and up into the court.

Once in court the waist chain was removed; the handcuffs and shackles remained. One by one prisoners were asked to stand up and the charges they faced were read out to them. They were then asked how they pleaded. Nearly all were facing cocaine-smuggling charges. The man beside me was charged with importing 200 kilos of cocaine; bail was granted. Then my name was called. I stood up. Across the crowded courtroom, a man closely resembling the actor Michael J. Fox stood up. This I realized must be the prosecutor Bobby O'Neill.

I was told that I was being charged with conspiracy to import hashish into the United States of America. How did I plead?

'Not guilty,' I said.

The judge then asked if bail was been applied for. Bobby O'Neill said that this was a very serious charge and I had had to be extradited from Spain. All eyes in the court turned on me. I wanted to scream out that I had only answered my phone in my house in Spain and said, 'My husband is out' or 'He'll be back in an hour' or some other such mundane thing. I wanted to tell them how much my children were suffering. But because I had been extradited, in their eyes I was a BIG bad wolf.

'Bail denied,' said the judge.

Back in North Dade detention centre I tried to get hold of Don Re, but again to no avail. I couldn't believe that I missed Yeserias and all its madness. Don Re had warned me not to discuss my case with anybody, that all too often snitches were put in cells to report conversations back to the government. North Dade was a Florida state jail, which housed offenders against Florida law. Federal and non-federal prisoners, by law, must be kept separate. Drug smuggling is a federal offence. There was no women's federal jail in Miami so the federal government, to house the increasing number of female federal prisoners, rented a part of the jail. The men's section was mainly to house federal prisoners the government wanted segregated for one reason or another from the prisoners at MCC, the large federal penitentiary in Miami. There were no facilities at North Dade except those needed for basic hygiene. The food was almost uneatable. Breakfast was served at 4.30 a.m., lunch at 11 a.m. and dinner at 4.30 p.m. I survived mainly on peanut butter and other bits I ordered from the commissary. The bed had a mattress less than an inch thick. The only good thing about North Dade was that I was allowed to receive phone calls every day. Inmates had an hour allotted to them for this. I had between 3 and 4 p.m. The children phoned, Howard phoned and many friends from England and Spain called.

Don Re finally called. He was trying to get O'Neill to let me plead guilty to the telephone count that had been discussed before I left Madrid in return for time served. O'Neill wanted me to plead to an interstate travel count, whatever that meant, also for time served. They were negotiating.

The women there were civil to me but I never got friendly with any of them, except a little with Melissa. She could be difficult to talk to as she had a big hang-up on Jamaica and often talked in Jamaican slang. Her Jamaican boyfriend worked on a late-night Miami radio station specializing in reggae. She spent hours on the phone to him in the middle of the night. Local calls were free.

Melissa's first brush with the law, she told me, was when she was eighteen. She was living at the time in the state of Arizona. She was giving her then boyfriend a blow-job when the police crashed through the door because of a misdemeanour on her boyfriend's part. She was arrested and sentenced to four years for 'crimes against nature'. While in the state penitentiary she had her womb removed without her consent. It was a horrific story. I was beginning to think the United States was seriously deranged.

Days dragged by. I spoke to Jude, who promised to come and see me soon. My brother Patrick phoned and we talked about the relief at his sentence and about our children. Ernie phoned. It was wonderful to hear his voice after so many years. He expressed concern for me and the children. He and Patti were due to be sentenced the following day. I wished him luck.

Don Re phoned me with the news that Ernie had been sentenced to forty years and Patti to eight.

'Someone doesn't like that guy,' commented Don. He then told me that O'Neill had backed out of his previous agreement under pressure from Lovato, and that O'Neill wanted me to plead guilty to Count Four of the indictment, the charge that had been read out in the arraignment proceedings. If I pleaded guilty to this charge, I would not be allowed back into the US. This meant if Howard was successfully extradited to the US, I would never be allowed to bring the children to visit him. Don thought I should go to trial and try again to have the telephone tapes thrown out of court. He said he would talk to O'Neill again.

Unfortunately, for me, Don Re was tied up in a large trial in LA, which made it hard for me, and presumably Bobby O'Neill, to get hold of him.

I stumbled out of bed one morning to get my breakfast tray. A woman said hello to me. It was a bit early for me so I merely nodded my head.

'Don't you want to know me?' she asked. I turned and looked at her; she had tears in her eyes.

'Patti, Patti, I'm so sorry – I didn't recognize you.' I stared at her in amazement before giving her a big hug. She looked almost as well as she did when I first met her.

'I guess we fell in love with the wrong guys, eh, Jude.'

Patti told me she had come from the Annexe jail in downtown Miami, where the conditions were appalling. I had heard horror stories from other women, including Melissa and some of the guards, about the Annexe. Patti and I talked non-stop. It was lovely to see her, but I wished it could have been on a tropical beach with piña coladas in our hands. Instead, we toasted each other with cough syrup that was handed out at night. After two days, she was moved to a women's federal prison in California to begin her sentence. Although she and Ernie were confident of getting their sentences reduced on appeal, she was frightened.

Days in North Dade were long. I couldn't concentrate well enough to read.

The television blasted out inane American rubbish all day and night. Outside in the patio I found it too humid and claustrophobic. Inside the cage I felt like a monkey, especially when inspectors wandered around peering in. I had a strong urge to climb up the bars and swing on them. It probably would have been another federal offence.

My emotions seesawed between wanting to fight and wanting to go to trial to plead guilty to anything that would get me home to the children.

Howard remained determinedly in Spain. The Spanish government had banned him from any further interviews with the press. The Spanish courts, closely observed by the American embassy in Madrid, systematically blocked and denied every motion and appeal that Muñoz presented to them. On 13 October 1989 Marcus phoned me and told me the final deciding authority, the Spanish Council of Ministers, had approved Howard's extradition. On 23 October Howard arrived in Miami. He was taken to the men's federal prison, where Ernie and Patrick and some other co-defendants were being held. He phoned me when he arrived and before he had met any of his other co-defendants. He hoped to be moved into the main part of the prison the following day. He sounded lonely and fearful. He hoped Don Re would have had me out by now. I explained to him about Lovato refusing to let me plead to anything but Count Four.

'He's a sad sadistic bastard,' he said.

'Yes, and a very powerful one,' I said.

Howard insisted that he was not going to hire a lawyer but defend himself. I felt frightened for him and longed to see him. He phoned the following day sounding upset and tearful.

'Jude, I've just seen Ernie. He was so angry with me. He said, "If the commissary sold guns, I'd go and buy one now and blow your fucking head off."'

'Howard, he's just been sentenced to forty years. Have you seen Patrick yet?'

'Yes, he was with Ernie.'

'How was he?'

'All right, not overfriendly. I probably won't see them again today. I'm being taken to court to be arraigned tomorrow.'

I knew from Patti that they were all angry with Howard. Ernie and Patrick were angry because Howard had carried on using our phone at home after having been told it was tapped, and because he had carried on having a relationship with Tom Sunde despite been told he was a double agent. They were also angry that Howard had sent Moynihan over to meet Patrick, even though he knew he was working for the DEA. This provided the nail in the coffin the DEA needed to make the RICO charge stick.

I guessed it was the anger she felt towards Howard that prevented Jude from visiting me. It upset me.

The following afternoon, Mary, a new woman in the cage, returned from court.

'Hey, Judy, I've just been in the van with your husband – he told me to let you know he's here.'

I looked towards the men's section and saw Howard being led to a cage. I waved but he didn't see me. I had not seen him for nearly six months.

I got in touch with the prison welfare officer. I explained our extradition and how we hadn't seen each other for months. She was sympathetic and said she would arrange a visit between us. We were locked up in cages 30 yards away from each other; it was frustrating. We could, however, spend time on the phone. I persuaded him he needed a lawyer. He finally conceded when I said we could interview them together.

My first sight of Howard was a shock. He was unkempt, and his hair was much longer. His hands and feet were blistering and oozing pus, a condition that had begun in Madrid. The jail doctor thought it was an allergy and was giving him a solution to put on it. I thought it was more likely a reaction to stress.

The welfare officer let us spend thirty minutes together in her office in her presence. We had a lot to discuss, but spent many of those precious minutes just gently holding hands and gazing into each other's eyes.

For the next week, we interviewed five or six lawyers a day. It didn't give us much time to speak together but the physical closeness to each other was comforting. Many of the lawyers we interviewed looked like they were on the wrong side of the bars. They would be dripping in diamond-encrusted gold Rolexes, medallions and rings. Most of them were only interested in arranging plea bargains; going to trial was too much work.

One lawyer was different from the rest. He was dressed smartly but conservatively and although his watch was undoubtedly expensive, it was not flashy. His name was Steve Bronis. We both liked him and Howard engaged him.

It was late November and the children were getting desperately worried I would miss another Christmas. I'd already missed another year of birthdays.

'We've got to get you home, Jude,' Howard said.

Bronis agreed. He thought Howard would be in a far better position to concentrate on his defence with me back with the children.

Don Re got in touch. He had heard from Bobby O'Neill. By mistake, the prosecution had not stated the amount of hashish in the charge (15,500 kilos); if they had, the charge carried a minimum sentence of ten years. I either pleaded guilty to Count Four and had time served, or they were going to change the wording of the charge so I would face the minimum ten years.

'That's blackmail, Don,' I said.

'It's the American government. You have a week to decide.'

I accepted but asked if in the plea agreement it could be established that I would be allowed back into the US to visit Howard. O'Neill agreed.

On Monday 4 December 1989 I was collected from North Dade at 5 a.m. by US marshals. I had dressed carefully for my court appearance. I had brought a smart grey conservative Calvin Klein dress and matching low-heeled shoes over from Spain. In the reception area, I was handcuffed and had the shackles placed around my ankles. On the way to the transit van, I discovered how difficult it is to walk in heels with shackled ankles. By the time I got into the van, my tights were ripped to shreds.

I was driven to Fort Lauderdale city jail, arriving early afternoon. It was not part of the federal system. Like in North Dade, two large cells were rented to the government. Unlike the guests of the federal system, bank robbers, arms dealers, racketeers and drug smugglers, the guests held in Fort Lauderdale were muggers, hookers, pimps and junkies. It was a godforsaken place, the conditions barely imaginable. In the reception area were women, some of them no more than girls, cuffed or chained to metal table legs or steel bars.

I was placed in a large cell on my own with the ubiquitous blaring television, and a toilet in a corner next to a tiny sink, from whose tap only the slightest drizzle emerged. The air-conditioning was freezing and I was given no blanket. The food was uneatable and stank. During the night I could hear the other prisoners fighting, howling and screaming.

The following morning the Palm Beach marshals collected me about 6.30 a.m. Twenty-four hours earlier, I had left North Dade looking presentable, ready to meet Judge Paine. I now had ripped tights, a heavily creased dress I had slept in, unbrushed hair, unbrushed teeth and I felt filthy.

I arrived at the West Palm Beach courthouse by 7.30 a.m. I was humiliated by how I imagined I looked and by how dirty I felt. I had left the ripped tights in the Fort Lauderdale jail. I had begged the marshals not to put the leg irons back but without success. My ankles were bruised and hurt.

At 9.00 a.m. I was taken into court. The courtroom was empty except for Craig Lovato, Bobby O'Neill and a few court officials. Mona, Don Re's Chinese partner, was there to represent me.

Judge Paine entered the room. He looked like a Southern gentleman. He was large and physically imposing with thick silver-white hair. He stared at me over his reading glasses.

I pleaded guilty to importing hashish into the United States of America. I signed a plea agreement and was sentenced to time served.

Back at North Dade, I was told to pack my belongings. All my jars of uneaten peanut butter and other commissary items I asked a guard to take to Howard. We were allowed two minutes to say goodbye. We kissed, not knowing when we ever would again.

'It'll be okay. You'll see, it'll be okay,' I said, trying hard not to sound as helpless and as hopeless as I felt as the salty tears ran down our faces.

At that moment if they had said I could stay there with him, I would have.

I was not allowed to take anything with me. My possessions I was told would be sent to my attorney. They never were. I was collected by two state police officers. I was no longer a federal prisoner and was taken to a downtown-holding cell, where all the women looked high, drunk or both. I was horrified. I had expected to be taken to an immigration centre.

From here, I was transferred to the dreaded Annexe. I have heard it said that how civilized a society is can be judged by how it treats its prisoners. If that is true, then the United States of America is an extremely uncivilized country.

The British embassy arranged for a new passport for me and friends in England paid for my ticket back to London.

On Monday 18 December 1989 I boarded a flight from Miami international airport to Gatwick, London, a free woman.

I was going home to my children for Christmas.

CHAPTER THIRTY
DIY Queen

Liz Denbigh met me at Gatwick with my onward flight ticket to Palma. She had brought a change of clothes for me from our flat in Cathcart Road. We shared a brief tearful reunion before I boarded the flight to Palma.

Despite all the worldwide press we had received on our arrest, there was only a small mention in the *Daily Express* of my release. For this, I was grateful.

Flying into Palma I felt a mixture of excitement and fear. It had been six long months since I had seen my children and over eighteen months since I had been taken from them. How would they feel having me home? How would people treat me? Would I be an outcast? Would people cross the street to avoid me?

I walked out of the arrivals hall and there was my beautiful daughter Amber, no longer a little ten-year-old girl, but a twelve-year-old, nearly my height and about to enter her teenage years. She ran into my arms. I clasped her tightly to me and buried my face in the scent of her silky long blonde hair. How I had longed for and dreamt of this moment.

'Where are Golly and Patrick?' I asked.

'Golls has a major part in the Christmas carol concert today and Patrick is at his nursery school,' Amber said as she raised her head from my shoulder. Marcus was behind her.

'We can pick Patrick up on the way home if you like, Judy,' he said.

'Yes, I'd like that.' I so longed to hold my baby in my arms. I wanted to take away his anger and make up to them all for my long absence.

I sat on the rear seat of Marcus's rented car on the way back to La Vileta with Amber cradled tightly in my arms. Mallorca looked little changed. It was late December but the sun shone like a summer's day. Was it possible I had been away only eighteen months? It felt like years. We drove up to Patrick's nursery school in the back streets of the village. Amber came into the school with me. On seeing Amber, Patrick stood up and went to get his coat off his coat peg.

'Pa, Pa,' he said, running to her on his three-year-old legs. He seemed oblivious to me. My dreams of him breaking into a smile and rushing into my arms were crushed. I stood and watched him run to Amber instead.

I crouched down. 'Hello, Patrick, do you remember me? I'm your mummy,' I said, trying to keep the tears away. He held onto Amber's legs tightly and turned his face from me. Amber picked him up and we walked out to the car.

It was strange walking back through the gates that I had been dragged out of eighteen months before. Natasha greeted me with tears running down her face.

'At last, Judy, welcome home,' she said. I was in a daze as champagne bottles popped and glasses rose. Patrick held his arms out to Natasha to lift him up.

'No, go to your mummy – your mummy's home now,' she said. Patrick started crying. An uncomfortable silence fell.

'Natasha, let him get used to me slowly, let him learn to trust me again.'

At that moment, I wondered if he ever would.

The sound of excited children's voices could be heard the other side of the gate.

'Here comes Golly, Albi and Thomas,' said Natasha. Her two boys had joined Amber and Golly at Queen's College. I felt nervous. I did not want to greet Golly in front of everyone. I left them sitting on the terrace and went to the sitting room.

Little Golly came flying into the sitting room. I scooped her up into my arms and hugged her so tightly I was frightened I would crush her.

That night I took Patrick up to bed. I washed him, brushed his teeth and tucked him up. My intention was to lie down beside him and read him a story. When I attempted this he became agitated and started screaming, 'Pa, pa!' Amber came running up the stairs. On seeing her, he calmed down.

'Mummy, I'll read him his story,' she said. With a heavy heart, I returned downstairs.

Back outside on the terrace with Golly on my knee, I realized what a dreadful state the house was. The courtyard looked more like a junkyard. The swimming pool was black with debris. Not one of the four lavatories in the house worked properly. Liz had warned me at the airport to expect to find the house chaotic. This was beyond chaos.

I phoned Howard at North Dade and let him know I was home. His relief was immense. That night I went to sleep with Amber and Golly cradled in my arms.

The following morning Golly made what I thought was a strange request.

'Mummy, will you wash me?' she asked, as her large turquoise eyes looked pleadingly at me.

'Of course, I'll wash you, Golly,' I said, thinking she wanted me to treat her as a baby like Patrick.

'I mean give me a bath and scrub me clean,' she said.

'I will do whatever you want, Golly,' I said. She nodded her head, went to the bathroom and ran a bath.

'Clean me please, Mummy,' she said.

I washed her gently from head to toe.

'Wash me again, Mummy.'

'If I wash you any more they'll be nothing left of you,' I said jokingly, not understanding the desperation in her voice.

She started crying. 'I don't feel clean, Mummy. I just don't feel clean.'

I didn't know what to say and so I held her tightly as tears fell down her face.

Christmas came. Money was tight; Natasha had offered the purse strings back to me; I did not think I was capable of handling them. Natasha had always been sensible with money and economical. I asked her to continue managing things until I had become used to living in the real world again.

She gave me the equivalent of £40 in pesetas to go Christmas shopping. I had been home five days and had not left the house. I was terrified.

'Judy, it's Christmas Eve, you have to go today,' Natasha said. Amber and Golly offered to come with me. We caught the bus into town and headed for Galerias, the biggest department store in Palma at that time. I kept my head down. I felt like I had 'prisoner' written all over me. In Galerias, I spotted Mrs Ramonell, Golly's former teacher, a kind Welsh woman, and I hid behind a pillar. I had no need to hide from her; she had written me beautiful letters in jail, and written references for me to say what a good and conscientious parent I was. I just could not face her. Over the following months, I noticed other changes in me. I became terrified of driving, especially at speed – which I used to love. I had developed a fear of heights. I used to love diving, but now I could not bear to have my head submerged.

With the excitement of my homecoming, Christmas and New Year over, it was time to face reality. Natasha wanted to get back to her husband Stuart in Florida, and her boys wanted their dad. There was no money to pay for their tickets. I put the flat that Howard had bought in Palma Nova on the market.

I set about sorting out the house. It was a huge task. Natasha, with five children aged twelve, ten, eight, five and three to look after on her own with little money, had had no spare time or money to look after the house. It was a large house to maintain, with four bathrooms and seven bedrooms, plus the garden and swimming pool. Before the arrest I had a cleaner come in every day for four hours, and even then keeping on top of the house was a lot of work.

Over the following weeks I became a proficient plumber, electrician and decorator. Whatever I was doing, Golly was always at my side helping me.

I sold the flat in Palma Nova at the rock bottom price of four million pesetas (about £20,000). Natasha and her boys were at last, after nearly eleven months, able to return home. Thankfully, Patrick was beginning to trust me more and no longer ran from me. However, there was a lot about him that worried me deeply.

For my sister Natasha's selfless devotion to my children, I will never be able to thank her enough.

With Natasha and her boys gone, I became more aware of the mess my children were in. I would discover Amber in the middle of the night wandering around the house sleepwalking. She, as the eldest, had felt responsible for Golly and Patrick; in her nocturnal walks it was as if she was checking on them.

Golly I would frequently find banging her head rhythmically and heavily against a wall. Her eyes would be wide and unblinking. The first time I witnessed the behaviour Natasha had still been with us. I asked her if she behaved like this often. Natasha said yes.

Patrick's lack of communication and withdrawal worried me deeply. He was three years old and didn't talk. He had not progressed in speech since my arrest. A parent from the girls' school suggested he might be autistic. I decided to go and see Dr Lee during the girls' half-term.

The flat in London was being rented for a nominal amount by some friends. All our personal belongings were still in it. I realized that this was foolish. If I cleared out our belongings and moved them to Palma, I could rent the London flat for more money, which would cover the mortgage and other bills. Even then there would be little left over.

It was strange being back in our flat in London. It was full of so many happy memories. I was reluctant to pack it up. Howard phoned about twenty times a day during this week. A private detective who worked for his lawyer had provided him with a phone card. It was almost as if he was there with us.

I went with the children to see Dr Lee. His delight at seeing me back with the children could clearly be seen on his face. The children waited in the waiting room while I voiced my concerns about them to him.

'Judy, I have to say that in all my years as a family practitioner I have never come across such a distressing case as when Francesca came to see me. I'm sorry I had to send you such a curt telegram.'

He arranged for Patrick to be seen by a child psychologist. With Amber and Golly, he felt that by having me home they would slowly recover from their trauma.

The child psychologist after examining Patrick ruled out autism and felt that he was suffering from severe trauma and that he had closed himself down for the eighteen months I had been away. She felt that with time he would be fine. We arranged for a follow-up appointment in a year's time.

Over the course of time, I slowly learnt of the appalling suffering the children had endured at the hands of Nigel. Nigel, apart from battering my sister in front of my children, kept Patrick locked in his room for hours and threatened the girls if they tried to go and comfort him. On one occasion he had taken Patrick out drinking with him; they were later discovered by the police, lying in a gutter, Nigel unconscious. In Amber's room, I found a poem she had written.

BROTHER
And still I hear you screaming.
Behind the wooden doors
With me standing on the tiles,
And my sister at my side.
He beat her all the time,
And though he never hit us,
We lived in the fear that he would.
He said he would,
If we opened the door
To the room in which you lay
Screaming in your cot.
At night they took you out,
And played with you till dawn,

DIY Queen

When you were placed again,
And quietly bolted in.
You lived your life in darkness,
Not uttering a word,
Only opening your mouth to scream.

A scream I could not answer.
No longer a baby,
But still you did not speak
And I was quiet also,
As she slapped your baby skin whilst soaking off
The excreta you seeked to hide in.
And desperately
You screamed.

Mummy home,
And slowly you began to speak.
No longer do you scream in pain.
And now I can always be with you.
You chatter away and smile all day,
Those days you never mention.
Yet still I hear you screaming.
Though I know your mouth is shut.

I listened in horror as more and more stories were revealed to me. Why had no one stepped in and removed them from Nigel's care?

The children and I had decided to stay in Mallorca rather than move back to London. The girls were happy and doing well at school and had no desire to leave. Although I had to pay the school fees, the cost of living was cheaper than London and the lifestyle was healthier. I decided to do up the house, sell it and buy one much smaller and more manageable, and pay off the mortgage in London. The rent from London would then give me an income. The children and Howard were happy with my decision.

I started to make new friends, in particular Anna Nielson and David Lightowler. They had just opened a bar in the old part of Palma called Latitude 39. They had both worked on luxurious yachts for many years, and with the money they had saved they bought a large apartment and the bar. The bar catered mainly to 'yachties', people who work as crew on luxury yachts. Yachties live onboard for much of the year, mostly tax-free. The majority of their expenses, including food, travel and accommodation, are paid for and hence they tend to have plenty of disposable income. Dave and Anna offered me the job of bar bouncer. This job, apart from providing a small regular income, also meant that I came to meet a vast number of people, which led in time to all sorts of other work.

Our Palma lawyer Luis Morrell succeeded in having the confiscated cars, a Ford Sierra and Fiesta, returned to me.

Howard phoned weekly. He was busy working on his defence. I missed him intensely and he was constantly in my mind. I often found myself making him a cup of tea as I had an imaginary conversation with him.

One night in May 1990 I had a nightmare that Howard had died. I awoke in the morning feeling bereaved and empty. When he next phoned, he sounded very depressed. Ernie had agreed to testify against him. He had agreed to testify in return for Patti's freedom, not for any reduction of his sentence. But he could not bear Patti being locked up for what he felt was Howard's fault.

Patrick had also agreed to testify against Howard. This upset me greatly and I didn't understand it. If he had only got three years, why was he going to testify against Howard?

Howard said they had given him twenty-one days to make up his mind whether or not to plead guilty. They had told him that if he pleaded guilty, and avoided the expense of a trial, they would ask for a maximum sentence of forty years under old sentencing guidelines, meaning he would be eligible for parole after serving a third. If he insisted on going to trial and lost, the government would demand under the new guidelines a sentence of more than one hundred years, meaning he would die in prison. They would ensure he spent his sentence in Marion penitentiary, which had been built to replace the notorious Alcatraz prison. Here the inmates are placed in solitary for more than twenty hours a day, often underground. It was known in the federal correctional system as being 'buried alive'. It wasn't much of a choice. I was petrified he would go to trial. But he realized that with Ernie's and others' testimony he had no chance. He was going to plead guilty and hope the judge would not give him forty years.

I heard from Natasha the intense pressure Lovato and Bobby O'Neill had put on Patrick. They were appealing his sentence. They argued that since some of the overt acts covered by the RICO charges had occurred after 1 November 1987, when the sentencing reform act became law, Patrick should be sentenced under the new guidelines, and his three-year sentence would be changed to twenty years with no parole. Also, the IRS (the revenue service) was bringing a case against him for defrauding the United States, and the INS (the immigration service) was going to prosecute him for illegally obtaining a green card. He could be facing years and years in jail. He didn't feel he could let Jude and his children suffer all that when Howard had introduced him to Moynihan knowing at the time he was a DEA snitch. So, like Ernie, he had agreed to cooperate. Both Ernie and Patrick felt that even without their evidence Howard would be found guilty. There were too many others also willing to testify.

On 13 July 1990, Howard appeared in front of Judge Paine and pleaded guilty to one count of RICO and one count of conspiracy. Sentencing was due to take place on 18 October. The children and I wrote letters to Judge Paine pleading for a short sentence. I rang up all our friends and asked them to do the same.

During the summer Amber fixed herself up with odd jobs such as babysitting to keep herself in pocket money. I was to discover she was an enterprising young lady. Golly wrote to Howard every single day for seven years without fail the entire time he was in jail.

In September, little Patrick, who had improved in leaps and bounds, began at Queen's College with the girls. Golly and Amber had also greatly improved. As the sentencing date got closer, Golly spent a great deal of her time in the village church praying and then came home and prayed to our Buddha in the garden. We tried to remain as positive as we could.

Julian Peto flew to Miami for the sentencing, promising to phone me the minute there was any news. We sat and waited for Julian to call.

The phone rang. 'Judy, it's amazing – it's only fifteen years. I'll call back after I've called his parents.'

I hung up and turned to Amber and Golly, who were standing nervously by me, with a big grin on my face. 'It's not too bad, it's only fifteen.'

The phone went again. It was a journalist from one of the tabloids, asking my opinion on Howard's twenty-five-year sentence. I told them they had it wrong. They said they hadn't, but at my insistence they said they would recheck and get back to me.

The phone rang again. It was my friend Anna, phoning to say how delighted she was that it was only fifteen years. She had just heard from Tom, the editor of the *Daily Bulletin*. I told her what the tabloid journalist had told me. She said she would get Tom to check again.

The phone went. 'Judy, isn't that marvellous news,' said Howard's mother.

I told her what I had heard.

Julian phoned back in high spirits. I told him what the tabloid journalist had told me. He argued with me. I asked him to go back into the court and check with Bronis.

The tabloid journalist phoned back confirming a sentence of twenty-five years. Anna phoned to say she was sorry. Amber and Golly cried.

While Julian rushed out of the court to phone Howard's parents and me, the judge decided he had made a mistake. He called everyone back into the court to amend the sentence to twenty-five years and a $50,000 fine. He recommended medium-security Butner prison in North Carolina as it had excellent psychiatric care, of which, in the judge's opinion, Howard was clearly in need.

The children and I consoled each other by saying it could have been worse. It could have been forty.

After a few days of deep depression, I began to feel that something would happen and he wouldn't do all those years. But however long it took, it was down to me to make my innocent children's lives as stable as I could after all they had endured. I was convinced that on appeal Howard's sentence would be cut. Within 120 days, Bronis had submitted a motion to reduce sentence. There was no time limit for Judge Paine to respond to the motion.

In the New Year, I put the house on the market and began looking for smaller properties. I also put a for-sale advertisement in the local paper for two fur coats I had. Two days later Spanish Customs arrived at the house and confiscated the coats. I told Luis Morrell. He was disgusted – he felt I was being victimized. He got them back for me a year later.

Howard phoned in January. He sounded terrible. He had been taken from Miami and was now being kept in a punishment cell ('the hole') in Atlanta, Georgia.

'Jude, they're sending me to a terrible maximum-security prison called Terre Haute in Indiana.'

'I thought the judge said you should go to North Carolina,' I said.

'He did, but it's not his decision. I told the guards that I had to go to North Carolina for the psychiatrist. They laughed and said there were psychiatrists at Terre Haute. Oh, Jude, I never thought anything like this would ever happen to me.' He broke down crying. It is a conversation deeply etched in my memory. I phoned Anna in tears.

He phoned a week later from Terre Haute. He sounded better.

'How is it, love?' I asked.

'I can manage it, Jude, as long as I know you'll be there for me when I get out.'

'Oh, Howard, don't be silly. You know I will be. And I'm sure it's not going to be as long as you think it will be. Your home and family will be waiting for you.'

A couple of months later, while the children were at school and I was sweeping the garden, the doorbell sounded. I opened the gate. It was an official from the Spanish court informing me that an embargo had been put on my house as the US government wanted to confiscate it. I went to see Luis Morrell. He said the Americans would not get away with it. However, while the embargo was in place, I could not sell the house. I asked how long the process would take. He shrugged his shoulders and said maybe a couple of years. All my carefully thought-out plans for surviving the next few years were wiped out.

I dared not sell the London flat in case the Americans succeeded in confiscating the Spanish house. Contrary to public belief, there were no large stashes of money hidden away. Howard had never been interested in saving or hoarding money. Howard liked to spend it. He had a theory that the more you spent, the more you got. He would spend as if there was no tomorrow.

Given that I could not sell the house, I had to think of another way to make money from it. I built a kitchen on the top floor and turned it into a two double-bedroom self-contained apartment and advertised it in the UK for holiday lets. It turned out to be successful. Meanwhile I had a string of odd jobs, from being Dave and Anna's bouncer to cleaning houses and yachts, ironing for film companies and waitressing, while trying to give my children as stable a home as possible. It was hard but we were surviving. Howard phoned weekly. I treasured the calls. The sound of his voice gave me strength.

Many of the children's friends and their parents had drinks in Portals on Sundays. One evening, Patrick and his schoolfriend Victoria were playing in the pedestrianized square at the back of the bar. At about seven o'clock I asked the girls to go and get him. It was Howard's and my wedding anniversary and I was expecting a phone call. They couldn't find him. Then I saw a cluster of people standing in a circle about 100 metres away and an ambulance with a flashing light. I ran down to the crowd just as the ambulancemen were lifting my little Patrick into the back. I leapt in after him and they closed the doors as Amber and Golly's faces appeared round the corner. Patrick had jumped off the balcony above the pizza restaurant and broken both his legs. Friends of mine drove the girls to all the hospitals in Palma to track us down.

The three of us spent two nights in hospital with Patrick. I knew Howard would be phoning, and he would be more worried than normal at not getting hold of me on our anniversary. When he eventually heard about Patrick he was distraught.

Patrick spent two months with his legs in plaster.

Howard seemed to be getting more and more depressed. He was suffering from shingles, skin rashes, tooth abscesses and prostate problems. Work had begun on building the first federal death row in the US. It was to be in Terre Haute. This distressed him terribly.

He was getting nowhere with being moved back to England. I started a petition. The children and I went around the island collecting signatures. I phoned everyone I knew in England asking them to do the same. Howard's parents went tirelessly to every house in Kenfig Hill. There was a tremendous amount of support. I wrote endless letters to Janet Reno, Clinton's attorney general, but never had an acknowledgement.

The children continued to do well at school, still consistently winning prizes. Often the emptiness and loneliness I felt would hit when I least expected it: driving along a road, or at the prize-giving ceremonies. I was so proud of the children and had no one to share that joy with. Been a single parent was lonely. I drove the girls mad by recording an entire side of a tape with Sinead O'Connor's 'Nothing Compares To You' and playing it endlessly in the car.

I was an extremely strict parent. Poor Amber spent many of her teenage years grounded.

In June 1993 Amber did her GCSEs. There was a recession in Europe. Unemployment was high. I was finding it harder and harder to pay the school fees and all the other bills. The rent from Cathcart no longer paid the mortgage; interest rates had risen from 9.5 per cent in 1988 to over 15.4 per cent in the 1990s. The embargo was still on the house in Spain. I decided I had no choice but to sell the London flat. I sold the flat at the worst possible time. I felt as if I was letting Howard down. We all loved that flat. I packed it up and shipped the furniture to Palma.

Amber did very well in her exams. In October, we went to London and stayed with Julian and Helen. I went to the US embassy to apply to go to the US to visit Howard.

'Have you ever being convicted of a drug offence?' was the first question on the form.

'Yes,' I wrote.

'Have you ever been deported from the United States?'

'Yes.'

I was interviewed at the embassy. They said they had no objection to me visiting on humanitarian grounds as long as Miami immigration had no objection. I phoned the US attorney William Pearson, who had replaced Bobby O'Neill. He was very helpful, and wrote to the immigration office on my behalf. After several weeks the Americans, despite having agreed in my plea agreement to let me visit Howard, turned my application down. Howard and I were convinced Lovato had something to do with it.

Julian Peto very kindly took Amber and Francesca to visit Howard. Patrick was too young to go without me.

Later on in the year, Howard was informed that 'his motion to reduce sentence' was to be heard in West Palm Beach. He was upset at being moved from Terre Haute. He had become institutionalized. Lovato and Julian Peto attended the hearing. The children and I wrote yet again to the judge. The judge did not rule for a few weeks but I felt optimistic.

Amber was offered a place at LSE to read law. I was so proud of her.

Liz Denbigh came to visit me.

'Have you heard about Nigel?' she asked.

I knew that Masha had eventually had enough and thrown him out. Now I learnt that he had been killed in a police chase after resisting arrest for attacking his mother. I felt no sorrow for his death.

The Spanish courts threw out the Americans' request to confiscate our house.

Judge Paine reduced Howard's sentence from twenty-five years to twenty years and said he was to be considered for immediate transfer to an English prison. The reduced sentence meant that Howard would shortly be eligible for parole. I was increasingly optimistic that the nightmare would soon be over. On 31 January 1995 Howard appeared before the parole board. The children and I prayed. Howard phoned that night and told us that he was being recommended for parole in March. On 14 February, the decision was confirmed. He would be released on 25 March. He asked us not to tell anyone; he was terrified Lovato would stop it.

I could barely wait to be lying in his arms again. It had been five years since I'd seen him, and I missed him as much as ever. He was the last person I thought of at night. In the morning my first thoughts were of him.

Near the beginning of March, Howard was moved to an immigration jail in Oakdale, Louisiana. His parents bought him an open ticket back to London because he would be given no notice of when he would actually be deported. It could be in two weeks, five, or more. He phoned me from Oakdale every Saturday morning.

I started spring-cleaning and making everything look as bright and fresh as possible for Howard's return. Golly had a wonderful Mallorquin boyfriend called Torres. He was a couple of years older than her and his handsome looks made even my girlfriends swoon. It was with his help that we got the house ready for Howard.

On Saturday morning, 7 April, Howard phoned me. 'Jude, guess where I am?'

Groggy from sleep I said I didn't know.

'I'm in Gatwick, trying to get a flight to Palma. I'll be home with you soon.'

'Oh, Howard, at last,' I said, as excitement coursed through me.

From now on, I thought, things could only get better. Couldn't they?